La Belle Époque

Eleonora Bairati • Philippe Jullian
Malcolm Falkus • Paolo Monelli
János Riesz • Brunello Vigezzi

La Belle Époque

Fifteen Euphoric Years of European History

William Morrow and Company, Inc.
New York 1978

Here below, Gustav Klimt, Danae, *oil on canvas, circa 1907–08. Frontispiece, ostrich feather fan with gold enamel handle and gold and enamel lorgnette by Carl Fabergé.*

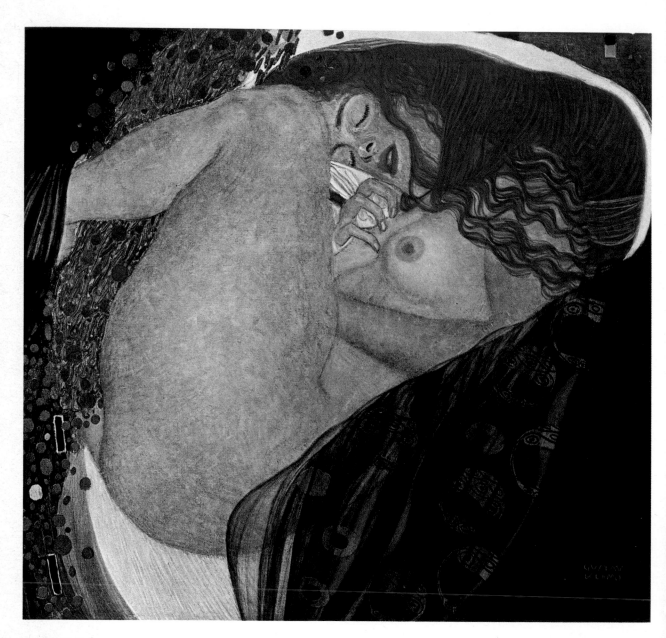

LA BELLE ÉPOQUE

Editorial Director: Enzo Orlandi
Editor-in-Chief: Lorenzo Camusso
Picture research and editing: Annalisa Romagnoni
Copyright © 1977 by Arnoldo Mondadori Editore S.p.A., Milano
English language edition copyright © 1978 by Arnoldo Mondadori Editore S.p.A., Milano
First published in the United States by William Morrow and Company, Inc., in 1978.
Originally published in Italian by Arnoldo Mondadori Editore in 1977.

Library of Congress Catalog Card Number 78-51813
ISBN 0-688-03327-X

Printed and bound in Italy by Arnoldo Mondadori Editore—Verona

Introduction
by Paolo Monelli   6
translated from the Italian by Olive Ordish

The Belle Époque: Trends and Developments   15
translated from the Italian by Olive Ordish

Can-can and Flappers
by Philippe Jullian   81
translated from the French by Jennifer Shipton

The Discreet Charm of an Epoch
by Eleonora Bairati   113
translated from the Italian by Olive Ordish

"A Mounting Fever . . ."
by János Riesz   177
translated from the Italian by Olive Ordish

Avant-Garde in Bowler Hats
by Eleonora Bairati   209
translated from the Italian by Olive Ordish

The European Economy in the Belle Époque
by Malcolm Falkus   257

Summer 1914
by Brunello Vigezzi   271
translated from the Italian by Olive Ordish

Chronology   291
translated from the Italian by Olive Ordish

Index   323

Photographic Sources   334

Introduction
by Paolo Monelli

Écoutez la chanson bien douce
Qui ne pleure que pour vous plaire;
Elle est discrète, elle est légère,
Un frisson d'eau sur de la mousse.

(Listen to the gentle song
Lamenting but to please;
Secret, light, and shimmering
Like water over moss.)
　　　　—*Paul Verlaine*

I could almost stop tapping the keys of my typewriter at this point, because those words have already said all there is to say of the *Belle Époque*, its sensibility and its total disappearance halfway through 1914. I have quoted the sweetest and most symbolist poet of France, and with his perfect quatrain have summed up his own art and that of other poets and artists whose lives spanned the nineteenth and twentieth centuries. He was the most representative artistic figure of his time and was justly accepted as the leader of them all: poets, novelists, painters, playwrights, designers, eccentrics, those who died young and those who lived to be ninety, the handsome, the plain, the athletic and the victims of mysterious diseases.

Verlaine had a varied and vagabond life, full of hardship and adventure. He was praised at one time, scorned at another, both in his own country and abroad. He had a wife, but fled with Rimbaud to Belgium, where he later fired two shots at him in a fit of jealousy. Verlaine was sentenced to two years' imprisonment, and served them in full. He wrote delicate and imaginative poetry and died in a hospital in 1896, composing verses to the end. The last word he wrote was "death": truly a shimmer of water over moss.

Then came France's happiest, craziest, most carefree years, in the course of which miraculous inventions became reality and revolutionized our lives: electricity, the cinema, the motorcar and the airplane. We enjoyed them prudently, without undue strain, without overexploiting or corrupting them. It was a splendid world and we genuinely believed we had thrown open forever the doors to perennial optimism, brilliant enterprises and lasting happiness.

Now that sixty years have passed, and only the disillusion of reality remains, we look back, whether old or young, with a sad feeling of regret; we were happy then and did not know it.

There is something pathetic in our nostalgia for that legendary epoch more than half a century ago. Today we are faced with thorny and increasing problems, a disturbed society and ever more straitened economic circumstances. Oceans are polluted by leaking oil tankers, mysterious and as yet incurable diseases lurk in the soil that grows our crops, hitherto unsuspected poisons are found to exist in colorants used to give food and drink a more appetizing tint. Human relations worsen from day to day; the sexes—now numbering three, if not four—struggle for an independence never contemplated before. Never a week goes by but the newspapers warn us of some new danger. We are no longer confident of our rural solitude, the vehicles that carry us or the wholesomeness of our food. And termites are eating the historic quarter of Udine.

On the right, Giovanni Boldini, Portrait of Count Robert de Montesquiou, or Portrait in Grey. Caricature by Sem (Georges Goursat).

7

The gentlemen of the *Belle Époque* rose late in the morning because they had gone to bed late after spending the night before at a dinner or theater, or in a café or one of the numerous or exclusive salons (and before retiring most of them seem to have made rather long-winded entries in their diaries). A large part of the day was spent in changing one's clothes and appearance. Men were tailored by Poole of London and sent their shirts to be ironed in England. Their sons were sent to Oxford or Cambridge to acquire the right tone of voice. They went regularly to the Derby at Epsom, and the Ascot races, where the Prince of Wales, later Edward VII, welcomed his friends from France in the Royal Enclosure, who soon, however, returned to their native country to enjoy delightful "cures" in fashionable resorts or even in Paris.

There they rode or promenaded every morning in the Bois de Boulogne for their health. The horsewomen wore tight-fitting habits as severe as those of the men, hats like theirs too, but even taller, multicoloured cravats, high-heeled boots, provocative veils and long, full skirts that had to be gathered up by an elegantly gloved hand when it was necessary to protect them from the dirt of the street. Many artists, such as Jean Béraud, Georges Seurat and Alfred Stevens, delighted to portray them in that guise. They may well have seen an eighty-year-old lady riding by, accompanied by a watchful groom holding a leading rein attached to her horse's bit. It was Maria Sophia, Queen of Naples and the Two Sicilies, the Amazon of Gaeta and the most celebrated of the many exiled princesses who held court in France. A gentleman was never seen outdoors without a walking stick held in one kid-gloved hand. From beneath the high, stiff collar a huge, voluptuous silk cravat flowed down to the white waistcoat; on his head he wore a shining top hat, glinting with reflections, as so often seen in portraits by Giacomo Boldini, born in Ferrara but Parisian by adoption.

When not dressed for sport on foot or horseback but receiving guests at home or lolling languidly in their carriages, ladies of fashion could not have been more elegantly arrayed. Sometimes, as in John Singer Sargent's portrait of Mme. Pailleron, a froth of lacy white underdress could be glimpsed beneath their long skirts or falling over their wrists. Over puffed-out hairstyles they wore enormous hats trimmed with everything under the sun, from ribbons and bows, foliage and flowers to feathers or even whole birds. In cold weather they were wrapped in costly furs with big muffs to warm their hands.

Thus we see them depicted in modish paintings and fashion plates, sometimes alone and full length, sometimes in a crowded drawing room with other women against a background of decorative draperies or wallpaper, rare furniture and sumptuous tapestries.

The men, too, are portrayed looking rather like tailor's dummies in their well-fitting tails or morning coats, exquisitely barbered, with impressive forelocks and long moustaches or prophetic beards.

For younger women hastening to amorous assignments there could be difficulties, and one of them was the corset. That ferocious armour of steel and whalebone might give them each a perfect line, but it was also a decided obstacle that needed skillful hands for its adjustment. If the love was young and impatient, the obstacle might take some time to overcome and longer still to replace. It is not impossible that in some dark alley a rare passerby might have observed a private carriage, a cockaded coachman, a liveried footman and a faithful lady's maid waiting for hours till their mistress returned, breathless, with the corset bundled up in a hasty parcel. She slips into the carriage and lets down the window blinds so that the maid, with patient skill, can replace the corset around her lovely waist.

Thus it seemed as if those twenty or thirty years—or, strictly speaking, the fifteen years between the beginning of the twentieth century and the middle of 1914—promised only increasing harmony and security, including rapid advances in surgery and science. Pasteur had discovered *Penicillium glaucum*, the Russian Élie Metchnikoff published his findings on phagocytes, and Jean Charcot was the master of neuropathology.

Other great cities outside France enjoyed their own *Belle Époque*, adapting it each after its own fashion and according to its special interpretation and idiosyncratic refinements, though always with an eye on Paris. There were Vienna, light and frivolous, with its four-month carnival, Budapest, with its amazing gypsy violinists, Bucharest, where a strange blend of Latin and Russian was spoken, Istanbul, then Constantinople, and, not to be forgotten, fascinating Asia, agreeably wild, slightly barbarous, immensely rich.

Paris was no paradise reserved exclusively for a select band of esthetes, writers, artists, French epicures and American or Oriental millionaires ever ready to spend their money and think up new, expensive crazes. The middle classes could enjoy it too, and so could the people working ten hours a day with no Sundays off, who had their own festivals, shows and inventions which they freely offered to the gentry: the circus, the cinema, billiards, the wall of death, cabarets and brothels (Toulouse-Lautrec, the gifted and nobly born dwarf, portrayed them with tireless energy and a very personal art that made the milieu seem picturesque).

A celebrated character of the period was painted by Boldini in a highly affected style. The painting is called *Portrait in Grey* and represents Count Robert de Montesquiou-Fezensac, one of the set in which Marcel Proust moved. It shows him in a languid pose, seemingly interested only in his walking stick, which slants across the foreground of the picture; his hat dangles from his elegantly gloved hand, his upper lip is adorned by pointed upcurving moustachios and a tiny imperial beard grows on his chin. He was the writer of a thousand sonnets, arrogant, decadent. The young Proust admired and envied him, and used him as the original of the Baron de Charlus, the homosexual character who figures so largely in his enormous novel. But the picture most representative of the epoch is not that of a woman, a hero or an adventurer. It is a photograph of the Count Boni de Castellane, who married the daughter of one of the richest men in America, Jay Gould. In this picture he looks tremendously elegant in his perfectly fitting brown morning coat reaching to below his knees, the corner of a white handkerchief drooping gracefully from an upper pocket. A top hat hangs loosely from his left hand, the right hand holds a stick firmly planted on the ground as he walks; a softly knotted cravat spreads into two points beneath his collar. His face is raised, a well-combed moustache embellishes his upper lip, his eyes look into the distance. It is the portrait of a Venus de Milo who has changed sex, and all Paris is his.

As soon as he could spend his wife's dollars he built a gigantic *palais rose* with a huge garden. One night they gave a reception there for which he ordered eighty thousand plants. When, a few years later, the wife decided on a separation, the numerous domestic staff grew anxious about their future employment, and the majordomo expressed their concern to their employer. "There is nothing to worry about," she replied with a smile. "None of you will lose your place. It is he who will have to go."

When in July 1914 officers of the reserve were being recalled to their units the colonel commanding a cavalry regiment remarked to his adjutant, "I don't know quite what to do. Boni de Castellane is coming tomorrow to rejoin this regiment and plans to introduce himself to all the officers. But, as you know, one of them is Prince X, whose wife he ran away with. Anything could happen." "Keep calm, sir," replied the adjutant, "they're used to that sort of thing. They'll know how to pass it off." Sure enough, next day when the officers were seated in the mess, Boni de Castellane appeared in uniform and began to present himself to the other officers, beginning, according to etiquette, at the bottom of the table. He finally came face to face with the prince whose wife he had seduced. There was a moment's hesitation. Then he stretched out his hand, saying, *"Je crois que nous nous connaissons déjà,"* to which the prince, stretching out his, replied, *"Mais oui, nous avons servi dans le même corps."*

The painters, designers and excellent caricaturists were the real stars of the epoch. They it was who recorded this mad, overdressed, overgroomed world that thronged to the annual race meetings where people of every nation gathered in the stands and clustered around the betting booths and the owners and jockeys with their mounts. The same world attended the salons of painting, came together in the latest fashionable restaurants and resorts or the Moulin Rouge or the circus with its acts from every land. Some were aristocrats—often with a mortgaged estate and crumbling mansion in the background—others were theater people, poets, novelists and those who called themselves the *monde* or the *demi-monde* and made no very definite dividing line between the two. Among the artists of brush and pastel, some born to the purple, like Toulouse-Lautrec, others risen from the ranks, or conscientious craftsmen "with all their papers in order," were Whistler, Sem (Georges Goursat), Puvis de Chavannes, Meissonier (a painter of detailed battle scenes), Carrière, who specialized in painting large families, Manet, Degas, Bonnard, Carolus Duran with his famous painting *La Dame au Gant*, Delaunay, Raffaelli . . . to name but a few of the many.

A major contributor to the idea of the *Belle Époque* was the Universal Exposition of 1900 in Paris, this grandiose undertaking inaugurated by the highest dignitaries of the Republic, the visitors ranging from the most exalted figures of Europe, America and Asia, citizens of every class and culture, to mestizos from the farthest reaches of the Empire (that a war was being waged at the other end of Africa, was of minor importance). The multitudes which flocked to Paris, almost doubling the city's population, laid siege to the exhibition from morning to night, invading every corner of the vast arena, drawn by the novelty, the incredibility of it all, carried along moving walkways, or riding in crested diligences with heavily moustached postillions. It held no less compelling an attraction for the more sophisticated members of society, although at times a smirk of condescension might be detected. Abel Hermant likened it to a gimcrack city; and Boni de Castellane saw it as a dirty cloth covering "poor Paris," attracting infected lice from every country.

At the *conversations* of the salons, wit was all (I have given an example of the brilliant repartee of Prince X). When it became known in Paris that the highly popular General Boulanger had failed in his foolhardy attempt to become head of state, he was suddenly abandoned by everyone. He went to live as a simple citizen in Brussels, and two years later committed suicide on the grave of his mistress, Marguerite de Bonnemain. Hearing the news, Clemenceau commented, "The general died as he lived, a lieutenant." "The Tiger," who in the meantime had become the head of government, was buttonholed in a bar about the rights of women by a well-known feminist. "There can be no doubt," she said, "that we are the equal of men, we can do anything they can, even better." Clemenceau heard her out, nodding his head, seemingly approving of everything she said. Finally, descending from his stool, he said: *"Eh bien, madame, allons pisser?"*

Just before the turn of the century important events occurred in France which thirty years earlier would have caused a riot among the populace or brought about a change of government. The defeat at Sedan that ended the Franco-Prussian War and led to the loss of Alsace-Lorraine was a blow that shocked and humiliated the nation. Public opinion was confused. In the Chamber of Deputies in 1875 the Republic survived by a majority of one vote. The failure of General Boulanger's royalist policy, the Panama Canal scandal, the five years of schism throughout the land between the pro- and anti-Dreyfus factions, all following in rapid succession, had left the people apathetic and put a curb on strong emotions. The only subject that roused any enthusiasm was France's colonial ventures into Tunis, Djibouti, Indochina, South America (Guiana) and Madagascar.

The scandal concerning the Suez Canal, which France had undertaken to build, entrusting the work to Lesseps, the man who cut through the Suez isthmus, lasted for two years. Lesseps had asked for only three hundred million francs, and was soon in difficulties. The health of the local inhabitants unexpectedly deteriorated, an epidemic of yellow fever broke out and claimed numerous victims (Dingles, director of excavation, and his whole family died of it), the place was invaded by prostitutes, adventurers, and men who ran gambling saloons, until, after two years, the Canal Company stopped payment and France lost one and a half thousand million francs.

Two years later the anarchist Sante Caserio assassinated Sadi Carnot, the President of the Republic, and the French thought all they had to do was to elect a new one. However, two years of political terror ensued and four hundred anarchists were arrested and executed.

In 1895 Staff Captain Alfred Dreyfus, who was a Jew and proud of it (whereas Jews in the worlds of literature, art, politics and finance tended to leave the subject untouched; who would think of insulting the wealthy Baron Rothschild by calling him a Jew?), was accused by Commandant Henry, deputy chief of the Intelligence Service at the Ministry of War, of sending an anonymous letter to the German military attaché in Paris, written in a hand asserted by Major Henry to be that of Dreyfus. Without any further proof Dreyfus was court-martialled and sentenced to life imprisonment for high treason, degraded from his rank and sent to die on Devil's Island off Guiana. Dreyfus pleaded innocent; his lawyer and his brother, Mathieu Dreyfus, appealed against the sentence. Colonel Georges Picquart, who was in charge of the inquiry, found a letter from Major Esterhazy, of French nationality but aristocratic Hungarian descent, which was equally compromising and was in handwriting very like that of Dreyfus—and he published it.

All France was split into two camps. Conservatives, anti-Semites and some of the nobility openly accused Dreyfus; liberals, socialists and most writers and artists declared him innocent. Finally three years after the verdict had been pronounced, Émile Zola, the novelist, intervened with a violent article in the socialist journal *L'Aurore*, which began with the famous words *J'accuse*, and was addressed to Félix Faure, the head of state. Major Henry committed suicide. A few weeks later Félix Faure suddenly died in his office during a private visit from a lady. His successor, Émile Loubet, immediately reprieved Captain Dreyfus, decorated him with the *Légion d'Honneur* and reinstated him in the army with the rank of major. He served in the 1914 war as a lieutenant colonel.

Marcel Proust too had a Jewish mother, although his father was a very rich and celebrated Catholic doctor. He suffered from asthma almost all his life and was told to avoid the open air at all seasons. From the age of ten onwards he was forced to lead a very sheltered life, but his health deteriorated. By the time he was thirty-five he was a great invalid and had to abandon all worldly activities. After the death of his parents, he abandoned the apartment where he had played host to the most illustrious figures, both French and foreign, among them aristocrats, scientists, diplomats, rich Jews, women famed for their wit and beauty, *jeunes filles en fleurs*, setting himself to recapture in a series of volumes his unsurpassed reminiscences of those guests, their witticisms, their remembrances. In his new abode, smaller and darker, in the intervals between illnesses, the windows closed tight against the air and scents of the outside world, he wrote, wrote and wrote on whatever sheet of paper that came to hand, even the backs of envelopes and invitations, erasing, correcting, adding. It was the task of his manservant to recover the scribbled notes left strewn over bed, furniture and floor when finally creation had to give way to exhaustion. He always got up, when his health allowed, late in the evening, and dressed with infinite care before going out to dine with friends, returning home with the dawn; or he invited them to supper, acquaintances of whom he had long made a study, providing him with inexhaustible material for his notebooks.

Finally, in 1913, appeared the first two volumes of *Du Côté de chez Swann*, a fact revealed to only a small circle of friends. The following year war broke out. Not until 1919 did the three volumes of *À l'Ombre de Jeunes Filles en Fleurs* appear, bringing the award of the Prix Goncourt. At last, success, fame, glory. He was France's most celebrated writer, his work translated into several languages. His career as a writer ended in 1922, eight years after the close of the *Belle Époque*.

The Italian contribution to the *Belle Époque* was very marked throughout. The famous Ferrarese painter Boldini has already been mentioned. Then there were the designer Cappiello, the painter de Nittis and several others, not forgetting the de Chirico brothers and Savinio. One name missing from this list of Italian participants in the *Belle Époque* is that of Gabriele D'Annunzio. That wild and restless character, early famous in Italy for his diverse and contrasting activities as poet, writer, politician and sportsman, might have replaced all by himself several of the figures chosen to represent the era, with his many women (the Comtesse Nathalie de Goloubeff, the Marchesa Casati, whom he immediately christened Cori, the artist Romaine Brooks), heavy debts, frequent polemics and the exalted, self-intoxicating confusion that expressed itself by thought, pen and deed. But in 1910 he suddenly disappeared from Italy. For months no one knew what had become of him, until the news leaked out that he had put the entire contents of his Tuscan villa La Capponcina—including three horses, seven dogs and a motorcar—up for public auction and gone to France.

The first thing he did there was to find an isolated house on the Atlantic coast. "I have come to work," he announced, "and to earn my living." Suddenly he became one of the most interesting and curious personalities of the world he had come to join. He worked tirelessly, writing novels, plays, stories and mysteries in both Italian and French, a perfect French, archaic for Sarah Bernhardt and modern for Pisanelle. He was hailed as the best writer in the two languages.

He was thinking of settling in Paris permanently, when the war broke out. Everyone, the French most of all, had thought that there would be no more wars. When, in 1915, he realized that Italy would soon be taking part in the war, he left for Genoa, made a belligerent speech in Quarto and declared himself ready to join the very new air force, on which, of course, he soon impressed his courage and zeal.

Five months before Austria's ultimatum to Serbia, caused by the assassination of the Crown Prince, the wife of the French Minister of Finance, Joseph Caillaux, went to Gaston Calmette, the editor of *Figaro*, and shot him dead with a revolver for publishing a series of articles attacking her husband's policy. She was immediately arrested and put on trial. The novelist Maurice Donnay wrote in his diary almost every day, and some of the entries show an ever-increasing anxiety about the news from Central Europe. On July 9 Donnay, who was on holiday, attended a small luncheon party given by the President of the Republic, Raymond Poincaré, and his wife, where he also met the "novelist of tailors and dressmakers," Marcel Prévost, with his wife. The newspapers were full of worrying reports from the Central Powers, from Serbia, Austria and Russia. Donnay describes the luncheon at some length, indulging in light and frivolous chatter and detailed descriptions of the ladies' dresses; he carefully avoids any mention of the international situation. Only at the end does he write that Poincaré, although he tried not to show it, had an anxious and troubled air. Perhaps the diarist thought that his host might still find an acceptable solution.

On July 29 Donnay, having read the newspapers, informs us in his diary that the trial of Mme. Caillaux "is put into second place, and only Austria and Serbia are thought worthy of the front page." Next day he adds no more than a few lines: "This morning at eleven o'clock the drum was beaten at Séraincourt; it has been announced that all those on leave must rejoin their regiments within twenty-four hours." Then he adds, "Mme. Caillaux has been acquitted. . . ."

By the first of August all hope had gone. "We can no longer conceal from ourselves that there is a 99 percent chance of war. I saw a huge man with a great pepper-and-salt beard and a large belly—a lieutenant in the territorials—dressed in uniform. That means mobilization."

He also writes a little later: "All night we heard trains passing through; and this morning the news is disastrous. A madman shot Jaurès, the socialist leader, at nine o'clock last night in a restaurant in the Rue de Croissant." He was the war's first victim.

The Belle Époque : Trends and Developments

At the beginning of the century nearly one out of every four inhabitants of this world was a subject of Queen Victoria (on the left, her portrait by Lady Abercrombie). Among the articles of faith bequeathed by the old century to the new, many were of English origin: belief, for instance, in the permanent value of the pound sterling, Savile Row tailoring, the Oxford accent, the White Man's Burden and the art of saying sweet nothings at the right moment with an air of detached elegance. Then the "old lady" died (January 12, 1901) and an era, the Victorian age, came to an end. Yet most of the old certainties lingered on.

On the other side of the Channel there were plenty of deep-rooted convictions too. Unfortunately, some of them were in mutual opposition (dividing society, for example, into pro- and anti-Dreyfus, or clerical and anticlerical

The Belle Époque: Trends and Developments

partisans. Below, an anticlerical cartoon). However, optimism was in the air, even if no one quite knew why.

May 1900: The British annexed the Orange Free State, but the Boer War continued.

June 1900: The Boxer rebels entered Peking and laid siege to the legations, which were not freed till August.

July 1900: King Humbert I of Italy was assassinated in Monza.

In the same year Europe celebrated the new century (only pedants maintained that it did not begin until the first of January 1901) with the opening of the Universal Exhibition in Paris. This wonderland of the twentieth century remained open from April 15 to November 12. An unbelievable number of people flocked to see it: about 40 million tickets were sold and receipts amounted to almost 130 million francs.

The public visited the many pavilions with their 76,000 exhibitors, 36,000 of whom were French. They were set up in the area of Paris bounded by the gardens of the Champs Elysées, overlooking the Place de la Concorde (where the exhibition's main entrance, the Porte Binet, was situated), the Trocadéro gardens, the Champ de Mars and the Boulevard des Invalides.

Almost in the center of the Champ de Mars rose the Palace of Electricity, its façade lit up at night by five thousand multicoloured lamps. "The forces of nature are

subdued and tamed; steam and electricity have become our obedient servants; the machine is crowned Queen of the World. Automatons of iron and steel are driving out the worker of flesh and blood, turning him into a mere auxiliary. ... Science serves us ever more diligently and is conquering ignorance and poverty." Thus, in his inaugural speech, the industrialist Prime Minister Alexandre Millerand interpreted a not uncommon conception of the contemporary world.

The Belle Époque: Trends and Developments

It was the dawn of the automobile age. A driver of motorcars was still a rarity, but for that very reason was well on the way to becoming a symbol, a model, a heroic figure. He wore what was more or less a uniform, consisting of goggles and a dustcoat, as in the Toulouse-Lautrec lithograph on the left, or in Albert Robida's cartoon ("Rue modern-style" for *L'Album*). A motorcar was undoubtedly a luxury. It was not until 1913 that Henry Ford started manufacturing them on an assembly line in his Detroit works. However, in 1903 there were already 13,000 automobiles in France and 1300 in Italy. Interest in motoring as a sport was considerable (the first race was held in 1894). Above is a snapshot of Lartigue driving in the French Automobile Club Grand Prix of 1912.

RUE MODERN-STYLE.

21

AL SECO

The twentieth century started off in an atmosphere of optimism. Social conflict was rife everywhere (the number of strikes in Italy during 1901 has been assessed at 1400), but it was a sign of optimism to have depicted the advance of the people, as did Pellizza da Volpedo in his work *The Fourth Estate* (a study made for it in 1892 is shown above). "I feel," he said, "that this is no longer an era of art for art's sake, but of art for humanity's sake."

It was also the time when the great art jewellery houses came into being. The shop of Georges Fouquet, the famous jeweller, was decorated with stained glass designed by a Czechoslovakian, Alphonse Mucha (on the right, two of his preparatory designs).

e ×× SALUTE !

One of the more solid foundations of optimism in the early years of the century was technical progress, a relatively new development in human history. By now a great deal of ground had already been covered. People could pride themselves on those achievements and yet feel there were no limits to the giddying leaps forward still to be made.

Radio, for example. William Marconi (shown below in a photograph of 1902) had been experimenting with wireless telegraphy in the attic of his father's house since boyhood. Since the Italian authorities showed no interest, he moved to England, his mother's birthplace, where he developed and perfected his invention. After demonstrations in London, on Salisbury Plain and by the Bristol Channel, he finally succeeded in transmitting the letter S in Morse code across the Atlantic from Cornwall. In 1909 Marconi won the Nobel Prize for physics, and the companies he had formed for the practical application of his invention were prospering.

Then there was photography. Seventy years after Joseph Niepce had obtained the first lasting photographic impression, the portable camera with film appeared. Instantaneous photography was now possible, and spread rapidly. Henri de Toulouse-Lautrec, acute observer of the *Belle Époque* scene

and designer of numerous posters,
drew this advertisement in 1894 for
his friend Paul Sescau.

If names can sum up an epoch, Maxim's is surely one of them. Here, seated on red divans, reflected in wall mirrors, one could see princes, politicians, financiers, artists—the "world," and everyone who hoped to appear a part of it—staying up till dawn with their champagne and their ladies dressed by Poiret.

High fashion invented its own mystique, celebrated by the great French stylists Paquin, Doucet and Poiret. Its brilliance penetrated to the provinces and crossed the frontier. Even the little Italian milliner, going her rounds with an apprentice carrying the hatboxes, caught something of its sparkle.

It was a world of aristocrats pretending to be middle-class, upper-middle-class people living like aristocrats and a lower middle class admiring them both. Meanwhile Lenin, who was thirty-two at the time, published his book *What Is to Be Done?* in 1902 (above right: the first page of the first edition).

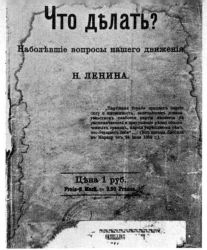

"Through the white, gilt-framed double doors, thrown open by invisible hands, their Majesties made their entrance. . . . The ladies sank into the curtsies etiquette demanded, the gentlemen bowed low. The two sovereigns advanced as if walking through a field of bending corn" (Joseph Roth, *The Thousand and Second Night*).

Grand balls took place at the court in Vienna, presided over by the aged but seemingly immortal Emperor Franz Joseph, who had been on the throne for more than half a century. The notes of the waltz echoed through the ballroom, while the Emperor of Austria-Hungary, already shattered by the suicide of the Archduke Rudolph, heir to his throne, awaited his inevitable end in a strange atmosphere of nostalgia amidst gleams of culture, nationalist tensions, legitimate and otherwise, and a cloying torpor.

Vienna and Paris: waltzes and cancan. The era is pervaded by their transient, contrasting rhythms. The painting on the right by Wilhelm Gause is redolent of an eighteenth-century imperial grandeur; on the left, Leonetto Cappiello's poster epitomizes the rakish acidity of nonconforming urban taste.

Cappiello, Gyp, Willy—the poster unites three names very typical of the *Belle Époque*. The first, a stage designer and commercial artist, was

LE FRIQUET
PIÈCE EN 4 ACTES DE WILLY
Tirée du Roman de GYP

a talented innovator in poster design; the second, Sybille-Marie-Antoinette de Riquetti de Mirabeau, though the author of a few rather sentimental works, wrote, above all, novels and stories of a worldly, satirical nature; the third, music-hall entertainer and husband of Colette, helped his wife write the successful *Claudine* novels.

The Belle Époque: Trends and Developments

"The flight lasted only twelve seconds but was, at least, the first flight in which a machine carrying a man rose into the air under its own power, soared upwards, advanced without losing speed and landed at a height above sea level equal to that of its point of departure...."

On December 17, 1903, the first engine-propelled machine (below), piloted by Orville Wright, succeeded in lifting itself off the ground. The feat aroused more skepticism than surprise. By 1905 the Wright brothers had completed over a hundred flights, but it was not until 1909, after European governments and the public had long shown their interest in the "technological miracle," that the authorities of the United States decided to pay it some attention. At Brescia in 1909 there was an international aeronautical competition. Kafka, who was among the spectators, noted the event in his diary. D'Annunzio flew with Glenn Curtiss.

In the summer of 1902 Venice was shaken by a mighty crash that echoed round the world. Her bell tower, the famous *campanile* of San Marco, worn out by the years and salty air, collapsed in ruins, fortunately without doing serious damage to the surrounding buildings. The debris once cleared away, the work of reconstruction was started almost immediately and ended in 1912 with the erection of an exact replica. On the left a curious trick photograph depicts the moment of the tower's collapse.

"... to live and love in happiness, free of the curse of knowledge and creative torment, in the contentment of the ordinary! ... I found myself between two worlds, without feeling myself at home in either of them, and that caused me some difficulty." Thus Thomas Mann in *Death in Venice* expresses his attitude to bourgeois values: art is life and privilege, but also a malady

and punishment. Below, a painting by A. Siebelist, *The Artist and His Disciples* (1902).

Technology had its disasters. Théophile-Alexandre Steinlen, Swiss-born but a naturalized Frenchman, was a draftsman, engraver and painter. He contributed to a number of satirical reviews, and commented with bitter sarcasm on the danger of the Paris underground railways. In August 1903, as the result of a collision between two trains, a terrible fire broke out in which eighty-four people perished. Above right: the Passy viaduct, now destroyed, built by Jean Camille Formigé between 1903 and 1905.

LE MÉTRO-NÉCRO-

N° 125   22 Août 1903   40 Cent

L'ASSIETTE
AU BEURRE

DESSINS DE
STEINLEN, WIDHOPFF, GALANIS
D'OSTOYA, FLORANE
VAN DONGEN, HRADECKY, POULBOT
CAMARA

In 1896 the French scientist Henri Becquerel discovered that uranium salts had the property of emitting radiation. Marie Curie devoted herself to the study of the characteristics and intensity of such radiation, establishing that the same phenomenon took place with thorium compounds. It then emerged that there existed a compound endowed with much higher radioactivity than that contained in the same quantity of uranium. With her husband at her side she intensified her researches, seeking to isolate from pitchblende the element she christened radium. The work took four years. For their discovery the Curies were awarded the 1903 Nobel Prize for physics (below, Marie's gold medal; she won another for chemistry in 1911).

Jean Jaurès (depicted here by Jean Veber as he lays down the law during an uproar in the Chamber) was the recognized leader of the French socialist deputies and one of the historic heads of international socialism. In France the political situation was somewhat unusual. After the 1899 elections the socialist Alexandre Millerand became a member of the government, an event that caused a great deal of discussion within the whole socialist movement. Paul Singer, representative of the German Social Democratic Party, remarked, "We cannot approve of a socialist entering a bourgeois ministry, but . . . now the Socialist Party has grown so big that in the moment of danger the bourgeoisie will be forced to run to one of us to save the cause of fundamental liberty." Jaurès defended the need for the Socialist Party to support republican institutions.

But the France of the *Belle Époque* is also the France of the Moulin Rouge (seen above in the painting by Charles Camoin, 1904) where dancers performed the frenzied, provocative cancan, the dance born in the night haunts of Montmartre frequented by *grisettes*, students, artists and models.

It was the France, too, of the Belle Otéro, a dancer and high-class courtesan who held princes and millionaires in her thrall. The Suicidal Siren, they called her in the United States, for between the twirl of a fandango and the turn of a roulette wheel she collected, with equal nonchalance, splendid jewels or the suicides of lovers, deceived or reduced to misery.

35

"I lead you towards a splendid era," announced the Kaiser in 1900. His subjects, or at any rate the classes typified in Max Slevogt's double portrait (1904), found it so, cushioned in the security of the Second Reich. The Germany of Wilhelm II was ultraconservative and disciplined, yet clumsy and boastful in its relations with other countries. Nevertheless it achieved impressive economic progress.

There was a war in the East. One read about it in the papers. The Russo-Japanese conflict of 1904–05 revealed three facts: that the Russian Empire was weaker than the one Europe had known a hundred years before, in the days of Napoleon and Alexander I; that modern war, with its machine guns, mines and torpedoes, was an unclean and tragic business; that the myth of the white man's supremacy was no longer convincing. Those concerned took none of these lessons to heart.

Below, Russia as a giant octopus, a Japanese cartoon that went round the world.

Anticlericalism was rampant. In 1901 a law was passed banning religious orders from teaching; in 1904 came the break-off of the relations between France and the Holy See. Pius X (seen here in a caricature from *Assiette au beurre*) issued the encyclical *Vehementer nos*, condemning modernism. In France, Church property came under severe penalties.

37

"At that time a deep and arrogant peace reigned in the world. The newspapers of the kingdom were filled with court circulars and society notes ..." (J. Roth). In an atmosphere of quiet self-satisfaction international "society," with its train of ladies' maids, Russian leather trunks, pet dogs and hatboxes, trailed through the chain of hotels founded by César Ritz in the great capitals of the West. The same set was to be seen at Cannes, Biarritz and Marienbad. Its members enjoyed the thrill of the tables at Monte Carlo; they dined at Demel's and ate cakes at the Hotel Sacher in Vienna, supped at Maxim's in Paris, went to the races at Longchamp and Ascot and, if they were invited, attended garden parties at Buckingham Palace.

On the right: the fountain in the Palm Court of the London Ritz, built in 1905; below, the stately Liberty-style staircase of a house in Milan, designed by the architect Alfredo Campanini.

Ladies at the races, wearing rustling trains and immense hats. Above: the fish market in Amsterdam, painted by Max Liebermann (1904). In the Dutch capital in 1904 the Congress of the Second International was held. There were violent disagreements among the socialist leaders about the motion proposed by Jules Guesde, who was in favour of rejecting any socialist participation whatsoever in the government of a capitalist country. After four days of hot debate, marked by some dramatic clashes between August Bebel and Jean Jaurès, the motion to refuse all compromise was passed by a large majority.

Still there today in the Montmartre quarter of Paris is the Lapin Agile, the famous tavern painted by Maurice Utrillo (above left; below, a photograph of its interior in 1905). It was a favourite meeting place of artists, bohemians and literary people. Writers and painters such as Francis Carco, Amedeo Modigliani, Maurice Utrillo (who painted it), Suzanne Valadon and Roland Dorgelès were all frequent visitors.

In the German-speaking world intellectual and scientific life was in a ferment. In 1900 Freud published *The Interpretation of Dreams*, and in 1901 *The Psychopathology of Everyday Life*. Einstein first set out the basis of his theory of relativity in his paper *On the Electrodynamics of Moving Bodies*.

On the right we see the scientist posing for a photograph in 1910, the year in which he left Switzerland to teach at the university of Prague.

On the right, below, a view of the Vienna Ringstrasse by Maximilian Lenz (1900).

"Thousands of workers—not social democrats but believers and loyal subjects—streamed, under the direction of Father Gapon, from all parts of the city towards its center, the square in front of the Winter Palace, to present a petition to the Tsar. The workers advanced, carrying the holy icons. . . . The troops were called out. Uhlans and Cossacks threw themselves sword in hand or firing on the unarmed crowd. . . . According to police records, there were over a thousand dead and two thousand wounded" (Lenin).

"Sunday, January 22. What a distressing day! . . . The troops were forced to open fire in different parts of the city. Many were killed or wounded. . . . Mamma had only just arrived in town and went at once to mass. I dined with the others. A walk with Mischa" (Nicholas II).

Thus Tsar Nicholas II recorded it in his diary and, some years later, Lenin recalled "Bloody Sunday." After the sanguinary repression of January 22, 1905, a series of strikes set in all over Russia. *Soviets* were formed in every province. A section of the navy at Kronstadt mutinied, as did the sailors on board the battleship *Potemkin* at Odessa. The Tsar had to sign the Manifesto of October 17, which, among other things, instituted a representative body, the *Duma*, whose power was largely with-

drawn as the revolution ebbed.

Below left: Fusillade in front of the Winter Palace at St. Petersburg. On the right: One of Fabergé's famous jewelled Easter eggs in gold, enamel and pearls. It was given by Tsar Nicholas II to his mother, Maria Feodorovna, probably in 1903.

AVANTI
DELLA
DOMENICA

"Liberty"—sometimes used as a synonym for Art Nouveau, though in England "Morris" is the more usual equivalent—is perhaps the most typical of all the *Belle Époque* styles. But the name itself goes back further than that. In 1875 Arthur Lasenby Liberty opened a shop in London, specializing in goods from the Far East: fabrics, jewels, draperies, screens and fine furnishings. Below: an advertisement for the firm, appearing in a 1906 number of *The Studio*, one of the most important art reviews of the period.

The Belle Époque: Trends and Developments

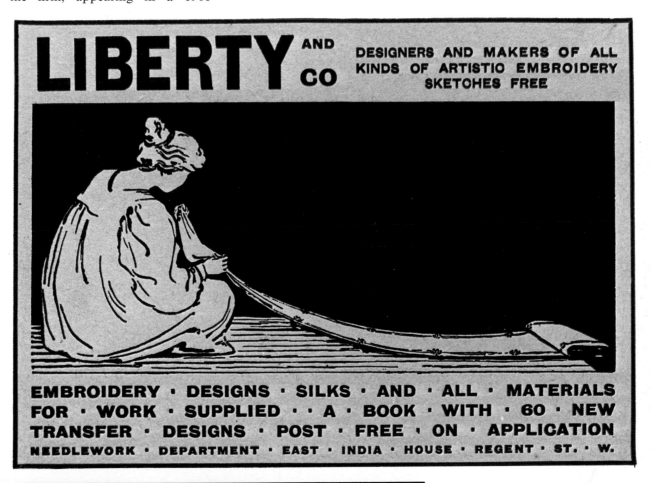

LIBERTY AND CO

DESIGNERS AND MAKERS OF ALL KINDS OF ARTISTIC EMBROIDERY SKETCHES FREE

EMBROIDERY · DESIGNS · SILKS · AND · ALL · MATERIALS FOR · WORK · SUPPLIED · · A · BOOK · WITH · 60 · NEW TRANSFER · DESIGNS · POST · FREE · ON · APPLICATION NEEDLEWORK · DEPARTMENT · EAST · INDIA · HOUSE · REGENT · ST. · W.

René Lalique, jeweller and goldsmith, gained a leading position in the production of Art Nouveau objects when his works were exhibited at the Salon du Champ de Mars in 1895. It was he that made the Florio Plaque (left) for the first motor race on the Madonie track, run in 1906.

On the opposite page: a cover design for *Avanti della Domenica* in the same year.

One day, just as in a fairy story, a little florist, daughter of a master builder, who had just occasionally sung popular songs in a small restaurant in the Piazza Navona, met her Pygmalion and so started the career that was to make her one of the most loved and renowned artists of the *Belle Époque*.

Lina Cavalieri (left, in a portrait by Cesare Tallone) was taken under the "protection" of Carlo di Rudini. She was ailing, but he brought her back to health, provided her with an elegant wardrobe and swept her into his life of luxury, travelling to and fro between Rome and Monte Carlo. Thrown headlong into the *beau monde*, she found an enthusiastic audience and achieved one triumph after another from Paris to St. Petersburg. There she married Prince Alexander Baryatinsky and became known as Princess Linochka. The marriage soon ended in divorce. A soprano, she specialized in opera and, perhaps more through her personal fascination than through the quality of her voice, met with success in all the leading opera houses, the San Carlo in Naples, Covent Garden in London and the Metropolitan in New York.

The other two leading ladies of the theater were made of different stuff. Sarah Bernhardt (center, in a bust by Gérôme), portrayed as Berma in Proust's *À la Recherche du*

Temps Perdu, figured frequently in the press for her sensational eccentricity, but also for the artistic quality that made her the most famous French actress of the period. But it was in Eleonora Duse (on the right) that the theater found its most spiritual and sensitive actress. She starred in plays by Verga, Goldoni, Shakespeare, Sardou and Dumas and was praised by Chekhov and Shaw. At the beginning of the century she was the impassioned interpreter of D'Annunzio's work and from 1904 to 1909 of Ibsen's. Always seeking to make her performance still more expressive, she followed closely all the innovatory movements of the European theater, collaborating with Gordon Craig and developing a very personal style of acting, outside the traditional framework.

The Belle Époque: Trends and Developments

In 1904 the Lumière brothers patented a new sort of photographic plate they called Autochrome, which made it possible to take colour photographs even before the advent of modern films. On the left is a composition published in *L'Illustration* in 1907 and relating to an article on unusual technical innovations.

Below, the international social set is satirized in a watercolour by Sem (Georges Goursat).

Famous journalists and titled nobility followed sport with attention or even took part in it themselves. Prince Scipione Borghese, together with Luigi Barzini, one of the most renowned special correspondents of the *Corriere della Sera*, competed in the Paris–Peking rally of 1907. The two Italians (seen below during a stop in Berlin) won the amazing race in their Itala.

The Belle Époque: Trends and Developments

"I have to confess that I search, search, search, but do not find. . . . I feel that I want to paint the new, the fruit of our industrial era."

Umberto Boccioni was describing his feelings on arriving in Milan in 1907, urged on by a desire to experience the essence of the great city in which he felt the breath of modern life. It was in 1908 that he painted *Factories at the Roman Gate* (below), in which his interest in the "modern idols" merged into a cer-

tain social enlightenment. A very different subject is treated in the gouache of Roger de la Fresnaye *L'Allée des Acacias* (on the right; 1908). Horses are hardly more than a symbol of the past. Now it is the motorcar, driven by an efficient chauffeur, that takes the lovely ladies with their silk parasols for a drive.

The Belle Époque: Trends and Developments

In December 1908, thirty-seven seconds of earthquake devastated Messina and Reggio Calabria (on the right: the ruins of Messina). The first helpers to arrive on the scene were the crew of a Russian warship, who shot down the looters scavenging among the fallen masonry.

Below: *Unemployed* (1908–09) by Rudolf Zeller. The figures represent the "victims" of a slump, or a local recessive phase in the economic cycle. One of the cultural

and political limiting factors of the society that supported the *Belle Époque* was to look on earthquakes and unemployment equally as inevitable natural disasters.

The "famous architect ... has divined that the human being, born in a clinic, dying in a hospital, must have his living space, too, designed with ascetic simplicity." "Then is art no more than a means of separating kitsch from life?... The more abstract art becomes, the clearer grows the air." So wrote Robert Musil. Those were the years when architecture was searching for a new language, inserting a new variable into the equation of building, namely functionalism. "Only what is practical can be beautiful," said Otto Wagner, chief of the generation of architects belonging to the Secession group, who was active in the Vienna of Musil. His Postal Savings Bank (1904–08) is shown below.

The Belle Époque: Trends and Developments

"At the Châtelet Theater at half past eight precisely, a gala performance, being the public rehearsal for the greatest spectacle of the Russian stage. The program will proceed in the following order: *Le Pavillon d'Armide, Le Prince Igor, Le Festin.*" With these words *Le Figaro* announced the first night of the Ballet Russe on May 18, 1909.

The creation of this company was an event of major importance in the history of music, ballet and design.

Serge Diaghilev collected round him the best soloists from the dance schools of Moscow and St. Petersburg. Anna Pavlova (shown in a poster below), Tamara Karsavina and Vaslav Nijinsky danced for him. The initial success was followed by a period of remarkable collaborations. Rimsky-Korsakov, Stravinsky, Debussy, Ravel, Mussorgsky composed the music; some of the great modern painters of the time—Bakst, Larionov, Matisse, Picasso and Derain among them—designed sets and costumes.

The opposition to conventionality in art and in the cultural situation was the distinctive mark of the Viennese Secession movement, which brought innovation not only in architecture but also in the graphic arts. Viktor Schufinsky designed the poster below for a nightclub. It differs from the French tradition of *affiches* in its clear-cut outlines, unusual shapes, contrasting colours, the white body and the intense erotic quality.

The *Belle Époque* was the time of the great fashion houses, but it also saw the first appearance of giant department stores: Au Printemps in Paris, and Selfridge in London. The latter shop opened in 1910. On the right, the big clock on its Oxford Street façade.

The Belle Époque: Trends and Developments

On February 20, 1909, *Le Figaro* (left, an advertisement by Pierre Bonnard) published the first *Futurist Manifesto* by Filippo Tommaso Marinetti ("We want to sing of the love of danger, the life of energy and daring").

Then, in 1910, the Venice Biennale, which until then had usually confined itself to the sphere of conventionality and provincialism, devoted an entire room to Renoir. Below: young girl seated, 1909.

Giovanni Boldini, who quickly took Paris as his adoptive city, was perhaps the most undeniably *Belle Époque* of all painters. In his pictures we see theater people, carriages, gentlemen, ladies—especially ladies. Luisa Casati, the "divine Marchesa," whose portrait, exhibited by the painter in the 1909 Salon, had inspired Montesquiou to some verses, insisted on being painted again in one of the extravagant poses she loved to assume.

The portrait below, presumably painted in 1914, shows her in an eccentric headdress of long-quilled peacock feathers. It was a bizarre, artificial image of the feminine type most admired in that world of orchids and Salukis.

The women, adorned with peacock plumes or their white throats encircled with ostrich feather boas; the men wearing an expression somewhere between dreamy and bored, elegant in their pale morning coats and gleaming top hats, carrying slender canes: those were the exclusive, frivolous outward insignia of the languid esthetes and worldly women that peopled the ambience of Swann, Odette de Crécy and Baron de Charlus. (Below right: Domenico Morelli, *Portrait of Bernardo Celentano*.)

The ballet *Schéhérazade* (music by Rimsky-Korsakov, 1910) had an enormous influence on scenic art and fashion. The set and costumes by Léon Bakst (his design for *Schéhérazade* is shown above right) affected the audience in the same way as the music and dancing, creating an atmosphere that suggested both aquarium and bazaar, "a greenhouse of the passions." Women especially were enthralled, and Paul Poiret quickly jumped on the bandwagon, creating clothes of Oriental cut made up in magnificent, brilliantly coloured materials.

The Belle Époque: Trends and Developments

Parisian nights: below we see *Le Jardin de Paris ou les Belles de Nuit* by Jean Béraud, the painter of Parisian aristocracy and high life in the early nineteen hundreds. Proust described him as the "young and glorious master, the artist acclaimed by both the new world and the old, a fascinating personality that everyone sought to capture, though none succeeded . . . the wittiest and most polished of men." Rows of electric lights illumine a vivacious evening gathering in the open air. Young dandies and their older companions observe the exceedingly elegant *belles de nuit* with appreciative but critical eyes. Paris is seen as the "center of the world," a medley of disparate attitudes, a bubbling caldron of culture and the favourite resort for a leisured or dissipated life. Mysterious ladies with flowery hats drive through the parks in their victorias while children of the nobility or upper middle classes play under the watchful eye of their impeccable nannies, as in the picture from *Novissima* (shown below right).

Portrait of a group with handsome carpet. All the others featured are monarchs assembled in London for the funeral of Edward VII in May 1910. In front: Alfonso XIII of Spain, George V of Great Britain, Frederick VIII of Denmark; in the back row: Haakon VII of Norway, Ferdinand I of Bulgaria, Manuel II of Portugal, Wilhelm II of Germany, Albert I of Belgium.

61

The *Belle Époque* invented holidays, too. They were the other aspect of the industrial society that saw people as "producers" (and soon everyone else went on holiday too). Above left, the Venice Lido in 1911; right: *The Holiday Guests* (1911) by Emil Nolde. The same set that patronized the Danieli restaurant disported itself on the Lido, those beaches described by Thomas Mann in *Death in Venice* as "corners of the civilized world, immersed in a light-hearted sensuality, where by the edge of the sea, on decked-out platforms like verandas, people dressed with careful morning elegance lay stretched out on deck chairs in the shade, while others, beside them, revelled, half naked, in the freedom of the place."

In homage to an ideal of feminine beauty that insisted on a white and delicate skin, and because a tan was looked on as a mark of illness, since only patients in sanatoria under-

In 1911 the pearl of the Louvre was stolen: the enigmatic and cloying smile of the *Mona Lisa* was gone. The theft caused a great stir and considerable dismay at the ease with which it had been accomplished. The French newspaper *Le Matin* offered "a reward of 5000 francs to any occultist, fortune-teller, chiromancer, diviner or clairvoyant" who could help to reveal its whereabouts, "since the keepers at the Louvre have been unable to preserve the *Gioconda*, and the police and judiciary have not known where to find it."

On the left below, the empty space in the Salon Carré at the Louvre.

went a sun cure, holidaymakers by the sea usually covered themselves at every point and, if they entered the water at all, wore heavy, clumsy bathing dresses.

Italy conquered Libya, thus belatedly entering the "noble" scramble to civilize the "natives" (above right, a biting comment in *Asino*, 1911). Gertrude Stein remarked: "Native always means people who belong somewhere else, because they had once belonged somewhere. That shows that the white race does not really think they belong anywhere because they think of everybody else as native."

Turkey lost the war. So Bulgaria, Serbia, Greece and company made another war on Turkey. Then Turkey, Greece, Serbia and company made war on Bulgaria, which lost the war. And so on.

In 1911 the statuette called *The Spirit of Ecstasy* was chosen as the symbol and mascot of Rolls-Royce Motors, the car firm dedicated since its beginning to the production of luxury automobiles of a superb technical standard.

On the left, the winged figure of Rolls-Royce; below right, a Vinot-Deguingand of 1912 which has another, if less famous, female figure on its radiator cap.

Around 1911 the tango, a popular Latin American dance, considered daring and rather scandalous, arrived in Europe. Women's dresses had to be slit at the back or side to allow for its fluidity of movement, while the men wore their hair swept backwards in the Argentine fashion. Below on the left: a little bronze of tango dancers by G. Eberlein, circa 1912.

"I only realized the gravity of the situation when I saw a third-class passenger on the first-class deck." On the night of April 14–15, 1912, the "unsinkable" transatlantic liner *Titanic*, on her maiden voyage, struck an iceberg south of Newfoundland and sank with one thousand five hundred people on board. A distress signal was sent out (the newly established SOS being used for the first time), but the wireless operator on the only ship within range had switched off his apparatus a few minutes earlier.

Above, on the right, an English magazine cover announcing the disaster; below, a French illustration depicting the *Titanic* as she strikes the iceberg.

MATA HARI (VENERE) nel BACCO e GAMBRINUS

TEATRO SCALA 1911-12

"... Since Picasso no painter uses a model ... and so they paint with what is inside them as it is in them and the only thing that is outside them is the painting ... Picasso had done my portrait ... he had asked me to be a model why this was an exception I do not know and as there was never any question there was never any answer."

Thus wrote Gertrude Stein in her *Everybody's Autobiography* on the subject of her portrait (1906; on the opposite page). In Gertrude's drawing room in Rue de Fleurus in Paris one met artists and intellectuals of two generations, from Picasso, Francis Picabia, Dalí, Thornton Wilder, Duchamp, Max Jacob, Braque and Matisse to Hemingway, Fitzgerald, Pound and Sherwood Anderson.

On this page, above, an advertisement for an Italian textile firm (1912); below, Mata Hari. The notorious Dutch dancer and adventuress, later accused of treason and spying and shot in 1917, had started by exhibiting herself in Parisian nightclubs in 1905 as a sacred Indian dancer. In 1911–12 she appeared at the Scala in Milan, where she played the part of Venus in *Bacchus and Gambrinus*.

"... the face with its curved nose and green eyes beneath a high forehead surrounded by hair combed *à la* Bressant": that is the description of Swann by Proust, who took his friend Charles Haas as a model. In *The Prisoner* there is an allusion to the painting *Le Cercle de la Rue Royale* by James Tissot (on the right, a detail showing the figure of Haas), and the writer admits that "some of his traits appear in the character of Swann."

On the left, a 1913 poster for an exhibition of works by Emil Pirchan, the German stage designer and member of the Viennese Secession movement.

During the years 1900–14 the theater played its part in the disintegration of traditional dramatic forms. In Germany and Austria the expressionist theater arose under the leadership of Frank Wedekind, Oskar Kokoschka (the painter Kokoschka's first play, *Assassination, Hope of Women*, was produced in 1908 and gave rise to heated argument), Walter Hasenclever (his *The Son*, 1914, presented parricide as the only solution of the father-son conflict) and Georg Kaiser (Pirchan designed sets and costumes for one of his plays). The movement developed further during and after the war, taking on antimilitarist and revolutionary overtones. The provocative innovations of the stage designs paved the way for the futurist creed of the value of progressiveness, suffering and terror.

It was during the *Belle Époque* years that the greatest number of emigrants left Europe. The average annual outflow was about one million persons, rising to a peak of 1,380,000 per year between 1906 and 1910. There was a difference in the new wave of emigrants when compared with the migratory trends of the nineteenth century: nearly all the earlier emigrants had been natives of northern and western Europe (the British Isles, Germany, Norway), but now they were coming from southern and eastern Europe (Italy, Spain, Russia and Austria-Hungary). Whole families left to seek their fortunes, or just to find a decent way of life, mainly to the United States, where there was a great demand for labour, but also to Canada, Latin America, South Africa and Australia.

Below: *Emigrants* by Angiolo Tommasi. Right: a 1912 camera.

The cinema now made its appearance: a mirror, an amusement and an art. In 1902 Georges Méliès produced *Le Voyage dans la Lune*, a mixture of trick photography, clever animation and ideas. *The Great Train Robbery* was made by Edwin S. Porter in 1903; 1912 saw the production of *Quo Vadis?* The theory of cinema was getting under way, too, with the *Manifeste des Sept Arts*, an essay on cinematographic esthetics by R. Canudo in 1911.

The Belle Époque: Trends and Developments

COLOGNE EXHIBITION
MAY TO OCTOBER 1914
DEUTSCHE WERKBUND-AUSSTELLUNG
EXHIBITION OF ART IN HANDICRAFT
INDUSTRIES & COMMERCE · ARCHITECTURE

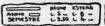

It is all too easy, in the light of hindsight, to see the warning signs. But 1914 undoubtedly dawned on a troubled world. What is he doing on the Cologne Crafts Exhibition poster, that curiously stiff, naked man astride a horse, holding a flaming torch in his hand?

It opened in May and closed in October. Our planet had already changed. It was not only the children that were playing at soldiers, but also the children in the children's books, as in Rubino's illustrations. In June came Italy's Red Week (above, the funeral of the three demonstrators killed at Ancona). Many feared and as many hoped for revolution. It was not revolution that came, but war.

Evening paper! Evening paper!
Italy! Germany! Austria!
And over the square, mournfully
edged with black,
Ran a rivulet of purple blood.

—Vladimir Mayakovsky

Above is an illustration from *The Dance of Death*, engraved by Paul Bürck.

On June 28, 1914, at Sarajevo, the Hereditary Archduke of Austria Franz Ferdinand of Hapsburg (seen on the right with his wife shortly before the attack) was assassinated. It was not the first time that one of the powerful ones of the earth had died a violent death; the diplomacy of the Great Powers had succeeded in solving more than one crisis— Morocco, the Balkans and the partition of Africa, for instance; there was an international pacifist movement; both the socialists and the church opposed armed conflict . . . and yet it ended in war.

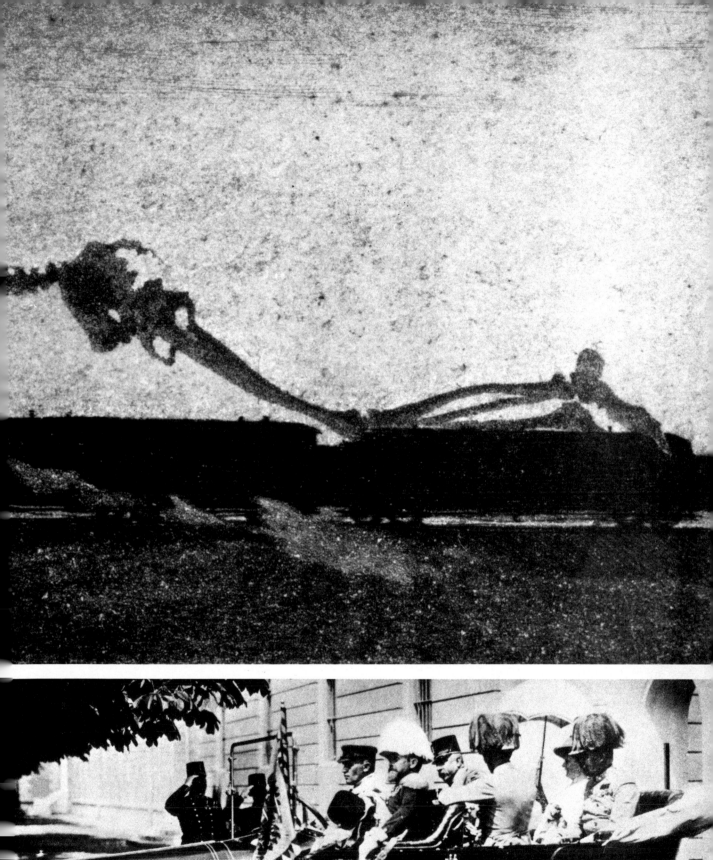

On the left, by A. Léveillé, *1er Aout 1914. La Mobilisation. Les Boulevards.* All the Great Powers had had their mobilization plans accurately planned for decades— ever since the end of the Franco-Prussian War, in fact. There were rigid and complicated strategies, never used or even tested, except perhaps by Russia during her war with Japan.

But on July 30 the Tsar gave orders for the general mobilization of his army in defense of Serbia, and that began a whole chain of declarations of war. Germany set about applying the Schlieffen plan against France. Italy, still neutral, could afford to mock, as in the cartoon on the right from *Numero* on the Germanization of the Moulin Rouge.

In the French capital, on the day of the Sarajevo murders, the glories of the Longchamp races were in full display. At the end of July

LA « GERMANIZZAZIONE » DELLA FRANCIA.   Disegno di MUSINI.

DOPO L'OCCUPAZIONE DI PARIGI. — Per dare un'impronta spiccatamente germanica alla capitale francese, Guglielmo II ha ordinato di sostituire alle « chanteuses » del *Molin Rouge*, i procaci ufficialetti dell'esercito conquistatore.

public attention was focussed on the Caillaux trial, which ended in the acquittal of the wife of France's ex-Minister of Finance. She had confessed to killing the journalist Calmette, who had been waging a bitter defamatory campaign against her husband. But the talk resulting from the verdict of July 27, however scandalous, found nothing more to feed upon. For on the thirty-first the German ambassador delivered an ultimatum to the President of the Council; on the evening of the same day, at the Café du Croissant near the headquarters of *L'Humanité*,

Jean Jaurès was killed with two shots from a revolver; on August 3 France went to war. The *Belle Époque*, whatever it may have been, was over.

The crackling of ephemeral events was muffled under the thunder of the shells. But even the accompanying picture of "the bullet in the heart," of fine, instant, clean and graceful death, was—in its dramatic unreality—a last legacy of the *Belle Époque* to the new age the world was facing, in which death was ugly, atrocious and mud-bespattered. *"Quelle connerie la guerre,"* said Jacques Prévert. But that was two world wars and several minor ones later.

Can-can and Flappers

by Philippe Jullian

Caricature by Sem (Georges Goursat).

The *Belle Époque*... Myth has replaced history to such a degree that these words immediately conjure up a music-hall scene: showgirls in black stockings, pink velvet bodices and feathered hats, dancing the cancan; their partners—English gentlemen in evening dress or uniformed Austrian officers, or even the artists of Montmartre. If the music hall can afford it, a hackney carriage drives across the back of the set, or perhaps one of the first motorcars. Regardless of perspective, the backcloth shows the Eiffel Tower and the Moulin Rouge together, or the Casino at Monte Carlo.

In the cinema, the *Belle Époque* style was much favoured by the Viennese directors Erich von Stroheim and Joseph von Sternberg working in Hollywood after the First World War. The films of Jean Renoir in France and later of Luchino Visconti in Italy made use of the images of a lost paradise.

As a subtitle, or on a band round a book, the words *Belle Époque* promise delightful evocations, whether true or false (it does not really matter, and in any case the difference is negligible): a lady from the highest society leaving her huge house to go to a party somewhere, a footman on the steps, an impeccable coachman or chauffeur in attendance. The sparkle of her jewellery, the rustling of her train contrasting with the evening suit of her companion who personifies the man on the de Reszke cigarette advertisements. Or, in front of a charming country house, small girls with golden curls under lacy bonnets playing diabolo with sailor-suited little boys who will be killed in the war. Or, again, in a box at the opera, superb women, their dresses a little too low-cut, listening to Melba singing *Thaïs* while in the stalls gentlemen in evening dress ogle the dancers' legs through their monocles.

For historians, the *Belle Époque* is the period when professional diplomats kept watch to ensure that nothing happened to upset the order established by the treaties initialled by respected monarchs, when ambassadors were still repeating the words of Disraeli and Bismarck. In the words Proust gave to the Marquis de Norpois, Turkey was "the sick man of Europe" and Austria the "double-headed monarchy." In spite of friction and rivalries, the "European concert" led the world.

As the witty English cartoonist Osbert Lancaster remarked in his memoirs, soldiers took a sporting attitude to war which came to an end only with the horror of the trenches in 1914. "If the relieving column did not arrive, or the ammunition ran out, so much the worse for the regiment; it was unthinkable, so accustomed to victory was that generation, that the ultimate outcome of the campaign would be affected. And even if by some extraordinary and terrible turn of events, or an act of betrayal on the part of Liberal politicians, the war itself should be lost, no threat to the British way of life would result; a whole battalion might be wiped out, national prestige sadly dimmed, but not a penny more would go on the income-tax, the Derby would still be run, and silk hats and frock-coats would still be worn at the church parade" (Osbert Lancaster, *All Done from Memory*, Houghton Mifflin Co., Boston, 1953, pp. 78–79).

To divide history from legend, this period must be placed exactly both in time and in space, for it was not equally glorious in every country in Europe, not to mention the rest of the world. ...

First of all, it must be said that the different social classes must have found it very different as regards happiness. Thus, the life of farm workers and country people remained much the same as it had been two generations earlier, in spite of some improvement in agricultural instruments. The very fast development of the industrial machinery which had caused so much upheaval in the nineteenth century finally led to a reduction in working hours, and trade unionism obtained definite advantages for workers. It was, however, in no way a *Belle Époque* for the Lancashire miner, the silk weaver from Lyons or any of those ranked among "the poor." No doubt the charity of "decent people" temporarily relieved these misfortunes, without doing much to eliminate their causes. There were the "honest poor," who worked hard and showed their gratitude, and the "idle poor," who drank and insulted the sisters of charity. However, under Tolstoy's influence, the hearts of the middle classes began to soften and

Max Nordau was able to write: "The worker today is what the noble savage was in the eighteenth century." A monument, alas since demolished, as a vestige of the paternalism of "decent people," was erected opposite the Bon Marché in Paris; it represented the owner of that shop and the Baroness de Hirsch in furs and muffs, leaning benevolently towards a beggar woman and her children. Nonetheless, before we sneer at them, we should remember the virtues of these "decent people." A family would bleed itself dry to avoid one of its number going bankrupt, or to provide a dowry for an ugly daughter. They were prepared to sacrifice a son for their country, a daughter to the convent; they paid wages to retired servants and invited their most tedious female relations to stay in the country. Family feeling extended far and wide—one needs only to read the interminable birth, marriage and death notices—and opposed any trend which threatened that institution however slightly. Hence Gide's words: "Family, I hate you." *L'Illustration*, which was the favourite magazine of "decent people," shows pictures of dynasties in front of their factories, congratulates heroic officers, charitable priests, daring leaders of industry and ladies of these families doing good works.

It becomes possible to refer to a *Belle Époque* when considering people who could afford to put money on one side or become landlords; in short, people who benefitted, however modestly, from capitalism, for, above all, it was a period when people had confidence in cash. The lower middle classes, clerks and primary-school teachers, had more days off and went away for their holidays—not very far away, it is true, but nevertheless no longer thought of themselves as being attached to the place where they worked and often finally achieved the ideal of living on their incomes. For those who had always lived on their incomes, the era was indeed a glorious one; we shall see later on who these people were.

In time, the *Belle Époque* covers the years 1900 to 1914. The tendency is to date it from 1880 so as to include the impressionist painters such as Toulouse-Lautrec, or even to turn it into a result of the Second Empire, when in reality it was more like a resurrection of it. The nineteenth century had ended badly. Its last decade saw a bitter realization of its own faults, and optimism at scientific progress gave way to a kind of disenchantment. Materialism undermined the marvellous but contributed no enthusiasm. Patriotism flung armies into colonial conquest before flinging them at one another which alarmed the "decent people" and exasperated the workers whom socialism was teaching to think. This disenchantment was reflected in two movements with frequent interruptions: the Decadent movement among intellectuals and the Anarchic movement among the masses.

Comparing the state of their society to what they knew of dying empires, writers were proclaiming themselves as decadent for the first time. All passions were permitted, as were daring styles of all kinds. The *avant-garde* dates from the nineties and to it we owe symbolism, that nebulous art, pursuing the dream, refusing to separate painting from music and from poetry, happily blending their values. A sad atmosphere originated in the damp plains of Belgium and spread like a cloud all over Europe, producing the occasional masterpiece and giving rise to countless failures. In his book *Degeneracy*, which caused a great stir at the time, the German journalist Max Nordau put all esthetic curiosities, vices and follies into one bag. Spiritism developed, strange sects abounded, esoterism occupied a place which religion, being too official, could not properly fill.

Anarchy was the violent expression of a hatred for the established order of things, for sacrosanct values: the monarchy, the army, the church. It was despair of ever achieving that happiness which too many forces prevented one from approaching. The Empress of Austria, King Umberto of Italy, President Carnot of France and various grand dukes were assassinated; a bomb went off in the Chamber of Deputies. The French anarchist Ravachol became a sort of hero, for memories of the Paris Commune uprising were not yet dead. There were also outrages during the *Belle Époque* but the bombs exploded in a sort of euphoria, without the slightest repercussion, except, of course, in Russia. But it would be as well to state from the outset that Russia experienced only the most distant echoes of gaiety.

Whereas outrages only made interesting news items, one peaceful death took on a symbolic significance: that of Queen Victoria on January 2, 1901. Once the woman who, somewhat arbitrarily, had represented moral values and adherence to principles in their strictest form had gone, it was permissible to enjoy oneself. Her heir lost no time in doing so, and the English equivalent of the *Belle Époque* was the Edwardian era. It was considered in bad taste to be indignant: scandal lost its edge. The last five years of the century had been shaken by two scandals the extent of which amazes us today when one gets to the bottom of them. In France the "Dreyfus Case" divided the country into two camps, the nationalists and the upholders of truth (who are too easily confused with the left). In Britain the trial of Oscar Wilde also represented the crushing of a minority (that of homosexuality; Dreyfus had been a Jew) by a society whose conventions were threatened. The Mayerling drama in Austria had struck a blow at the monarchy. The Panama Canal affair discredited the parliamentary system.

The Boers' resistance held British power in check and earned the old Queen the insults of the rest of Europe. China rejected colonization. The century did indeed finish badly and "decent people" had plenty of reason for anxiety. "Decent people"—that is to say, people of note, the establishment for the British, those who clung to their privileges because of their responsibilities, mainly landowners and clergymen who were then in their service as the army is in the service of democracy today. Anarchists cursed "the alliance of army and church." The judges and heads of commerce and industry consisted almost entirely of "decent people"—the world of banking a little less so, as it was international and often Jewish. Paul Bourget wrote for his readers, who were "decent people," that the pillars of the European order were: the House of Lords, the body of Prussian commissioned officers, the Académie Française and the College of Cardinals. And,

reassured, they proceeded to buy Russian stock.

The year 1900, which was the year of the Universal Exhibition in Paris, really does mark an overturning of European attitudes and is not just a convenient reference point. The pessimism of the end of the century gave way to optimism: the twentieth century would be the century of electricity, that "fairy" who would bewitch the exhibition's fantastic pavilions, where the nineteenth century had languished under the black sign of coal, painfully extracted from the earth. Electricity, in contrast, came from water, was clean and flexible and had unlimited power. This quotation from Gustave Geoffroy's artistic criticism clearly expresses the optimism tinged with estheticism and socialism released by the exhibition: "The masses should also look at themselves. They are the essence of life, the mainspring of all this work, the *raison d'être* of all this art. Let them listen to the educators sprung from their own midst; they must realize their destiny and the part they have to play. ... It is a coming together of peoples, a universal harmony. May this force give the reason to art and ideas against the missiles of steel."

In politics, the great powers were watching each other and arming themselves, but still respected the decisions of the Congress of Berlin, which, twenty-five years earlier, had established a balance between the two powers of Great Britain and Germany. It is true that Russian imperialism and French *revanchisme* were threats, but the Franco-Russian rapprochement was no more of a threat to peace than the Triple Alliance among Germany, Austria and Italy. And when the Kaiser denounced the Yellow Peril, politicians whispered: "Let him enjoy himself." It was therefore possible to believe that a period of peace was beginning, and the illusion continued until the Balkan wars and Wilhelm II's "coups" shook this optimism. But the progress of socialism seemed worrying in a different way.

This euphoria was encouraged by improvements in standards of living which filtered all through the social strata to the lower middle classes, thanks to electricity, running water, speed of transport, etc. and, as we shall see, the ever increasing forms of recreation. So the *Belle Époque* was born with a century the first ten years of which fulfilled all that people expected of it, "people" here being mainly the "decent people," then the workers risen from the proletariat; it lasted exactly fourteen years.

Now is the moment to point out that this era was not equally happy and glorious in all countries. France, to whom the expression the *Belle Époque* belongs, experienced euphoria more flamboyantly than other nations. Great artistic creations developed there in that atmosphere of well-being, which means that it can no longer be considered as superficial. Proust and Debussy, for example, were part of the *Belle Époque* inasmuch as their estheticism extended over a society for which beauty was the prime consideration. In 1900 France was rich, her political dissentions calm. She was becoming a republic and believed in a future of social justice. It is true that there were several scandals, but none of them became as vitriolic as Panama.

They always involved the discovery of a woman somewhere among the files, just as a woman was always discovered under the bed in Georges Feydeau's farces. President Félix Faure, who died in his mistress's arms, had a very *Belle Époque* death, inspiring the popular songwriters without plunging the nation into mourning. England smiled in the end at her King's escapades and the Belgians were happy to think that King Leopold was entertaining the most beautiful dancer in Paris. The statue of the Parisienne above the triumphal gateway to the Exhibition, her arms open wide, dressed in the latest fashion, clearly expresses the supremacy of woman (or, rather, of love).

The Exhibition, which drew millions of visitors, was an act of homage to the working world as much as the expression of a new form of art. Witness the words of the poet and journalist Jean Lorrain, who was at the same time the strictest and the most dazzled of the *Belle Époque*'s critics, firstly about the new beauty: "At last the water tower begins to work, and with a glow of stained glass, frames within its multicoloured façade fountains and cascades first of liquid sapphire and

ruby, then of topaz and sardonyx. But the most beautiful sight of all is the dark, reflecting span of the river, the Seine suddenly constricted between the Palaces of the Rue des Nations and the greenhouses of the Rue de Paris, bearing reflections and flames in its waters, the Seine transformed into a stream of incandescent lava flowing between the stones of the embankments and the pillars of the bridges. Oh! The magic of the night, night with its everchanging forms! Then the Porte Binet and its grotesque towers changes into translucent enamel and assumes a certain grandeur."

Then Lorrain gives us a description of a fairground: "In an apocalyptic frenzy, roundabouts peopled by pigs, giraffes, camels, cars and bicycles, and with the mountains of Russia painted on a circular backcloth, turn and pass, blaze, glow and flash, sparkling with tinsel, gilt and mirrors in a truly Dantesque whirl, with a rustle of skirts, the flash of a breastplate, the shine of a helmet, a fluttering of blouses, the occasional flame of a silk scarf or of hair, manes, tippets and chignons. The electric light whitens colours and flattens silhouettes."

Paris has never had so many theaters, music halls, large restaurants or cafés. The provinces, the South in particular, followed the movement; Toulouse, for example, was known as the Athens of the Third Republic. "Decent people" kept their appearance of being in power and the mode of life that goes with it. The middle classes were at last learning to spend in the face of so many temptations, the most pressing of which, after 1910, was the motorcar. The workers, listening to Jaurès, believed in a better future.

After Paris, Vienna was a *Belle Époque* capital, even more so than Paris if we are considering only the world of pleasure. The waltz, the operettas and masterpieces such as *Der Rosenkavalier* tend to make us think today that the old Emperor reigned over subjects who cared for nothing but dancing. One need only read Musil and Rilke to realize the profound malaise which was preparing the collapse of the Austro-Hungarian Empire. But Vienna—such a provincial town today—is still living on the memory of its *Belle Époque*, like

those prima donnas who give a farewell concert every three or four years. In Vienna as in Paris, the Second Empire tradition persisted, without the interruptions of a war and a revolution, but shaken by the terrible economic crisis of 1873.

In the Stadtpark there stands a monument to Johann Strauss, who is the perfect symbol of Viennese sensuality. It shows the composer playing the violin, stepping out of a sculpted frame of intertwined women, some veiled and some less so, with fine profiles and superb bosoms, representing the Waltz. This huge trinket contains elements of Rodin and closely resembles Klimt.

As has been said, the *Belle Époque* was a new Second Empire with Franz Léhár as Offenbach, and the world of *The Merry Widow* was the same world as that of *La Vie Parisienne*. The *Orient Express*, linking the two pleasure capitals of Europe, was full of Rumanian princes, Turkish pashas, Polish noblemen, Balkan royalty, all determined to "drink their fill of it," as Offenbach's characters sang in 1867. Sometimes the operetta world turned sour, as when the Serbs threw their King and his wife Queen Draga out of the palace windows, and it is a fact that that famous day in Sarajevo began like an operetta: folk dancing, a flamboyant royal couple in love ... The members of a royal court and the archdukes gave Vienna great style and society was exclusively aristocratic, although everything of interest was patronized by Jews. In Paris not all the elegant women who set the fashion came from the Faubourg St. Germain—far from it—and the smart world was much more closely connected with the world of art. The old Princess Metternich, who had shone at the court of Napoleon III, gave parties which, with charity as an excuse, united different circles, and the Mayor of Vienna, Lüger, saw to it that there was dancing everywhere, especially in suburban pleasure gardens and open-air cafés. They sang:

"*Wien, Wien, nur du allein
Wirst stets die Stadt meiner Traüme sein.*"

("Vienna, Vienna, you alone will always be the city of my dreams.") They adored fancy-dress processions like the one, around 1880, for which the painter Mackart designed the costumes. The most sumptuous was held in honour of the fifty years of Emperor Franz Josef's reign and the greatest names of the Empire capered about dressed in costumes of the time when their ancestors had made their names. There were processions of flower-decked carriages on the Prater. Masked balls were all the rage and served as subject matter for Hugo von Hofmannsthal and many librettists. Frequently, a kind of premonitory sadness crept into these celebrations, that basically rather pleasant anguish expressed so languorously by the gypsy violins. Around 1900 these gypsies began to appear everywhere in France. One of them, called Rigo, with smouldering eyes and enormous whiskers, carried off Clara Ward, a splendid American woman, who had just married the Prince de Chimay. The ex-princess appeared in a figure-hugging costume beside her lover on the stage of the Folies Bergère. There was a terrible scandal.

Even without its masquerades, Vienna was the most colourful capital in Europe because of its Balkan and Hungarian elements and the variety of its uniforms. Its restaurants were almost as good as those in Paris and its cake shops were better. Even today there is still a "pre-1914" feeling about Sacher and Demel's. It need hardly be said that Professor Freud did not join in the fun.

In London there was hardly any connection between the social and intellectual worlds, but in contrast the political and social worlds were intimately linked. Power was still in the hands of the great families, and "political hostesses" made and unmade ministries in the course of a weekend; the great noblemen shared out government posts between them. In his memoirs, Somerset Maugham recalls having heard someone saying: "Jimmy can have India, Tom can have Ireland and Archie can have the Exchequer ...." César Ritz founded the first of his great hotels in London because, as he said, "I realized that here were a great many people ready to spend huge amounts for the best that was obtainable." After 1900, money began to have the edge over aristocracy while at the same time assuming its habits and titles. The "decent people" who had owned the land and held the power for so long felt themselves overtaken by the arrival of Chamberlain and Asquith. They were not good at resisting the attacks of those who resented their vast fortunes. Victorian integrity disintegrated. In 1913 some ministers, of whom Lloyd George was one, had to admit that, although they had not actually accepted bribes, they had unduly favoured the Marconi Telegraph Company in which they held large numbers of shares.

London was truly the capital of the world during Edward VII's reign. One could live magnificently there, but it was still difficult to enjoy oneself and people went to Paris for real pleasure and to Italy for the esthetic life. Provincial England remained Victorian and religion retained its importance—chiefly a decorative religion: "There goes God's butler," said a great lady, watching the Archbishop of Canterbury pass by. The church parade after morning service on Sundays was one of those rites, simultaneously sacred and profane, which enable sociologists to define a social group. Osbert Lancaster draws this sketch of a parish frequented by the middle classes of Kensington: "... the verger opened the doors at the final verse of the closing hymn. Then a short pause, a rustling murmur as the congregation rose from its knees gathering up prayer books and feather boas and adjusting veils and gloves, and the first worshippers would emerge blinking a little in the bright sun pursued by the rolling chords of the voluntary. Soon the whole churchyard and street was a mass of elaborate, pale-shaded millinery, great cart wheels a la Lily. Elsie decorated with monstrous roses and doves in flight, old-fashioned bonnets trimmed with Parma violets, among which the glittering top hats, ceaselessly doffed and replaced, provided the sharper, more definite accents" (Osbert Lancaster, *All Done from Memory*, Houghton Mifflin Co., Boston, 1953, pp. 72–73). Nowhere more than in England did an official clergy composed of rich men not

overconcerned with metaphysics give "decent people" the assurance that everything was for the best in the best of all possible worlds.

The young German Empire, wholly concerned with acquiring the biggest army, the biggest factories, only participated in the *Belle Époque* through increased prosperity. The Germans were moral and megalomaniac like the Emperor Wilhelm, and the aristocracy was too sure of its importance to bother about being smart. With an admirable organization, few painters except those of an obscure *avant-garde*, the cult of Wagner followed by the dictatorship of Strauss, the importance still accorded to the philosophers Schopenhauer and Nietzsche, the Germans could not allow themselves the wasteful and carefree attitudes typical of the prewar period. No one in Berlin would have said, *"Après nous le déluge."* The sense of humour was confined to the Munich newspaper *Simplicissimus*. There was, however, a Viennese operetta feeling about the scandals, such as the musician Tosti carrying off the Queen of Saxony. The quality of life was improving rapidly. Town planning was the most advanced in Europe and methods of transport the quickest. Germany was the most modern country by far and her progress alarmed other countries even more than her armaments. Paul Valéry wrote an article entitled "A Methodical Conquest" about it, which gave much more food for thought than his early poems.

Far more than elsewhere, the ruling class favoured the new art. Thus, the Grand Duke of Hesse encouraged the Darmstadt school and had a whole district of his capital built by Joseph Maria Olbrich. Weimar remained an intellectual center. The *Blaue Reiter* group was formed in Munich, the official artistic capital. The German *Belle Époque* was opulent and serious but scarcely international. The euphoria of the first years of this century depended greatly on pleasant relations (from banking to ballet) between people from every corner of Europe. Excessive ideas of grandeur, a lack of tact and a basically moralistic attitude prevented Berlin from becoming a happy capital on the level of Vienna.

If opulence was present in Russia it lay in

90

Caricature by Sem (Georges Goursat).

disorder and waste. As to serious matters, it turned quickly to mysticism if not nihilism. "We are dancing on a volcano" was the refrain of a sumptuous and unbalanced aristocracy. As for professional dancers, it took the genius of a Diaghilev to teach them to dance to any music other than Tchaikovsky's. Fabergé's creations—precious, amazingly intricate, in appalling taste and utterly useless—are archetypal *Belle Époque* trinkets. The boyars who colonized the French Riviera and settled in Paris and Rome brought their panache and a kind of madness to the life of pleasure and laid the foundations for the arrival of the Ballets, which were the greatest esthetic creation of the age.

Where Scandinavia, sinking quietly into democracy, took no part in the festivities, Italy on the other hand behaved like a woman who is always a little overdressed to hide the fact that she is rather hard up. There was a desperation in her enjoyment as there is in the novels of D'Annunzio. That the great poet should have thought of himself as a great nobleman clearly shows the unbalanced state of the country. But for wealthy foreigners, Rome, Venice and Florence, each offering different delights, were like so many heavens. The Italians brought beauty to the European party. Thus the Marchesa Casati travelled through the *Belle Époque* in a wake of orchids, inspiring masterpieces, causing suicides, planning extravagant "years of madness." Of Spain there is as little to be said as of Portugal. No one would have dreamed of going there except as a tourist. On the other hand, thanks to a few madly Parisian noblemen, Bucharest was a citadel of elegance facing a fast-decomposing Orient. The India of the viceroys and the maharajahs also took part in the Edwardian fun. For Americans, London was the place to spend one's money and marry one's daughters.

Having placed the *Belle Époque* in time—a period of fourteen years at the most—and on the map of Europe, we should now, if we are to understand its various aspects, ask ourselves who it was that benefitted most from it, who, because

of exceptional circumstances of culture and fortune, was able to instigate works of art, inspire a Proust or a D'Annunzio, applaud a Hugo von Hofmannsthal or a Diaghilev. As this period was the last still ruled by precedence, we shall begin with the royal families who benefitted from it between assassination attempts, but who, for a long time now, had only inspired official painters, the librettists of operettas and academicians. We can receive an idea of this separate world by looking at magazines which devoted so many pages to royal celebrations: coronations, jubilees, weddings, christenings and funerals. Looking at the photographed groups surrounding a monarch, a connoisseur could recognize a Bourbon, a Hapsburg or a Hanover by his Roman nose, protruding lips or bulbous eyes. Most people copied the style and dress of King Edward and Queen Alexandra, but often, beneath their English veneer, their Germanic haughtiness or joviality, their Austrian foolishness or their Russian neurasthenia was soon apparent. Royalty filled the sleeping cars. The *Orient Express* carried Fürstenburg and Hohenlohe to Vienna, Coburg to Sofia and Danois to Athens. The *North Star* took Würtemberg and Hesse to St. Petersburg. Cannes and Marienbad, Venice and Biarritz, were linked by special trains. Red carpets were cheerfully rolled out at railway stations, and the "august passengers" followed by ladies-in-waiting and aides-de-camp graciously received their greetings. Their royal highnesses were always charming, but the Grand Duchess Vladimir was the most elegant, the Empress of Germany the least fashionable, Queen Marie of Rumania the most beautiful, the King of Belgium's daughters the most unhappy and the King of England's the most childish. The Infantas were often flighty, whereas the Savoy princesses aspired to sainthood. As for the men, the Battenbergs were splendid but penniless, the Bourbons—both the Neapolitans and the Carlists—extremely pious, the Braganzas were gadabouts and the Orléans very intelligent.

The visits rulers paid one another became the occasion for retinues, processions, fireworks and festivities in which the whole population took part. We have lost this sense of occasion, which is one of the things dividing us from the *Belle Époque*. The French Republic also knew how to receive guests; when Nicholas II, Edward VII, and Alfonso XIII came to Paris, the town was decked with flags and thousands of onlookers waited for hours to cheer a king.

The arrival of a ruler, even if incognito, always caused a stir. The Comtesse Edmond de Pourtales and the Countess Greffulhe gave sumptuous and intimate lunches (only twenty guests) for Edward VII in Paris; for Don Carlos, King of Portugal, Count Boni de Castellane posted a footman on every step of his marble staircase. The arrival of a royal personage in a spa caused disturbances in hotels and casinos alike. With Edward VII always in the lead, Hamburg, Marienbad, Cannes and Biarritz experienced brilliant seasons, and each time a Congress of Vienna in miniature gathered around the fat but well-dressed gentleman: highnesses, ambassadors, famous beauties waiting to be noticed or remembered, ladies ready to spend millions to be seen beside the King, like the famous Mrs. Moore, an American, of whom the King said: *"Il y a trois choses auxquelles on n'échappe pas: l'amour, la mort et la Moore."* (There are three things from which one cannot escape: love, death and Mrs. Moore.) In Biarritz the beautiful Mrs. Keppel kept guard over the King and Mrs. Moore despaired of ever meeting him until the day she thought up the idea of giving the royal chauffeur an enormous tip. The large Mercedes broke down in the middle of an outing and "by happy chance" the American, driving in the opposite direction in her De Dion-Bouton, offered to give the King a lift to Biarritz.

Gloomy under Victoria's reign, the English palaces became models not only for other courts but also for the houses of the millionaires whose company the King enjoyed so much. What Queen Marie of Rumania wrote about Windsor could almost equally well have been written after a visit to the Duke of Marlborough at Blenheim Palace, to the Duke of Westminster at Eaton Hall or to the Rothschilds at Waddesdon or Ferrières:

"There is nothing more perfect down to the smallest detail than the Court of the King of England, a sort of aristocratic opulence where everything was easy with not the slightest false note and no time was wasted. From the handsome and splendidly dressed gentleman who welcomes you to the solemn yet affable footman who precedes you into the galleries, everything enchants even the most difficult of people."

Edward VII said to the keeper of his art collection: "I don't know anything about pictures, but I know how they should be hung"—a remark typical of royalty who, mostly, had their apartments arranged in a vaguely Louis XVI style which became that of the Ritz Hotels. The damask walls were hung with portraits by Philip Alexis László de Lombos, a Hungarian who was a genius at painting the sparkle of tiaras and medals.

Royal courts were naturally magnificent, the Kaiser's among others, with ceremony comparable to a grand military revue, but the court of Edward VII was elegant as well. Not even St. Petersburg could offer so many beauties or so many exotic costumes. Diamonds sparkled on the shoulders of peeresses and the turbans of maharajahs and gold on the uniforms of ambassadors and field marshals. The guests of honour opened the ball by dancing a quadrille or a polonaise with the sovereign; then, one on either side, preceded by chamberlains, the King and Queen slowly made the tour of their guests and, as they passed, heads bowed like ears of corn in a wind. After this, the orchestra attacked a waltz or a Boston two-step. At midnight the royalties followed the King and Queen to have supper in a more intimate dining room and the guests moved into a gallery where a buffet was set out between pyramids of roses and exotic fruit, peacocks fanning out their tails and boars' heads. Gold plate glittered on the sideboards and people danced until dawn. Presentations of debutantes and Buckingham Palace garden parties were the occasions for enormous social upheaval and offered the crowd a sparkling—and free—spectacle. The toing and froing of impeccably harnessed carriages announced the royal presence in the streets. The court added a sparkle to every capital such as we can hardly imagine, and it was one of the many faults of Nicholas II to neglect St. Petersburg because the Tsarina disliked parties. It is true that in poor countries, such as Portugal, the pomp and show of a court which had scarcely changed since the eighteenth century impelled the people towards anarchy.

As France had no court, the aristocracy took its place and, having no longer any political power, became purely representative because of its great fortunes in land. About ten families, intermarried and related to foreign royalty by marriage, supplied Marcel Proust with the originals for the Guermantes family. One need only reread *À la Recherche du Temps Perdu* to realize that the life of the Guermantes, with their balls, grand lunches, visits to one château after another, created a luxury movement which one could not help admiring even without being as snobbish as Proust. The carriages and horses, a magnificent outfit glimpsed in the street or in front of a house, a coming and going of superb footmen, plume-decked dowagers or young officers with bird of prey-like profiles gave a party atmosphere to the Faubourg St. Germain where the Guermantes lived, as well as to their village church or a concert which would otherwise have been very dreary. Proust saw very clearly that the Guermantes lived on familiar terms with ordinary people and were friendly with everyone as long as they did not try to force an entry; in short, they gave society an image of Beauty and a reminder of History. The same applied to the Italian aristocrats described by D'Annunzio in *Il Piacere*, and one needs only to see a Visconti film like *L'Innocente* to realize that a stylish aristocracy at least helped to make the world a little more amusing and much less ugly.

Did people really enjoy themselves when being entertained by the Guermantes or the Roman princes or English dukes? One would hardly think so from reading the novels which take us into their drawing rooms; but writers, even when they were quite definitely guests, were still too much like spectators not to be severe critics of an allusive type of wit and expensive, monotonous pleasures. We need only call to mind some of the rules which dominated the society world to realize that so many constraints, even if they had the

advantage of filling in people's long hours of leisure, would soon seem unbearable to us. One had to leave visiting cards, pay visits, attend all the weddings and funerals, be seen at horse shows, at the opera, at the races, at exhibitions, at charity bazaars, wearing a different outfit every time. Such a mechanical way of life caused what we should today call alienation in society people, a loss of individuality, turning them with the passing years into caricatures of themselves. Elegance and grotesqueness are never far away with Proust. Two typically Parisian artists, Helleu and Sem, precisely represented these two attributes. In a hundred sketches, Helleu, painter of yachts and young girls in bloom, captured the elegance of famous beauties such as the Duchess of Marlborough and the Comtesse Greffulhe. They are goddesses raised above the masses on marble steps and surrounded by a court in which it is no easy task to distinguish the admirers from the parasites. The engravings show them reclining on a Louis XVI chaise longue, leaning on a parasol to inspect a Watteau drawing, their noses tucked into a muff or half hidden behind a fan. Ah, yes! It was indeed a *belle époque*!

Sem, who observed them without tenderness, depicted the famous beauty as the tired old woman she would become. As for women who had never been beautiful, he stresses the obscenity of a mouth, the avariciousness of a glance. The Marquise de Villeparisis and the Marquise de Ste. Euverte, whose feather headdresses, trains and makeup-plastered faces Proust describes so amusingly, are found again in Sem's drawings, wild with the vanities of this world, beside shifty-eyed gentlemen, seedy gigolos and monolithic grand dukes. A *belle époque*, was it? One wonders as one leafs through Sem's albums of drawings.

When overwhelmed with nostalgia for the *Belle Époque*, one should read the memoirs of those who lived through it with all its advantages. Two women have left particularly delightful ones: the Duchesse de Clermont-Tonnerre *Au Temps des Marronniers en Fleurs* (*When the Chestnuts Were in Flower*), and the Comtesse de Pange *J'ai vécu 1900* (*I Lived in 1900*). In their pages the world of Proust lives again, a happy mixture of worldliness and intelligence. In spite of the conventions of the time, a woman of spirit could easily make an interesting life for herself if she did not waste too much time visiting, attending fittings at her dressmaker's or engaging in love affairs. With a little intrigue, a good table and plenty of wit she could manage to run a salon, a typically Parisian institution and one possible only in a leisured society. There were as many originals for Proust's Mme. Verdurin as there were for his Duchesse de Guermantes. Examples were Mme. Armand de Caillavet, who exhibited Anatole France as if he were an unusual animal, Mme. de Loynes, in whose salon right-wing policies were forged, and Mme. Menard-Dorian, at whose house (in spite of the fact that she was a millionaire) left-wing policies were hatched. There were musical salons, artistic salons (the least smart). Each had its own Academician and fought to obtain the election to the Académie Française (which has a maximum of forty eminent members elected for life) of other members of the faithful. These ladies had their "days" when almost everyone they knew came to call between five o'clock and seven; then they gave grand dinners, leading the conversation like a conductor, their musicians taking care not to miss a single word uttered by the "resident" great man. The lady of the house had frequently captured him by means of love, and she retained him with good cuisine and by arranging a sort of court around him. We have no idea today of the degree of importance which could be attained by a writer such as Paul Bourget or Pierre Loti. When D'Annunzio came to Paris, delirium ensued. André Gide, who loathed these dramas and intrigues, is not a *Belle Époque* writer.

These ladies also had to fill their homes with old furniture and knickknacks. The *Belle Époque* of "decent people" on the whole (except in Belgium and Germany) turned its back on contemporary art, hoping to hide its defects under the cast-off clothing of more gallant or glorious days. When Boni de Castellane built a palace with his wife's dollars, he had a copy of the Grand Trianon made. In this taste for the past and this refusal to live in the present can be seen a society nearing its end.

Where French memoir writers were impregnated with literature, English ladies—far more numerous but less witty, with the exception of Margot Asquith—were almost equally preoccupied with politics as with society. Their sphere was more likely to be a country house than a salon. In the country they had ministers and deputies, dukes and bankers, ambassadors and journalists in their hands. A few beauties warmed these gatherings with their presence. Sport occupied a more important place than conversation unless one belonged to the kingdom of the "souls," a group of cultured aristocrats who professed scorn for the rather vulgar luxury of the Edwardians. In 1906, Lady Londonderry succeeded in breaking the alliance between the Conservatives and the Liberals through her hatred of Lloyd George; the old Duchess of Devonshire had pushed her husband into all the ministries in spite of his indolence, and Margot Asquith managed to make hers Prime Minister.

Enormous fortunes made it possible to maintain two country houses, a house in London, a shoot in Scotland, a villa in Cannes, a yacht and a racing stable. Lord Tredegar and Lord Bute between them owned almost all the coal in Wales. Already very rich, Lord Derby inherited £300,000 from an uncle on condition that he distribute £67,000 among the 763 servants, stablemen and gardeners. If the Guermantes had a humourous insolence, their British equivalents were in such a majestic position that they would never have had the opportunity of using that kind of wit. The Duchess of Devonshire offered either one or two fingers to the ladies who visited her when shaking hands, according to their rank or virtue, rarely her whole hand. In her palace on the Mall the Duchess of Sutherland received her guests in three stages: first, a dinner given for the King and a few dukes and ambassadors; then about a hundred friends came for coffee; lastly, at about eleven o'clock, came the "crush," that is, "everyone who was anyone." Woe betide anyone who arrived too early!

A lavish society, nonintellectual, but containing many beautiful women. Sargent's famous painting of the Wyndham sisters, a symphony in

white, is the perfect image of the Edwardian style, just as his portrait of Lord Ribblesdale is an example of perfect elegance not without a certain ease and grace. The women of the world whose photographs appeared in tobacco kiosk windows were known as "professional beauties"; some of them, like Lillie Langtry, were on the fringes of the *demi-monde*. Lady Randolph Churchill had many affairs but without the slightest scandal. The model for these ladies was the honoured Mrs. Keppel, as clever as she was beautiful; she managed to occupy first place in the King's heart as well as in society. Princess Daisy of Pless, equally intimate with the King and the Kaiser, dreamed of an Anglo-German rapprochement. She left memoirs which endlessly describe parties and palaces, a delight for lovers of past glories. Two words consistently recur in them: "lavish" and "pageant."

Edwardian society was in fact a prodigious procession with which the newspapers kept their readers in touch hourly. One is amazed, leafing through the newspapers of the day, at the amount of space occupied by society events. The public followed these reports with as much interest as the fans have today in their favourite stars.

Accounts of weekends at Chatsworth, the Duke of Devonshire's house, filled whole pages. It is true that there were good reasons for this. Fifty guests arrived, each with his valet or her lady's maid; the duke himself had over two hundred servants. These "upper servants" were served in a separate dining room seated in exactly the same order of precedence as their masters; amongst themselves they called one another by the same titles as the people they served. The party arrived by special train with two extra wagons for the vast amounts of luggage. It seems that much of the time was spent changing one's clothes. From breakfast on, one wore country clothes, then lunch was eaten round small tables, with the ladies who were not going hunting that afternoon in town clothes. After the hunt came tea. If the King was present, a lobster salad was served, the gentlemen in morning coats, the ladies in tea gowns. Then bridge was played until it was time to change into evening dress for dinner—a different dress each evening, of course, and the gentlemen in knee breeches or uniform. Theater occupied the evening with singers from London, unless there was a ball. At midnight a cold buffet was served: plovers' eggs, grouse, salmon. The King was very difficult to entertain. One day, having been invited to visit the pretty Mrs. James, he found an enormous Easter egg on the step, out of which his hostess jumped dressed as a chick. He gave her Victoria's look when she uttered her famous "We are not amused."

The best witness of Edwardian ostentation was Vita Sackville-West, a very young girl, whose father owned the fabulous Knole Castle. Her novel *The Edwardians* is as pitiless an account as that of the Guermantes but lacks the esthetic sparkle which enabled Proust to give his duchess a place among the great figures of literature.

The author's mother, Lady Sackville, was the leading figure of a shocking trial from which, thanks to her beauty and insolence, she emerged with her head high. A rich old gentleman who had inherited all the millions of Sir Richard Wallace (of Wallace Collection fame) was in love with Lady Sackville. He left her a fortune and his fabulous furniture. The old gentleman's family went to court to try to recover their inheritance, but lost the case because they could not prove that Lady Sackville had been the mistress of Sir Murray Scott. Lady Sackville was a great admirer of Rodin, who sculpted a beautiful bust of her.

Generally speaking, in such a well-organized society the scandals did not reach the public at large but produced situations which, after Oscar Wilde, dramatists such as Somerset Maugham and Arthur Wing Pinero made the most of. One of the most famous stories is that of the rivalry between Lady Grey, a great beauty who launched the Ballet Russe in Paris, and Lady Londonderry. Both were in love with a very handsome man, Harry Cust, who left several descendants among the great families. Lady Grey had Lady Londonderry's letters to Harry Cust stolen from his desk, and sent them to Lady Londonderry's husband. He read the first, gave the packet to his wife and said, "From today on I shall never speak to you again." And, putting up an impeccable front in public and continuing to receive, the couple lived as strangers in their Park Lane house and their Irish castle.

Blackmail was the worst danger facing these privileged existences. The indiscretion of a rival, the revenge of a servant or the schemes of society people in need could, with the threat of scandal, if not ruin, at least poison these people, who were well known to the general public and respected by them, because their photographs had appeared hundreds of times in magazines like the *Tatler* and *Vanity Fair*.

The aristocracy, because of its attachment to the land, remained much more nationalist than royalty. Another international class should now be considered whose alliance with the aristocracy had happy results, esthetically at least.

International high finance served as a link between London, Paris, Vienna and, to a lesser extent, Berlin and Rome. The Rothschilds, with relations in the great capitals, were the most famous example of an environment whose splendour added to the brilliance of the *Belle Époque*. There were the Cahen of Antwerp, the Deutsch de la Meurthes and the Foulds in Paris, the Bleichroders in Berlin, and in Vienna so many bankers whose wives posed for Klimt. In London the King imposed two financiers on a society which was not, however, much impressed by wealth. They were Baron de Hirsch and Sir Ernest Cassel. The latter built himself a Carrara marble palace in Park Lane. His granddaughter married Lord Mountbatten, a great-nephew of the King's. The Prime Minister, Lord Rosebery, had married a Rothschild. Even if they did not enjoy it at all, bankers, wishing to become part of Europe's most brilliant aristocracy, kept racing stables and went fox hunting. They also became collectors to furnish their homes. Sargent painted them, dark and powerful against a damask background, and their wives like peach Melbas—an Edwardian invention—heavy with roses on creamy cushions. In Paris, Sem sketched Semitic profiles at the races or at Deauville, inhaling the air rich with worldly promise, and Proust chose a Jew, Charles Haas, for the most elegant man in his great work, under the name of Swann.

Immense fortunes were then at the disposal of women for whom beauty and elegance were one. The most intelligent of them bought paintings, gave marvellous parties, made a success of an opera or a couturier. Boldini painted them playing with their long strings of pearls. Baron de Meyer photographed them in shades of grey reminiscent of Whistler. The most marvellous and the most extravagant was the Marchesa Casati, daughter of a Milanese banker, "the only woman who has ever surprised me," said D'Annunzio, who drew this portrait of her in *Forse che sì, forse che no*:

"She also enjoyed enhancing the freshness of her twenty-five years with red and black; her eyelids were always in mourning around their bright irises, and sometimes she blooded her mouth with vermillion. But her alchemy was much more intricate and produced yet greater wonders. What magic did she use to transmute the matter of her life into charms of such touching power? Some of her facial expressions condensed the poetry of a garden, a tragedy, a fable. Some ordinary, everyday action—slowly removing a glove, sliding the kid over the light down of her arm; sitting on her bed, taking off a long silk stocking as delicate as a flower which fades in an instant; removing the pins from a hat, lifting her arms in an arc and letting her sleeve flow down her arm to the curled gold of her armpit." Never has anyone written better about women.

The extravagances of la Casati continued into the "mad years," whose fashions she had foreseen. Others, like the Princesse Edmond de Polignac, *née* Singer, of sewing-machine fame, served Beauty by ordering the composition of ballets or sonatas by Ravel, Fauré, Falla, Stravinsky, while her brother gave Isadora Duncan the money she needed to open her schools of dancing. A very musical Polish woman, Missia Gobedska, having married the founder of *La Revue Blanche* and been a visitor to Mallarmé and Vuillard, married the proprietor of a great newspaper whose millions she merrily spent helping artists, Diaghilev in particular.

The Ballet Russe owed the *Belle Époque* a success in which estheticism and snobbery held equal shares. It was supported by those whom capitalist society considered most intelligent and yet it was too modern, too different from the usual taste of the rich to be thought of as a product of the period. Quite the contrary, the time seems affected, pompous or tasteless compared with Diaghilev's brilliant creations. Beside the Russian composers, the Mascagnis, Leoncavallos and Massenets seemed very insipid; compared with the tutu-clad ballerinas so dear to opera lovers, Tamara Karsavina or Ida Rubinstein, enturbanned, almost naked under their gold veils, were like the clash of cymbals in a serenade. The stars of that euphoric world were much more the great opera singers like Nellie Melba and Mary Garden. *Bel canto* suited their imposing presence; they appeared at the Ritz as if on the stage of the opera house. An Edwardian expression to describe the way these women made their entrance at a ball or a theater in their plumed headdresses was "They sailed in." They lived, as the French would have said, "in full sail."

The only port in which these fair vessels would consent to stay for longer than one season was Venice, capital of estheticism, in an aristocratic milieu maintained by capitalism and brought back into fashion by D'Annunzio, about which Proust wrote some famous pages.

One is forced always to come back to Proust when discussing this era to which he gave so much prestige. When he has finished showing us the almost regal way of life of the Guermantes and the elegance of Swann, we can follow him into the milieu of the wealthy bourgeoisie, his own, that of Mme. Verdurin and Dr. Cottard. For anyone who did not know the so-called *Belle Époque*, the most difficult thing to grasp is the number and importance of servants; without them, Proust's society could not have existed. The Prousts kept a butler, a cook assisted by a kitchen maid, and a lady's maid. Once a week a man came in to polish the floors, and a young man did the errands. This was the minimum for the proper maintenance of the vast apartment. The upper middle class added to this list a coachman and a laundress. This small world led a life reflecting that of its masters,

dependent but lacking in privacy and often loathsome. The intrigues were similar to those of the drawing room and linked houses from kitchen to kitchen. The children, whose mothers were busy with "social obligations"—there was nothing funny about the juxtaposition of these two words fifty years ago—lived much of the time with the servants. Thanks to their nannies they had some idea of country life. Familiar lady's maids and brazen valets very often taught them "the facts of life."

The circle of acquaintance had to be wide, as the time-honoured expression was, and this was not so much an expression of snobbery as an insurance against "reversals of fortune," a tribal interaid system. "Decent people" knew that somebody's uncle, a councillor of state, someone else's brother-in-law, a banker, or yet another person's nephew, the heir to an important legal practice, could one day help a husband or marry a daughter, and they paid visits and gave dinners to consolidate links with these connections and to create a milieu.

In order to lead this social life one had to have a complete accounting system as well as a large apartment and a well-organized staff. Our grandmothers' and great-grandmothers' address books were strongly bound volumes. Acquaintances were listed in three orders: first, alphabetical; second, by days: Mme. Cottard on Tuesdays, Mme. Legrand on the first Thursday. Some were extremely complicated, such as Mme. Ganderax, the wife of the proprietor of the *Revue de Paris*, who was at home to visitors at four o'clock on the first Thursday in every month and every Friday except the first. Thirdly and lastly, the names were listed by streets; thus, without wasting time, one could "do" all the Mondays in the Rue de la Bienfaisance, all the Tuesdays in the Avenue de Messine, and so on. The salon directories, the real *Almanachs de Gotha* of that society, gave details of changes in families, addresses and "at home" days. Every day the *Figaro* and the *Gaulois* devoted a whole page to social events and aspirants for membership to society carefully scanned the lists of people seen at teas, young ladies' dances or funerals. Mothers were fasci-

Helleu

nated by lists of wedding presents: Mme. Jacquemart-André, a britannia-metal teapot, the Baronne de Salomon de Rothschild, a pair of Louis XV sugar tongs; young girls devoured descriptions of fashions: Mlle. Lucie Félix Faure in a puff of lilac tulle, the Baronne Hottinguer in a black-on-black visiting gown trimmed with black.

The elements most determined to enjoy themselves among this rich bourgeoisie found in Paris, much more easily than in other capitals, aristocrats bored by the conventions of their environment. And so we come to the *demi-monde*, to the world of the theater, which with official painters, actors, clubmen and the upper middle class made up that famous *Tout Paris*. *Tout Paris* ate at restaurants, launched Maxim's, went driving in the Bois de Boulogne in the first motorcars, decided the success or the failure of a play. In several novels Jean Lorrain, whose pen was as cruel as Sem's pencil, describes a grand first night at which the plumed and painted guests with their servile or avaricious expressions are reminiscent of a sequence from a Fellini film. An author of light comedies, more kindly disposed than Lorrain, draws a pretty picture of Parisian restaurants:

"Paris prepares for dinner . . . out of doors. And at Laurent's, in front of the bourgeois Le Doyen, around the Folie-Paillard, through the bushes glows the green light of the lamp shades. In the candlelight the tablecloths are as white as sheets. From a distance, when the people make to sit at table, they look as if they were about to start reading in bed.

"This is the moment when the Champs Elysées, from the Place de la Concorde to the Étoile, and especially around the Rond-Point, gradually awakens to a night life quite different from that of the daytime. Alone, near the calm upper part of the avenue of which one can make out neither the beginning nor the end, the Palace draws a double row of strollers towards its illumined windows, their eyes filled with ecstasy or loathing. Behind the windows, two steps away, one can see foreigners sitting as clearly as if they were outside, still rich, eating to the sound of the czardas snatched specially for them from the hearts of violins and zithers by gypsies with walrus moustaches and aubergine cheeks, their languorously lustful eyes rolling towards the shoulder of an American woman flowing with pearls, one can see the valets in their knee breeches, the haughty attitude of the butlers, hands weighed down with rings tremblingly raising an overfilled glass of champagne, the smell of gutted poultry stuffed with a wealth of truffles, sheaves of roses, the block of ice illuminated from within like the thick glass of a lighthouse lantern, and the teeth of the beautiful girl in the act of preparing a flower for a buttonhole." (Henri Lavedan)

The *demi-mondaines* loved making theatrical entrances into these restaurants, and especially into Maxim's at suppertime, in very light coloured dresses standing out clearly from the dark suits of their admirers massed behind them and over whom they towered with their plumed hats or lofty sprays of feathers. If every head did not turn on recognizing her flourishing soprano laugh, her entrance had failed.

The same performance could be seen in the Bois de Boulogne in spring. Let us turn again to Jean Lorrain:

"Half past twelve. Pavillon d'Armenonville. It is cool, the lighting is soft, dimmed by great, deep shadows, a scene of refined elegance, the height of luxury; the gleam of silver and glass through the plate-glass windows of the veranda, the shadowy green of the leaves reflected in the pale-blue lacquered tables, and among the snorting of horses, the clanking of bits and curb chains, the grinding of wheels and the flash of harness, one can observe hand shakes, charming laughter, desultory conversation, 'good mornings' said for the pleasure of showing the teeth and holding out a delicate little hand laden with rings, a toing and froing of bright dresses and supple waists sheathed in embroidery beneath unexpectedly twirling parasols."

The delightful theater in Monte Carlo was one of the places where these ladies, who would not have had a box at the Paris Opéra, displayed their jewellery. During one particular season the public was thrilled by the rivalry between the beautiful

Otéro and Liane de Pougy. If one evening Otéro brought out her rubies, Liane would sport even bigger ones the following day. If Otéro's pearls reached to her waist, Liane could make a belt out of hers. Finally, it became known that Otéro had been given a diamond rivière beside which Liane's diamonds would pale into insignificance. However, Liane appeared in her box dressed all in white without a single jewel. Behind her came her lady's maid covered in diamonds easily worth the same as Otéro's.

Liane de Pougy was by far the more elegant and the more intelligent of these two famous courtesans, who attracted so many people to Paris and whose names, infinitely better known than those of Pasteur and Degas, inspired the dreams of gentlemen from Caracas to Vladivostok. Liane was entertained simultaneously by distinguished foreigners, Baron Bleichroder in Berlin, Lord Carnarvon in London, Prince Strozzi in Florence, and in Paris (among others) the young Maurice de Rothschild. The brother of the King of Portugal spent fortunes on her. But she preferred women, and had a stormy relationship with a young American, Nathalie Barney. Jean Lorrain, who himself preferred men, nearly married Liane de Pougy. He described her as follows:

"Taller, slenderer, more refined than ever, with that transparent complexion and those blueish circles round her great frightened doe-eyes, Liane receives her visitors today reclining on a snowdrift of white furs thrown over her famous white satin chaise longue. She wears a sumptuous dress with overfull sleeves of white brocade, the material and the lining patterned with lilies. Six rows of pearls encircle her fragile neck, one of those pretty necks destined for the executioner's ax and, amid all the furry whiteness, the glassy satin and the orient pearls, she looks like a sickly, delicate Infanta."

To amuse her girl friend, Liane gave strange parties to which she invited suspicious-looking wrestlers and at which she served strawberries in champagne and ether. To round off the evening, they went to nightclubs in Montmartre to dance with artists and ruffians and sometimes stayed until dawn if a famous murderer was being guillotined in the la Roquette prison yard. Such sights provided a new thrill for these ladies and their companions. A *belle époque*?

Never has prostitution been so well organized or offered so many variations as in the Paris of 1900. From the great courtesans who could be seen driving down the Champs Élysées lolling back on the seats of their carriages to the bareheaded girls in shawls who strolled the outer boulevards, there was something to suit all tastes and every purse. The "demicastors" were middle-class women who, through go-betweens, found gentlemen only too willing to buy them dresses and jewellery. These gentlemen were old reprobates or, if they liked extreme youth, "nice, clean old gentlemen." This is the world Colette depicted in *Gigi*. It was Georges Feydeau's source of many of the characters in his comedies—the "creatures" discovered in their corsets hiding under a bed, who turn up in a ball gown at a small family reunion, who are pursued with much shrieking and yelling down sleeping-car corridors. Nice girls at heart, and preferable to the permanently cantankerous, avaricious and stupid wives accompanied by formidable mothers.

The Feydeau farce atmosphere reappears even in the most shady affairs. The pretty Mme. Stenheil, in whose arms ten years before President Félix Faure had expired, was accused of murdering her mother and her husband with the complicity of her valet. A complicated setting, contradictory witnesses, magistrates determined to find out as little as possible, all led to an acquittal which shocked "decent people." And, Parisian to her fingertips, Mme. Stenheil lost no time in marrying a Scottish lord.

A stranger arriving in Paris had only to take a few steps on the Boulevard des Italiens to be accosted by plumed prostitutes or more subtly inveigled by correct-looking people. If he suspected some sort of trap (and not without reason), he would go to the famous brothels. The Chabanais, started by the Prince of Wales and still visited by him as King Edward VII, was extremely luxurious with its Gothic and Arabian rooms and its sleeping car. The ladies received their customers in evening dresses. In the less classy establishments they wore dressing gowns, as painted by

Toulouse-Lautrec. Then there were the frankly popular houses in which the women were virtually prisoners. The traffic in girls developed and became highly organized; the "white slave trade" sent large numbers of unfortunate girls mainly to South America. In *La Maison Philibert*, Jean Lorrain paints the portraits of "these ladies in a provincial brothel."

Venereal disease cast a shadow over this *Belle Époque*, which sometimes appears to have been irrigated by a bidet. One need only read the pages of advertisements in magazines such as *Le Rire* or *La Vie Parisienne* to realize that the promises of amazing cures were usually only booby traps. To receive a true impression of a period, the small advertisements in a paper are much more useful than articles aimed at giving the reader a rosy view of life. Better than the "glamorous" photographs, for example, provided for all tastes. Those available to us now in the form of postcards generally provoke laughter because the decor and accessories are an ill match for the beautiful girls posing with such lack of conviction.

Lesbian scenes abounded. Pierre Louÿs had just published the *Chansons de Bilitis*, and much was done in the name of Antiquity. And yet when, seminaked, Colette danced a sort of Sapphic dance based on a scenario by her friend the Marquise de Belboeuf, she caused a scandal mainly because her protectress was the daughter of the Duc de Morny. A vast fortune usually enabled one to surmount the most difficult situations. A millionaire baroness, so fat that she was nicknamed *La Brioche*, entertained a young poetess, Renée Vivien, and kept her prisoner in a huge apartment full of Oriental *objets d'art* where boredom induced her to take drugs. Another American woman, young and beautiful this time, Nathalie Barney, was also in love with Renée Vivien but could not communicate with her. So she paid an enormous fee to the singer Emma Calvé to disguise herself as one of the street singers of whom there were so many in Paris, just like the "German bands" in London and the Neapolitan "musicos" who overran Italy. Only, instead of singing a popular song, Emma Calvé

sang the great aria from Carmen. The whole street ran to its windows, Renée recognized Nathalie standing on the pavement and realized that she was still loved. Alas, the opium and the baronne's champagne did not go well together and Renée Vivien died very young in circumstances never properly explained.

Whereas Lesbos was treated with amused indulgence, Sodom was frowned upon. For the benefit of Anglo-Saxon tourists visiting Taormina, the Baron de Gloeden introduced young Sicilians of dubious purity disguised as Virgilian shepherd boys. Even in the heart of Paris, Jean Lorrain, Proust and their model, the Comte Robert de Montesquiou, had to make a show of having female attachments. There was only one homosexual scandal in France, that of the young Comte d'Adelsward de Fersen, a member of the best Protestant society. He celebrated "pink masses" in his apartment in the Plaine Monceau and exiled himself to Capri. There he met again one of the directors of the Krupp armaments firm, who shortly afterwards committed suicide. In fact, what happened was that people committed suicide when threatened with a scandal or simply on becoming aware of tastes which were called "unnatural." A young man, appalled by his proclivities, went to ask the Abbé Mugnier, a great friend of Proust's and one of his models, whether he should enter holy orders or join the Foreign Legion, as his religion debarred him from committing suicide. The drawing-room chaplain gave him this wise advice: "Continue with your life, and try not to do anything definite in either direction."

Proust clearly depicted the part played by obliging servants or go-betweens. It was the same in all aristocratic societies, but in England convention refused to allow women to know that such things could exist. Thus, when Lord Henry Somerset's wife began telling everyone that she had surprised her husband in the arms of a footman, doors closed on her and her husband retired to Florence.

Germany experienced scandals poisoned by the left-wing press to discredit the Emperor. The endless trial of Prince Eulenburg from 1907 to

1909 was the more regrettable in that the facts denigrated Wilhelm II's most sensible councillor. Shortly afterwards the head of the Emperor's Military Household danced in a tutu before his master, who wept with laughter at the sight. Either the effort or the success was too much for the general, who died of an embolism. It was only with the greatest difficulty that they managed to get him back into a uniform. Then two young Hohenzollern princes were caught in a similar scandal to the great delight of the press: "Really, Willy is too clumsy," sighed Edward VII. In England, in fact, scandal never touched a member of the royal family. In Vienna a few years earlier the Emperor's brother, the Archduke Ludwig-Victor, nicknamed Luzi-Wurzi, was compromised by the masseur at a Turkish bath. And has not too much been said about the friendship of the Empress for an *haute-école equestrienne*? In France, without scandal but not without roars of laughter, the Rumanian actor De Max personified transvestism. He took himself for Sarah Bernhardt and, covered in jewels and dragging yards of velvet, he acted the parts of Bas-Empire princes. He presented transvestite and literary productions in the little theaters of Montmartre at which Jean Cocteau recited his first poems.

Tout Paris pursued the amorous low life in Montmartre at the Moulin Rouge, then at the Bal Tabarin or the Casino de Paris. The Montmartre myth dates from the last decade of the century. The fact that the church of the Sacré-Coeur crowned this hill consecrated to the pleasures of the flesh gave it a very decadent ambiguity. Singers, somewhat anarchistic, rather mystical, usually smutty, made the most of what the English referred to in French as *la nostalgie de la boue*. This time, so self-confident, so wealthy, had a weakness for representations of poverty. Just as people liked to hang on their drawing-room wall a painting—in a nicely gilded frame—representing beggar children, so they liked listening—while eating oysters—to singers such as Bruant or Jehan Rictus singing about tramps, prostitutes, convicts or drunkards whose presence could be sensed in the shadows as one left the Cabaret du Chat Noir, dark and disturbing as in Théophile Alexandre Steinlen's lithographs. This longing for the low life had been the making of La Goulue, so often painted by Toulouse-Lautrec, and who inspired so many imitators throughout the *Belle Époque*.

"'Huh! Haven't you got wives at home?' Jostling the mob of idlers, flashy adventurers and provincials out on a spree who crowd around her as she tries to pass, La Goulue, fat, white, moulded into her little black dress, pushes impassively through the crowd, her hand on the shoulder of La Môme Fromage, insolently surveying all these rutting males with the look of a beautiful, self-confident girl who has experienced every degradation. The setting: the Élysée Gardens, the mirrors of the Moulin Rouge or the brilliantly lit Jablockhof in the Jardin de Paris. La Goulue! Bursting from her abundant clusters of petticoats in a rustle of lace and expensive underwear, heightened here and there by soft-coloured ribbons, a leg appears, pointing straight at the chandelier, shining and silky, gripped above the knee by a diamond buckle; the leg flutters about, joyous and witty, lascivious and teasing with its mobile, dislocated foot, miming what look like greetings to the oglers crowding round. La Goulue is the star of the dance halls, those gigantic meeting places for bored men and prostitutes, the star of Montmartre rising in the moonlight of the Pierrot de Willette above the mound of the Sacré-Coeur and the ghostly sails of dead windmills, a cynical glory made of fancy and filth, a flower in a lavatory pan caught in a ray of electric light and suddenly made all the rage." (Jean Lorrain)

Even today, the French cancan is still an absurd and solemn rite, now devoid of any eroticism, practiced every night in the music halls of Montmartre for an audience of foreigners attracted by a spectacle described as *Belle Époque*, one of the few French expressions they understand.

This somewhat sordid *Belle Époque* of Montmartre has nonetheless left us some pleasant memories, thanks to some of Colette's writings, Leautaud's *Petit Ami* and Francis Carco's *Jésus la Caille*. We still sing Yvette Guilbert's songs, we still admire the posters of Jules Chéret, which, after Lautrec, and more cheerfully, covered the walls with frenzied pictures to the glory of some ephemeral star, some aperitif or some remedy. In about 1910 the great painter Bonnard was inspired by this atmosphere of pleasure which lit up the evenings around the Place Pigalle. By the light of electric signs and the headlights of cars, revellers went from one nightclub to another. Girls painted by Kees Van Dongen, naked in black stockings, their eyes made up in green. But Picasso and Modigliani, who were also then painting in Montmartre, were in no way a part of the *Belle Époque*.

The world of pleasure was less well organized, less socially stratified, in the other capitals. In London, the *nostalgie de la boue* led to the worst kind of trouble: blackmail, prison . . .

This was the town where the music hall assumed enormous importance and is still the symbol of Edwardian fun. Enormous Coliseums and Alhambras were built. They could be seen in the streets, where Walter Sickert went to find the subjects for his best paintings. Marie Lloyd sang cockney songs and after 1910 Gaby Deslys had more success there than in Paris, plumed and naked under the pearls given her by the King of Portugal. This charming girl, who died very young, sang in the language of the Entente Cordiale:

> "Sur la plage, sur la plage,
> Men are full of persiflage.
> When I take my bain de mer
> All the boys just stand and stare."

To sing this, she wore a bathing costume. People loved postcards of bathing belles. Her songs were all recorded and have withstood the test of time better than the voices of Caruso and Melba. The horn gramophone so quickly adopted by the British, along with the mutt of His Master's Voice, became one of the symbols of their *Belle Époque*.

Another passion, this time from the United States, the Gibson girls, was to some extent the equivalent of today's "bunnies." Showgirls with incredibly slim waists, superb chignons, dressed in evening gowns as depicted in Charles Dana Gibson's drawings, they were a mixture of the erotic and aristocratic ideals, ideals which Gladys Cooper brought to the stage, for obviously the public hardly liked anything but representations of the "high life." Only farces were given wealthy bourgeois settings. Men were usually comedians, but the handsome Lewis Waller, who in 1902 created M. Beaucaire (later one of Rudolph Valentino's great roles), was the first man to have a fan club, the members of which sported buttons engraved "K.O.W." (keen on Waller). An absurd sort of dandy nicknamed the "knuts", always impeccably dressed, would stroll the lounges of the great music halls and sometimes had the honour of dining at the Savoy with a star. But there was no room in London for the great *demi-mondaines*. They would not have been admitted to the Ritz or the Savoy, their carriages would not have been allowed to parade in Hyde Park and only men with no reputation would have been seen in their company. For that, one went to Paris.

Vienna, as we have seen, was very comparable to Paris, but people had less money there; the Sacher was not as elegant as Maxim's, although most of its customers were more aristocratic than the upper middle class who formed the basis of the French clientele. Its women were entrancing, if Klimt's drawings are to be believed, and the erotic drawings of the strange Marquis de Byros, showing opulent creatures in rococo-*Jugendstil* beds surrendering to a thousand fantasies with hussars, little girls or poodles. Sacher-Masoch was far more Viennese than Freud.

St. Petersburg had its famous island restaurants with their gypsies, but true connoisseurs sent for their mistresses from Paris or for preference went to join them on the Riviera.

The French and Italian Rivieras formed a separate country whose entire upper class came from practically everywhere to spend its money on pleasure and whose native population was engaged in waiting on the visitors, on selling them salads or all sorts of services at very high prices. The country only came to life in the winter. Villas and hotels were closed between Whitsun and All Saints' Day. It was not a haven, as Switzerland is today, for tax-threatened fortunes or from

106

Paul Helleu, study.

changes of government, but one had to be rich there, or at least appear to be so. As we have said, royalty paid long visits to the Riviera and mixed with Prussian princes disturbed by despotism, lords threatened by some scandal, Americans fleeing from Puritanism and looking for brilliant company, French ladies with good incomes and lovers too young for them, bankers who became respectable there, retired prima donnas, Egyptians and Turks on the spree. But it was the Russians who set the tone, from the Grand Duchess to the most broken of gamblers. There were also Rumanians and Italians, all of them some kind of prince. No fuss was made about the origin of titles in Rivieraland; the important thing was to have one. No one worried about the origin of fortunes either, as long as they were liberally expended. *Tout Paris* met one another there, all spruced up in the February sun. The *demi-mondaines* rented villas or apartments there according to their means. D'Annunzio travelled there from Florence for brief visits, Jean Lorrain wrote scandalous reports of its goings-on, but the gaming table was cultivated there in preference to literature. The nucleus of café society, which died away after the last war, was formed there. In July the habitués of the French Riviera met again happily in St. Moritz or Deauville but they had been to London for the season and in Paris until the Grand Prix (the first Sunday in July). September would find the most delicate in Venice and the richest in Biarritz. Abel Hermant's novels entitled *Trains de Luxe (Luxury Trains)* and *Transatlantiques (Transatlantic Liners)* give us an idea of this itinerant world which had the pretensions of high society and the facilities of the *demi-monde* and who treated palaces like luxury hotels.

The *Belle Époque* was indeed the age of the grand hotels; they became enormous, their entrance halls were floored with marble and walled with Gobelin tapestries, in that style cautiously known to Americans as "Louis." The Ritz, the Claridge, the Carlton and the Savoy still retain an echo of the *Belle Époque*, and the Plaza in New York more than any other with its Viennese palm court orchestra. The same decor was found in less important spas and gave "decent people" an idea of international life. In the Grand Hotel at Balbec, Proust noticed relationships between the social classes which would never have had the opportunity of meeting elsewhere. That the Marquise de Villeparisis, the banker Nissim Bernard and a presiding judge should be staying under the same roof would have been unthinkable thirty years earlier.

Alongside the development of grand hotels and for a comparable clientele, transatlantic liners grew enormous. A nation's prestige depended on its degree of luxury. The same as for naval fleets, rivalry was great between the German Nord-Amerika Line and the British White Star Line. The White Star had built a 46,000-ton ship called the *Titanic* whose progress could not be slowed down even by the fiercest storms. An iceberg cut it in two on its maiden voyage on April 14–15, 1912, and 1635 people's lives were lost. Announcing the news, the headline in the American newspapers read, "Mr. Astor drowned in mid-Atlantic," the 1634 other victims being of so much smaller importance than the millionaire! Incidentally, the second-class corridors were blocked to make room for the first-class passengers in the lifeboats. It has been said that the orchestra played the hymn "Nearer, My God, to Thee" as the ship was sinking. In fact it played Viennese waltzes. The catastrophe shook European optimism. Man had in fact not become master of the elements, as a generation fed on the novels of Jules Verne had been led to believe. The engulfment of the floating palace seemed to many like a warning.

However, this catastrophe in no way slowed down the taste for machinery, which had taken a hold on society, and the motorcar was soon to upset the rhythm of life completely. Speed became a new pleasure. In the nineties the bicycle had already given people an appetite for sport. It was a smart sport to begin with, because before the advent of mass production a bicycle cost as much as a small car today, but by about 1905 only the "poor" could not afford a "bike." Bicycle races attracted a huge public and a far more democratic one than race courses. Horseback riding became an upper-class sport.

The car took longer to be democratized. Until the 1914–18 war it was an expensive and complicated machine. A mechanic—he was not yet known as a chauffeur—was needed to take care of it continually. And yet by 1910 in the moneyed classes, cars had almost completely supplanted horses. A statuette by Charles Sykes called *Spirit of Ecstasy* was chosen in 1911 to decorate the bonnet of the Rolls-Royce.

In capital cities, taxis and buses replaced hansom cabs and horse-drawn omnibuses. Life speeded up. People went for a day in the country instead of going to stay there for a week. Tourism began to grow. Edith Wharton took Henry James on a tour of French churches, D'Annunzio plowed Tuscany on the track of pretty women or in search of a ruin. Soon he would own an airplane. The lyricism of the hero of *Forse che sì, forse che no* flying towards the sun pushes to a climax the happiness which was to be that of sports lovers twenty years later. Skiers too—but not swimmers—began to discover that intoxication of the senses. The sport that developed fastest was tennis. Diaghilev created a ballet about it to music by Debussy. Perhaps Europeans of today could get the truest idea of a placid, middle-class *Belle Époque* from a game of tennis played in the garden of a country house: the players impeccably dressed in white, refreshments awaiting them in a pavilion where the older people in light-coloured clothes watch them, chatting. How many novels have described such summer scenes in the gardens of Richmond or St.-Cloud? Golf remained a smart sport, and to have an idea of the most luxurious sport, one must read the description of a polo match in a novel by Princess Bibesco. No yacht had a crew of fewer than ten.

· Thus the *Belle Époque* witnessed the change—thanks to a certain euphoria due to the plentiful circulation of money and the impression of a lasting state of equilibrium in spite of a few foreign wars (Cuba, Japan)—of an aristocratic society into a capitalistic one, the latter adopting the habits of the former. Ease of transport, big hotels, sport, the passion for theaters and parties brought together social groups very different in both upbringing and origin. There was an international pleasure group, the same stars were acclaimed in every capital, the same painters received orders in London, Paris and New York. Another very important element in this popularizing of taste was the development of the illustrated weeklies with photographs supplied to them by international agencies. The readers of *L'Illustration* and the *Illustrated London News* were interested in the same things and wanted to see the same spectacles. The more expensive magazines, such as *Les Modes*, *Vanity Fair*, and *Vogue* in America, popularized a certain notion of "chic" with photographs and mainly through artists who presented an idealized image of the "high life." Court life seemed inaccessible fifty years earlier, but to lead the grand hotel life one needed only to earn enough to buy a good car and have a well-dressed wife.

This brings us to one of the most typical phenomena of the *Belle Époque*, the importance given to *haute couture*. It is true that Charles Frederick Worth had dressed the Empress Eugénie and her court and that around 1900 there were some very famous couturiers, such as Doucet and Redfern; but it would never have been believed that they would become the international figures they are today or even that they would be received in "society." Paul Poiret changed all that, and with his reign the *Belle Époque* announced its "years of madness."

The four years leading up to the 1914 war were exceptionally brilliant from the artistic and social points of view. There had never been so many new and sparkling spectacles, such unexpected colours and sounds. Never had so many strikingly elegant women received so many artists. The framework of the old society of vast fortunes and the introduction of a foreign element allowed productions to be staged which seemed like theatrical parties in their setting, the luxuriousness of their costumes and the beauty of their stars. The theater, the arts and society, united at last, shook the public, who were at first shocked or amused and finally dazzled. These years were more like a fireworks display than a party with dazzling colours, rockets like osprey plumes, long necklaces of stars, flares like gauze veils. The wonder workers were called Diaghilev and Poiret. Everything has already been said about the Ballet Russe, their stage designers, their musicians and their dancers. Poiret, his designers and his customers are just beginning to be rediscovered. Both were despotic in the accomplishment of their dreams, impatient with anything that hindered their whims, unfair and generous, adored or mocked.

The fashion of the party years freed women from corsets and ankle boots, reduced the mass and weight of cloth and the volume of hats. Alone, Paul Poiret achieved this miracle of transforming the plenteous and corseted lady of 1900 into a slender veil-draped houri. The most daring women even began to wear trousers. So Diaghilev dressed the stage and Poiret the auditorium. In a single season the women not dressed by him looked out of date. The misogynist Diaghilev left Nijinsky practically naked but stifled his women in jewellery; Poiret, who adored women, allowed the shapes of their bodies to be guessed at at last.

On June 24, 1911, the couturier astounded his establishment in the Faubourg St. Honoré, but let us allow Poiret himself to describe to us this One Thousand and Second Night, so often to be imitated: "The guests entered a drawing room where a half-naked Negro, draped in Bokhara silks and carrying a torch and a yataghan, gathered them together and led them to me. Then they crossed a sanded courtyard where, beneath a blue-and-gold awning, fountains played in porcelain basins. A multicoloured light descended through the colours of the awning. They climbed a few steps and found themselves in front of an immense golden cage latticed with twisted fittings inside which I had locked my favourite (Mme. Poiret), surrounded by her maids in waiting, who were singing real Persian songs. Mirrors, sorbets, aquariums, small birds, veils and feathers, these were the amusements of the queen of the harem and her attendants. Carpets covered the tiles of the doorstep and the sand of the pathways so that the sound of steps was muted and a profound silence reigned. The visitors, impressed, spoke in

low voices as if in a mosque. In the middle of flower beds of embroidery stood the white cornelian vase. Lights hidden among the surrounding leaves lit it strangely. A thin jet of water escaped from it and pink ibises walked all around to take their share of the coolness and the light. Some of the trees were covered in luminous dark-blue fruit, others bore berries of purple light. Live monkeys, macaws and parrots enlivened all this greenery, which looked like the entrance to a great park.

"When my three hundred guests were assembled, I arose and, followed by all my wives, I advanced towards the cage of my favourite whom I set free. She escaped just as a bird would. . . . Then a cataract of fire crowned the palace and suddenly the air was filled with a tearing sound. From the terrace overlooking the garden burst a rain of fire which cascaded down the steps. Now silver, now gold, this thrilling storm electrified the crowd and when it subsided it left phosphorescent insects everywhere, caught in branches or suspended in midair."

The following year, two society women, Mmes. de Chabrilland and de Clermont-Tonnerre, gave Persian parties in their turn, and there all the jewels were real. Members of royal families followed the entertainment from galleries. And *L'Illustration* published four pages in colour of the costumes. A year earlier there had been an article about coloured wigs. That the "decent people's" magazine should suggest so many frivolities was very characteristic of the times; there were also articles on fashion, some illustrated with delightful drawings by Barbier, Lepape and Marty, heralding the coming of Art Deco, and others with Sem's caricatures. There were reports of smart events at Deauville and at the races; chic became the ideal, as did speed. Both were offered by the motorcar.

Then there was the tango! It originated in the depths of Buenos Aires about 1910 and two years later it reigned supreme in the drawing rooms, having dethroned the more elegant Boston two-step. "Tango teas" were given in London. The tango was danced at noon on the boardwalk at Deauville. In short, it was a

Caricature by Sem (Georges Goursat).

Among the "minor masters" of Parisian graphic art of the Belle Époque, should be mentioned Georges Goursat, better known by his pseudonym Sem, and Paul Helleu. Their respective attitudes to life at the beginning of the century could hardly have been more divergent: Sem, a pitiless observer of humanity; Helleu, more sophisticated and attuned to his environment, perfervid admirer and painter of the beautiful and elegant of high society.
Georges Goursat (1863–1934), examples of whose work
appear on pages 82, 90, 95, 103 and above, came from Perigueux. He captured Paris with the publication, in 1900, of Les sportsmen, *his barbed caricatures of the gay world whose Mecca was Maxim's, appearing in the* Journal, Figaro *and* Gaulois. *Helleu (1859–1927), painter, engraver and worker in ceramics, brings to life in his delicate pastels, the titled ladies from the drawing rooms of Proust. See examples on pages 87, 99 and 106.*

madness much more than a fashion, and belonged to the "mad years" much more than to the *Belle Époque*. People began to talk of gigolos, and Latin American rhythms began to supersede Viennese melodies (the first jazz bands began to cross the Atlantic at the same time). The success of the lascivious dance alarmed the Pope, and *L'Illustration* shows us Pius X watching a couple in black dancing the old and respectable Venetian forlane, which, if one had listened to him, would have supplanted the tango. Bridge reached us from Argentina, too, a development of whist. In Buenos Aires there was a glittering monument to that era, the Jockey Club. Eva Perón had it burned down.

Hobble-skirted dresses and enormous hats which left the face in shadow suited the *femmes fatales*. They often met with sad ends. The actress Lanthelme, wife of an extremely rich newspaper proprietor, fell or was pushed into the Rhine during a cruise. She had the most beautiful eyes in Paris. In Venice during the trial of a Polish countess accused of murder, the guard had to be changed every two hours, as one look from the beauty was enough to make them lose their heads. The "vamps" dated from before 1914 and were destined to be used by the cinema ten years later. But here again, do they really belong to the *Belle Époque*? Not really. "Decent people" had an ideal much nearer to that of the eighteenth century. We shall not find the *Belle Époque* ideal described in the great novels of the time—Thomas Mann of *The Magic Mountain*, John Galsworthy of *The Forsyte Saga* and Roger Martin du Gard of *The World of the Thibaults* were too serious to linger over such matters—but rather in the novels and drawings published in *L'Illustration*.

The Parisienne is always in the foreground in drawings idealizing reality. She appears cool and impeccable, in Trans-Siberian Railway stations, blushing slightly as she congratulates bathing-costumed athletes in the Reims stadium, plumed on an icy road, the limousine which was to have taken her from her château to the Opéra having broken down, about to climb into the Santos Dumont airship or examining Louis Blériot's airplane. Parisiennes feature again in Gaston Latouche's great picture, *The Casino*, reproduced in colour after its success at the 1914 Exhibition. Beneath a flowered pergola, sitting at small tables by the light of blue and pink lamps, women in evening dress dine with men in white tie and tails, in the distance the lights of a port, in the darkness, the rockets of a firework display. Thanks to advances in photographic reproduction, even in colour, after 1910 magazines became much closer to what they were to be thirty years later than to what they had been ten years earlier.

Looking through copies of *L'Illustration* from the years before the Great War, it seems that Europe was in the grip of a sort of fever; confidence gives way to a kind of agitation—brilliant, it is true, but worrying. Many pages are devoted to cars and airplanes, but also to the new armaments being tried out in the wars ravaging the Balkans. For a time attention is focussed on Albania, which has been given a German ruler—another operetta—then on Morocco, where "our brave Senegalese soldiers are fighting alongside the Legion" to retain dominion for France of an area Germany had tried to snatch from her by sending warships to Agadir. This failed coup meant that a Franco-German confrontation was inevitable. Ridiculous photographs of the Kaiser were published: at the time of the erection of the enormous monument commemorating the Battle of Leipzig, *L'Illustration* showed a photograph of the Arc de Triomphe, a "Latin taste," commemorating "172 French victories as compared with the German government's celebration of 350,000 allies who managed to polish off 157,000 Frenchmen." But here again, society keeps its oar in. A large drawing shows a reception at the German embassy in honour of the new President, Poincaré, one of the men chiefly responsible for the war. Mme. Poincaré, divorced after leading an eventful life, looks somewhat ill at ease. When Alfonso XIII of Spain visited Paris, it was alone. The Queen of Spain could not be asked to meet such a person. The British rulers were less difficult. Anxious at the growth of the German fleet, the British transformed their cautious Entente Cordiale into a tacit alliance.

Scandals grew apace, and after looking at the

pictures in *L'Illustration* one should read the memoirs of Léon Daudet, who was the St.-Simon of the *Belle Époque*, with its injustices, its gripping accounts, and its larger-than-life portraits. The dubious members of parliament, the ruined members of the bourgeoisie and the corrupt judges on whom "decent people" did not wish Daudet to open their eyes were brought into the foreground of reality on March 21, 1914, when Mme. Caillaux, wife of the Minister of Finance, arrived at the offices of *Le Figaro* and coldly shot six bullets into the proprietor of that newspaper, M. Calmette, who had been leading a tough campaign against her husband, the Calmette who is remembered chiefly because Proust had just dedicated his book *Du Côté de Chez Swann (Swann's Way)* to him—but let us allow *L'Illustration* to express its own indignation: "Paris has just lived through a week of stupor. An unheard-of murder—a journalist shot down with an automatic to prevent the publication of political documents, the arrest of the wife of a Minister, a man in the forefront of public life cast precipitately from the political scene, the revelation to the court of a scandalous document. A noisy and sinister hearing reminiscent of the darkest hours of the Convention—all these extraordinary events one after another have thrown public opinion into an incredible state of moral disarray. Never before in the history of our society has the voice of the pistol produced such profound and alarming echoes."

The verdict acquitting Mme. Caillaux seemed to D'Annunzio like the sign of a national decline of which his own decline was the reflection. The poet had lived in France for three years. Countless feminine conquests in every milieu did not compensate him for the failure of his plays. It should be remembered that in spite of Debussy's music and Bakst's costumes, *The Martyrdom of St. Sebastian* had seemed unbearably boring. After several meetings with "a lady above all suspicion," D'Annunzio discovered that he had caught a venereal disease. He immediately proclaimed the news. Wasn't it extraordinary, at the age of fifty and for the first time, after leading such a life as his? But for himself he wrote: "I feel that I have received the truly degrading badge of Paris, the truly unspeakable and undeserved punishment." The year 1914 began very badly: "Life in Paris is a ferment of decay." The Caillaux affair, like an abscess, served to drain away all its degradations and allowed a sweet bitterness to be drawn from it. "Eternal France" seemed to him at its lowest ebb. Had she not voted to the left, which meant reducing the length of military service and bringing her closer to Germany? During a conversation with Maurice Paléologue, the ambassador in Russia, he made no attempt to hide his disappointment with his adoptive country: "The crisis which France has just undergone has shaken every fiber of my patriotism. We are living in an infamous time under the tyranny of a proletariat. Never has the Latin spirit sunk so low. ... A great national war is the only hope left for salvation. Only war can stop the decline of a degenerate race."

The Discreet Charm of an Epoch

by Eleonora Bairati

The expression *Belle Époque* is nowhere to be found among the many different names applied to the artistic groups and movements of that period. Art Nouveau, *Jugendstil*, Modernism, Liberty style, *Sezession Stil*, were the labels most often used to describe new phenomena not only in the field of art but also in fashion and manners, all based largely on the same theoretical assumptions but differing stylistically. If there is one main thread connecting these varying aspects, one that can be identified as the spirit of the *Belle Époque*, it is the utterly new mass use during those years of the same ideal image at all levels. The work of architects, sculptors, painters, commercial artists, cartoonists, craftsmen and decorators was not only a reflection of prevalent taste, an answer to the demands and expectations of the contemporary public. It seems also to have been the expression of a true "cultural strategy" proposed and orchestrated by the upper middle classes, which, during the years before the disaster of war, enjoyed the happiest period in their history.

THE DAWN OF THE NEW CENTURY

"Peace, prosperity, progress" — the positive ideals of the new century are symbolized on the cover of the first number of the 1900 *Domenica del Corriere* (left) by three women holding respectively an electric battery, a classical cornucopia and an olive branch, against a distant background of smoking factory chimneys. The surge of innovation that swept Europe at the beginning of the century recalls the quotation from Dante ("The century renews itself") attached to the print by Aleardo Terzi (below) that appeared in 1901 in the first number of the Italian review that called itself— not without good reason— *Novissima*. Indeed, at that time the theme of the new and the youthful was a constant in the wide field of European art, taste and fashion, stressed time and again in the names bestowed on their movements: Art Nouveau (new art), *Jugendstil* (style of youth) or, in regard to Italian literature, *Stil Novo* (new style), and so on.

The amiable idiom of that most popular illustrator, Achille Beltrame, seems still to be linked to the naturalism of the nineteenth century in the way, for instance,

that he treats flower subjects realistically rather than in the manner already widespread in Europe, as stylized decoration (irises were one of the favourite floral themes of Art Nouveau). A subtle draftsman such as Terzi, on the other hand, used an up-to-date technique based on the *Jugendstil*, aiming for a synthesis of line and colour.

In his sketch for a poster (above) Alphonse Mucha—a Czech artist active in Paris, and the creator of an ideal of female beauty that became enormously popular—draws with a soft, flowing line typical of French taste. The poster was to advertise an event which, more than any other, symbolized the burgeoning myth of the *Belle Époque*, namely, the Universal Exhibition of Paris in 1900, the buildings of which can be seen in the background.

THE AGE OF ELECTRICITY

The reigning deity of the new Olympus of twentieth-century myth was without doubt electricity, and the *ville lumière* celebrated its triumph. In the watercolour below, taken from a souvenir booklet, representing *The Exhibition at Night*, the Eiffel Tower, that most potent artifact of nineteenth-century engineering (1889) and crowning symbol of technological progress, seems transformed by its raiment of lamps into a sort of lighthouse for the new "century of electricity." This glowing and fanciful picture is nothing but the idealized projection of a reality which at that moment was massively assailing Europe: the industrialization for which electrical power was one of the determining factors.

Industrial constructions became the new "monuments" of the age of progress, and the architect Gaetano Moretti used monumental forms when he designed the electric power station (below) at Trezzo d'Adda, his most original work (1904–06).

More directly, in his poster for the Brescia Exhibition of 1909, A. Sala exploits the immediate charm of his design with its Latin mottoes and innocently symbolic figures to advertise the new technological and scientific realities.

LVX

SONVM

MOTVS

CALOR

ESPOSIZIONE INTERNAZIONALE
di APPLICAZIONI dell'ELETTRICITÀ

SOTTO L'ALTO PATRONATO
DI S.E. COCCO ORTV
MINISTRO di AGR.IND.e COMM.
PRESID. del COMITATO d'ONORE:
GORIO AVV. COMM. CARLO
SENATORE DEL REGNO
PRESID. del COMITATO ESECVTIVO:
MAINETTI CAV. DOMINATORE
PRESID. della CAMERA di COMMERCio

BRESCIA 1909
AGOSTO — OTTOBRE
INAUGURAZIONE 8 AGOSTO
RIBASSI FERROVIARI

MOSTRE SPECIALI : IGIENE
FLORICOLTVRA e FRVTTICOLTVRA
LAGHI e VALLI=SCVOLE PROFESS.
FOTOGRAFIE = AVIAZIONE.
CONCORSI GINNASTICI=CONV.
CICLISTICI = TIRO a SEGNO =
TIRO a VOLO=CONGRESSI=CONFE-
RENZE=FESTEGGIAM. PATRIOTT.ecc

COLORI LORILLEUX

UNIONE TIPO=LITO BRESCIANA BRESCIA

PIETRE LITHOS

THE GREAT EXHIBITIONS

From the mid-nineteenth century onwards, universal exhibitions were considered incomparable vehicles for the advertising and diffusion of new advances in technology, science and industry. Moreover, they also served as testing grounds for technical innovations of fundamental importance to the development of modern architecture. At the Paris Exhibition of 1900 some very advanced technical solutions were masked by the festive exuberance of the decorative pavilions, which were a convivial jumble of nineteenth-century eclecticism and "new style" (the watercolour below gives a view of the *Palace of Instruction—Arts, Science and Letters*).

The pavilions of the International Exhibition of Decorative Arts held in Turin in 1902 (an original sketch for the main entrance is shown above) were designed by the gifted architect Raimondo D'Aronco. In their colouring and attractive combination of geometrical patterns of the Secessionist school with "floral style" decoration, they represent the highest point and greatest stylistic coherence of the style known in Italy as Liberty, which seems so exactly right for the ephemeral and transitory constructions of all those national or local exhibitions, shows and fairs. Only a few years later, however, when a great exhibition was held in Milan in 1906 to celebrate one of the most moving events of the decade, the opening of the Simplon Tunnel, the curve of style seems to have taken a downward turn into the heavy and pretentious. The contrast is plain when one compares the clumsiness of the building (designed, like most of those in the exhibition, by the architect Sebastiano Locati) depicted on the book cover on page 120 with the graceful and flawless graphic solution above.

This rapid turnover of styles was characteristic of the exhibitors themselves, who, in the cause of commercial competition, continually changed the appearance of their wares and products, and therewith the architectural "wrappings" that enclosed and advertised them. Here we approach the roots of the consumer society.

The Discreet Charm of
an Epoch

MILANO e la ESPOSIZIONE INTERNAZIONALE del SEMPIONE 1906

MILANO
FRATELLI TREVES
EDITORI

THE CULT OF SPEED

One distinguishing mark of the new century's rhythm was speed. The progress of means of communication sensationally diminished distances—physical and psychological—between nations. It was the era of new motor roads, extended railway lines and increased steam navigation, of fraternization between peoples under the symbol of winged Mercury, the god of trade.

Just as industrial buildings gave rise to a new type of architecture, so the railway train, motorcar and airplane became new subjects of the century's iconography.

In the painting on page 121, *The Pacific Line* by Gaetano Previati, a train has been chosen as the symbol to glorify commercial communications. It was one of a series (other significant titles are *Tunnel Through the Alps* and *The Suez Canal*) executed for the Milan Chamber of

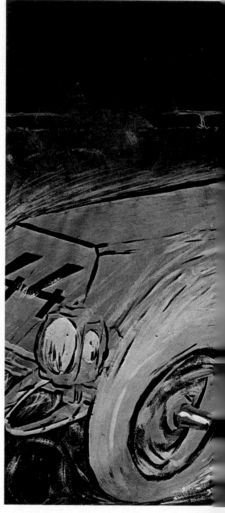

Commerce in honour of progress and technical achievement. The artist, one of the major Italian pointillist painters of the symbolist school, continued right up to 1916 to use the same technique in which to translate literary or symbolical themes into pictorial art.

It was the motorcar, however, that occupied the place of honour in the taste and fashion of the period we call the *Belle Époque*. The automobile industry was flourishing. Fiat started manufacture in 1899, Lancia in 1902, Ford in 1903... In 1907 an Italian model, the Itala, driven by the journalist

Barzini and Prince Borghese, won the famous Peking–Paris race. In 1906 the Palermo industrialist Vincenzo Florio instituted the Florio Shield motorcar race, of social and European renown. The enthusiasm for automobile racing influenced clothes (those long dust-coats), created a vogue and imposed its own social pilgrimage of race-tracks on its well-off adherents. That atmosphere permeates the poster (left) by Marcello Dudovich—one of the most prolific commercial artists of the period— advertising the Brescia races (1907); it is there, in a less worldly, more cutting version, in the sketch on the right by Umberto Boccioni. As with Previati's work, the latter is one of a series (seven tempera paintings of motor-driving scenes) and in it, in spite of its rather slick commercial style, the futurist-to-be already reveals (it was only 1901) something of the basic trend of his poetic art.

In his watercolour of 1914 the architect Silvio Gambini casts this fragile aircraft—greatly resembling the monoplane in which Louis Blériot flew the channel in 1909—as the newest symbol of technical progress, and displays it in front of a magnificent architectural conception of the Austrian school. We are on the eve of war: all too soon the messenger of peace will turn into the bringer of death.

DREAM CITY

The modern city produces a lively, highly characteristic impression: glittering, colourful, dynamic, a place in which prosperous town dwellers can recognize and create a suitable setting for their own social prestige.

In the *Belle Époque* streets were the dominant feature of the city: streets brightly illuminated by electric lights and reflections in shop windows, thronged with cars, carriages and pedestrians in constant movement, the attention ceaselessly spurred by multiple distractions.

(Below, a station on the Vienna metropolitan railway, reserved exclusively for members of the imperial family.)

The Discreet Charm of an Epoch

The traffic also descended into the bowels of the city, and underground-railway stations became a characteristic feature of the urban scene. The simple but lively outlines and delicate decorations of the Vienna metropolitan's twenty-five stations—the most famous of which appears on page 125—were the work of Otto Wagner. The stations were originally part of a general plan of urban expansion which was never carried out, although studied and projected by the great architect between the years 1894 and 1900. Fantastic and transfigured underground stations designed by Hector Guimard, founder of Art Nouveau architecture, contributed so much to the special appearance of Paris that they were accredited with a style of their own—the *style métro*. The roofing was in iron-framed glass, taut and transparent as a moth's wing; lamp holders in bulbous cast-iron-supported buds of coloured glass, as beautifully exemplified in the Gare de la Porte Dauphine (1900–01, shown on the left). A repertory of Parisian urban furnishings— canopies, kiosks, roofing, balustrades—was made in the same style, though in shapes often vulgarized by mass production. A charming example is seen in the sketch (above) of an electric tramway station by A. Laverrière, published in 1903 in *Moderne Bauformen*.

On a minor scale, urban equipment consisted mostly in a sort of cosmetic treatment of the street or building, of decorative signs, plaques, and entrances attached to shops and restaurants. There was a rich design vocabulary ranging from the free, dynamic line of the Frenchman Maxime Roisin (above right) or the subtle adornment of the hotel entrance below, by the Viennese Marcellus Kammerer (both taken from *Moderne* *Bauformen*, 1902 and 1903), to the modest, anonymous sign (below right) on a small Italian café, poor in material but well designed. Applied to older buildings, the springing, whiplash stylistic elements, the curls or spirals, Secessionist geometry or floral patterns, flowed impartially to cover the urban spaces with a veneer of modernity.

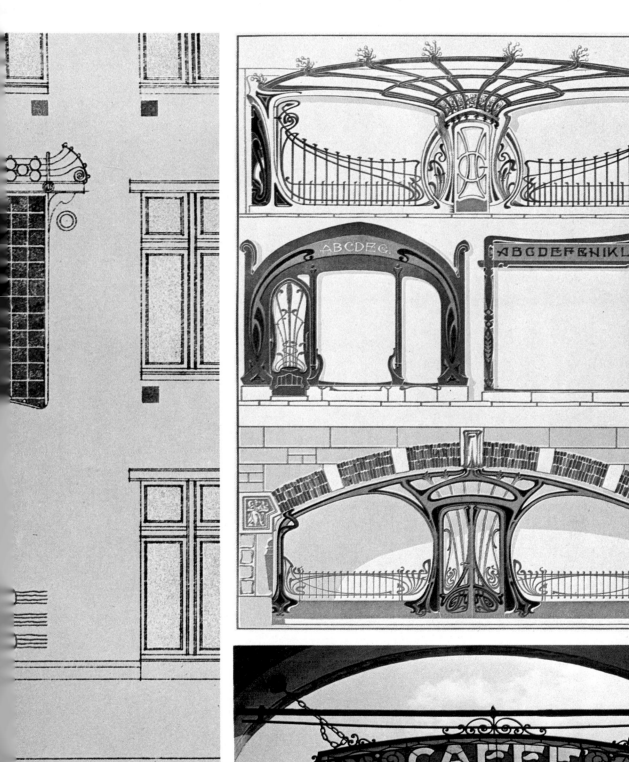

However, when new commercial buildings were in the planning stage, the greatest care was taken to ensure that exterior and interior should be properly related to one another. The interior design of shops and big stores—a branch of architecture that developed notably during those years—extended to the outside in the form of tempting window displays, signs and advertisements.

An example of absolute stylistic austerity and clean functionalism is seen in the display cases (below) made for Philippe Wolfer's jewellery shop by the great Belgian architect Victor Horta, who specialized in commercial design and to whom, in great part, the outward appearance of modern Brussels is due. But the combination of the symbolic form and functional needs of a building was not always realized with such exemplary coherence. All too often the "picture

values" and formal assertion of the style were allowed to mask the technical and functional content. Railway stations provide a prime example of that tendency. These symbols of swift transportation and accelerated rhythm of life, with their technically advanced solutions of vast, cantilever roofing in glass and iron, were frequently loaded with monumental shapes and exuberant decoration. One of the worst instances is Milan Central Station (right) designed in 1912 by Ulisse Stacchini, who with this work won a national competition and established his reputation as an architect. It was not actually built until 1923–30, by which time, in any case, the style was outdated.

The architecture of European towns during the *Belle Époque* was, at least in the outward appearance it presented, very much of its period. The technical advances in constructional methods and the very individual style in vogue encouraged both major architects and ordinary builders to concentrate on external embellishment: wrought iron, ornamental work in moulded cement or coloured majolica with matching floral designs covered the façades of the houses, as in the terraces of the Via Pisacane (left), a street like many others in the middle-class districts of Milan, built between 1900 and 1907 as if to parade the whole decorative repertory of contemporary urban building.

Town life for the moneyed classes during the *Belle Époque* was largely externalized and public, governed by very precise and codified rhythms, times and places: the parade of fashion in London, Vienna and Paris, meetings at the Ascot and Longchamp racecourses, interludes at the boulevard cafés, appointments at smart restaurants or nightclubs, evenings at the theater or opera.

The painters were faithful interpreters of this urban scene, judging by the spate of representations of the high life of the day, already in full flood during the late nineteenth century; indeed, ever since the impressionist revolution. The best known of these reporters in paint was perhaps the Italian Parisian Giovanni Boldini, who was a celebrity on the European scale. His unmistakable style, together with the worldly sophistication of his work, presents a glamorous picture of Parisian life, as in the painting *Walk in the Bois de Boulogne* (1910, on the right).

Architects and designers commissioned to decorate the amenities of the town were skilled in translating a bygone style into the idiom of the day. In his project for the interior (below) of a new room for the Brasserie Pousset in the Boulevard des Italiens in Paris (1900)— illustrated in *Décoration Ancienne et Moderne*—the architect Édouard Niermans has most ingeniously translated the artistic convention of the French rococo into the latest floral motif and soft, winding lines of Art Nouveau.

A minor work such as the new front of the Filodrammatici Theater in Milan (1904; page 137), designed by the architect Giuseppe Giachi in the Liberty style, has nevertheless in its proportions and decoration a distinct suggestion of the "mannerist" period. The fine iron canopy over the entrance is the work of A. Mazzucotelli, Italy's leading craftsman of wrought iron.

NOUVELLE SALLE

RASSERIE POUSSET

Cavazzoni

THE RESORTS OF THE BELLE ÉPOQUE

Town, however, was not the only setting for the leisured life of the *haute bourgeoisie* during the *Belle Époque*. There were other settings, too, where the more prosperous inhabitants of Europe performed their social rituals. The early years of the century saw the beginning of the holiday cult. Seaside towns, watering places and mountain resorts flourished as never before; touring and excursions expanded into a mass phenomenon; it became a matter of prestige, an absolute necessity, to have a villa—or a "cottage"—by the lake or sea.

In Italy entire holiday areas such as the Ligurian and Adriatic Rivieras and the Lombardy lakes were sprinkled with trim or brash little villas, built in a somewhat indefinite style, but one very indicative of a certain taste and way of life. One such, designed by the architect A. Cavazzoni, is seen in his attractive watercolour on the left. The illustration is taken from a collection devoted to the subject of the weekend villa. In a casual style that borders on indifference they sprout excrescences, such as this turret, inspired by models from all over Europe.

O. Schönthal

The design of one-family houses was one of the chief preoccupations of the architects of the period. Only the most socially and professionally conscientious applied themselves to the problem of the housing needs and living standards of the less well-off elements of the population. From the angle of outward appearance, the industrial villages, working-class settlements and garden cities that did indeed come into being—the most progressive developments, in fact—were given much less prominence than the typically middle-class detached houses that were built in profusion and a wide variety of styles. In the examples that follow (taken once more from *Moderne Bauformen*, 1902 and 1903) one can compare the pleasing, if modified, Art Nouveau versions by the Parisian architects Sauvage and Sarrazin (below) with the flawlessly elegant design on the left by Viennese Otto Schöntal.

The Discreet Charm of an Epoch

In both cases the impression is more one of brilliant graphic exercises than of genuine projects, in striking contrast to the very English standards of comfort and habitability expressed in the one-family homes planned by C. F. A. Voysey. He was an architect and interior decorator who devoted nearly all his planning activities to the traditional English theme of rural housing (below, two of his projects, 1903).

In holiday resorts the privately owned villas were rivalled by that equally popular and status-enhancing but public institution, the grand hotel. The whole complex of the Grand Hotel Tre Croci at Campo dei Fiori above Varese, was the work of Giuseppe Sommaruga, one of the most creative architects of the Italian Liberty school. It was built between 1908 and 1911 and is one of the most impressive examples of its kind. Commanding a superb view,

it includes, in addition to the main building, the funicular arrival station and a restaurant extending onto terraces, as well as a private road to the beach and up the slope dotted by villas and cottages, some of them also designed by Sommaruga. The original plans—which were modified in the final version—are to be seen in Ugo Monneret de Villard's *L'architettura di Giuseppe Sommaruga* of 1909 (on the right, two drawings of the hotel).

Thanks to the complete and delightful integration of the architectural and interior design by Ernesto Basile, and the decorative wall paintings by E. de Maria Bergler, the drawing room of the Grand Villa Igiea Hotel at Palermo, first intended as a private residence for the Florio family (1899–1903), is one of the happiest creations of the Italian floral idiom (on these pages) and a charming composition that hands down to us intact the atmosphere of a whole epoch.

On quite a different level we have the pompous decorative *mise-en-scène* of the main staircase of the Spa Hotel at Berzieri di Salsomaggiore (below) planned by Ugo Giusti in 1913, but not carried out until 1923, with decoration by Galileo Chini. Style is sacrificed to the architectural object as symbol. It is a backcloth to the section of society for whom it is intended. Indeed, we can imagine it inhabited by elegant ladies of the type portrayed on the opposite page: *Isa and Her Friends* by Aroldo Bonzagni, one of the most perceptive illustrators of the current social poses. But the gulf that divides the two architectural conceptions—though both intended for the same social purposes—is more than a mere matter of style. In the Italy of 1923 it underlined the distance between the progressive prewar middle class and those who were to become the main support of Fascism.

The Discreet Charm of an Epoch

CULTURE AND INTERIOR DECORATION

One of the most striking aspects of the renaissance of applied art that took place around the turn of the century is undoubtedly the concept of interior decoration as the planning of a unified whole. The overloaded and stifling ornamentation, the tasteless bric-à-brac of the Victorian age, were swept away to make room for clean lines and clearly defined spaces with an imprint of stylistic unity characterizing every detail of architecture and interior design. But while the principle was generally accepted, its application could vary greatly in different parts of Europe. The sumptuous dining room shown on the preceding two pages, made in about 1905 and kept intact in the Nancy School Museum, is the work of one of the greatest French cabinetmakers. It is an example of the Art Nouveau that found its inspiration in natural forms and gave it plastic and dynamic shape. The same free metamorphosis of natural elements, extending to sculptural effects of the utmost originality, is evident in the dining room (below left) on the first floor of Casa Batallo in Barcelona (1905–07). It was designed—as was the whole house—by perhaps the most original and independent figure in modern European archi-

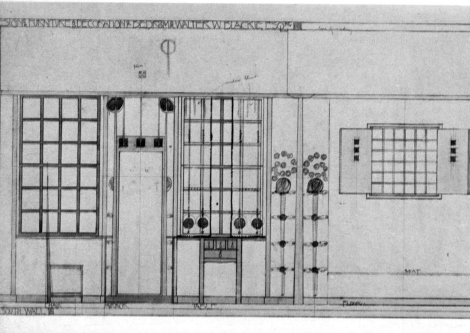

tecture: Antonio Gaudi.

In English-speaking countries the taste in interior decoration was different: clear-cut spaces, delicate decorative elements, sparse furniture with simple lines, pastel shades. An almost rarefied atmosphere and a high stylistic level typify the interiors of the Scottish architect Charles Rennie Mackintosh. The design for the walls and furniture of a bedroom (above left) is part of a detailed study for the internal decoration of Hill House in Helensburgh, first planned in 1902. The sketch for a dining room (below) by the British architect M. H. Baillie-Scott—published in 1900 in *The Studio*, the first and one of the most influential reviews of modernism in Europe—is, on the other hand, typical of the "medium" style of English interior design, adapting traditional elements to the "modern" taste.

The Discreet Charm of an Epoch

References to the national traditions of separate countries were much more evident and more explicitly folkish in character in the decoration and furnishings of lands on the "fringe" of international modernism than they were in the English-speaking countries. That was the case with Holland (though here there were also borrowings from their eastern colonies, mostly Javanese-type decoration, ceramics, materials and patterns) and

ELIEL SAARINEN ATD

150

with the northern countries, especially Scandinavia, as well as Russia and Hungary. "Folk" furniture by the Hungarian craftsman-decorator Odön Farago met with great success in international exhibitions. Even in Italy Basile was designing furniture in the Sicilian cart tradition.

The revival of popular art is evident in the coloured drawings of interiors (left)—published in the 1902 *Moderne Bauformen*—by the Finnish architect Eliel Saarinen, who was also a designer of furniture and the creator of the Finnish Pavilion at the Paris Exposition of 1900. There is some doubt as to whether the ornamental window-panes (above) designed by the Russian S. V. Maljutin can be classed as Art Nouveau. He was a student of folk art and director of the engraving workshop at the Talaškino artists' colony, which, together with the better-known one at Abramtsevo, was the chief center of what in Europe was rather freely called Russian Art Nouveau. The illustration comes from a 1903 number of *Mir Iskusstva* (*The World of Art*), one of the most important Russian art reviews of the period.

Apart from these special instances, however, European interior decoration appears to follow two principal stylistic lines: on the one hand, the naturalistic and transfigurative line of French and Belgian Art Nouveau, German *Jugendstil* and Catalán "modernism"—similar to the "floral" idiom of Italy—and on the other, the abstract, geometrical style of the British experiments, realized at its most extreme in the Austro-German area.

The austerely decorative design for a music room (left) was executed in 1902–03 by Joseph M. Olbrich, an Austrian architect and one of the masters of the Vienna Secession. It was intended, among many others, as an interior design for houses belonging to the "artists' colony" at Darmstadt, founded by the Archduke Ernst Ludwig of Hesse, and one of the centers in which the subject of architectural design for industry was developed with great consistency.

The importance of furnishing and decoration to the life of the *Belle Époque* is evident in the special attention given to the depiction of indoor environments in pictures of the *bourgeoisie* at home. Admittedly, that was not a twentieth-century invention. The domestic portraiture of the late nineteenth century produced a whole range of works—particularly in France, where the names Vuillard and Bonnard spring to mind—but the *Belle Époque* paintings of interiors have a conspicuous "slice of life" feeling missing in the earlier works. Momentary gestures and attitudes, unguarded moments in drawing room or bedroom are caught with the immediacy of a snapshot, as in the picture *Late* by Camillo Innocenti (1910; on the right).

THE IMAGE OF WOMAN

In the iconography of the *Belle Époque* the female image plays a leading part, portrayed in many different aspects, from the angelic lily-woman of Pre-Raphaelite romance to the *femme fatale*, arouser of tragic passions, the elegant ladies of the fashion plate and advertisement, and finally the decorative portrayals of women seen in mouldings on house fronts, in prints of all kinds and in a wide variety of ornaments and jewels.

Among all these fancies there was very little sign of the real-life woman, the one that worked, that fought for her rights, that started on the long and wearisome march towards emancipation. The discovery of a different, authentic image of herself, not conditioned by current social myths, was to be a slow, hard conquest of feminine consciousness.

The *Belle Époque* was the age of the great actresses and opera singers. The most famous of all for the fascination she exerted over her contemporaries was the "divine" Sarah Bernhardt. Her successful career began when Alphonse Mucha drew for her a series of splendid posters that diffused an image of the great actress as a figure at once popular and legendary. We see her in the poster on the left transformed into a fantastic queen of the snows! And for her—a passionate lover of jewellery and a client of the famous craftsman René Lalique—Mucha designed the superb brooch (above right) carried out by the goldsmith Fouquet, and inset with a Medusa head bearing the idealized features of the actress.

The publicity that spread the image of the divine Sarah, and even of the trappings imbued with her personality, naturally permeated the world of the upper-class woman, who absorbed, transformed and adapted for herself the mythic model set before her.

Typical of this kind of publicity is the advertisement by Manuel Orazi (below right) for the Maison Moderne with its artificial, almost abstract, female silhouette displaying combs and jewels in the same style as the vases and figurines spread across the background.

While it might be said that Sarah Bernhardt projected an image of the *femme fatale* in tune with the symbolist and decadent tradition of the nineties but no longer typical of the new theater, there was another female image that could be accepted as the essence not only of the taste but of the whole figurative style of the era: the most renowned dancer of the turn of the century, Loie Fuller. Nothing better summarized the swirling, fluid lines of French Art Nouveau than the waving and flowing of the veils used in her celebrated dances. They were even captured in cement on the pavilion theater dedicated to her at the 1900 Paris Exposition.

Loie Fuller's dances provide one of the earliest examples of the mass production of an image, repeated in endless variations from the most commonplace (advertisements for her performances at the Folies Bergère) to the finest (Chéret and

156

Toulouse-Lautrec designed posters for her) and in numerous little sculptures, bronzes, china ornaments and so on, turned out in every shape, size and material. Illustrated here are the strangely abstract watercolour by Koloman Moser (on the right), a subtle draftsman of the Viennese Secessionist group and the lampstand made by Raoul Larche in about 1900 (left), a perfect example of the flowing lines typical of artifacts of the French school.

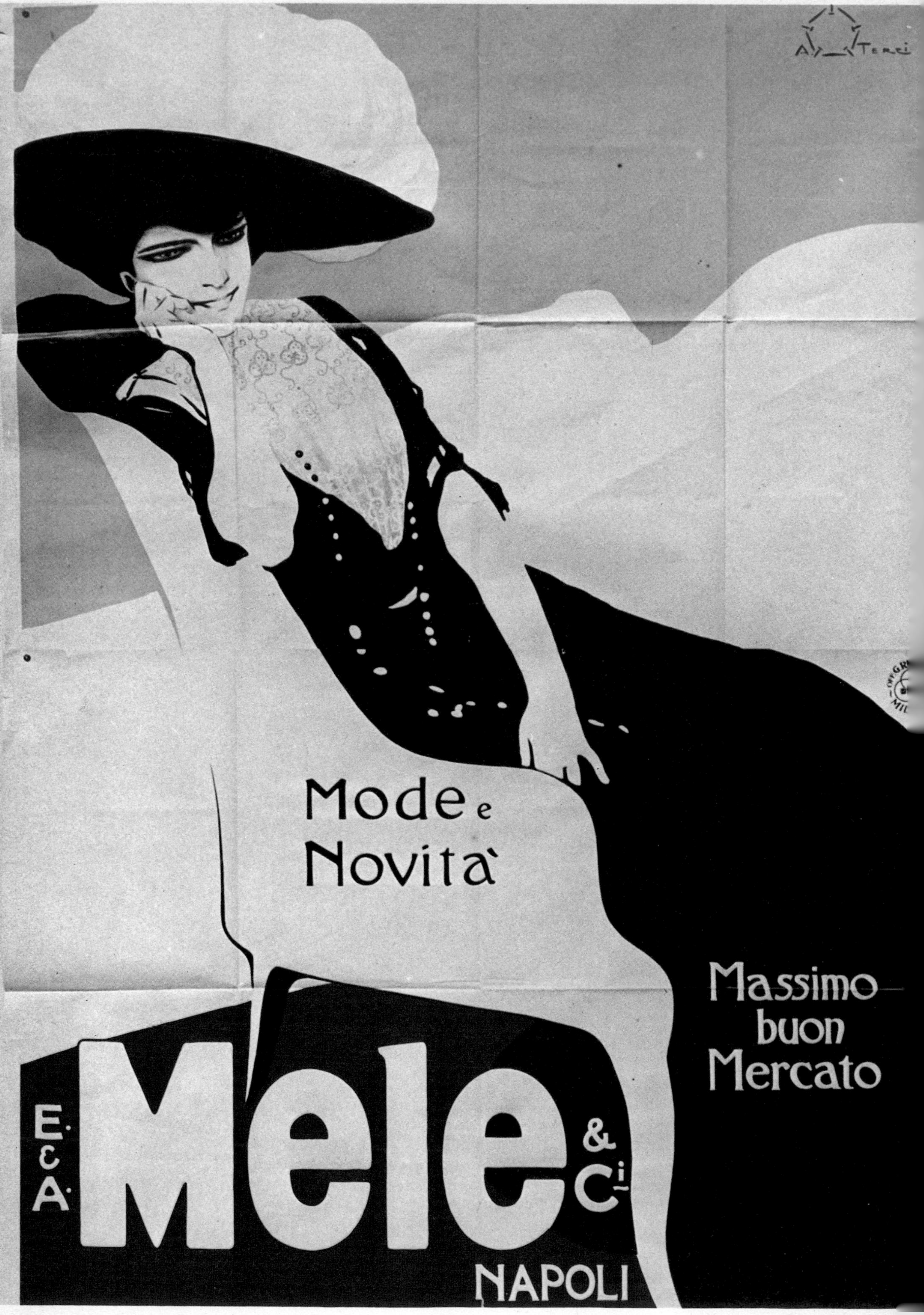
A Terzi
Mode e
Novità
Massimo
buon
Mercato
E. & A.
Mele
& C.i
NAPOLI

From these models of high drama and glamour we turn to their mass-produced derivative: the fashionable "look" for the refined, elegant woman of the middle classes. We cannot speak of clothes in the Art Nouveau style, in spite of the close connection between style, fashion and taste typical of the period, and in spite of artists such as Van de Velde having designed women's dresses. The prevailing fashions can be better seen in women's magazines, fashion plates, advertisements for department stores and dress shops, in which woman is the subject-object. They are pictures of herself as she would wish to be, and conveyors of the message—buy, buy, buy—directed at the great feminine public.

Two examples from different countries: the rather French and richly coloured picture on the right by the Hungarian painter and designer Géza Faragó, advertising the big fashion house of Holzer in Budapest; the poster (1912, on the left) designed by Aleardo Terzi for the important Mele clothes shops in Naples (a firm that employed the best graphic artists in Italy, from Dudovich to Metlicovitz and Cappiello), an attractive composition of clear colours following a clean, witty line.

Another rich source of female images can be found not in the applied but among the fine arts in painting. Portraits of women of the epoch present a wider variety of interpretations and obviously much less standardized types than those exhibited in the posters and popular prints.

In his *Portrait of Frau Eläge* (1902; on the right) Gustav Klimt, a leading Vienna Secessionist, gives the dress and background a superb-ly decorative abstract quality similar to that with which he surrounds the fatal and barbaric woman-idols in his many pictures of Salome and Judith. Nothing is allowed to distract from the pene-trating vitality of the face or the aristocratic bearing of the body.

In *After the Concert* (1905, left), a painting by the Russian Michail A. Vrubel of his wife, the singer N. J. Zabella, the flickering firelight falling on the subject endows it with iridescent colouring and an evoc-ative enchantment. It is a remark-able example of the "portrait of an ambience."

Although not always of the same rich pictorial quality, the portraits of an ambience, in which the female sitter is seen in the intimacy of her own home, among her own possessions and wearing her favourite clothes, were nevertheless the way in which the woman of the period best liked to be portrayed. Works of this sort show an explicit relationship to the better examples of graphic advertising and fashion plates. The resemblance is plain in *The Bird of Paradise* (1910; left)—the title refers to the feathers in the voguish hat worn by the young woman—one of a series of portraits of Parisian ladies painted by the Italian Emilio Rizzi during his stay in the French capital (1909–14). A typically middle-class composition, it compares interestingly with the high-society figures portrayed by Boldini, and is very descriptive of a period and its dress.

On the right is a picture in which figure, objects and background are so stylistically uniform as almost to amount to the "portrait of an ambience," or at any rate an accomplished example of window dressing. It is, in fact, a full-page advertisement from a sales catalogue (1905) of the London firm Liberty. The woman in the foreground is wearing a graceful gown called Josephine. She is an image advertising both herself and the products created for her and her surroundings, all representative of a certain social status. Liberty's shop, already active in the second half of the nineteenth century, later became a producer of fabrics, draperies, jewels and furniture well ahead of current taste, which spread to the continent and contributed to the formation of the new style. In Italy they were so successful that the name "Liberty" was applied to all modernist productions. It is a term still used in the antique business. "Morris" is the more usual corresponding description in England.

The fashion industry underwent an amazing growth during the first twenty years of the century. In Paris—then the undisputed Mecca of Mode—in about 1906 a young and still unknown dressmaker called Paul Poiret brought about a veritable revolution in clothes. He invented the original "free" dress, which by releasing women from the straitjacket of the corset and the burden of multiple petticoats became the symbol of emancipation and the harbinger of more free-and-easy behaviour. The success of Poiret's creations was, however, partly due to the extraordinary graphic skill of Paul Iribe, who in 1908 illustrated them in an exquisite album entitled *Les Robes de Paul Poiret*. What a contrast the boldly assymetrical composition, the subtle colouring and the witty conjunction of figures and traditional background furniture make with the charming but commonplace effect of the Liberty advertisement on the preceding page!

Women's faces changed too. Cosmetics improved enormously and were applied with greater art to accentuate or rejuvenate the wearer's features, especially eyes and lips, as she desired. Hair was cut and dressed in new ways that altered her whole appearance.

Another French fashion artist, Georges Lepape, provides us with the delicious female head with

turban (right) taken from another collection of Poiret's creations, *Les Choses de Paul Poiret* of 1911. It is not hard to trace in them the influences of contemporary art, from the colour revolution of the Fauves to the orientalism of the Ballet Russe and the costume designs of Léon Bakst—but also a certain resemblance to the pale face and heavy makeup of the first film stars.

During those few years fashion evolved rapidly. In 1911 deep "toques" covered the head, in 1914 skirts were worn startlingly short; the Latin American tango arrived in Europe. Even before the outbreak of the First World War—a looming tragedy that was to strip away the last illusions of the *Belle Époque*—the soft and languid lady of the century's beginning was already transforming herself into the vigorous, aggressive, boyish girl of the twenties.

The Discreet Charm of an Epoch

DESIGN FOR LIVING

In no other field is the diffusion and success of the new century's style so evident as in that of the so-called applied or decorative arts. Their revaluation was among the most cherished assumptions of modernist theory. The worldwide projection of the new ideas meant a change of appearance in all household articles, even those in everyday use, for an ever wider consuming public. Unfortunately the progressive and democratic ideal of an "art of living" was not always successfully realized. There was an inherent contradiction between the desire to "beautify" an object and the needs of its commercial mass production. The original esthetic quality designed for an elite was often imitated and debased to a point of utter stylistic banality.

The principle of artistic unity in the decorative arts was one of the factors at the root of the profound sense of consanguinity pervading the representational climate and even the "fine" arts of the *Belle Époque*. In his painting *The Pearl* of 1904 (below) the Russian painter Mikhail A. Vrubel—also a creator of elegant pottery at the Talaškino workshops—treated his subject as if he were decorating an object, gracefully draping translucent siren figures along the edges of an oyster shell. In style it is very similar to the ceramic ornament made at his Zsolnay pottery by the Hungarian potter Pécs (1900–10; above right), in which the line of the female figure continues into the curving bowl shaped like a shell. It is also related to the gilded bronze ornament (below right) designed by R. Carabin, a French craftsman specializing in precious objects depicting every possible variation of that favourite Art Nouveau–*Jugendstil* theme, the woman holding or turning into a flower.

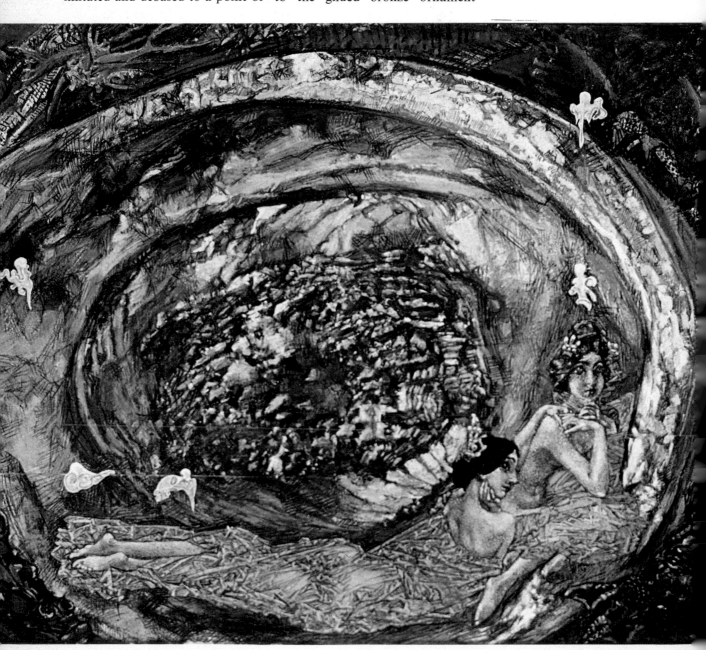

The taste for metamorphosis in Art Nouveau expressed itself with inexhaustibly inventive imagination applied to every conceivable kind of object and involving a varied selection of animal and vegetable species. The favourites were symbolic animals with literary connotations, capable of being adapted to the graceful, flexible line of the current style, such as the swan, or richly and variously coloured, like the peacock, highly symbolic, like the iridescent snake, or fragile creatures, such as the moth and butterfly.

The fascinating theme of the butterfly-woman, pursued with almost surrealist effect by the painter and illustrator Alberto Martini in his pastel *Gilded Butterfly* (1913; above left), was transformed into a semiabstract image in a beautiful brooch of translucent enamel set with opalescent stones (1900; below left) designed by Eugène Feuillâtre, a French goldsmith.

In this type of jewellery, however elegant, it is notable that the symbolic effect of the design takes precedence over the value of the materials, which are chosen less for their intrinsic worth than for their qualities of transparency, light and colour.

Two extreme examples of the passion for depicting animal or plant metamorphosis are seen in the following pieces of furniture. First

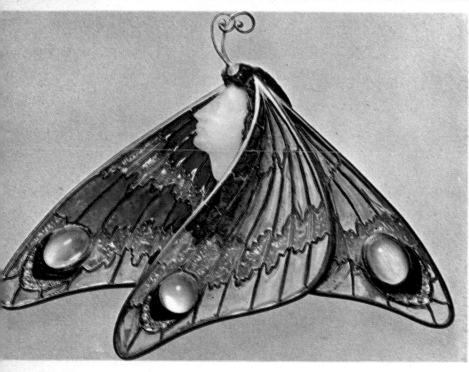

is the fantastic *papillon* bed (1904; right) by Émile Gallé—one of the most remarkable craftsmen of French Art Nouveau, creator of furniture and glass objects of the finest workmanship, and founder of the famous School of Nancy—in which butterflies fashioned out of precious inlaid woods and mother-of-pearl represent Dawn at the foot of the bed and Dusk at its head. (We should observe, in passing, the fungoid bedside lamp.) The second (on page 170) is a writing table, the work of Henry van de Velde, a Belgian architect and designer, as well as the leading theoretician of modernism. Unlike the first, it does not actually imitate the natural subject, but transfers it to the functional level, so that although the vibrant line of the butterfly wing is evident in the coloured-glass insertion, it becomes an abstract element of design foreshadowing the functionalism that was to come.

The Discreet Charm of an Epoch

The Discreet Charm of an Epoch

But from the late nineteenth century onwards no animal was so admired for its esthetic appeal— especially in the England of the Pre-Raphaelites, Morris and Liberty— as the divine bird, Juno's favourite and the symbol of pomp and circumstance, the peacock. Its sinuous and graceful form, the iridescent splendour of its plumes— often compared to a woman's hair—encounter us in the most varied selection of objects, from lace to pottery, from wallpaper to wrought iron, from every kind of print, whether as subtle as the cloak with which Beardsley adorned his Salomé or as ordinary as advertisements and textile patterns. It was not by chance that the wall decoration in one of the precursors of the modernist cult of esthetic unity, the famous *Peacock Room* (1876) by James McNeill Whistler, consists of peacock feathers.

Two English examples: firstly, the marvellous dish in brilliantly coloured enamels, one of the last works of the English potter William de Morgan, who was already active at the end of the nineteenth century, and in close touch with the Pre-Raphaelites and the crafts fellow-ship of William Morris; secondly, the delicate pendant in gold, silver and pearls (1902; on the left), made by the writer and architect Charles R. Ashbee, who founded the London Guild of Handicrafts, a body for developing artisanship, not unlike Morris's Arts and Crafts fellow-ship.

(Above left: the butterfly writing desk designed by Henry van de Velde.)

As well as the butterfly-woman tradition, there was the swan-woman of legend, a widely diffused theme in the folklore of Germanic and still more of Nordic and Slavonic lands. The charming picture of the Swan Princess (below right), as glowing in colour as cloisonné enamel, comes from a series of illustrations for the fairy tale *Tsar Saltan* (1905) by the Russian artist I. J. Bilibin, an impassioned student of popular tradition.

Similar in decorative effect, because it also consists of areas of flat colour bordered by black outlines—justified in this case by the technical needs of the final product—is the sketch of a swan preening. It might almost be another illustration for the same story, but it is, in fact, a design for stained glass taken from the collection *Examples of Decorative Art* (1911), by the Italian decorative artist Giovanni Buffa, who was particularly fond of using gay and colourful plant and animal subjects in his ceramics and stained glass.

The same theme was immensely popular in French and Belgian Art Nouveau articles, but there the swan-woman was often fantasized and transfigured, as in the plated

172

bronze grill (1900; right). The enormously prolonged, transparent wings give it lightness and elegance. It was created for the great jeweller Lalique in the Place Vendôme, Paris.

A popular Art Nouveau style, charming though too often vulgarized, was known in Italy as "floral" for the ubiquity of flowers in the design. The flowers might be chosen for their symbolic value or because they lent themselves particularly well to the demands of the style. Thus a whole range of long-stemmed plants, naturalistic or formalized, played their decorative role: Pre-Raphaelite lilies, irises, tulips, roses; also pretty, ephemeral flowers such as violets, cyclamen or lilies of the valley, the undulations of water lilies and aquatic plants, drooping wisteria, sprays of orchids and clusters of mistletoe.

The Discreet Charm of an Epoch

The motif of hanging blossoms was used for a great variety of decorative purposes. An unpretentious but pleasing example is seen in the stained-glass window on the opposite page. It was probably made at G. Beltrami's Milan glassworks after a design by Giovanni Buffa, who exhibited similar wisteria-patterned windows at the Milan Exhibition of 1906.

Given a more stylistic treatment, wisteria appears again in a brooch (1900; above right) designed by the famous French jeweller René Lalique, who, together with Émile Gallé, was much given to phytomorphic themes in the applied arts.

Lalique's extraordinary mimetic skill is evident in his small masterpiece of an orchid in ivory and horn (1897–1900; below), the lifelike rendering of which attains an uncanny, almost surreal, level.

The glass jar decorated with a delicate wood anemone pattern (left) is by Émile Gallé, rivalled only by the American Tiffany, who was undoubtedly the most accomplished master glazier of the modernist school. Unlike other contemporary European craftsmen in glassware, who aimed for effects of transparency or iridescent colour, Gallé created a thick, opalescent type of glass on or into which, by some special, secret process, he modelled, incised or enclosed floral patterns of ever fresh invention.

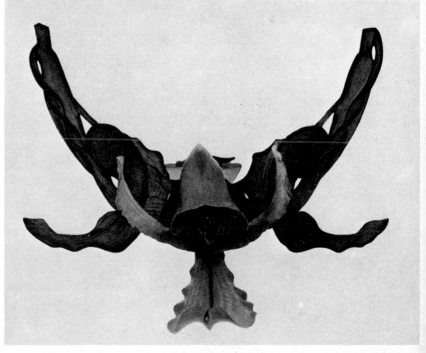

We may talk of the formal quality of a style, but the real touchstone of the degree to which it truly represents an era—and the examples on this page illustrate the point—is its prevalence in every sort of artifact, however unpractical (the feeling that a thing of beauty should be useless was a legacy from the estheticism of the nineties) or seldom used. Most of the personal possessions made during the *Belle Époque*—on whatever qualitative level—had the subtle fascination of the ephemeral, the transitory, accentuated by their delicacy and fragility, and by the inclusion of floral motifs.

So it is with these two objects—very divergent in value, but intended for the same social environment—both the precious gold-and-enamel brooch by Paul Albert Beaudoin (left) of a girl's delicate face emerging from among the violets, symbols of transience; and an article as trifling as the Hungarian dance program on the right (1910), adorned with a girl's head in floral style, framed in Secessionist decoration, all quite commonplace, but endowed with the gentle, evocative appeal of a time in which each revolution of the dance floor was consuming its own history and its own fate.

"A Mounting Fever . . ."

by János Riesz

At first glance the *Belle Époque* seems far removed from our own day, yet when one calls to mind the names of the authors writing then, and the titles of their works, it is remarkable how near to us that era becomes and how modern.

Many writers already famous at that time lived on until and beyond the middle of our century: Heinrich Mann (1871–1950), Thomas Mann (1875–1955) and Hermann Hesse (1877–1962) in German literature, for intance; Claudel (1868–1955), Gide (1869–1951) and Colette (1873–1954) in French; Shaw (1856–1950) and John Masefield (1868–1967) in English. Parallel names are Croce (1866–1952) and Giovanni Papini (1881–1956) in the literature of Italy, Pío Barroja (1872–1956) and Ortega y Gasset (1883–1955) in that of Spain, and Ferenc Molnár (1878–1952) in that of Hungary. If we turn our attention to writers who died during the early years of the twentieth century, we notice how many names from the previous hundred years survived into our time. Nietzsche died in 1900, Zola in 1902, Chekhov and Jules Verne in 1904, Ibsen in 1906, Carducci and Huysmans in 1907, Tolstoy and Mark Twain in 1910, Strindberg and Giovanni Pascoli in 1912.

Add to that list the names of authors born at the beginning of this century on whom the years in question exercised an inescapable influence, and we end with an extremely heterogeneous collection. Leafing through the pages of French literature alone, we find Adamov, Anouilh, Aymé, Beauvoir, Beckett, Camus, Duras, Genêt, Gracq, Green, Leiris, Malraux, Prévert, Queneau, St.-Exupéry, Sarraute, Sartre, Simenon, Claude Simon, Weil. This generation is deeply rooted in those earlier years, as Sartre reveals in the autobiographical description of his childhood in *Les Mots*. And so the first decade and a half of the twentieth century, seen as the point of intersection of so many generations, so many different trends of opinion and modes of thought, appears to us both far in the past and near to our own times.

One bridge that provides a shortcut over the long time gap separating us from the *Belle Époque* is its living presence in our paperback collections, theater repertories, cinema and television programs, and even comic strips. Without the plays of Shaw, Ibsen, Chekhov, Strindberg, Wedekind, Hofmannsthal and Pirandello we should lose a large part of our regular repertoire. The same could be said for cinema and television without filmed versions of novels by Colette, Gide, Conrad, Kipling, H. G. Wells, Thomas Mann, D'Annunzio, Karl May, Jack London and Gorky or adaptations in the style of *The Forsyte Saga*, Father Brown, *Buddenbrooks* and Sherlock Holmes. Even strip cartoon characters such as Superman and the Incredible Hulk are descendants of Tarzan, Jekyll and Hyde and so on. Thus something of that past permeates our present, a pervading essence that arises not only from continuity but also from a sort of nostalgia based as much on a feeling of ideal affinity as on a yearning to live again in a past that can never return: at the same time near, and yet far.

In trying to compose an overall picture of the *Belle Époque* in its mental and spiritual aspects a question arises as to which generation of writers was the most significant, those whose creativity was at its peak, those who were just beginning to be known, or those who still stood for the traditions of the nineteenth century? Even within the compass of a general characterization it is permissible to distinguish between the period as seen by itself and the image it presents to our eyes after more than half a century. For the affluent classes it was a beautiful epoch in the true sense of the term, contented, carefree and seemingly destined to last forever. Stefan Zweig's description of the "world of yesterday" under the Hapsburg Empire applies equally to other European countries: "When I try briefly to describe the years before the First World War it seems to me fair to say that it was the golden age of security. Everything seemed destined to endure indefinitely under our nearly thousand-year-old Austrian monarchy, and the state appeared to be the guarantee of that stability. The rights granted to the inhabitants were underwritten by parliament, the freely elected representatives of the people, and the duties of the subject were clearly defined. Our currency, the Austrian thaler, circulated in the form of gleaming gold coins, apparently undebasable. Everyone knew the extent of his own patrimony, what was expected of him, what was allowed and what forbidden. Everything had its standard weight and measure. Anyone possessing capital could calculate the yearly income from it with exactitude. An official or clerk could tell from his calendar, without a shadow of doubt, when his next promotion was due and the date of his pensioned retirement. Each family lived according to a precise budget, knew how much it spent on board and lodging, on holidays and entertainment. Without fail a moderate sum was set aside for emergencies, illness and doctors' fees. House owners felt they had a secure home that would still be there for their children and grandchildren; estates and businesses were passed down from generation to generation; a little nest egg was laid in the newborn baby's money box or bank account as a provision for the future. Everything was solid, immutable and in the right place in that vast realm, and in the highest place of all sat the old Emperor. One knew that after his death there would be another, and nothing would be changed in the well-run order of things. No one thought of wars, revolutions and upheavals. Radicalism and violence were unthinkable in that age of reason." (Stefan Zweig, *The World of Yesterday*.)

Did we not know how it all ended, we might say it was a most enviable state of affairs. But calm and security are only one aspect of that era, a middle-class façade, as it were. Musil, another Austrian, saw the same period in quite a different light. He spoke of spiritual unrest, a mysterious malady of the age, an atmosphere of revolt and awakening: "In the last twenty years of the nineteenth century, from beneath a calm as smooth as oil, there suddenly surfaced currents of impelling force that swept all over Europe. No one really knew what would happen next. Perhaps a new art, a new type of man, would emerge, or the social order be turned upside down? Everyone said what suited him best. Creative talent flowered that would once have been stifled at birth; individuals who would formerly have played no part in public life

assumed great roles." (R. Musil, *The Man Without Qualities*.)

The epoch appears as a mass of contradictions and opposed opinions. Musil catalogues a series of catchwords and trends that characterize the multiple aspects of the time, tiny pieces in the mosaic that will finally make up the whole picture.

Superman and brute force appealed, health and sunshine were worshipped—but so also was the tradition of young women whose life was threatened by mysterious illnesses. Enthusiasm for the heroic legend vied with the cult of the "little man." People of the period were at once credulous and skeptical, naturalist and artificial, strong and frail. They daydreamed of ancient castles, autumnal gardens, glassy pools, precious stones, hashish, mortal disease, demon-haunted nature, but also of prairies, wide horizons, forges and factories, naked wrestlers, the revolt of slaves, primitive human couples and the destruction of society.

And yet, for Musil, there was a unity in this multiplicity, a common spirit animating the whole epoch: "Through this tangle of beliefs stirred a steady wind, bending the branches in its path, a spirit of faction and reformation, a glad consciousness of change and new beginnings. It was a modest renaissance telling of better times to come. Anyone born into the world in those years felt its breath on the cheek wherever he or she might be."

To understand the *Belle Époque* it will not do to take into account only the feelings of those who lived through it, still less the backward glance that so often sees it through a golden haze. With hindsight we observe the projects and terrors that obsessed it. We know what was in store, what was being prepared but had not yet come to fruition. The *Belle Époque* came before the First World War, before the Russian Revolution and, in the artistic field, before the golden age of the cinema. All three events loomed on the horizon as vague shadows at once desired and feared. In 1915, soon after the outbreak of the Great War, Rilke sent a letter to the Princess Marie of Thurn and Taxis-Hohenlohe, in which he wrote, "Was it this, I ask myself a hundred times a day, was it this that weighed so horribly on our spirits during these last years, that terrifying future which is now our cruel present? Whatever happens afterwards, the worst is that that innocence of life in which we grew up will never come again for any of us."

While for Rilke the shadow of war loomed as a dark foreboding, a "horrible weight," Lenin's solution to the question he was asking himself in 1901–02, "What is to be done?" appeared in his manifesto as a rational, well-thought-out program that, according to historical necessity, could find its sufficient realization in the October Revolution. Seeing that the majority of Russian workers would benefit from economic and political education, Lenin wrote of the need to found a newspaper. It should not confine itself exclusively to increasing political information, finding comrades prepared to fight, organizing propaganda and framing plans for collectivization. It should also act as a catalyst of the revolutionary movement. "Through and around this journal," Lenin wrote, "a permanent organization will spontaneously arise. That group will occupy itself not solely with social activities but also with activities of a general and continuous nature. In this way the members will become accustomed to concerning themselves with political events, adequately evaluating their significance and the effects they may have on different classes, and working out methods by which the revolutionary party can sway those events to its advantage." (Lenin, *What Is to Be Done?*) Even this passage is not entirely rational or founded exclusively on logical reasoning. In that "spontaneously arise" there is a hint of the Hegelian belief in the "spontaneous evolution of world history": "And if we combine our forces to publish a journal for all, that work will bring together and train not only our cleverest propagandists, but also efficient organizers and the most gifted members of the party, who, at the right moment, will know how to summon and guide the others to the decisive battle."

In the artistic field we are in the years preceding the flowering of cinematic art, which reached its best moments during the twenties. In 1895 the brothers Lumière had exhibited their first film, *Products from the Lumière Workshop*. The early science-fiction films of Meliès, interesting from a technical point of view, were soon followed by films of artistic merit. The first result was a transformation of the artist's vision of the world. The rapid succession of images, the fleeting quality of the impressions, brought about a profound change in perception, what Walter Benjamin called the "form of dispersive perception." Reality is too complex to convey by simple imitation. It can be reconstructed, it seems, only through details and fragments. But let us return to the history of ideas in the *Belle Époque*.

Marx's thesis, according to which "the dominant ideas of an era are always the ideas of its dominant class," may seem a platitude today, but the passage that follows it is often forgotten: "We are speaking of ideas that revolutionize a whole society, bearing witness to the birth within the old society of the elements of a new social order, a decay of the old conditions of life that marches in step with the decay of traditional thought." (*Communist Manifesto*.) Dominant ideas as ideas of the dominant class or, in opposition to those, revolutionary ideas pointing towards the future? Unfortunately, neither provides the ideal solution that will enable us to reconcile all the contradictions of the time in one all-inclusive picture.

A great divergence yawns, however, between the products of intellectual activity that seemed to its contemporaries superior and significant, and the works that have survived into our own times, between official culture and the so-called masterpieces. It is a distinction that can be found in every sector. In the theaters of Paris the public was applauding pale neoromantic and realist pastiches, not Maeterlinck, Claudel or Jarry. With sarcasm André Gide reported, "Today there are two types of dramatic work: those which are written but not played, and those which are shown in the theater but have no importance." These last appealed to a middle-class public that could not tolerate revolutionary innovations or accept new forms aimed at shaking their convictions.

The same applies to the Nobel Prize for literature in those years. The choice of winning authors was, to quote Erwin Koppen, "catastrophic." "At that time," he wrote, "the prize went to Sully-Prudhomme, Björnson, Echegaray, Sienkiewicz, Kipling, Eucken and Heyse. No one thought of Tolstoy, Zola, Unamuno, Ibsen, Strindberg or Mark Twain, to say nothing of younger authors such as Hofmannsthal, Rubén Darío and Paul Valéry or of Thomas Mann, Gide and Pirandello, who received their prizes much later. It constitutes an enigma not yet explained from the historical or theoretical angle." The answer to that "enigma," according to Koppen, lay in the "theory of an ideal literature," a concept typical of conservative European bourgeois poetry in the second half of the nineteenth century. "Literature and poetry belong to the world of ideas. The poet, son of the Muses, is a being gifted with supernatural talents; art should concern itself with truth, beauty and goodness with the purpose of ennobling mankind."

The positive character, supporting the establishment and sometimes directly pro-imperialist, of this pseudo-idealistic view of literature was expressed most clearly by the Kaiser Wilhelm II, who had no hesitation in publicizing his personal opinions on literature and art: "Art should contribute to the people's education, offering even the lowest strata the chance to improve themselves through its ideas after their hard day's toil." He had it publicly proclaimed that poetry required "greatness of spirit, exceptional characters, splendour and total beauty." And there was no lack of authors, even in other countries, who obeyed his instructions and produced literature that was "opium for the people," pro-imperialist and sympathetic to the establishment. The officially approved literature sold well. It was easy to read and easy to sell. It is enough to know that the highly popular novelist Hedwig Courths-Mahler produced an average of two books a year, with a circulation of over a million copies.

How, then, can we judge what were the ideas and intellectual trends consistent with the more progressive aspects of the epoch and historical situation? With regard to art the imperative of Rimbaud is still valid after more than a hundred years: "It is essential to be absolutely modern."

But what was modern between 1900 and 1915? It is certainly not the same as to ask what was fashionable, up-to-date and popular, nor a matter of best sellers and West End hits. In relation to the time in which they lived, we can define Freud, Einstein, Bergson, Unamuno, Lenin and Veblen as modern. But how shall we place and classify Hofmannsthal, George, Barrès, Alain-Fournier, D'Annunzio and Pascoli? In the sphere of art and ideas, too, progress does not necessarily advance in one direction only, but is dual and undergoes considerable regressions, retreats to the past and "the contemporary in the noncontemporary." But history does not repeat itself, and the neoromanticism and neoclassicism of this century's beginning have little but the name in common with their models from the past. T. W. Adorno speaks of two criteria by which we may judge what is genuinely modern, two standards which will indicate the spirit of true progress (T. W. Adorno and P. V. Haselberg, Sull' adeguatezza storica della coscienza [On the historical adequacy of conscience]). The first, and positive, one is innovation, that is to say the strong nervous reaction of the artist or philosopher to the present; the second, and negative, criterion, a spontaneous reaction of distaste, an inability to tolerate certain linguistic forms, certain subjects, a sort of "sense of historical rightness," as summarized, for instance, by Hölderlin, when he says, "This can go no further." These reactions, at first blind and instinctive, must eventually rise to the conscious level and leave the sphere of spontaneity, for "the subjective reaction is justified only when it is the result of conscious thought."

Can we, who do not belong to the epoch, identify with the spirit of that time? Is it possible to think ourselves back into those years to define what was then modern and progressive? Or should we start by accepting in principle the inadequacies of their cultural aims when applied to real life? Is what Piero Melograni wrote of the world of politics and power equally valid for that of the arts? "Cultural patterns, whether related to interpretation or planning for the future, usually emerge as obsolete when compared to the ever-

Aubrey Beardsley, John and
Salome, *illustration for* Salome *by
Oscar Wilde, omitted from the 1894
edition and published only in 1907.*

changing pattern of reality. Contemporary society alters rapidly. Ideas change more gradually. Those in authority are usually of mature age and tend to perpetuate the ideas of the past. The world in which they grew up and achieved their success is the world of yesterday. The younger generation, on the other hand, expresses its ideas in a fragmented and confused manner; its experience of the world is necessarily limited. Thus it happens that both old and young, the rulers and the governed, nearly always find themselves disarmed in the presence of real life. In its pursuit of reality, society tends culturally to trail a long way behind."

The problem becomes even more complex when one looks at Europe as a whole, and at the varying stages of development existing in the different countries. On one side we observe an inequality of level between them, some being in the vanguard of literature and the arts, others still immersed in the culture of the nineteenth century. On the other side, one could already speak of a sort of Common Market of ideas, with many elements shared, even the choice of themes and patterns of thought. Thus two opposing aspects must be borne in mind, firstly the internationalism of literary and artistic processes, and secondly national autonomy. For the first time political and cultural history involved the whole planet: Europe, through her colonies and ex-colonies, extended into every continent. Goethe's ideal of a world literature achieved through improved means of communication, as foreseen by him in a conversation with Johann Peter Eckermann in 1827, seemed about to come true. "National literature," he maintained, "is no longer so important. The age of world literature approaches, and every one of us should do what he can to hasten its coming." According to Goethe, who had a sharp sense of the practical, it was the natural consequence of the growth of international traffic and the increased number of translations.

A true representative of that "world culture" of the *Belle Époque* was Filippo Tommaso Marinetti, "inventor" and propagandist of futurism. A well-to-do man, he could afford the luxury of travelling all over Europe, often in the company of futurist painters, of whom he made himself the patron and manager. Wherever he went, whether to Paris, London, Berlin, Munich, Moscow or St. Petersburg, his presence was a provocation, both in his manner of introducing himself and in the audacity of the ideas he propagated. In every place he visited he ignited violent discussion, found disciples, made enemies. They called him "the caffeine of Europe," or, alternatively, "the intellectual Cromwell of our time." He succeeded in attracting public attention so exclusively that during his stay in London, for example, everything new created in the field of art was dubbed "futurist." There is no doubt that Marinetti was the first man fully to exploit the railways of Europe for artistic ends.

It was not only the means of communication, however, that created new opportunities for cultural exchange. Important new inventions in the printing industry also caused considerable transformations. In 1870 the rotary press was invented, followed by improved methods of typesetting. The production of printed texts was enormously speeded up by these devices. The following dates and figures refer to Germany, but are significant for other nations as well: in 1860 the number of books printed was 7284, in 1890 it was 18,875, while by 1913 the figure had risen to 35,078. The rate of increase in the production of printing paper between 1860 and 1927 was 2000 percent, from 96,000 to 652,000 tons. Productivity growth in the printing industry, increasing industrialization, urban agglomeration, the growing prosperity of a wider spectrum of the population, and attempts to improve the level of popular education, were also factors of great importance in the birth and development of the epoch's cultural movements. Literature became an object of financial speculation and an instrument for manipulating the masses, though it had already been so to some extent in the preceding century. Great publishing houses catered to a huge public by producing cheaper books, lower prices and superior editions, while readership increased enormously.

Here we must take into consideration the

sudden proliferation of literary and artistic reviews, a phenomenon common to all the European nations. These journals were often the rallying point and official organ of some literary school or group. There was lively competition among them, controlled by, among other things, the market economy. If they wanted to sell, they had to be forever finding something new to attract the public. The picture of the *Belle Époque* as "the golden age of schools and manifestos" arose partly from new material and economic opportunities. The age was characterized above all by its multiplicity of intellectual movements, trends, styles, moods, groups, schools of thought, statements of belief, attitudes, programs, messages … (the literary terminology offers an infinite choice of names).

In looking through the history of the thought and literature of those years one is struck by the way the most disparate cults and movements are all described as typical of the period: estheticism, idealism, paganism, subjectivity, vitalism, intuitionism, mysticism, occultism, spiritualism, esoteric philosophy, pragmatism, the doctrine of immanence, the study of psychology, individualism, the cult of heroism and the myth of Superman, Art Nouveau, reform, regional literature, biology as universal explanation, racism, neoclassicism, neoromanticism, nationalism, militarism, Darwinian socialism … and so on, with all their national variants.

Even within a single work one detects elements of different trends and attitudes. Is there one common denominator underlying all these trends, a unity enclosing the multiplicity? In the German literature of the time Jens Malte Fischer distinguishes four basic attitudes, four different ways of reacting to contemporary problems, namely, a reactionary stance; individualistic concern in psychology; pseudoreformist proposals; evasive solutions. Common to all these, according to him, was a regressive tendency that separated them from the social commitment characterizing the naturalism that preceded them. Fischer writes, "Typical of the beginning of the century was a withdrawal of attention from social and political reality through a process of in-dividualization that manifested itself in a growing interest in psychology and in a new esthetic creed of the beautiful and supertemporal."

Regression, individualism, psychology, estheticism: basically these tendencies can function only on an abstract level which does not reflect the unique character of the epoch in its diverse and changing reality. Such abstract definitions fail to take into account the development of a new approach in the natural and moral sciences; to say nothing of the feminist movement then expressing itself in both literature and militant action, regional art that was more than merely backward-looking, and the many novels, so typical of their time, whose protagonists were adolescent.

In the first place, to speak of the "ideas" of a particular period does not mean that they are to be looked for only in texts where they are expressed explicitly and with purpose. They must also be sought for beneath the surface, or where they are embodied in the characters, implicit in the subject matter or even present without the author's being aware of them. In this context it is relevant to quote the famous letter from Engels to Margaret Harkness in 1888, referring to the novel *City Girl*, which she had just written. "I do not think it was a mistake at all for you not to have written an openly Socialist novel … extolling the author's social and political views. That is not important. The more concealed are the ideas of the artist herself, the more successful will the work of art be. The realism of which I speak will manifest itself even in spite of the author's declared opinions." Engels illustrated his statement by citing Balzac, whose political views were royalist and legitimist, and yet who, in his novels, made all his interesting and admirable characters republican representatives of the people.

The same can be said of the writers of the *Belle Époque*. The theories of art and political ideology of a Thomas Mann, for instance, did not necessarily coincide with what he put into his poetry. It is the very authors who see themselves as outside the political fray and pose as representatives of purely esthetic individualism, whose works most betray the futility and questionable quality of such a stance, sometimes carrying it to the point of absurdity. In our context that means that the themes and currents of thought we seek to describe remain abstractions and have no direct correspondence with concrete facts and conditions. They are not to be found isolated in certain texts, but always appear in company with other problems and elements. The selection we shall have to make is of a somewhat arbitrary character, and is only one of the possible selections. The basic criterion it follows is the international representation of separate trends of thought. If, in the exposition that follows, an undue amount of space has been given to writers in the German language, it is only for practical reasons (availability of texts) and not with the intention of stressing a nonexistent hegemony.

Changes in the Scientific Conception of the Universe— Crises of Language and Cognition

Education and the arts in the second half of the nineteenth century had broken the mould of traditional encyclopedic knowledge and were turning ever more to the world of exact science. The numerous publications devoted to popular science bear witness to that. *The Riddle of the Universe* by Ernst Haeckel (1899) went into numerous editions and became a truly popular work. Other of his texts that appealed to a vast public were *The General Morphology of Organisms* and *The History of Creation*. The starting point of this phenomenon was Charles Darwin's *Origin of Species*, published in 1859. His theories on selection and evolution soon became popularized and trivialized. "The fight for existence" and "the survival of the fittest" became catchphrases. The application of the evolutionary theory to man was treated with caution by Darwin, but became the basic theme of Haeckel's books. The desire for a unitary, monistic conception of life, scientifically proved, went hand in hand with attempts to grasp by means of a few general principles the infinite quantity of new scientific ideas and contain them within the ideal construction of a coherent vision of the world.

By far more revolutionary than the theses of Haeckel, whether in practical consequences or in the changes they brought to our understanding of the universe, were the quantum theory of Max Planck and Einstein's theory of relativity, both of which originated early in this century. From the times of Galileo and Newton one ruling principle of physics had remained valid, the conception of a causally derived continuity: nature never made jumps. Then Planck demonstrated that nature did just that: light did not radiate in a continuous stream but, as it were, "dripped" in single "quanta" which moved at the speed of light, and possessed measurable quantities of energy, weight and dimension. Light, like matter, had an atomic structure. From the difference of quality described in classic physics we have advanced to the difference of quantity laid down by modern physics. The new world of physics can no longer be conceived in concrete images, but only described by mathematical formulae.

The same goes for Einstein's $E = mc^2$. Here, too, fundamental principles of classical physics have been overtaken: the laws of the conservation of mass and the conservation of energy. Einstein's formula demonstrates that one force can be transformed into the other, and that in the course of that transformation enormous quantities of energy are released (c^2 is the square of the speed of light). The formula belongs to the system of the special theory of relativity, which extends the law of relativity of classical physics to all natural phenomena. Relativity of space: the laws governing all physical phenomena are the same for two observers moving in relation to one another; relativity of time: light travels through space at a constant speed in all directions, independent of the different states of motion of the source or the observer. From that it follows, among other things, that each system has its different way of measuring the duration of time. Two observers situated in two different systems will obtain different coordinates for their position in space and different values for calculating an event in time.

The theories of Planck and Einstein met with much the same treatment as had distorted that of

Aubrey Beardsley, illustration for the story The Murders in the Rue Morgue *by Edgar Allan Poe, 1894–95.*

Darwin. Taken out of the clearly defined context of physics, they were simplified and generalized. It was not long before they were supposed to have confirmed the existence of a fourth dimension, to have endowed space and time with a new significance and shown that everything in nature and morality was relative to this world. Finally they became the source of jokes like that of the passenger in a train who asked the ticket collector when the next station would be stopping. Neither Planck nor Einstein had expected such public reactions to their investigations. In an address given long after his "Significance and Limits of the Exact Sciences," Planck emphasized the strictness of the scientific ethic, which demanded constant work and continual amendment and improvement of the results that were obtained from time to time. He insisted in particular that "the continuous sequence of reasoning required in the transition from one view of the world to another does not arise from fluctuating states of mind, or in a superficial manner, but is an unavoidable necessity. The necessity becomes a bitter one every time research uncovers a new fact of nature that does not fit into the traditional system. The old conception of the universe is not simply set aside as being obsolete, but is seen as part of a larger picture, more extended and at the same time more homogenous. Thus the evolution of research does not mean an irregular and arbitrary swing to and fro, but a progress and bringing to perfection." (Max Planck, *Lectures on Theoretical Physics*.)

In the world of letters we find movements parallel to the scientific and pseudoscientific trends of the period. In that age of naturalism and positivism the exact sciences enjoyed undisputed prestige. The literary historian Wilhelm Scherer described them as "conquerors riding in a triumphal chariot to which all the rest are chained." E. Wilhelm Boelsche, who was fighting for a new form of culture that would no longer be literary in the accepted sense, wrote his chief work, *The Scientific Basis of Poetry*, in 1887. In it he described the need to align the ideas and methods of poetry with those of the natural sciences. He envisaged poetic creation as "an experiment in the scientific sense of the word." His idea of the natural world was of course still that of classical physics: "a picture of the immutable regularity of all cosmic phenomena." After Planck and Einstein it was no longer possible to think in those terms.

Analogous to the disorientation caused by their theories was the profound crisis of language experienced by poets in the early part of the century, a crisis involving knowledge itself. The doubts which shook the national certainty of their world extended to a belief, hitherto unquestioned, in the power of human language to communicate. The crisis affected linguistic philosophers as much as poets. In his philosophical essays, Gottlob Frege, striving after an unambiguous clarity of expression, went so far as to propose that ordinary prose should be replaced by "ideographs," a formalized language of pure thought comparable to that used in arithmetic. Linguistic and cybernetic science and the theory of information later took up the idea. Still more radical is the opinion of Fritz Mauthner, who considered understanding and communication through language quite impossible. It expressed individual ideas, always subjectively and metaphorically. Communication was not its function. He writes: "Human beings, possessing only language, live in the unrealizable longing to know more of the world about them. The words of a language are little suited to communication, because they are the products of memory, and two people never share the same memories. Words are little suited to communication, in that each is obscured by secondary associations of sound and meaning accumulated through the years. Finally, words are not suited to the task of penetrating the essence of reality, because they are no more than memories of impressions received through our senses, and our senses are affected by chance. They know as little of reality as the spider knows of the palace on the walls of which it spins its web." (Fritz Mauthner, *Contributions to a Critical Essay on Language*.)

Poets, too, began to despair of their power to express themselves through language, in which they had lost confidence. It was so with Paul

Valéry, whose creative ability, after its symbolist beginnings under the shadow of Mallarmé, grew steadily weaker during the nineties, then lapsed into silence for twenty years until it returned to life in *La Jeune Parque*. The poets of the decadent Hapsburg Empire were the first to feel profoundly the inadequacy of language. Rilke described with deep emotion the futility of the faith humanity set in the meaning of words:

I fear the words of men.
They state everything so clearly:
This is a dog, and that a house,
Here is the beginning and the end is there.

The clearest evidence of this crisis of language is the imaginary letter written by Hugo von Hofmannsthal in 1902. The supposed date is 1603, the imaginary author the young Lord Chandos, a writer of recent renown, the recipient his old friend, Francis Bacon. In many of its aspects the letter is a paradox. Lord Chandos speaks of his malady: "I have completely lost the ability to write or think coherently on any subject." Nonetheless he meticulously describes all the stages of this loss of his world and language in an exact and concrete prose. "The abstract words block up my mouth like decaying fungi." He can no longer take part in simple, everyday talk. "It all breaks into fragments, ever smaller pieces, and I can no longer grasp anything in a single phrase. Words drift around me, they materialize in eyes that look at me attentively and force my attention: they are wildly swirling vortices through which one reaches emptiness." Giving up all hope of finding a new equilibrium, the poet is engulfed in a fearful solitude. Only at rare moments does the sight of an object or a human being distract him: "a watering can, a harrow left in the field, a dog lying in the sun, a neglected cemetery, a cripple, a farmhouse; all these things can be the starting point of revelation."

The experience of loss of language is not solely negative; it can even be one of joy, not so much an attitude of skepticism in face of every experience as a feeling of the inadequacy of words that have become unusable through their unthinking usage and dreary rationalism. In moments of ecstasy the poet feels he is transcending language: "It seemed to me then that my body was composed of so many coded signs that explained everything to me. Or as if it could enter into a new relationship of intuitive understanding with the whole universe if I could but begin to think with my heart." This is the new language the poet is looking for, "neither Latin, nor English, nor Italian, nor Spanish, but a tongue in which dumb objects speak to me, in which I shall have to defend myself before an unknown judge in the tomb."

These experiences, which Hofmannsthal attributes to a fictional seventeenth-century character, are indicative of the state of mind of many of his contemporaries. It can be traced in the works of Kafka, Arthur Schnitzler and the young Gottfried Benn. Years later Sartre, in his novel of the thirties, *La Nausée*, echoed the general crises of language and consciousness typical of the century's early years. It seems to me significant that in this novel too the only way out of the hopeless situation is to write. At the end of *La Nausée* Antoine Roquentin perceived a glimmer of light. "Behind the printed word, behind the pages, we must discover something that does not exist, that is above existence. A story, for example, such as could not happen, an adventure. It must be beautiful and strong like steel, and make people ashamed of their own lives." Hofmannsthal published the Lord Chandos letter in one of the most widely circulated newspapers of the time. With that gesture he was justifying in advance to his readers the temporary silence to come, for he was turning to new poetic forms. In tragedy he reconstructed models of antiquity; in other theatrical works, such as the *Rosenkavalier*, he used new forms of expression, new ways of deploying music, dance, design and gesture.

New Beginnings—Autonomy in the Arts—Estheticism

The turn to natural science, the attempt to adopt its methods, a sensation of the inadequacy of language, failure of efforts to grasp the essence of reality, doubt, skepticism, resignation—all these make up one aspect of the period we are describing. But there was also the endeavour, carried on from the preceding century, to base experience and knowledge of reality on a nonscientific foundation. In 1883 Wilhelm Scherer published his history of literature in which he used the methods common to the natural sciences. The same year saw the publication of the first volume of Wilhelm Dilthey's *Introduction to the Sciences of the Mind*. In this work Dilthey seeks to define in theory the method appropriate to psychological science, which he saw as essentially different from that of the exact sciences. While the latter analyze the objects of their investigation by means that can be rationally verified by observation, experiment and mathematical calculation, the former's point of departure is the personal experience of the inquirer. The object of his study, especially if it be literature, consists in a cognitive act that cannot be reduced to any lesser elements. Experience and understanding fuse into a self-governing entity. Its interpretation becomes a separate work of art, its result depending on the talent and capacity for identification of the one who interprets. The first essential is a certain

Edvard Munch, Dread, *lithograph, 1896.*

sympathetic affinity between interpreter and author, an affinity that can be augmented and developed through "living in depth with the author" and "continuous study." "From which," he continues, "arises the intuitive character of the interpretation . . . but . . . as soon as it concerns an exceptional talent less gifted individuals will need to turn to the work of interpretation, to exert themselves to study. And to fulfill that need, the subtle perceptions of the original interpreters must rise to the surface embodied in rules appertaining to a method. . . ." But neither Dilthey nor those that followed have specified those rules. How can one confine such intuitive elements within fixed and iron-bound standards?

Dilthey's theory was not a closed and self-sufficient system, and the same can be said for the historico-esthetic method of Benedetto Croce, whose writings constitute a corpus of encyclopedic proportions. His first important work, *Esthetics*, contains his basic theses of the autonomy of art, the fundamental unity of all the arts and the meaning of intuition and artistic expression. Intuition and expression as the paired product of the artist's imagination became the favourite subject and central point of his philosophy of the spirit and of "absolute historicism." Croce's esthetic criticism is guided by an unlimited faith in the supremacy of the empirical faculty of taste. Although his critical values are intuitive, they rest on a firm foundation of historical learning and universal literature, which saves him, in general, from pronouncing false judgments. The opinions which now strike us as mistaken stemmed from Croce's personal dislike of some phenomena he felt unable to accept, especially those of his own day. One has only to think of his adverse judgment on futurism, seen as the spiritual precursor of Fascism, or on Pascoli, D'Annunzio and Pirandello, mere philosophizing poets in his critical eyes. In other areas his esthetic activity played a leading part in the history of literary criticism, as demonstrated by his essay on Goethe published during the First World War, and by the revaluation of the literature of the baroque, of which he laid the foundations in 1911.

Croce's work of esthetic criticism was above all one of inexorable destruction, ceaselessly attacking the old positivist positions and the views of the literary establishment. The activity of readers and critics was itself esthetic, repeating the intuition-expression of the artist. All the elements that were not directly dependent on that esthetic act were cast aside. Literature's didactic content, its social significance, problems of style, meter and rhetoric, divisions into periods and schools, literary labels such as comedy and tragedy—what did all that signify in the end? The distinction of poetry from nonpoetry, that is to say the esthetic judgment of a work of art, finishes by being only an establishment of poetic quality reached by identification with the creative act.

Although he neither laid down a set of rules by which to interpret works of art nor founded an actual school, it must be admitted that Croce had an immense influence on Italian critics and readers. Philosophers, historians, men of letters and art critics assigned to him the position held in other countries by a whole generation of scholars. They spoke later of a "dictatorship of idealism." Looking back after the Second World War on the cultural atmosphere of the past, it seems clear that, while Croce's anti-Fascism was based on moral and humanitarian grounds, Fascism was not in principle contrary to his system of philosophy. The philosophy of idealism had conditioned people to conformity and contained nothing they could use to oppose Fascism. But we must do justice to Croce—as did Antonio Gramsci, giving him credit for his power as historian and biographer, and seeing in him the man who gave Italy her most valid ideology of the bourgeois era and brought her closer to the cultural world of Europe.

The autonomy of art and letters postulated by Croce, their detachment from all other spheres of life, had its counterpart in the estheticism of many poets of his time. It was expressed in the cult of beauty, an inward-turning, an escape from life into art culminating in an estheticization of every aspect of life, even war and violence. Let us take D'Annunzio as the extreme personification of this school of thought. His novel *The Flame of Life* (1900) was written at the peak of his career as an esthete, in the sense that he had arrived at a glittering command of language and music. To illustrate his conception of art and man I will quote a passage central to the theme, a description of the crisis in the amorous relationship between the two leading characters, the poet-musician Stelio Effrena and the actress Foscarina. The conflict is brought into the open by a scene depicting Foscarina's jealousy, but the underlying cause is the totally differing views of life held by the protagonists. "The will of the one was crying out, 'I love you and I want you for me alone, body and soul.' The other's will answered her, 'I want you to love and serve me, but I cannot renounce in this life anything that rouses my desire.' The struggle is unequal and appalling. . . ." One can guess the outcome of that conflict: the ultimate complete submission of the woman.

The inhuman poetics of this superman are displayed more clearly still when he writes of his visit to the glassworks of Murano, during which D'Annunzio expounds his thoughts on the connection between poetic activity and human relationships: "'The power of fire!' mused the author, distracted from his agitation by the miraculous beauty of the element which was as familiar to him as a brother. . . . 'Ah, could I but give to the life of the creatures who love me the perfection of form I long for! Could I but purge them at white heat of all their weaknesses, and mould them to a compliant substance on which I might imprint the commands of my heroic will and the images of my purest poetry! Why, why, my love, will you not be the divine moving statue of my dreams, the work of faith and suffering by which our life could transcend our art?'" The beloved woman and all humanity are seen as raw material to be moulded by the writer's heroic will, which reduces everything to himself and his art, and knows human relationships only as bonds of despotic command and blind submission.

Another aspect of this attitude appears in the scene at the glassworks. A glassworker of the Seguso family, which has passed down the art of glassblowing for hundreds of years, moulds and offers to Foscarina a miraculously beautiful goblet. Stelio Effrena continues his reflections on the mysteries of artistic creation. "'Imagine the sum of human experience that has gone into the making of this beautiful object!' he cried, amazed. 'All the generations of Segusos through the centuries have contributed their breath and touch to the birth of this creation—the goblet—at the joyous moment when this unknowing little glassworker followed that distant impulse and transmitted it unfailingly to the material. The flame was steady, the blend was rich, the air temperate: every condition was favourable. The miracle happened.'" While the artist-superman, guided by his heroic will, may use others as clay to be moulded by his inspiration, the little glass-blower, bent with fatigue, appears as the human instrument divested of will by a "distant impulse."

To him this division of humanity into those who die below decks and those who live above at the helm seems to be an immutable fact of nature. In the poetry of Hofmannsthal, on the other hand, the two groups are linked together.

Some, it is true, must die below
Where men strain at the heavy oars.
Others live above at the helm,
Know the flight of birds and the realm of stars.

Some lie always with heavy limbs
Inextricably caught in the roots of life.
For others couches are prepared
Where sybils are, and queens.
There they sit as if at home
With light minds and a light touch.

Yet from their lives a shadow falls
On the other lives in the other place,
And to the heavy the light are bound
Like earth to air.

The weariness of forgotten people
Will not shift from my heavy lids,
Nor the soundless fall of distant stars
Keep away from my shaken soul.

Many fates entwine with mine.
Existence weaves them through each other.
My part is more than the thin flame
And feeble song of this my life.

193

In D'Annunzio there is no longer any relation with a social struggle or a reading public, with a social class, the nation or humanity itself. Physical reality he transmutes in order to construct an artificial world for display in a shop window. Indeed he himself became an object of display in the eyes of his contemporaries. Marinetti tells an anecdote that illuminates this side of D'Annunzio's personality: "Gabriele D'Annunzio, dressed all in white (boots, jacket, tie and hat) rears up vertiginously on a great horse as white as Carrara marble; Gabriele D'Annunzio, handsome and elegant, white as the snow, holding the white reins close in his white-gloved hand, comes here like this every Sunday, they say, to listen to the municipal band playing in the sunny square of a little Tuscan village ... And they say too, the peasants, when they see him sitting there so upright, proud and silent with his feet in the white stirrups, 'Oh, look ... there's the poet rehearsing for his equestrian monument. ...'" (F. T. Marinetti, *Les Dieux s'en vont, D'Annunzio reste*.) Decaying estheticism has stiffened into a decadent pose, a false front.

The world of art had nothing more to do with the world of work. This process of isolation from the rest of society could take the form of haughty arrogance as with D'Annunzio, of sadness and troubled conscience, as in Hofmannsthal's poems, or end in an attempt to isolate oneself with a few of the faithful in an "artificial paradise" (as did Stefan George and his group). In Thomas Mann's works, for instance, the world of art becomes a refuge, the ultimate retreat of the disillusioned, of those who do not know how to cope with the difficulties of life. The little Hanno Buddenbrook, in Mann's novel, finds in music a means of escape from the restraints of real life: with music, screens are torn down, doors flung open, thorny hedges broken through, walls of flame overcome. At least in art he can free himself from the fetters of reality for a few moments.

Thomas Mann's position, however, was opposed to estheticism. Characterizing the poetic Spinell in *Tristan* (1902), he wrote that the poet's lifework consisted of a few descriptions of sublime and intoxicating beauty to be read in an idle quarter hour. In his story *The Prophet* (1904) an esthetic individualist who poses as the saviour of mankind appears as a dangerous madman. Thomas Mann deals mainly with the artist in his relationship with the bourgeois world. The "bourgeois" in the traditional sense of the word had relationships in active and practical life with his fellow men, and a naturally positive attitude towards them. The new bourgeois was no more than a function. He had lost the positive and essential basis of human contact; he had become depersonalized. The artist sought escape from this process of depersonalization by removing himself from society. His problem was that he was unable to define his position with any certainty, or to keep in touch with nonalienated humanity and establish himself through an activity recognized as useful by the rest of the population. And therefore the bourgeois world still held a secret fascination for him. In *Death in Venice* (1904), a novel with autobiographical overtones, Thomas Mann carries this bourgeois-artist dialectic to its extreme. Kroeger, the protagonist, is "a bourgeois who has lost his way in art, a bohemian who yearns after good manners, an artist whose conscience is uneasy." But at the end of the novel there is a gleam of light: the utopia of an art with social purpose, as formulated by the Russian painter Lisavetta Ivanovna. Thomas Mann, however, is far from sharing that conception of art.

New Ideas in the Field of Psychological Investigation: Bergson—Freud—Proust—Gide—Pirandello

Bergson's philosophy, too, can be seen as idealism in opposition to the positivist doctrines of Taine, Renan and Spencer, and to the materialist-mechanist trend in the second half of the nineteenth century; or, in more general terms, as a philosophical reaffirmation of psychic and spiritual power in the face of the predominating ideas of the epoch. However, his philosophy is also a scientific inquiry into the consequences of the mental split lying at the root of his theses on the existence of spirit apart from matter. Bergson's works embrace more than one philosophical discipline: the theory of consciousness in his *Essay on the Immediate Data of Consciousness* (1889), psychology in *Matter and Memory* (1896) and metaphysics in his principal work *Creative Evolution* (1907), "the poem of the life force." The basis elements of Bergsonian intuitionism are borrowed from the philosophy of Schopenhauer. The intellect is related to the perceptible form of space. It is an instrument of organization, incapable of reproducing the interior treasure or of understanding reality except in mathematical symbols, whereas intuition is related to time, to its indivisible flow, and becoming to pure duration; only intuition is capable of perceiving the riches of the mind's inner life.

Bergson became the fashionable philosopher of the early years of the century. The most elegant members of Parisian society flocked to the hall of the Collège de Paris, where he gave his public lectures every Friday afternoon. His philosophy suited the spirit of the time and expressed his generation's feelings about life: life as a free progression to an unknown destination, as a transcendence of the limits imposed by matter, a

THE KISS OF
JVDAS

Aubrey Beardsley, The Kiss of
Judas, *illustration for a story
published in* The Pall Mall
Magazine, *1893*.

passing beyond determinism and a realization of dormant potentialities, a vital force, instinct, desire, will. There are many points of contact with other philosophical and literary trends of the period, such as the influence of Nietzsche, or the naturists, futurists and all those who felt an aversion for the humdrum daily round and longed to depart for distant horizons. It is not easy to distinguish the influence of Bergson from what was simply in the air. Gide wrote in his diary on the first of March, 1924: "Later, people will think they see his influence on our time everywhere, but it is he himself who is a part of our time and unceasingly follows its intellectual movements. That explains his importance."

Sigmund Freud's starting point was in natural science. The young doctor devoted himself at first to the study of physiology and neurology, in Vienna under Josef Breuer and in Paris under Jean Martin Charcot. His masters, in carrying out research on hysteria, were using hypnosis. Breuer describes the case of one patient who, when hypnotized, remembered her illness beginning at a time when she was nursing her sick father. Charcot investigated the neurosis of a young woman and established the importance of sexuality in that type of ailment. Two precepts were fundamental to Freud's work: therapy through memories no longer present in the conscious mind and the dominance of sexual appetite over every other instinctive drive. Unlike his masters, Freud renounced hypnosis. His method was free association. The patient said whatever came into his head; from the discontinuity of the narrative and from details superficially without importance Freud put together the elements of his theory, which can be condensed to two main postulates: the primal reality of sexuality and the importance of the unconscious. It was the development of a project already outlined by Nietzsche in *Gaia Scienza*: "The whole of psychology is still enmeshed in fear and moral prejudice. No one has yet dared to plumb the depths." Freudian psychology, originally conceived as a therapeutical method, had, in the first decade of the twentieth century, become a recognized school of psychology, and later even an intellectual philos-

ophy. In 1900 he wrote *The Interpretation of Dreams*, in 1901 *The Psychopathology of Everyday Life* and in 1905 *Humour and the Unconscious.*

At a conference held in 1914 Freud made an attempt to define the part played by his discoveries in the development of European cultural movements. Between the end of the Middle Ages and today self-conscious man had been shaken by three fundamental discoveries: the Copernican cosmology, which displaced the earth from the center of the universe, Darwin's theory of evolution, which dethroned mankind from its privileged position among other living creatures, and finally Freudian psychology, which showed *Homo sapiens* as ruled by unconscious levels of his own mind that could not be controlled by reason. Freud's contemporaries did not look on him with a favourable eye. The scientific world rejected his hypotheses. At a conference in 1910 it was maintained that the subject of his research was more a matter for the police than for science. Here the very mechanism of repression described by him in *The Interpretation of Dreams* came into operation. The diagnosis that society was sick and itself the cause of sickness could not be accepted. This reaction of the patient can be considered as final evidence of the truth of Freud's theory.

Allied to this scientific investigation of the human mind was the interest apparent in contemporary literature concerning psychic areas till then disregarded. Dreams, desires, anxiety, forgotten memories of childhood, psychic conflicts and illnesses, neuroses, phobias, psychoses—all these were now fit subjects for literary works. Scholars of Proust have often pointed out that the reading of Bergson could explain many aspects of *À la Recherche du Temps Perdu*, the first volume of which was published in 1913. One of Bergson's central concepts is *duration*, time experienced internally, in contrast to the measurable succession of years and days. Bergson produced the concept to which Proust gave literary form. There are, he feels, two kinds of memory: memory directed by will, which registers external events, and involuntary memory, *souvenir*, which reawakens experience in all its original freshness and vitality, independent of will, a recollection imprisoned in an object of physical reality. Without direct contact with the object in question, the memory linked with it would remain forever buried in the unconscious.

The episode of the *madeleine*, an integral part of Proust's novel, is well known. On a cold winter's day the narrator returns to Combray, his childhood home, where his mother offers him a cup of tea and some little cakes, the *petites madeleines*. The miracle occurs when his palate comes in contact with the tartlet dipped in tea. "A delicious pleasure suffused me, isolated, with no clue as to its cause. Suddenly the vicissitudes of life lost all importance, its disasters appeared innocuous, its brevity illusory. It affected me in the same way as falling in love, filling me with a precious essence: perhaps the essence was not something in me but was myself. I no longer felt myself to be mediocre, a creature subject to chance, mortal. Whence could that powerful joy have come? I sensed that it was connected with the taste of tea and cake, but surpassed them utterly. It was not of the same nature. From where did it come? What did it mean? Where could I find out? Then all at once the memory came. It was the taste of the little piece of *madeleine* Aunt Léonie used to give me on Sunday mornings after having dipped it in tea or *tisane* when I came to say good morning to her in her room. ..." Thus life relived as memory flowed into the present and halted chronological time. The past returned with all its detailed memories. Time no longer has only one dimension and is no longer irreversible, but has real duration and psychic reality. It is closely linked with atmosphere, surroundings, sentiments and sensations. In Proust's novels there are no exact dates, but states of mind. Time and space are ways in which memory can exist.

The art of Proust is a synthesis of the French psychological novels of the time of Mme. de La Fayette. He wants to depict total reality: life, intellectual and biological, feelings, instincts, the unconscious and subconscious, the different stages of awareness, the perceptible world in all its multiplicity. But there is no connection with social reality. Proust, too, was caught up in an individualistic estheticism. For his readers Proust brings to life a universe seen through the prism of esthetic perception, devoid of any real social context. It is an artificial world, closed in on itself, functioning according to laws of its own and strangely separated from the world outside. It is a world with no way out.

André Gide's attitude to life expressed in his early works, his "immoralism," has also been connected with the Bergsonian philosophy of the "life force." But Gide considered himself more a follower of Nietzsche and contributed greatly to the diffusion of the German philosopher's works in France. Gide, who like Proust was comfortably off, was in an ideal position for devoting himself to the "cult of the I," eager to assimilate and elaborate all the newest trends. That may be why, to a superficial view, the necessary distinction has not always been drawn between his life and his works.

In *The Fruits of the Earth* (1897) he explains his new concept of life. In lyrically inspired language he describes a life of the emotions in which all rules are cast aside and sensual ecstasy is exalted. *The Fruits of the Earth* hymns the gratitude of a young man who, on his way to recovery after a long illness, finds himself changed. Suddenly he has become "the person whom everything around me—books, masters, parents, even myself—had sought to suppress." Now he discovers the joys of the senses: the sun, the sea, flowers, fruits, his body. Gide's "immoralism" appears in an explicit form: "to love, without caring whether it is right or wrong."

The Immoralist (1902) develops the theme. The book's subject is the liberation of a personality at first oppressed and atrophied. It tells the life story of a twenty-five-year-old intellectual, Michel, a student of history and archeology, who promises at his father's death bed to accept a marriage of convenience. During the honeymoon, a journey across North Africa, he contracts tuberculosis, and is on the point of death. Once again, recovery is accompanied by a new zest for life, for the pleasures of the senses and the body. He finds in himself capacities hitherto repressed and turns away from the dusty world of books that had been

The Norwegian Edvard Munch (1863–1944), examples of whose work appear opposite and on pages 178, 185, 191 and 205, by reason of his training, artistic experience covering both centuries, and the influence he exercised on painting, especially German, of the twentieth century, remains a key figure in the artistic and cultural phenomena of the "other face"—which is far removed from the stereotypes evoked by the name—of the Belle Époque.
Contemporary and friend of Ibsen and Strindberg, his early forays were into Scandinavian naturalism. He studied Impressionism in Paris, came under the influence of Toulouse Lautrec, his painting verging more and more towards the symbolistic. In Germany, where he mainly lived from 1892 to 1908, he was active in the Berlin avant-guard and the breakaway movement. His works, "tormented and pregnant with the silence of death," mark him as a pioneer of Expressionism.

his only source of experience. Michel's transformation is symbolized in an episode of "a symbolico-narrative nature" (Hans Hinterhaeuser). It is April, and he is bathing in a mountain stream near Amalfi. "From a hollow in the rocks of which I speak flowed a clear spring. It was little more than a trickle, certainly, but it had carved out a deep basin down below to receive its sparkling waters. Three times I had come there, bent over it full of thirst and desire, and gazed long at the smooth stones on the bottom. There was neither mud nor weed there and the vibrant sunlight penetrated to the rock, lending it colour. ... Suddenly, without hesitation, I plunged into the clear, pure water, letting it cover me entirely. Quickly cold, I left the pool and stretched myself out on the grass in the sun. Aromatic mint was growing around me. I picked some, crushed the leaves and rubbed them all over my damp but glowing body. Then I looked at myself for a long time without any feeling of shame, only joy. I saw myself not yet strong, but soon to become so, and harmonious, sensuous, almost beautiful."

It is instantly clear what the scene is about: the rising above a Puritan morality that could make even one's own body an object of fear. The passage is an affirmation of life in all its sensuous fullness, and the body as a promise to be fulfilled. It is a denial of musty intellectualism, a no to decadence, disease and *fin de siècle* weariness.

However, the novel also describes the dangers and limits of this new feeling for life. Occupied with the achievement of his new, unfettered freedom, the hero has no thought for anyone else. He will trample over the dead, if need be. Marceline, the wife whom he does not love, is the victim of his unconditional will to live and express himself. Later, people were to speak of the "criminal folly" of *The Immoralist*. The public was still more scandalized when it read *The Cellars of the Vatican* (1914), in which the author described and glorified (or so his readers understood) a murder without motive as a "free action," the final product of an individual's total liberation from the chains of morality and the traditional view of life. But here, too, it would be wrong to give a simplistic interpretation of the contents of literature. Rather, it puts forward an antithesis to be overcome and is, at the same time, an exorcism of the forces unleashed by his new ideas. Gide said later of *The Immoralist*, "I wrote that book to get over it: I had suffered it as one suffers an illness."

The Late Mattia Pascal (1904) by Luigi Pirandello is also the story of a man's attempt to throw off the yoke of a life hemmed in by work and family. Michel, the "immoralist," could free himself because he was financially secure. Pirandello makes the same thing possible for his hero, Mattia Pascal, by a happy combination of circumstances. A sum of money given him by his brother enables him to travel. At Monte Carlo he wins a fortune at the tables and becomes a rich man. Reading a newspaper in the train, he sees that a man has been found drowned near his home, and that everyone supposes it to be himself. Although it looks as if everything is in his favour, his attempt to start a new life under the name of Adriano Meis is a failure. The hero, thought to be dead, returns to his native land like a ghost and finishes his life working in an old ruined library.

Pirandello's pessimism (or his psychological realism?) does not admit a positive solution, a happy ending. In his view, human nature has not changed up to the present, in spite of the revolutions in our vision of the Copernican universe, nor has humanity taken any real step forward. "Even today," he maintains, "we believe the moon is there only to light up our nights as the sun does our days, and that the stars revolve merely to offer us a splendid spectacle. No doubt about it. And we often and gladly forget that we are infinitesimal atoms, in order to revere and admire one another. We are capable of going to war for a morsel of ground or distressing ourselves about matters which, if we were truly aware of what we are, would appear to us insignificant trifles."

Notwithstanding all that, Pirandello's world is richer in reality, more concrete, and so more true, even in details and in his way of continually revaluing ideas, as it were casually and as a matter of no importance. He interprets them in a material key, whereas the heroes of so many other

books of that era have nothing else in their heads but their "ideas." For example: "I had then, or thought I had (it's the same thing) so much going on in my head. I had some money, too, which—apart from anything else—provided me with certain ideas which I would never have had without it." The hero of the novel sees himself as "an actor in a tragedy more ridiculous than one could ever imagine."

In *The Late Mattia Pascal* Pirandello's humour appears under various guises. It lies in the comicality arising directly from the situations and in the perception of their contradictory quality. But there is also an awareness of the underlying causes of that contrariety which permits the author to analyze the situation in depth and show its tragic, negative aspect. How many platitudes that remorseless "humour" destroys! What, for instance, is left of the edifying pictures of "fraternal love" and "innocent childhood," etc., after one has read Mattia Pascal's description of his first sight of the twins just born to him? "I seem to see them still, lying side by side in their cradle. They were scratching at one another with their tiny hands, so delicate, yet almost clawing, from some savage instinct that aroused both horror and compassion. Poor, poor little creatures, even more so than those two kittens who were there every morning in their cage. The little cats at least could miaow, but these had hardly strength to whimper—and yet they were scratching each other!"

One could hardly be more pitiless and implacable in describing the human condition. And it seems no coincidence that at least three writers in the first decade of the century wrote with humour, and through their humour exposed the abyss that separates appearance from reality.

Towards a Transcendence of Individual Values: Theory and Social Criticism in Literature and the Social Sciences

The *Belle Époque* was also the golden age of sociology. Many of the classics of modern sociology were written during the first years of the century. Let us choose three of the more important authors: Émile Durkheim, Max Weber and Thorstein Veblen. Durkheim's dogma can be explained most readily by comparing it to that of Bergson. Whereas for Bergson the fundamental essence of life lies in the spontaneous expression of individuality, and the ideal is the greatest possible emancipation of the "deep-lying I that is liberty," for Durkheim the basic principle is "the collective conscience of the group to which one belongs," "the bringing to light in ourselves of essential characteristics of a collective type." Bergson fights for an open morality and society and interprets these from the viewpoint of creative evolution. Durkheim insists on the need for integration and consolidation.

His position has been interpreted in its political aspect, and some have professed to see in Durkheim's sociology the desire to add to the strength of France's Third Republic as a deliberate swing away from the exaggerated demands of individuals critical of society, or one motivated by fear of the anarchy that could arise from an excess of individual rights. In view of the struggle for power in foreign policy and the worsening social problems inside the country, contemporary theories that trusted in an almost natural evolution of society must have seemed scarcely valid or even tenable.

Durkheim's basic theme is thus the "social fact," the morally and spiritually superior human unit (role, function, group or institution) to which the single person must submit himself. Only through society can the individual attain order, truth, moral superiority and a better and richer life. Durkheim is a dualist radical. In his essay on *Sociology and Its Scientific Domain* he invests sociology with a scientific justification, starting from the principle that the social fact is an object of clearly defined cognition, in contrast to the independent, individual "fact," and that sociology has the task of studying its specific characteristics. The difference between general and individual is inherent in human nature. Man contains two natures: his consciousness as an individual is quite distinct from that as the member of a community.

In considering the problem of education, he demonstrates the externally compulsory nature of the social fact. To educate means to teach the child a certain way of seeing and feeling that would not develop spontaneously. As part of that process the pupil eventually internalizes what he learns, which is to say identifies himself with social constraint. In time this comes to dominate him from inside and finally to govern his way of thinking. Taking religion and morality as examples, he expounds his theory of the predominance of the social fact over the individual. In religion it is not God that directs the people, and in morality it is not human integrity. In both cases it is society that directs the elements of which it is composed. Religion is a symbol of society: that is to say, society can "set up an idol or invent a god." Clearly the weak point in Durkheim's sociology is its failure to give an answer to the question of how the single person can succeed in accepting the social norms, or causing them to be accepted, or of whether all hierarchies of social values are equally valid, or to what point the individual should submit to them.

What for Durkheim is the social fact is for Max Weber the concept of "action." Collective concepts such as status, society, groups and so on are referred back to the actions of the individuals concerned. Sociological investigation should begin with the analysis of the single person's motive. It is not the "social fact" that raises its hat, but the single person who does so for motives of his own. Max Weber wanted to put an end to the "fantasy of collective names"; according to him "sociology, like other disciplines, can take as its point of departure only the action of the individual, whether one of few or many; in other words, the individualistic method." The purpose of sociological research is thus not the identifi-

cation of general laws, but the investigation of the singularity of definite historico-cultural phenomena and of the cultural significance of particular social phenomena. The best-known example is his attempt to give a rational explanation of the phenomenon of capitalism. He does not deny the influence of economico-technical factors, but he also searches for the cardinal point accounting for the establishment of capitalism, and finds it in the Protestant ethic, in the disciplined desire of people to behave rationally as instruments, first in the service of God and later in that of the earthly powers that be. The cultural importance of capitalist economy is explained by the wish to rule the world by reason. The development of that wish can be seen as the result of Christian teaching, especially of the Puritan, Protestant kind.

Let us take as an example of Max Weber's interpretative sociology his analysis of the origin of the Lutheran-Prussian spirit of submission, which runs parallel to his investigation of capitalism: "The phenomenon of the division of labour and the organization of trades and professions in society was already familiar to Thomas Aquinas (and others) as a direct emanation of the divine cosmic order. The fitting of individuals into that cosmos occurs *ex causibus naturabilis* and is a matter of chance. . . . For Luther the division of people into classes and trades consequent on objective historical order was a direct expression of the divine will, and it was the religious duty of the individual to remain in his place and within the limits that God had assigned to him." (Max Weber, *Sociology and Analyses of Problems of Universal Political History*.)

In describing post-Civil War American literature, it can be said that it deals not so much with ideas and "beauty" as with the immediate observation of hard facts. It is also clear that the works of American sociologists and philosophers did not arise from theoretical reconstructions and interpretations of historical development, but were related directly to American society and are of a pragmatic nature.

In his first published work, *The Theory of the Leisure Class* (1899), Thorstein Veblen criticized with considerable sarcasm the financial aristoc-

AUBREY
BEARDSLEY

Aubrey Beardsley, drawing for the frontispiece of A Full and True Account of the Wonderful Mission of Earl Lavender, Which Lasted One Night and One Day, *by John Davidson, 1895.*

racy of the America of his day. His point of departure is the thesis according to which human behaviour is conditioned by certain instinctive inclinations which cannot be reduced to other factors, the most important being the instinct of workmanship. Everyone likes to achieve something concrete, objective, and thus has a natural inclination for productive work and an aversion to useless activity. The conflict between this tendency and unproductive activity is the heart of his book. By unproductive activity he means any that does not have goods for necessary consumption as its end product. The parasitical existence of the upper classes seemed to him particularly reprehensible, because not only did they fail to take part in production, but also weighed down the conditions and standard of living of the working class by their extravagant consumption and habits.

The aristocracy of wealth has taken over the functions invested in the nobility and clergy of feudal times, and has a similar hierarchy of values. At the top come "useless" activities, to which importance and prestige are attached, and at the bottom lies the humble activity of production. The striving for wealth is no longer primarily related to the fulfillment of natural needs.

In his critical attitude one recognizes the sincerity of Veblen's feelings about social justice and its incompatibility with a scale of values that relegated productive labour to the lowest level of society. However, Veblen, in his efforts to reevaluate efficiency and utility, was basically in agreement with American commercial morality, according to which time is money and should not be wasted. The reversal of these values in his time was to Veblen a serious obstacle in the path of social progress. The institutions and morality of society were not keeping up with technical and commercial advances, thus inevitably causing crises which could be dissolved only by reform. Veblen took up a position that was later to make others' fortunes under the heading of "technocratic" thinking. Workmen, engineers, technicians, as representatives of reason, should put themselves at the head of institutions. Veblen was

to be mentioned and quoted by experts and non-experts for decades every time there was a discussion of the American world of business.

Pragmatism is considered even today as the sole philosophical trend born and developed in America. It is distinguished from similar European schools of thought by its antidogmatic stance and its activist content. The attitude of skepticism in the face of theories and systematization becomes an object of reflection and is made into a basic principle. Abstract theories are important only insofar as they increase our practical knowledge; ideas and concepts are tools for the active comprehension of reality. In *Pragmatism* (1906–07) William James holds that what is useful, anything with an exact monetary value, is true. General concepts are only symbolic abbreviations representing concrete facts, actually composed of details, psychological particulars. The aim of scientific research, then, must be to collect particular facts and investigate their interconnection, not to proclaim laws of general validity, which would be truth independent of real facts. In contrast to the deterministic view of the world typical of the nineteenth century, William James emphasized the utilitarian and activist aspects of his doctrine. The acid test of our scientific hypotheses as well as of our moral convictions, he considered, must be their social usefulness, moral and biological. William James's philosophy finally emerges as a conception of functional socialism, and the portrayal of a society in which individuals, freed by scientific planning, achieve a peaceful coexistence.

The literature of the early 1900s, both European and American, contained elements of social criticism and analysis, either in the form of a direct criticism of contemporary society or an indirect one of an imagined new, Utopian reality.

In his book *The Heart of Darkness*, Joseph Conrad, a Pole by birth, bitterly attacked the brutality and cruelty of colonial imperialism. John Galsworthy, Arnold Bennett and E. M. Forster arraigned the anti-intellectual attitude of the world of business. Others turned their fire on sharp practice, fraudulent enterprises and modern methods of commercial publicity. In *Mrs.*

Warren's Profession (1902) Bernard Shaw describes prostitution as the symbol of the capitalist system. The millionaire figured frequently in popular literature and works of social criticism. According to Oscar Wilde he was the only person who achieved complete self-realization in the new century; in Joseph Conrad's view, the millionaire was the true anarchist.

Most of the writers concerned with social problems chose comedy as their medium. The greatest success went to the traditional comedy of manners, a form that Wilde had renovated and brought back into fashion. The success of Ibsen's theatrical works and the interest aroused by his realistic plays lay at the root of the "new" English and Irish theater. The meticulous description of a special social environment, so fashionable during the reign of naturalism, gave way to plays dealing with a particular social problem. John Galsworthy, for example, took as his themes justice in relation to class, the unfairness of the penal system, class prejudice and the conflicts of the working class, while Harley Granville-Barker wrote about the separation of church and state, dishonest administrations and unsuitable marriages.

The plays which have best survived their period are those of George Bernard Shaw, which do not so much criticize particular aspects and negative qualities of society as expound ideas and fundamental ideologies, to be treated with a pungent, biting skepticism. They are less dated, because they deal with basic problems and do not refer to specific levels of society at one particular moment of history. While he keeps to the traditional rules of dramaturgy, Shaw introduces social questions both in plays with a historical background and in plays set in modern times.

His comedy *Candida* (1900), for instance, seems at first sight to be based on the banal situation of a *ménage à trois.* The chief characters are the Protestant vicar Morell, a Christian socialist who is fighting for the reforms he considers necessary; his wife Candida, younger than he, who is always at his side to free him from the petty worries of everyday life; the young, still immature poet Marchbanks. In the first act Morell, in a speech

blown up with pathos, extols his happy married life. The young poet protests, and describes the marriage from the point of view of the wife who for years has patiently put up with her husband's ineffective reforming zeal and empty rhetoric. At these words the parson loses his temper completely and is ready to come to blows. He throws himself on the young man, but recovers his self-control when Marchbanks screams and, having evaded Morell's anger, gives in abjectly. Thus begins the open conflict of ideas, which is also a conflict between two types of rhetoric, the Bible-inspired language of the priest and the idealistic metaphors of the poet. The time comes for Candida to decide between the two men, and Shaw allows her to justify her choice rationally. She says she will choose the weaker one, and that turns out to be, not as one might suppose, the poet who appeals to her feelings, but the husband, who continues to talk in fine phrases of his spiritual strength and role of protector. But it is Candida who is the stronger and makes her husband see their married life in a truer light: it is he who is in need of her help. Her decision also helps Marchbanks to accept real life and take a step forward in his development. The end of the play also seems conventional on the surface: the marriage does not break up, the couple remain united in spite of the intruder who nearly divided them. But the audience sees the result of the conflict in another light, thanks to Shaw's arguments. Personal liberty may be preferable to a marriage based on love, and Ibsen's "life lie" is inherent in every form of bourgeois "idyll."

Dubliners, a collection of short stories by James Joyce, introduces us to characters drawn from life among the lower middle class of Dublin. These people cannot free themselves from the sad realities of work and family life. They see no way out from the conventions and coercions that hedge them in. Joyce presents these characters to us with distant irony, but not without sympathy for their yearning for a life worth living and their reactions to the world that oppresses them, expressed according to temperament by aggression, resignation, apathy, or despair drowned in alcohol. He varies his style of prose continually.

Stream of consciousness alternates with ordinary dialogue, the pages of a diary with philosophic argument. In *Portrait of the Artist as a Young Man* (1914–15), also situated in Dublin, Joyce depicts the development of Stephen Dedalus, his conflict with his provincial environment, his rebellion against religious and social conventions and the awakening of his artistic consciousness and discovery of reality.

Jack London's novels are certainly among the most widely circulated, and are still read today all over the world. The main theme of his work is the contrast between the comfortable middle class and its repression of individual personality on one side, and on the other the untamed lands of North America and men who have turned their backs on civilization. His heroes are often so-called savages—Amerinds or Pacific Islanders—whose character and way of life he idealizes. They are distinguishable from civilized people by their courage, the tenacity they show in the struggle for life, and the depth of their feelings.

In the partly autobiographical *Martin Eden* (1909) he describes the tragic experiences of a young and talented writer of humble birth in the society in which he finds himself. His love for a refined young girl of middle-class origin spurs him to action. . . . But Martin Eden soon realizes that the opulent façade of the bourgeois society he is forced to move in conceals greed for money, poverty of spirit, stupidity and philistinism. Even Ruth Morse, the girl he loves, succumbs to the materialistic mentality of her class to the point of not believing in her lover's talent until the day when bourgeois society offers him the mark of its official approval: money. She deserts the young man at a time of peculiar difficulty for him, but is prepared to return to him later, when Martin Eden is a rich and famous author.

Like Jack London, other American writers chose their principal characters from the lowest levels of society, as did Theodore Dreiser in *Sister Carrie* and Upton Sinclair in *The Jungle*. The latter novel depicts life in a poor quarter of Chicago populated by immigrants and workers in the tinned meat industry. These authors are different from the realistic novelists of the past,

most of all in not describing their heroes from a distance, without fellow feeling, as a scientist might observe the objects of his research. On the contrary, these new authors sought to awaken their readers' interest in and understanding of life in less privileged environments.

Compared with the Russian novelists of the previous century, Maxim Gorky appears a revolutionary if only by virtue of his life. He grew up in difficult and straitened circumstances, far from the nation's cultural centers. In the course of trying one trade after another and tramping through Russia and the Ukraine like a barefoot friar he acquired a high degree of self-education. These experiences are naturally reflected in his work. His characters—tramps, gypsies and pilgrims, embody his protest against society. Unfettered by worldly goods, they are not prepared to submit to social discipline. *The Lower Depths* (1904) is a series of scenes depicting a community of homeless wretches in an almshouse. The characters are grouped around two opposed figures: Luka, "the consoler," who thinks that this "human refuse" has need of illusions, and Satin, the cynical rebel who, in drunken monologues full of passion, emerges nevertheless as the strong man unafraid of reality.

His novel *The Mother* (1906) was written in support of the workers' party struggle. It is the story of the mother of Pavel Vlasov, a revolutionary, tracing his development up to the moment when he joins, actively and fully aware of what he is doing, the fight for socialism. Gorky follows his theme with openly didactic aims perceptible even in the novel's structure, the grouping of the characters and the affecting expressiveness of the style. Because of these "artistic" defects and the lack of "realism," *The Mother* was at first bitterly criticized by orthodox Marxist critics such as G. V. Plekhanov and A. V. Lunacharsky. After they had observed the power of its message among Russian revolutionaries, however, the once despised book was declared to be a model of socialist realism.

For Gorky the Russian Revolution and the struggle to achieve a socialist society took the place occupied for writers of other nations by

Aubrey Beardsley, The Black Cape,
illustration for Salomé by Oscar
Wilde, 1894.

collective supra-individualist ideals such as the nation, homeland or religious faith. The subjects are international, but each country marks its works with its own characteristic imprint.

Let us take as an example Spain, where particular historical events have so clearly shaped society. The country's defeat by the United States in 1898 resulted in the loss of Spain's last remaining colonies and the development of a serious political and spiritual crisis. The nation's ruin and the various means by which it might be overcome were the subject matter of a rich "literature of regeneration." It was, above all, people aged between twenty and thirty that were most badly hit by their country's misfortunes. Some of them reacted sharply by banding themselves together under the title "generation of '98" to find a remedy for Spain's decadence and help towards her revival. The radicalism of that generation was especially clear in its hostility towards the political restoration that had recently taken place, and the powers that sustained it: Catholicism on the right and positivism on the left, the ineffective parliament and, in the literary world, the naturalism and encyclopedic learning of men such as Marcelino Menéndez y Pelayo. After that first phase of general hostility and will to destroy, they restored those "true" values of the Spanish soul, which had in the past earned Spain her grandeur and her place in the world.

Miguel Unamuno, in his *Life of Don Quixote and Sancho Panza* (1905), held that there was a need for Quixote to come back to life in contemporary Spain. A delirium, a heroic madness, should flow through the whole land, sweeping away the decadent old Spain of academic culture, priests, dukes and hairdressers. The authentic traditions of the people, ruling justice and the solitary activities of individuals, should return in honour. Again, in his work *The Tragic Sense of Life* (1913), Unamuno extols Quixotic madness, faith for the sake of faith, the heart opposed to reason. In spite of the particularly Spanish slant of his and his contemporaries' attitude, one can recognize points of contact with the European situation. The unmistakable influence of Nietzsche is present everywhere and there is a whiff of Bergsonian vitalism too. The literary scene in Spain was populated by supermen vibrant with vital force and indomitable will who loved danger, declared war on decadence and sought adventure under the aegis of Don Quixote.

Which brings us back to the rest of Europe, where the theme of the superman (a pattern for the *Fuehrer*) appears in literature in the most varied forms. We might look for his origin in Darwin's theory of evolution and borrow words from Nietzsche's *Zarathustra*. When we recall Nietzsche's statement that Superman is to the man of our time what the latter is to an ape, one sees how the idea of the superman grew from an extrapolation of evolutionary thought.

From the wide range of authors who devoted themselves to that subject during those years we will select F. T. Marinetti and his *Mafarka the Futurist*, published in French in Paris during 1909. This "African novel" combines in its pages all the weak points and absurdities typical of the bourgeois European intellectualism of the period, from D'Annunzio to Zarathustra, but it also looks forward in time—especially in its Utopian aspect—to our own days.

In the last chapter Marinetti describes the creation of a new sort of human being, Gazurmah, the unsleeping hero who can lift himself up into the air like an airplane. Gazurmah kills Colubbi, his "mother," because she witnessed his birth from a hiding place; Colubbi, who also wanted to be his lover. "One huge blow. Surges of shrill crying and sobs ... a massive jet of blood spurted like a red plume against his chest. With a mighty flap of his wings Gazurmah rose into the sky ... So rapidly that he scarcely heard from far below him the dying voice of Colubbi gasping, 'You have crushed my heart beneath your ribs of bronze! ... But in killing me you have killed the earth ... the earth! ... In a little while I shall hear the first tremor of its death agony.'"

There is, perhaps, no passage in the literature of the time that states so clearly and without any equivocation just where the frenzied hubris of mankind is leading us: the greedy, heedless exploitation of the earth and the lack of respect for nature that was the actuality of the *Belle Époque*.

Avant-Garde in Bowler Hats

by Eleonora Bairati

The years between the beginning of the twentieth century and the outbreak of the First World War were fundamental to the development of modern art. That was when the groups and movements since known as the historical avant-garde arose. The name indicates a systematic search for the new, a break with the past, the proposal of a new and different content and form based on the more advanced ideas of the epoch. Art in the *Belle Époque* entered another world, antithetical and disturbing; a continuous and increasingly urgent investigation of extended possibilities of expression produced an astonishingly rich and fecund artistic culture.

All the same, the members of that vanguard belonged to their time and were part of the society that was shocked by their work; the pictures they created—sometimes deliberately provocative—yet contain a flavour of the *Belle Époque* they spurned. A telling piece of evidence is the famous photograph of the Italian futurists in Paris, dressed in the overcoats, bowler hats and ties of the very *bourgeoisie* they wished to *épater*.

THE IDOL OF MODERNITY

Faced with the same subject—modernity—the vanguard produced a mirror image of the captivating, propagandist, accepted vision of the *Belle Époque* almost picture for picture with its own aggressive, penetrating version, profoundly innovatory on the visual plane.

Two examples of this are provided by the paintings of Umberto Boccioni, the Italian futurist who most clearly interpreted the content of the age of progress both theoretically and in avant-garde pictorial terms. It is extraordinary how, in his *Modern Idol* (1911; left), he has, by his lurid colouring, transformed a typically *Belle Époque* subject—lady in a flowered hat—into an expressionist mask violently illuminated by beams of light (street lamps or spotlights?) that draw us into the disquieting, equivocal night

life the futurists admired so much.

The City Rises (1910; detail above), now acquired for the Museum of Modern Art in New York through the Mrs. Simon Guggenheim Fund, is a complex work. Prepared for by numerous studies and preceded by several other paintings of the outlying parts of Milan, it is the major pictorial product of Boccioni's expressed wish to paint "the fruit of our industrial age."

Against a background of half-finished buildings ancillary to the smoking factory chimneys, swirls a seething tangle of forms—men and horses, emotionally involving the spectator and expressing symbolically the dynamic rhythm and impetuous growth of the modern city in its inextricable maelstrom of movement, light and din.

(How tame and oleographic in comparison appear most contemporary illustrations of the same theme! One has only to think of Beltrame's cover design for the *Domenica del Corriere*.)

211

"LET'S SWITCH ON THE MOON"

Referring perhaps to the painting opposite, *The Arc Lamp* (1909) by G. Balla, F. T. Marinetti named one of his futurist manifestos written in that year *Let's Switch On the Moon*. He had adopted as his own the creed of progressive technology, which he saw in an antiromantic, anti-bourgeois light.

The art-technology-industry relationship was differently worked out by the German Peter Behrens, who took a direct part in the manufacturing process. He worked for the firm AEG, designing for them lamps (1911; on the right), logos (1912; below), and finally the turbine factory in Berlin (1908–09; shown at the bottom of the page), which was bare of all merely ornamental features, functionalism being the prime consideration.

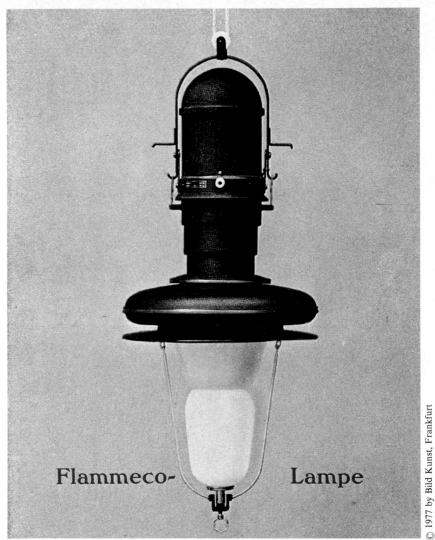

Flammeco- Lampe

213

THE CITY OF THE FUTURE: BETWEEN UTOPIA AND REALITY

Boccioni's romanticization of the industrial town in *The City Rises* was the painter's homage to a theme that other members of the vanguard tackled from a more technological and planning point of view.

Rejecting on principle all the useless ornamentation typical of *Belle Époque* urban building, the avant-garde architects gave first place to the mechanical and functional values of the great dynamic, pulsating "machine" that is a city.

"We must invent and remake the city of the future in the likeness of an immense, uproarious construction, flexible, movable, dynamic in every part, and we must plan the futurist house as a gigantic machine." That statement was published in *The Manifesto of Futurist Architecture* (1914) by Antonio

Sant'Elia, the talented forerunner of modern architecture, who was killed in the war, still too young to have been able to carry out any of his fantastic projects. In Sant'Elia's designs and visionary drawings of the "new town" (none of his technical plans survives) the traffic is accepted as an integral part of the city. Huge, terraced buildings rise to an enormous height, bereft of any ornamentation, connected horizontally by galleries and passages at different levels, as well as footbridges with moving gangways, and traversed vertically by external, glassed-in elevator shafts (left).

The heart and dynamo of this dream city were to be the electrical generating stations for which Sant'Elia made numerous studies (one of them on the right). Admittedly, his visionary plans betray a monumentality heavy with symbolic and expressionist overtones—very different from the protorationalism of a Behrens—but, nevertheless, every decorative detail has been eliminated, and the contrast with, for instance, Gaetano Moretti's power station at Trezzi shows how far ahead he was of his time.

Sant'Elia's work is difficult to judge dispassionately. Was it Utopia or reality to come? An inspired leap in the dark or clear, conscious rationality? (But we should not forget that quite recently Corbusier described houses as "machines for living.") On the other hand, beneath all the reasoned researches of the avant-garde lay a stratum of Utopia. We detect it even in the projects of Tony Garnier, the French town planner, otherwise so firmly based on reality. His "industrial city" (below), studied between 1901 and 1904, was planned for a population of 35,000, but provided for a possible increase along radiating axes. It was only partially translated into reality—and not very well—in the architect's additions to the town of Lyons. However, in its strictly functional distribution of the various elements of urban structure (residential areas, official and public-service buildings, parks and gardens, industrial zones), its accurate analysis of urban requirements, the lavish use of reinforced concrete in severe simple shapes and the attention bestowed on traffic problems, it remains the best and most concrete anticipation of future, rationalist town planning.

TWO TOWERS BETWEEN PAST AND FUTURE

In two phrases written on his first study for *La Tour Eiffel* (1909; below) Robert Delaunay clarifies the symbolic meaning of the bridge between the past (*Exposition Universelle 1889—La tour à l'univers s'adresse*) and the present (*mouvement profondeur—France-Russie*) of the new avant-garde art, alluding to the intervening relationship between French and Russian artists.

Ten years later a Russian artist seems to be recalling Delaunay's message by creating his model of a monument to the Third International (left), a tremendous steel spiral, a synthesis of architecture, sculpture, technology and symbolism, the tower of a new historical era, constructed to commemorate not the magnificence of the bourgeoisie but the triumph of the proletarian revolution.

Avant-Garde in Bowler Hats

217

THE FORCES OF THE STREET

In the spirit, the vanguard—painters equally with architects and town planners—took the town as a central theme, interpreting it in its most violent and futurist aspects. For them the street is no longer the place appointed for worldly rituals, a background for the elegance of prosperous town dwellers. It is the theater of unceasing contrast, witness to encounters and violence, throbbing with the feverish tensions that Boccioni called "forces."

That was how the vanguard painters chose to interpret urban life: in pictures such as *Street Brawl* (1910; left) by Boccioni (significantly, the street is one of the most important in Milan, the Galleria Vittorio Emanuele, also used as a background in 1912 by another futurist painter of Milan, Carlo Carrà) and others by the same painter, for example *Dragnet* (origi-nally called *Dear Whores*) and *Scuffle*, or Carrà's *The Funeral of the Anarchist Galli* (1911). In the foreground are the characters excluded from respectable society, the dregs of the city—night walkers, alcoholics, prostitutes. By means of a language of dynamic forms, lurid colours and disharmonies, the painter transmits to the viewer a sensation of conflict and violence.

Ardengo Soffici, a Tuscan and temporary fellow traveller of fu-

turism, who was trained in Paris but left the movement in 1915, interpreted the street scene in a different way. His *Lines and Volumes of a Street* (1912; right) expresses the futurist poetic creed of "simultaneity," in which the picture is intended to be "the synthesis of things remembered and things seen" (Boccioni). In this case, for example, the letters represent memory, the persisting visual impressions of notices, signs, métro station names, gathered while passing through the streets. But we must also take into account the contemporary cubist investigation of the breaking up and intersection of planes. It was during the same years—when Delaunay, too, was painting his unorthodox and cubist-oriented views of Paris—that another Parisian-minded futurist, Gino Severini, produced comparable works, such as *The Autobus* and *The North–South Métro Line*.

In contrast to the vital energy of the futurists, who exhibited—albeit in an aggressive and often profane form—a positivist optimism and faith in the technical progress of the new century, stood the pessimistic and dramatic vision of the German expressionist painters. Probing beneath the positive, propagandist surface appearance of the prosperous city, they crudely revealed the reality as a place of stress and alienation: town squares, streets, human figures were distorted in a sulfurous tension of forms. These seem like projections of an inner anxiety and dread, sometimes reaching the condition of nightmare. Ernst Ludwig Kirchner, cofounder of the *Bruecke* group, was the questing and angry poet of a denatured, mechanized city through which haunted, emblematic figures of rakes and prostitutes move like zombies, as in his *Five Women in the Street* (1913; left;

from the Ludwig Museum in Cologne). But the *Street by Lamplight* (1913) by Otto Dix, is empty, a desolate, hostile place, pierced by elongated beams of light. In mid-*Belle Époque*, the "scream" of expressionism seems like a prophetic but unheeded premonition of the epoch's tragic end. The hallucinatory atmosphere of these townscapes was to reappear in postwar German expressionist cinema.

SPEED AND MOTOR POWER

"We maintain that the splendour of this world has been enriched by a new beauty: the beauty of speed ... the roaring motorcar, which seems to run on machine-gun fire, is more beautiful than the Winged Victory of Samothrace."

This profane and programmatic declaration comes from *The Futurist Manifesto* that appeared in the Parisian *Figaro* on February 20, 1909: the subject of speed and motor power could not but be central to futurist art, but supporters of the movement confronted it from different theoretical angles.

Boccioni's interpretation of the theme is adopted in *Dynamism of an Automobile* (1912–13; left) by a minor futurist painter, Luigi Russolo.

The Roman branch of futurism followed a different line, setting

against the Boccionian synthesis concerned with dimension and space the analytical breakdown of movement through time, expressed by a sequence of the positions of which it is composed, a process closely related to photography, chronophotography (a succession of photograms) and the cinema. That relationship is very apparent in the picture *The Hands of the Violinist* (1912; above right) by Giacomo Balla, who was deeply immersed in the analysis of movement. Another example is the photograph *The Violinist* taken from the treatise *Photodynamism* (1911) by Anton Giulio Bragaglia, pioneer of experimental research on photography and the theater. The film he directed in 1916, *Perfido incanto*, was the first sally of the avant-garde into the history of the cinema.

NU DESCENDANT UN ESCALIER

Boccioni's researches into plastic dynamism reached their peak in his bronze figure *Single Forms Continuing in Space* (1913; below), which emanates a prodigious sense of vitality. The exaltation of the human anatomy takes one back to certain classical artists—the giganticism of Michelangelo, seen again in Rodin's work, for example—but suggests still more a mutual relationship with the studies of Marcel Duchamp, illustrated here by his *Nude Descending a Staircase* (1912; left). The French artist has clearly adopted the futurist theme of the splitting up of movement into a succession of momentary stages, though less analytically than Balla. But one feels that his attitude to Boccioni's vitalism is subtly ironical, in that his subject, the nude, is peculiarly academic, and hence detested by all good futurists.

The Roman futurist group also—especially in the work of Fortunato

Avant-Garde in Bowler Hats

Depero—accentuated the mechanical aspect of movement, extending their interest to the creation of puppets and "mechanistic" stage scenery. This aspect was developed in various sorts of experimental work in different parts of Europe, because it seemed to form a bridge between futurist dynamism and cubist disintegration.

Indeed there was an avant-garde school in Russia that called itself cubo-futurism. One of its members was Kasimir Malevich, who, in works such as scissors *Grinder* (1912; detail below) propounded an explicit identification of man with machine. This came very close to the ideas on which Fernand Léger, a cubist fascinated by the futurist imagination, was working at that time. His interest in "mechanicism" is expressed in his studies *Contrasting Forms*, juggling with intersecting solid geometrical forms vaguely reminiscent of human shapes.

The transformation of the human figure into a mechanical puppet could be done in a lighthearted way, even in regard to the material used (painted wood) and a simple toylike shape, as in *Carrousel Pierrot* (1913; above right; Guggenheim Museum, New York) by Alexander Archipenko, a Russian artist who had become completely French in his ideas and worked in Paris from 1908 to 1914; then in Berlin, and finally in the United States from 1924.

GROUPS, MANIFESTOS, EXHIBITIONS AND SCANDALS

The manifestos of avant-garde art were—almost by definition—turbulent and provocative, and aroused endless argument and scandal. Very often it was the artists themselves who publicized their work with declarations and controversial writings. At other times critics, writers, friends and supporters of the artists—Guillaume Apollinaire, for instance, seen in the photograph below left with Francis Picabia and Gabrielle Buffet—minted definitions and invented labels for the new movements. It was the age of isms—futurism, expressionism, cubism, etc.—following one another at a bewildering pace.

For the artists it was also important to find new outlets for the distribution of their work, in place of the usual official channels.

Consequently there was a rapid increase of shows and exhibitions in private galleries or improvised settings, as well as participation in official events. Owing to these new sales outlets, Paris became a veritable market for modern art.

The most impressive was probably the Paris Salon d'Automne, founded in 1903 as a revival of the traditional nineteenth-century exhibition center (on the left, a catalogue of the first show). It was at the

exhibition there in 1905 that the expression *fauves*—and one of the major scandals concerning the Parisian vanguard—arose. A conservative critic, noticing a small academic sculpture in a room filled with paintings by Henri Matisse and André Derain, exclaimed, "*Donatello parmi les fauves!*" ("Donatello among the wild beasts"). On the right: paintings by the fauves reproduced in an *Illustration* of 1905; on the left page,

above, a woodcut by Derain for *L'Enchanteur pourissant* by Apollinaire, 1909. The nickname survived and was carried like a banner by members of the group. In reality, however, the fauves were a group without manifestos or declarations of intent. Their short-lived unity lay in the use of brilliant and sometimes discordant colouring. Some of the fauves became cubists; conversely many great cubists passed through a phase of fauvism.

Avant-Garde in Bowler Hats

HENRI MANGUIN. — La Sieste.

M. Manguin : progrès énorme ; indépendant sorti des pochades et qui marche résolument vers le grand tableau. Trop de relents de Cézanne encore, mais la griffe d'une puissante personnalité toutefois. De quelle lumière est baignée cette femme à demi nue qui sommeille sur un canapé d'osier!

LOUIS VAUXCELLES, *Gil Blas.*

GEORGES ROUAULT. — Forains, Cabotins, Pitres.

Il est représenté ici par une série d'études de forains dont l'énergie d'accent et la robustesse de dessin sont extrêmes. Rouault a l'étoffe d'un maître et je serais tenté de voir là le prélude d'une période d'affranchissement que des créations originales et des travaux définitifs marqueront.   THIÉBAULT-SISSON, *le Temps.*

M. Rouault éclaire, mieux que l'an passé, sa lanterne de caricaturiste à la recherche des filles, forains, cabotins, pitres, etc.   GUSTAVE GEFFROY, *le Journal.*

M. Rouault... âme de rêveur catholique et misogyne.   LOUIS VAUXCELLES, *Gil Blas.*

HENRI MATISSE. — Femme au chapeau.

ANDRÉ DERAIN. — Le séchage des voiles.

M. Derain effarouchera... Je le crois plus affichiste que peintre. Le parti pris de son imagerie virulente, la juxtaposition facile des complémentaires sembleront à certains d'un art volontiers puéril. Reconnaissons cependant que ses bateaux décoreraient heureusement le mur d'une chambre d'enfant.   LOUIS VAUXCELLES, *Gil Blas.*

LOUIS VALTA. — Marine.

A noter encore : ... Valtat et ses puissants bords de mer aux abruptes falaises.   THIÉBAULT-SISSON, *le Temps.*

M. Louis Valtat montre une vraie puissance pour évoquer les rochers rouges ou violacés, selon les heures, et la mer bleue, claire ou sombrie.   GUSTAVE GEFFROY, *le Journal.*

HENRI MATISSE. — Fenêtre ouverte.

M. Matisse est l'un des plus robustement doués des peintres d'aujourd'hui. Il aurait pu obtenir de faciles bravos, il préfère s'enfoncer, errer en des recherches passionnées, demander au pointillisme plus de vibrations de luminosité. Mais le souci de la forme souffre.

LOUIS VAUXCELLES, *Gil Blas.*

M. Henri Matisse, si bien doué, s'est égaré comme d'autres en excentricités coloriées, dont il reviendra de lui-même, sans aucun doute.

JEAN PUY. — Flânerie sous les pins.

M. Puy, de qui on a vu au bord de la mer évoquer le large schématisme de Cézanne, est représenté par des scènes de plein air où les volumes des

But it is not always necessary to classify works of art according to critical definitions and polemical declarations: here are two unwritten manifestos, two famous paintings composed in 1907.

Henri Matisse was the leader of the fauves, but remained an extraordinarily independent character. In *Luxury* (left) he expresses through his personal poetry of sinuous line and glowing but harmonious colours, a happy hedonism.

In contrast, we have the provocation and discord of *Les Demoiselles d'Avignon* (detail below; Museum of Modern Art, New York) by Pablo Picasso, whose name is indissolubly linked with cubism, the origin of which has been traced back to this very painting—profane even in its title (the *demoiselles* were prostitutes from a brothel in the Rue d'Avignon at Barcelona) —because of its breakdown into counterposed geometrical planes.

Avant-Garde in Bowler Hats

In 1903 there arose in Dresden an arts group called *die Brücke* (the Bridge), which shared many of their ideas. It was the first group to take an organized form, translating into creative works the complex whole of cultural assumptions and existential behaviour to which the name expressionism has been given.

According to a declaration of the founding nucleus—which included the painters Ernst Ludwig Kirchner, Erich Heckel and Karl Schmidt-Rottluff—the purpose of the Brücke was "to gather to itself all revolutionary elements and those in ferment, as the name itself indicates." By intention, the art of the group was antiart, the art of opposition. The explosive charge of the fauves was largely expressed at the level of form combined with violent colour, whereas for the German expressionists colour and form were the means of bringing to light a deep inner tension, a dramatic conception of life, often imbued with explicit social criticism.

This stance was made by the Brücke artists even in their selection of technical means. They used a great many woodcuts, a technically "poor" method but highly expressive and typical of German folk tradition. The group's pamphlets and signs, designed by Kirchner, were rough but effective in their simplification of the picture, the choice of typography and the placing on the page (right).

The Brücke fellowship split up in 1913. In 1911, while still in Munich, Vassily Kandinsky and Franz Marc founded the *Blaue Reiter* (Blue Rider) group, which adopted, within the compass of expressionism, a very different if not totally opposite

position. Kandinsky, the tireless leading spirit of the movement, had by then already achieved the final goal of the first "abstract" painting and was writing his most famous book, *The Art of Spiritual Harmony*. Now his aim was to express the ineffable, the deepest "resonance" of the spirit, in response to the dominant principle of the "inner necessity": a sort of lyrical expressionism—Franz Marc and Paul Klee were nearing the same point, though with different results—trusting above all to evocative qualities, like those of colour,

and to his ability to produce an inner resonance, as with music.

The group's knightly symbol, designed by Kandinsky for the cover of the *Blaue Reiter Almanach* (right) published in 1912 on the occasion of his second show, appears as a romantic hero riding in search of the new and unknown world of free form.

DER
BLAUE
REITER

Manifestos, declarations of principles, groups, associations, shows: all these were still not enough for the futurists. Not only art but life was to be taken over. Provocative gestures, a special pattern of behaviour, conflict—even physical—with opponents, were essential. Every channel must be used to spread their ideas, including leaflets, booklets and the daily press (it was not fortuitously that Marinetti had his first *Futurist*

Manifesto of 1909 published in France's most influential newspaper, *Le Figaro*). Thus the notorious "futurist evenings" came into being. These manifestations caused scandal (but scandal intentionally provoked) and consisted of lectures, recitals of literary works, musical interludes, slaps—usually figurative, but sometimes real—in the face of the right-thinking audience. They often ended in rowdy scuffles. The *soirée* at the Costanzi Theater in Rome has gone down in history, but there were many others in various towns, such as Milan, Florence and Venice. The atmosphere at these meetings has been recorded with pointed irony by Boccioni in a drawing made in 1911 (left): on the stage are Boccioni himself, the musician Balilla Pratella, Marinetti declaiming, Carrà, and Russolo beside his "noise tuner." Curiously, nothing of this uproarious spirit is discern-

Avant-Garde in Bowler Hats

ible in the famous photograph of the futurist artists (Severini, Boccioni, Marinetti, Carrà, Russolo) taken in Paris in 1912, where they look like sober civil servants, or at least strictly academic (above). On the top of the left-hand page is the catalogue of the futurist exhibition at the Bernheim-Jeune Gallery that year.

In contrast to the first group photograph is another, showing some of the same characters (Marinetti, Boccioni, Sant'Elia, Sironi) in uniform at the front (below, left).

At first sight, the futurist movement might seem ephemeral and transient, especially in view of the theoretical paper and propaganda it engendered, but in fact it had a profound influence, especially if one takes account of the dadaists, a similar but more bitterly iconoclastic group that arose in Zürich about the year 1916.

235

ЛУЧИЗМЪ

МОСКВА
1 9 1 3

Even though when Marinetti toured Russia he was greeted with catcalls, an analogous movement already existed there. Russian futurism was founded in 1911–12, independently of its Italian equivalent, but with a similar vitalist philosophy and desire to shock.

Vladimir Mayakovsky, the great poet and playwright of Russian futurism, wanted to "remake life." Before the Revolution, he desired to revolutionize his own life and habits and, in the futurist manner, to provoke, use a declamatory style and wear strange clothes (such as his famous yellow jacket). It is true that this form of Russian futurism was predominantly concerned with literature, poetry and the theater. Productions in the field of representational art were very complex and varied. On one side they seemed to be independent of the European canon; on the other, they were continually oscillating between an Oriental "barbarism" and adherence to the principles of Western Modernity.

The middleman of the fruits of this fertile grafting was Serge Diaghilev, the editor of *Mir Iskusstva* and great theatrical impresario. His crowning achievement was the introduction of the Ballet Russe to Western Europe, where its first appearance was an enormous success in the Paris of 1909. Diaghilev was in touch with all the Russian artists in Europe: painters, illustrators, stage designers (such as Léon Bakst, midpage) and composers such as the great Stravinsky. It was he who had summoned Natalya Goncharova and her fellow artist and life's companion, Mikhail Larionov, to Paris in 1906, because their works were being exhibited at the Salon

d'Automne. The two artists (below, left) returned to Russia, where, with Malevich and Tatlin, they initiated an original avant-garde movement which, from a fauvist and cubist basis, passed through a stage of folk "primitivism," reached cubo-futurism, and finally "rayonism," the Russian form of futurism—a "mixture of cubism, futurism and mysticism," as Larionov defined it (above, left, the manifesto *Rayonism*, published in Moscow in 1913).

The earliest of Larionov's rayonist paintings, such as *The Cockerel* (right) are dated 1911–12, and show how far the Russian vanguard had advanced along the road to abstract art. In the same year Malevich reached geometrical abstraction by another route, starting the "suprematist" phase in which, for a short time, Tatlin was at his side. The latter soon dis-associated himself, however, in order to found constructivism.

Avant-Garde in Bowler Hats

PARIS, CAPITAL OF THE AVANT-GARDE

In 1900 an unknown Spanish painter arrived in Paris. (Below on the right is a photograph of him as he was in 1912.) At much the same time two French provincials, Georges Braque and Fernand Léger, came to the capital to seek their fortunes. It was many years before the future masters of cubism met, but the results of their artistic experience grew inextricably interwoven.

That was only one of the golden strands which made the Paris of the first two decades of this century the undisputed capital of the avant-garde, a springboard for the most important intellectual movements.

After the sensation of fauvism came the new provocation of cubism (1908) and the futurists' challenge to the world (1909). Cubism gained official sanction with a large show at the Salon des Indépendants (1911) and the publication of its first theoretical paper *Du Cubisme* (1912). Soon, however, the movement was split by civil war with the desertion of Léger and two irreverent and experimentally minded spirits, Marcel Duchamp and Francis Picabia (in the photograph on the left), the future leaders of first dada and then surrealism. Painted in the same year, 1913, as *Bicycle Wheel* by Duchamp was *Udnie* by Picabia (right), in which futurist com-

position and mesmeric colouring combine to form an abstract synthesis.

But apart from these events, now recorded in every history of modern art, there was the legendary life led by the writers and painters of Paris in their favourite haunts of Montmartre and Montparnasse and the cafés where they met. Obscure then, these places have now become famous, as have the artists' studios. The best known of those is the Bateau-Lavoir in Rue Ravignan (below left), a great wooden barrack resembling a boat, with a washhouse in the basement. Picasso lived there from 1904 to 1909 with his companion Fernande and a large dog; studios and rooms in the building were let to the painters Kees van Dongen and Juan Gris, and the writers André Salmon and Max Jacob. It was there that a banquet was held to honour that strange character, Le Douanier Rousseau, the "naïve" painter.

Avant-Garde in Bowler Hats

239

In 1906 Kandinsky (below right) was also in Paris, as were many other Russian artists. In the same year a twenty-one-year-old Italian, Amedeo Modigliani (below left), joined them, to burn up the rest of his short life there—he died in 1920—producing impassioned, existentialist works of art. Two incomparable talents, quite distinct yet closely interconnected—in life, art and legend—were the two "poets" of Montmartre, namely Modigliani and Maurice Utrillo. Friends, drinking and brawling companions, they were drawn together by their addiction to alcohol and drugs, but still more by their dedication to modern art. Utrillo and Modigliani depicted Montmartre, its inner spirit and its outer appearance, with a persistent, loving, almost craftsmanlike devotion. The feeling of humility and desolation revealed by the infinite vista of streets and squares painted by Utrillo finds its exact equivalent in the human understanding of the model never absent from Modigliani's portraits, which never lose the piercing individuality of the sitter. In *Madam Pompadour* (1915; detail right) we see the tenderly ironical grace with which Modigliani could translate the intellectual dogma of cubism into emotive sensitivity.

241

THE DESTRUCTION OF THE REPRESENTATIONAL

Perhaps the most obvious characteristic of modern art, if not the most relevant from the critical point of view, then at least the one that struck—not to say shocked— public opinion most forcibly, was the ever-increasing abandonment of the traditionally representational in regard to the subject of the picture, or of any form in it that remotely resembled a real object. It was the fiercest and most radical weapon in that "battle of paintings" waged by the vanguard against the massed and propagandist representational art of the *Belle Époque*. In the face of a pictorial tradition of such long standing and richness, the rejection of the image was a bold and organized attack on accepted artistic values.

First came impressionism. That was a slow and gradual development, starting underground and culminating in the glory of modern painting at its best in the mature works of Cézanne and Monet. In the numerous *Water Lily* studies painted by Monet around the turn of the century (the example below dates from 1910) the progressive withdrawal from naturalism became an almost total dissolution of form in a blazing aurora borealis of colour. It was the first road—lyrical and emotive—leading to abstraction. Kandinsky, the creator of abstract painting, may well have been influenced by Monet's work. "Abstraction" was more than a movement. It was a trend, the lyrical, nonrepresentational constant of many interpretations; without theoretical unity, but rich in developments. His first abstract watercolour (right), a free play of line and colour, in which every remnant of the representational has been thrown overboard, was painted in 1910 and marks a watershed in the evolution of the avant-garde.

The great qualitative leap forward was completed. From that time forward a picture would have a value within itself as an act of creation, and not for what it represented.

243

On the other slope of the impressionist mountain we find the work of Paul Cézanne. He responded to Monet's chromatic dissolution with a solidification of impressionism into a dense, concrete composition made up of shapes expressed in geometrical planes, as seen in his landscape *Mont Ste. Victoire* (below; he made several versions between 1904 and 1906). As an intellectual exercise, it forms the source of cubist disintegration, while the cubo-futurists, Picasso, Braque and Léger, took it to extreme lengths. They were deeply impressed by Cézanne's work in the retrospective show at the Salon d'Automne in 1907, the date of Picasso's *Demoiselles* and one year after the name "cubism" had been coined. Only a few years later Georges Braque, the most intellectual and dogmatic of the cubists and the true originator of the movement, working in close

contact with Picasso, passed beyond the peak stage of the disintegration of the subject to arrive at so-called "synthetic cubism," in which the essential contents of the picture are reassembled at the pictorial level without any reference to traditional perspective. The composition was now nothing but a surface bearing freely arranged elements which, in reality, have only a slight, allusive connection with one another, as in *Still Life with Playing Cards* (1912–13; on page 246), one of Braque's many works of the static, abstractly objective kind he liked to paint.

It was not only in France that the works of Cézanne and cubist disintegration marked the way towards the nonrepresentational picture. Their influence enriched the imagination and performance of artists from very diverse cultural backgrounds and stimulated them to diverging interpretations of abstract art.

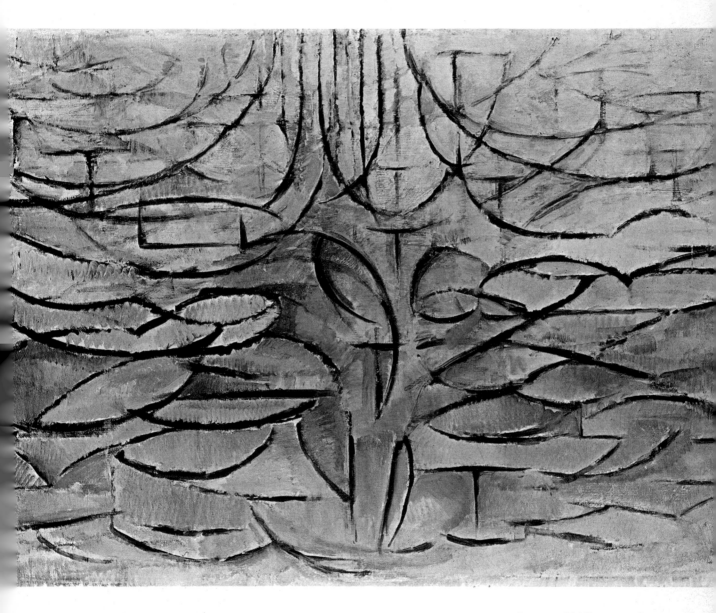

The Dutchman Piet Mondrian arrived at pure geometrical abstraction by slow degrees, in which the cubist phase was fundamental. During the years 1909 to 1912 he continued to elaborate one single theme—a tree—in a series of drawings and paintings. Progressing by way of colourful fauvism and the plastic structures of a Cézanne to ever more pronounced cubist disintegration of form, he arrived with the painting above, *Apple Tree in Flower* (1912), on the very threshold of abstraction. Towards 1915—at the same time as the Russian Malevich—Mondrian reached purely geometrical abstract art and—with the publication of *De Stijl*, an authoritative review—originated the strictest form of abstraction, known as neoplasticism, in opposition to Malevich's suprematism.

Less basic was the technique of cubist disintegration derived from Cézanne's work, as practiced by Paul Klee, a German artist keenly interested in the colour studies of the nonconforming "mystic" cubist Delaunay, friend of Marc and Kandinsky at the time of the Blaue Reiter, and sympathetic to the latter's "lyrical abstraction." But Klee's work is intimate and self-contained in comparison to the emotional impetus and "spiritual" elation of Kandinsky. For him art is the "allegorical image of creation," a means of penetrating the secrets and re-creating the processes of evolution, of reaching—as is written on the epitaph on his grave— "nearer to creation than is general," even though "still not near enough." In none of his delicate watercolours does Klee entirely suppress the subject, but reassembles it in subtle parallels under the fanciful titles he gives his compositions, such as *Green X Above on the Left* (1915; above), in which X, indicated with lightly ironical precision, becomes a personality, an odd, fantastic character.

Two compositions of the cubist school are shown for comparison: on the left-hand page the "intellectual" type by Georges Braque; above, the "poetic" work of Paul Klee.

247

Thus the mainstream of non-objectivity, flowing from Kandinsky's work in 1910, consisted from its early days of two separate currents: the lyrical and emotional; the intellectual and geometrical. On this second component —certainly the more austere, though not essentially the predominant one—the last word (before Mondrian's explanation of 1917) was spoken by the Russian Malevich. Associated with the most vital elements of the Paris avant-garde, he passed through a stage of cubo-futurism in 1913. Drawing from it only the purely geometrical forms, he took the final step towards absolute abstraction. His picture, consisting only of a black square on a white background— pure geometry, devoid of symbolism or suggestion—was followed by others of the same type, such as *Blue Triangle on Black Rectangle* (about 1915; left) and

finally a white square against a white background, a sort of immaculate shroud for the concept of representational art. During the same years Malevich was working on his *Manifesto of Suprematism* (1915), meaning by suprematism the "nonrepresentative world," the supremacy of the pure "sensibility of inobjectivity."

Malevich's radicalism seems to have led the whole artistic vanguard up a blind alley. Beyond that white canvas there seemed no possibility of advance.

However, the irrepressible Marcel Duchamp found an ingenious way out of the impasse by standing the trend on its head. If nothing now remained of a picture but its pure objective entity, he reasoned, if art had a value as an object "in itself," then the *real* object "in itself" could be valued as art.

During the years 1913–15

Avant-Garde in Bowler Hats

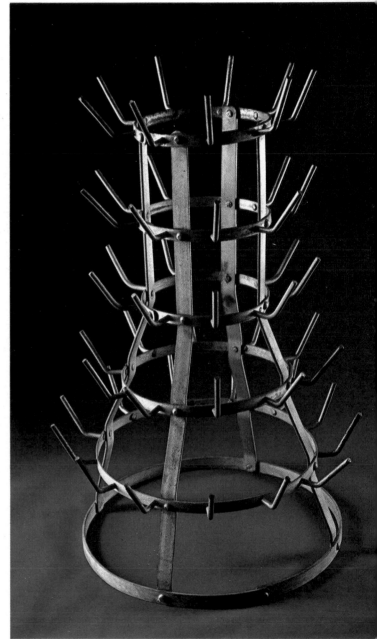

Duchamp affixed his signature to a *Bicycle Wheel* and a *Bottle Rack* (below), raising them by this simple act to the status of works of art. But curiously, these objects, wrenched out of their proper context, made into museum pieces as a joke, turned into an irreverent, controversial parody of artistic creation, assumed a disturbing ambiguity and a lacerating irony.

There was only one more year to run before 1916, when the most destructive movement in the history of the avant-garde, the mocking nihilism of dada, exploded in the Cabaret Voltaire in Zürich ("Dada means nothing," stated their *Manifesto* of 1918). Just over the horizon lay surrealism.

ORNAMENT AN OFFENSE

In his *Manifesto* of 1914 Sant'Elia wrote, "Decoration as something superimposed on architecture is an absurdity . . .," but before that, in 1908, another architect had written a celebrated essay called *Ornament an Offense*, in which he said, "I have discovered this piece of wisdom and proclaim it to the world: the evolution of civilization is synonymous with the exclusion of ornament from articles of use." On the one hand we have the vitality and intuitive dash of the Italian futurists, on the other the strict, almost religious asceticism of the Austrian Adolf Loos. From 1910 onwards, in the Vienna so recently under the decorative spell of the secessionists, he started the era of the new, severe, protorationalist architecture.

The wish for simplicity and uncluttered lines in architecture at that time was not his alone, but whereas in Sant'Elia's work there is still a monumentality and a strong symbolic content, the architecture of Loos has the purity and hardness of crystals. Bare surfaces, devoid of any modulation, intersect at sharp angles, and even traditional features are reduced to purely geometrical elements. Thus, for instance, the columns holding up the portico of the corner house in Michaelerplatz (1910; right), a building that caused

a great deal of controversy at the time, become a frame defining a geometrical space in the historic heart of Vienna.

But the true unwritten declaration of Loos' faith, of his thirst for the absolute of pure form, is the Steiner house (left) built in the same year, with its clear-cut articulation, impeccable proportions of volume and the (then) whiteness of its surfaces.

The future that awaited these buildings in a negative way bears witness to the profound originality of the architect. The splendid interior of the Michaelerplatz corner house was destroyed by the Nazis in 1938; the Steiner house was defaced after the war by a ridiculous decoration on the outside wall. It was as if a sort of posthumous vendetta of anticulture and speculation were being waged against the moral rigour of a true civilization.

Avant-Garde in Bowler Hats

Loos' architectural taste corresponded with the nonrepresentational trend in painting; colour, too, was banished from his formal universe. As with Malevich, the only contrast was between black and white. Black marble frames the Knize shop front (1913; left), its extreme sobriety of line enriched by the materials. It still stands today, the interior unaltered. It can be compared to the best examples of the rationalism of the twenties.

During the same prewar years the first master of architectural rationalism, the German Walter Gropius, was at work on the earliest of his great constructions: the Fagus shoe factory (1912; below and on the right), a fruit of the seed sown by Behrens—who was Gropius' master—only a few years earlier, when he designed the AEG turbine factory. But the solutions arrived at by Gropius were newer and more revolutionary than his

master's, uncompromising in form though these latter were. With its vast, shedlike shape, and mighty columns set into the walls, the AEG building gives an impression of tremendous power. Gropius, on the other hand, achieves an effect of functional strength with the bold and controversial use of transparent glass on a grand scale. Enormous vertical glass window sections project beyond the main outside walls.

The most important thing that

Gropius inherited from Behrens, however, was an all-absorbing interest in the relationship between art and industry. In 1919, soon after the war, he founded the Bauhaus, a school of architecture and industrial design, a crucible of ideas for the modernist movement.

But the Bauhaus did not arise from nothing. As early as 1907 an experimental association was formed that can be considered its immediate ancestor: the Deutsche Werkbund. It was founded by Behrens, and Gropius was one of its members.

It is no use searching the Werkbund program for the controversial spirit and manifestos of the artistic avant-garde. The association's aim was to reorganize and solve the contradictions pervading industry by designing objects, "bringing together the forces and trends existing in the world of industry so as to produce work of quality."

Avant-Garde in Bowler Hats

An example of the scrupulous integrity of design through which the Werkbund hoped to achieve a coherent organization of the environment and the objects of use contained in it is furnished by the projects of Richard Riemerschmid, architect, town planner and designer. His designs were clear, accurate and legible, nearly all for practical use, and all making the object's function the prime concern. It was the same whether the subject was new compartments for the state railway (1908) or a coffee service (1910), since both were subject to the same standard, that of a "work of quality." (The two designs are shown below.)

WAR, "THE ONLY HYGIENE FOR THE WORLD"

In his *Futurist Manifesto* of 1909 Marinetti wrote, "We desire to glorify war—the only hygiene for the world—militarism, patriotism, the destructive act of anarchists, the beautiful ideas for which one dies...." Consistently, the Italian futurists were nearly all nationalist and eager for Italy to enter the war. In 1914 the Roman group even designed an "antineutralist suit" in white, red and green, accompanied by yet another manifesto. The futurists of Milan, with Marinetti at their head, enlisted in the Battalion of Volunteer Cyclists, a suitable choice when one remembers how much study Boccioni bestowed on his *Dynamism of a Bicyclist* in 1913. A snapshot of Marinetti, Boccioni, Sant'Elia and Sironi together at the front is shown on page 234.

The Bayonet Charge (1915; right) by Boccioni is a work of considerable interest both for its use of collage and because the subject was treated by other futurists (Carrà and Severini) in the same year. In the violent tangle of lines and the evocative power of the newspaper cuttings bearing war news inserted in the composition, it expresses the surge of enthusiasm that inspired the painter and permeates his letters

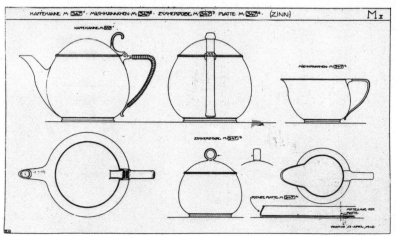

254

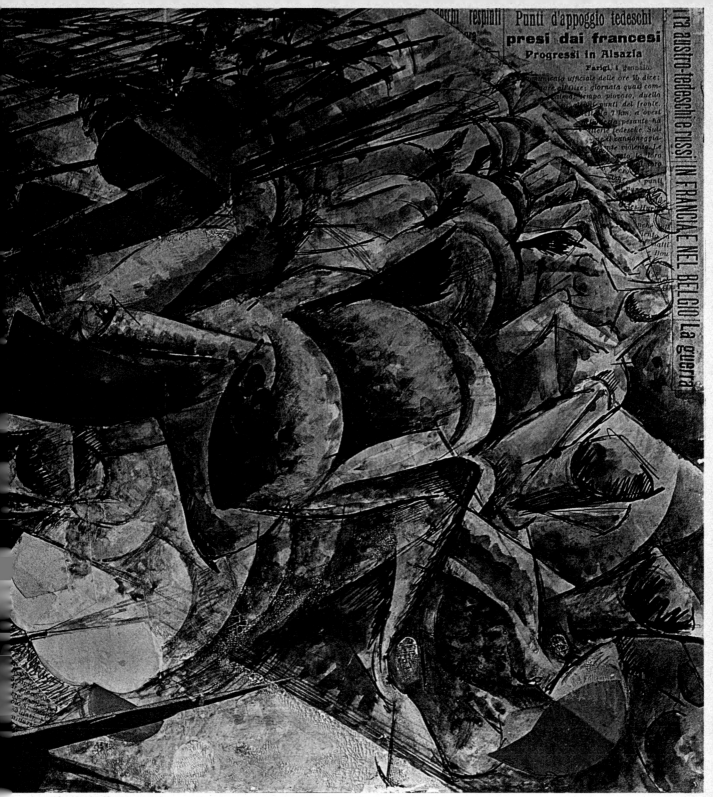

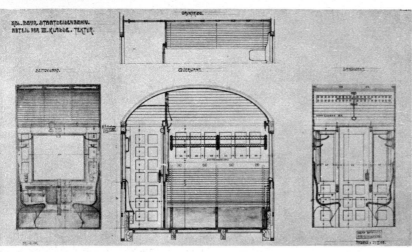

and war diaries. But war was not "a beautiful idea" even though one died for it (as died, in the trenches of opposing armies, the Italian Sant'Elia and the Germans August Macke and Franz Marc, comrades in life and art in the Blaue Reiter group). Boccioni, too, came to understand its full horror. A few days before he died of a fall from his horse in 1916 he wrote—as if destroyed: "I shall leave this life with a contempt for everything that is not art. There is only art."

But there were artists who saw war differently, among them the German Otto Dix, who in this *Self-Portrait of a Soldier* (1914) shows us his own face transformed into a tragic mask that seems to anticipate the images of the best German expressionist cinema.

The experience of war pointed the way clearly to the future destiny of Dix, man and artist. After the war he described all the horror of that experience in harshly crude pictures, identifying in it the germs of the moral disintegration, crimes and perversions of postwar German society, which was hastening straight towards National Socialism, of which in the twenties he was one of the most implacable critics. The look that impales us from this despairing portrait—a fragment of the appalling tragedy that was ravaging Europe—seems to speak not only of horror in the past but of other horrors to come, a message of revolt and liberation to the new forces entering history. A pamphlet written by Dix and other artists connected with the Berlin "revolutionary" *Novembergruppe* (an organization founded by Max Pechstein and César Klein in 1918) reads: "Adherence to the revolution, to a new society, is not a matter of formal declarations. Our immediate task is to put it into practice, to work together to build a new human society, the society of the workers!"

The European Economy in the *Belle Époque*

by Malcolm Falkus

From the economic point of view the Belle Époque *was a short-lived boom, which profited, in an unstable equilibrium, from the fruits of industrialization based on coal and steel, and the growth of international trade. Below: a train crossing the Forth Bridge in Scotland.*

When President Harding coined his famous phrase "back to normalcy" in the early 1920s he was certainly expressing a very general longing to return to prewar conditions. Yet historians have always had difficulty reconciling the popular image *la Belle Époque* with reality. These years had witnessed growing unrest, discontent, and often street violence throughout Europe: in Britain, France, Germany, Italy, and elsewhere, while Russia had been torn by revolution in 1905 and the following years there saw no more than surface normality.

From the standpoint of the 1920s, however, some aspects of the pre-1914 era seemed golden indeed. The years following 1918 saw the collapse of the delicate network of international economic relations. Economic nationalism, currency disorder, reparations arguments, and the poverty of primary producing nations all plagued the postwar world economy. No wonder, therefore, that statesmen looked back to the years before 1914 as a halcyon period, and if the image of this period does coincide with economic reality then it is to be found in the economic relations between nations.

It would be wrong to think of the period 1900–14 as forming any distinct epoch in economic affairs. For many decades the various strands that made up the international economy had been maturing and strengthening, and, as we shall see, the foundations of the system rested ultimately on the industrial revolution pioneered first in Britain over a century earlier. Yet it is certainly true that the period after 1890 saw in many respects a culmination: the greatest volume of trade, the largest flow of international capital, and the biggest outpouring of international migration. It is this culmination that the present article sets out to explain and describe.

The world economy of 1913 was a complex affair, and is best understood if from the outset a number of general points are kept in mind, points which will be elaborated later. In the first place, the world economy was dominated by international trade. Trade grew rapidly throughout the nineteenth century, and it was generated by two unique features: the spread of industrialization in Western Europe and in the United States and the coexistence of large areas outside Europe which could be brought into cultivation in response to the demands of the industrializing regions. Industrialization, because of technological advances, and the opportunities brought by specialization, meant growing wealth in the industrial centers. The "new countries," hitherto largely unexploited, also became richer as mechanized agriculture and improved communications stimulated development. Older primary producing areas and tropical countries too were drawn more closely into the world economy, but since their output growth was not usually the result of any technological revolution, an ever-widening gap appeared between rich and poor nations. This gap encouraged the growth of colonialism.

In 1913 nearly two thirds of all the world's trade was accounted for by European nations, that is, trade between European countries themselves and between Europe and non-European regions. The growth of the world economy was Europe-centered and can be thought of as resulting from a huge imbalance being created by the appearance of modernizing industrial economies. For not only did the products of these European industries seek outlets abroad, but the industries themselves required raw materials and the urban manufacturing populations needed foods. Industrial specialization therefore resulted in growing demands for primary products. Food could come from the new temperate lands, but only if populations there increased in order to exploit the natural resources. Such opportunities attracted a vast influx of European migrants during the years before 1914. Europe's population itself grew by leaps and bounds, stimulated in part by growing incomes and the medical benefits brought by industrialization. Labour was not the only productive factor required to translate Europe's demands into real output. Capital too flowed in a mounting stream to open up and exploit resources. It poured into railways, mines, plantations, docks, harbours and industries not only in the new countries but in the old primary producing areas as well. The availability of capital was partly a result of wealth-creating industrialization, and the flow, along with that of population, can be thought of as a response to the international imbalance caused by industrialization in Europe. But the flows did not produce equilibrium. In turn they triggered further wealth creation. Spectacular growth took place in the United States, and by 1900 that country was the largest industrial power in the world. The international economy had taken on a very different appearance to that existing in 1850 or even in 1875.

Industrialism, international specialization, economic growth and flows of productive factors: these characterized the international economy of 1914. No disruptive monetary crises interfered with the process. Trade and capital flows operated in an environment which by 1900 was one of currency stability and convertibility, based on an almost universal gold standard.

It is justifiable to think of the period between 1870 and 1914 as marking the high tide of the world economy. Two very different events in the year 1869 are a useful reminder of the increasing interrelatedness of the economic affairs of nations. The opening of the Suez Canal greatly fostered the use of steam shipping between Europe and the Far East; journeys were shorter and cheaper, and trade expanded in response. The year also saw the completion of America's first transcontinental railway, linking the Pacific and Atlantic coasts. Soon railways were opening to cereal farming vast tracts of new land, and by the mid-1870s huge quantities of American grain were reaching Europe's markets.

As the year 1900 approached, Europe's imports were coming more easily and cheaply from every continent. The 1870s initiated a period of painful readjustment for Europe's farmers. No longer did European food prices necessarily rise in years of bad harvests, since imports from the United States, Australia, India, Canada, the Argentine and elsewhere could meet a deficit.

Integration in the world economy led to an international trade cycle where business depressions in one area could be felt worldwide. Trade and capital flows dominated such a cyclical pattern, and the gold standard and the adoption of free trade by some countries (Britain above all) heightened the simultaneous experiences of prosperity or depression. Thus most countries in the world benefitted from an international boom which set in after 1896, and, after a few checks, grew rapidly again after 1908. In output and profits 1913 was itself a peak year nearly everywhere, and memories of this fostered the image of the period as the *Belle Époque*.

To these general elements may be added three further points. The first two are significant because they are often overlooked, with the consequence that the true nature of the international economy between 1900 and 1913 is frequently misunderstood. They are, firstly, that the structure of 1914 was in some essential respects a very recent creation. This is most clearly seen in the adoption of the gold standard, which only became generally accepted after 1890. To this extent Harding's term "normalcy" is misleading, for normality, if such it was, had been only short-lived. Second, the international economy was not stable. Many important changes were taking place in the years before 1914, and some were undermining the very basis of the international economy. To present too sharp a contrast between the "anarchy" of the interwar years and the golden prosperity previously is therefore misleading. We must understand that even before the war the walls of the imposing edifice were showing cracks, even though the structure was not yet crumbling.

The third point is fundamental. Between 1900 and 1914 the world economy revolved around Britain. Britain's role is therefore the obvious starting point for a closer look at how the economy functioned.

The Role of Britain

Britain's position at the center of the world's commercial wheel rested on her early industrial revolution. Even in 1800 agriculture contributed only about one third of the total national product, while more people worked in nonagricultural than in agricultural occupations. Thereafter rapid industrial development and the growth of commercial and other service occupations brought the proportion of farmworkers inexorably down. After 1850 the agricultural population fell absolutely as well as relatively. At mid-century agriculture was contributing about one fifth of national output, and by 1913 the share was only 5 percent. By this latter date for every hundred British workers only eight were employed in agriculture. With the rise of industry came the growth of large industrial towns such as Manchester and Birmingham.

Britain's pioneer position had two important international consequences. First, the early start quickly gave Britain a dominating position in world manufacturing output and trade. Second, Britain's supremacy was founded on a rather narrow range of commodities: on those products which arose from the comparatively primitive technology of the early days of industrialization, and for which demand existed at a time when incomes were generally low and when world economic growth had not itself begun to transform demand and technology elsewhere. Thus Britain's industrial structure was founded on cotton and woollen textiles, coal, simple iron products, and, later, on shipbuilding. In 1907 three basic industries, coal, iron and steel, and textiles, together formed 46 percent of net industrial output, and accounted for 70 percent of all exports.

Fast as Britain's real national income grew, her foreign trade grew faster. By the 1870s exports and imports combined were about 50 percent of national income, whereas in 1800 the proportion had been only about 20 percent. Britain's growth and prosperity was therefore integrally bound up with commerce, and British exports conquered world markets to a quite astonishing extent. Between 1850 and 1913 never less than 40 percent of Britain's manufactured goods was sent abroad, and most of the major industries were heavily dependent on foreign markets. Of total exports in 1850, some 63 percent consisted of textile products, and in 1890 the proportion was still 43 percent. Lancashire's dependence on foreign markets was reflected in the steadily increasing share of output sent abroad, and in 1913 over four fifths of cotton textile output went overseas. Britain's preeminence can also be seen by her share of world trade. In the 1870s, when Britain alone accounted for about one third of the world's manufacturing output, Britain accounted for no less than 40 percent of the world's trade in manufactured commodities.

This industrial growth led to an equally dramatic rise in imports. From the outset Britain's principal industry, cotton textiles, could not expand without foreign supplies of raw cotton. As the century progressed, increasing quantities of other raw materials—wool, iron, timber, copper, rubber, and many more—bought as home supplies were either nonexistent or inadequate. Moreover, Britain's commitment to industrialization meant growing urban centers whose populations could no longer be fed from home sources. This factor, coupled with rapid population growth that took the total in England and Wales from 9 million in 1800 to 36 million in 1911, meant huge imports of grain and meat, especially from the 1870s, as well as traditional imports such as tea, coffee, tobacco, and cane sugar.

Britain's industrialization therefore influenced directly other areas of the world. Her exports entered overseas markets in ever greater quantities, while her own market provided an outlet for the produce of other nations. Specialization led to an expansion of trade impossible before the advent of the industrial revolution. The interchange was fostered by Britain's adherence to free trade throughout the years between the 1840s and the First World War. This policy maximized Britain's imports and in turn provided other countries with earnings, part of which would inevitably raise demand for Britain's manufactures at a time when Britain held a virtual world monopoly.

We can see, therefore, how Britain's industrial revolution stimulated international trade, and provided an opportunity for nations like the United States, who could supply Britain with cotton and grain and whose resource endowment was favourable, to grow and industrialize too. In addition, of course, the technology pioneered by Britain—steam-driven machinery, railways, steam shipping, and a host of other developments—could spread elsewhere and promote industrialization.

A further point needs to be stressed. The dominant position in world commerce attained by Britain by about 1870 gave to that country a natural supremacy in international finance and in the various services connected with trade. Sterling, which was based on a gold standard, was the chief currency of world trade. Foreign governments held sterling in London, while even transactions not involving Britain were often settled in sterling. Shipping services, bullion and commodity markets, and insurance were likewise centered in London, and specialist banks and other financial institutions grew up to deal with them. The soundness of Britain's banking structure and the preeminent security of the Bank of England all made London the leading financial center. This position was strengthened by, and in turn stimulated, the willingness of Britons to invest overseas as opportunities developed. Just as Britain pursued a free-trade policy, so British nationals were free to invest in countries throughout the world.

More will be said about international capital movements later. But so far we are able to answer one very fundamental question: Why did Britain's industrial strength not lead to an international balance-of-payments crisis as Britain's exports flooded world markets? Why, in other words, did not all the world's gold tend to accumulate in London and weaken the economies of the other nations? The answer is that Britain was also a huge importer, a position inherent in the composition of her own manufactures and in the extent of her industrialization, and a position strengthened by a policy of free trade. It is, indeed, a strange and important fact that throughout the nineteenth century Britain never had a balance of commodity trade surplus. Imports always exceeded exports, and by an increasing amount after 1870. True, Britain had large noncommodity earnings from shipping, insurance, and investments. Her balance of payments was sound. But Britain's vast overseas lending, made possible by these various earnings, helped to ensure that growing countries such as the United States and Australia did not have their development stunted through foreign currency shortages. In turn, of course, British capital, insofar as it went into railways, mines, industries, and other forms of productive enterprise, helped raise the capacity of foreign countries to export (or substitute for imports) and so help pay off the debts.

It should be unnecessary to add that all this was not the result of conscious policy. Investment and trade decisions were taken by private individuals, based on personal calculations of profit and risk. Free trade was a deliberate policy; so was the maintenance of the gold standard. But we should not, as contemporaries often did, attribute the harmonious consequences solely to these institutions. We should remember also the favourable and unique conjuncture of circumstances within which they operated.

The Spread of Industrialization and Trade

The second half of the nineteenth century was marked by a rapid growth of industrialization in a number of European countries and in the United States. Between 1870 and 1913, manufacturing industry surpassed agriculture in its contribution to national output in the United States, Germany, France, Belgium, Switzerland and Sweden. By the end of the nineteenth century, industrial development was growing significantly in northern Italy, in European Russia, and in Austria; in Asia the first glimpses of industrialization in a nation not part of Europe or European culture and background were to be seen in Japan.

With growing industrialization went growing world trade. Between 1840 and 1880 the volume of world trade tripled, while from 1880 to 1913 the volume tripled again. In the years 1900–13 alone the quantity of goods traded internationally more than doubled. These increases were far greater than the growth of world production, so that an increasing proportion of the world's goods were traded across national borders in this period. The ratio of trade to production probably increased more than threefold between 1815 and 1913 and trade was, in the words of the well-known economist Ragnar Nurkse, an "engine of growth."

Fundamental was the growth of transport and communications. The spread of railway networks all over the world opened up new regions to productive investment and trade. The railways themselves were giant consumers of coal and iron and so gave rise to trade in these commodities and their exploitation in new countries. The railways also absorbed investments on a scale hitherto unknown. They revolutionized capital markets, created a new role for state economic action (for only in Britain could the railways be built entirely by private enterprise) and fostered the international flow of investment from advanced to backward nations to finance the railways.

Between the opening of the first railway in Britain in 1825 and 1840, well under 6000 miles of track were opened in the world, nearly all of it in Europe and North America and about three quarters of the total being in Britain and the United States alone. Thereafter came a spectacular advance: 220,000 miles were in operation in 1880 and over 500,000 miles in 1913. By this latter date railways were revolutionizing economies in every continent. Germany, for example, possessed 7000 miles of track in 1860; by 1900 the figure was 32,000 miles. India had no railway until 1853, but by 1900 some 25,000 miles were open. In the Argentine the network grew from under 2000 miles in 1880 to over 10,000 in 1900.

The growth of steam shipping also added an immeasurable impetus to the world economy. Freight rates fell, journey speeds were increased, and times made more regular. Britain dominated world shipping. Even in 1914 Britain owned about half of the world's steam tonnage. Table 1 shows the growth of Britain's tonnage, and it is interesting that sail tonnage did not decline absolutely until after 1880. Alongside these developments went many other improvements in

communications, such as the telegraph and the spread of postal services, which helped further to encourage the growth of the international economy.

Against this background the role of the European industrial revolutions becomes clear. Industrial and urban growth and rapid population increases created a growing demand for foodstuffs and raw materials, while manufactured products could be sold in return. In the thirty or forty years before 1914 the share of primary products in international trade remained remarkably constant at about two thirds of the total volume: the impact of industrial on nonindustrial countries needs no further stressing.

Of this vast array of primary products, foodstuffs, as might be expected, provided the main part. Wheat was the single most valuable commodity traded, and wheat exports gave a marked stimulus to economic development in a number of countries, the United States after 1870, Australia after 1880, and Canada and the Argentine after 1890. The United Kingdom was the world's principal market for wheat, as it was for many of the other principal traded commodities, such as cotton, wool, meat, tea, sugar and tobacco. The sources of the foodstuffs were varied. Wheat came not only from Russia, the United States, the Argentine, Canada, Australia, but from Rumania, Hungary and India. It was sold in every country in Western and southern Europe. In general the areas of provenance were more limited than the final destinations of primary products. In 1913 India, Ceylon and China provided over 80 percent of all the world's tea exports, while Brazil accounted for more than half the coffee. Denmark and Russia supplied over one third of the butter, Italy and Spain over 90 percent of the citrus fruit. The leading sugar exporters were Cuba and the Dutch East Indies, and the Gold Coast and Brazil monopolized cocoa.

Even more in the case of raw materials did rising demand and limited sources of supply ensure that the needs of industrial countries would influence a widening area, for the variety of such products was bewildering and their sources

Table 1
British Merchant Shipping Tonnage
(millions of tons), 1850–1910

	1850	1880	1890	1910
Sail	3.4	3.8	2.9	0.8
Steam	0.2	2.9	5.0	10.4
	3.6	6.7	7.9	11.2

scattered. Europe's needs found echoes in the distant rubber plantations of Malaya, in nitrate mines in Chile, and in the frozen meat industries in New Zealand. Of the principal raw materials, by 1913 cotton came chiefly from the United States with significant quantities from Egypt, India and even Uganda. India exported over 90 percent of the world's jute, while Australia and the Argentine were by far the leading exporters of wool. Japan was the leading exporter of raw silk. Iron ore came chiefly from Spain, France and Sweden, copper ore from Chile, Peru and Mexico, and tin from Bolivia and Malaya.

Coal and petroleum presented a rather different pattern. Coal was present in a number of advanced industrial countries (its presence going some way, of course, towards explaining the origins of their industrial power), and it was traded mainly from these nations to other less well endowed European countries. Britain was the major coal exporter in the years between 1900 and 1913, followed by the United States, Germany and Belgium. The principal importers were France, Italy, the Netherlands and Austria. The United States and Russia were the leading oil exporters in this period, although oil from Borneo, Sumatra, and Persia was appearing on world markets before 1914.

The basis of growing trade was industrialization, and Table 2 shows the industrial growth rates achieved by certain nations after 1860. The list is by no means exhaustive, for we have mentioned already the strides made in Switzerland, Belgium, Sweden, Japan and elsewhere. But the table does show a number of interesting

features. Some of the highest rates of increase were recorded by the most backward countries, Russia and Italy, although we must remember that these nations were industrializing from a very low base. Even such rapid rates of growth did not result in fully industrialized economies before 1914. Indeed in Russia some 80 percent of the population by 1914 still earned their living from agriculture.

Particularly striking were the achievements of Germany and the United States, whereas in Britain growth was relatively slow. Table 3 shows how differing growth rates resulted in the changing division of industrial power. It was inevitable, perhaps, that Britain could not maintain the extraordinary early ascendancy. Rapidly growing populations and abundant natural resources elsewhere were bound to foster industrial expansion. Moreover, the "second industrial revolution" after 1870, based increasingly on science-based technology instead of the rather simple technology of earlier phases, was suited to the intellectual and economic environments of both Germany and the United States. The result was that by the 1890s the United States was the world's foremost industrial power, with Germany strongly challenging Britain. By 1913 coal and iron and steel output in the United States was considerably ahead of Britain's production, while Germany produced twice as much steel and the United States four times as much as Britain.

Table 2
Annual Rates of Industrial Growth,
1860–1910

	1860–1870	1870–1880	1880–1890	1890–1900	1900–1910
Great Britain	2.6	1.9	1.6	2.4	0.7
Germany	2.5	3.3	4.8	5.0	3.2
France	2.7	2.4	2.7	1.7	3.0
Russia	5.0	2.7	4.7	8.5	3.2
Italy	—	3.1	5.7	3.4	5.9
U.S.A.	3.2	4.4	8.6	3.3	5.1
World	3.1	3.2	5.2	3.4	3.9

Table 3
Share of World Industrial Production
(Percent of Total)

	1870	1913		1870	1913
Great Britain	31.8	14.0	France	10.3	6.4
United States	23.3	35.8	Russia	3.7	5.5
Germany	13.2	15.7	Italy	2.4	2.7

Table 4
Share of Manufactured Goods in Exports,
1913

Share of Manufactures			
	%		%
Great Britain	77	Japan	49
Switzerland	77	Italy	45
Germany	72	United States	34
France	58		

Growing industrialization brought in all industrial countries an increasing concentration of manufactured products in exports, as Table 4 shows. Such exports were matched by a growing share of imports of foodstuffs and raw materials. For example in the single decade of the 1870s Germany changed from a net grain exporter to a net importer, and in 1913 grain ranked third behind cotton and wool in Germany's imports. In the same years leading French imports were wool, coal, cotton and grain; while in Belgium wool was the leading import, followed by grain.

European grain imports would have been higher had most countries not protected their agricultural sectors with tariffs in response to the flood of American products in the last quarter of the century. Only Britain of the major European industrial countries clung to free trade, and the British agricultural sector was relatively far smaller than that of any other country by 1913.

During the 1870s most European countries, again with the notable exception of Britain, fostered their industries with protective tariffs. In France there were a number of tariff increases in the 1870s and 1880s culminating in the high Méline tariff of 1892. In Germany, Bismarck ended free trade in 1879; in Austria major increases in tariffs took place in 1875 and 1878; in Russia there were steady increases after 1877, while Spain too became protectionist in the same year; Italy adopted high protection in 1887. Outside Europe, the United States was also industrializing behind growing tariff walls.

The Flow of Capital

The development of the world economy brought growing opportunities for the flow of international capital investment. Generally investment flowed from the rich industrial countries to the developing regions. A partial exception to this was the United States, which, despite its economic strength, was a huge debtor in 1914. The reason was that the United States was growing so rapidly that profitable investment opportunities could absorb domestic savings and still attract capital from abroad.

Exports of capital were very much a Western European monopoly. By far the major capital exporter was Britain. It is estimated that in 1914 the total stock of long-term foreign assets held by British nationals was about £4000 million, some 41 percent of all such investment. Next in importance, perhaps surprisingly in view of the low growth rates shown in Table 2, was France with about 20 percent. But a moment's thought will tell us that the low industrial growth rates shown by both Britain and France were indicative of a lack of investment opportunities at home, and it was not unnatural for private investors (for these were the majority of the capital exporters) to prefer the high yields abroad. After France came Germany with about 13 percent of the total, while Belgium, the Netherlands and Switzerland combined added a further 12 percent. Thus these six

265

nations contributed no less than 88 percent of total foreign capital investment in 1914.

International capital flows rose quickly after 1880 and reached a peak in the decade before 1914. British investment is estimated to have grown from about £200 million in 1850 to £700 million in 1870 and £2400 million in 1900. By 1913, when the total reached £4000 million, the annual flow was an astonishing 9 percent of total national income. The main directions of investment are shown in Table 5. Especially notable is the relative decline in Britain's investments in Europe. The United States continued to be a major recipient, but the chief areas of growth were in the Empire, with India taking a lower share and the dominions (mainly Australia, Canada and South Africa) a much larger proportion. In Latin America the Argentine was the heaviest borrower.

Over 40 percent of Britain's foreign investments in 1914 was in railway companies. A further 30 percent was invested in government bonds (central and local), a considerable proportion of which went to finance or subsidize railway construction also. Indeed, perhaps 70 percent of all British investments helped finance railways and public utilities of various kinds (such as harbour and dock improvements and gas and water undertakings).

French investment was of a somewhat different character. It too grew rapidly, multiplying some threefold between 1880 and 1914, but the French colonies absorbed relatively little, and French capital was concentrated in Europe. In 1914, under 10 percent was invested in the colonies, whereas some 60 percent was in Europe. The largest share was in Russia, about one quarter of the total. Especially after 1890, considerable sums were invested by Frenchmen in Russian industries and in Russian government bonds. A number of large French metallurgical and mining concerns were set up in Russia in this period, and by 1914 France held about one third of the large Russian foreign debt.

The significance of these international capital flows was great. Railways brought new areas within the orbit of world commerce while British capital developed tea plantations in India, rubber plantations in Malaya, gold and diamond mining in South Africa, and iron mines in Spain; French capital helped build Spanish railways and the Ukrainian coal and iron industries; French, Swedish and British capital created Russia's oil industry in the Caucasus. Such examples could be multiplied a thousandfold.

With capital went techniques and enterprise. Many French firms in Russia, for example, used French technology and equipment and employed skilled French workers. British capital too had a direct consequence in raising demand for British capital equipment. In this manner capital flows were a potent force in diffusing Western technology.

A further consequence of capital investment was that it not only directly stimulated economic growth, but provided foreign exchange for essential imports. Thus Australia, Canada and even the United States could sustain balance-of-payments deficits on current accounts as they laid down the railways and imported the capital equipment necessary for future development and growth.

Table 5
British Foreign Investment by Region, 1870–1914 (Percent)

	1870	1914
Europe	25	5
United States	27	21
Latin America	11	18
India	22	9
Dominions	12	37
Others	3	10
	100	100

The Gold Standard

Central to the flow of international capital and to the smooth functioning of the world economy was the widespread adoption of the gold standard. The gold standard meant guaranteed convertibility of currencies into gold at fixed exchange rates (since values of currencies were tied to gold). This encouraged investors to lend abroad since their dividends would not fluctuate with currency movements.

The international gold standard was a product of the last thirty years of the nineteenth century. Before this time several countries had experimented from time to time with a gold standard, but in 1870 only two, Britain and Portugal, had their currencies tied to gold. Most other European countries were on a silver standard, as were the United States, India and China. However, in the 1870s silver prices began to tumble, bringing considerable problems to silver standard countries. European industrial nations in particular were hit by relatively rising costs of imported raw materials. At the same time a number of primary producing countries, such as Russia, Japan, Hungary, India and the Argentine, began to see the advantages of attracting foreign capital with a stable gold-backed currency. As a result many countries joined Britain on the gold standard. Germany led the way in the early 1870s and by the time Russia and Japan went onto the full standard in 1897 most of the world's major trading nations had gold-backed currencies.

The gold standard did not lead to stable international prices. On the contrary, its adoption meant that price trends tended to move up and down together in various countries. The period from the 1870s to the 1890s was one of severe deflation, but from the mid-1890s, spurred by the huge gold discoveries in the Transvaal, prices rose once more. From this time until 1913, prices of primary products rose more steeply than prices of industrial products. Europe's farmers prospered again, and the favourable movements in the terms of trade encouraged yet more capital investment in developing countries. This high tide of prosperity stimulated the sense of well-being which characterized the *Belle Époque* before 1914.

The Migration of People

Alongside the international movement of goods and capital went a massive movement of people. The nineteenth century was a restless age. People moved within nations from countryside to town, and they moved also between country and country. The driving force was of course the opportunities opened up by industrialization and trade, and it was in the period between 1900 and 1914 that the international flow of migrants reached a peak. In the five years before the war some 1.5 million annually left their homelands to settle permanently abroad.

The major immigrant-receiving countries were those empty regions in temperate zones whose agricultural and mineral resources were now able to be developed. The United States absorbed about one half of all migrants, and at no period before 1914 did the foreign-born population of America comprise less than 13 percent of the total population. In the single decade 1900–10 more than 9 million migrants entered the United States. Australia, New Zealand, Canada, the Argentine, Brazil, and South Africa, also attracted large numbers, in many cases proportionally to their sizes even greater than to the United States.

As in the case of capital, it was Europe which provided the bulk of migrants. Between 1850 and 1914 about 40 million Europeans migrated. After 1890 the majority of entrants to the United States came from the poorer nations of southern and Eastern Europe, especially Austria-Hungary and Italy, in contrast to the earlier migrations which came chiefly from Great Britain and Ireland, Germany and Scandinavia. After 1890 many Germans settled in the Argentine and Brazil, while British migrants went increasingly to the Empire countries.

Another type of migration should be mentioned. Labour forces for the mines, plantations and railways that were being opened in tropical regions were often drawn from other nations, usually under contract. China and India provided large numbers of such labourers, the Chinese going principally to Malaya and the Dutch East Indies, and both Indians and Chinese going to the plantations of the West Indies and southern Africa.

Cracks in the World Economy

In retrospect, it is possible to see that all was not well with the world economy in the decade before 1914, despite the seeming prosperity and tranquillity which characterized international economic relations in the period. The problems can best be understood by focussing on Britain. Britain was central to the system, yet her position was steadily being eroded. We have seen already that Britain's industrial leadership was lessening, and this was reflected in world trade too. Whereas in 1840 Britain had accounted for about one third of world trade, by 1913 the proportion, though still greater than that of any other nation, was only 17 percent. Between 1880 and 1913 Britain's share of world exports of manufactured goods fell from 41.4 percent to 29.9 percent. By contrast, over the same period the share of Germany climbed from 19.3 percent to 26.5 percent, and that of the United States from 2.8 to 12.6 percent.

In the face of growing international competition from newly industrializing rivals, and the growth of protection in the leading manufacturing countries, Britain's exporters retreated increasingly towards the markets of primary producers, especially in the Empire. In other words, Britain's export industries, instead of developing new products, turned to the underdeveloped areas for export markets. By 1913 some two thirds of Britain's exports went to primary producing countries and one quarter of all cotton textile exports went to India alone.

In the complex system of multilateral payments that emerged, Britain depended increasingly on the Indian market. By the beginning of the twentieth century Britain had a huge trade surplus with India, but deficits with industrial Europe, with the United States, and with the temperate agricultural regions of the Argentine and Australasia. India in turn had surpluses with the United States and with continental Europe. In this way debt settlement could be made on a multilateral basis.

But such a pattern could not endure. It depended on the free entry of British goods into markets like India, and it depended on Empire countries being willing to continue importing British goods in preference to those of Britain's rivals. It depended also on the continued limited development of native industries, for example of Indian cotton textiles. By 1914 there were signs that Britain's position was being eroded in all these respects.

Certainly London remained the world's banking and financial center in 1914, its strength resting on returns from foreign investment and huge earnings from shipping which helped keep sterling a stable and attractive currency. On the other hand, by 1914 nations like Germany, the United States and even Japan were fast developing their own merchant shipping fleets. Moreover, by 1914 New York was becoming a major financial center as the United States economy prospered.

This was the essence of the problem. As long as free-trade Britain, with large capital exports and vast imports of food and raw materials, was the center of the world economy, the system could function reasonably well. The gold standard could be maintained, since there was no permanent drain of gold to one or two centers. But the United States was protectionist, and in any case was far more self-sufficient than Britain in food products, raw materials, and even many manufactured commodities. Once the United States built up large trade surpluses it was difficult for other countries to earn dollars to pay for them. This became the intractable problem of the 1920s, but some hints of difficulties to come are evident long before the Great War.

The Role of the Colonies

There is no clear connection between the growth of colonies and the expansion of the world

268

economy. After all, the history of European colonization stretches back to the sixteenth century and beyond. But it is undeniable that the expansion of trade, involving the growing search for markets and supplies of food and raw materials, greatly stimulated interest in colonies. At the same time the growing gulf between rich and poor nations encouraged the wealthy to colonize the weak, and in addition to formal acquisitions, "informal" colonies existed in China and in parts of Latin America.

Table 6 shows the growth of Europe's formal colonies. From the point of view of the world economy Britain's imperial connection was the most significant for, as we have seen, the Empire countries were increasingly important for Britain's trade and capital investment, while the surpluses with India underwrote the whole system of multilateral settlements.

Conclusion

Nostalgia is a natural emotion, and it is hard not to sympathize with those who regretted the passing of an era after 1914. There is no doubt that the problems of the interwar period made all the more attractive memories of the earlier years. There is no doubt also that the cataclysm of the Great War was so abrupt that it masked the fact that major changes in the international economy were taking place already; that the system was in 1913 of recent origin, and that it might in any case have proved only short-lived. But impermanence does not make less valid the real achievements. Between 1900 and 1913 the world was close-knit as never before or since. Western and Eastern Europe, the United States and China, the tropics and the new temperate regions all shared in a brief era of growth and, for some, prosperity. They shared an illusion of stability and permanence. It was *la Belle Époque*; but it was also *l'Époque Éphémère*.

Table 6
European Colonial Possessions, 1860–1914
(Area in Million Square Miles, Population in Millions)

	British Empire		French Empire		German Empire		Others		European
	Area	Population	Area	Population	Area	Population	Area	Population	Population
1860	2.5	145	0.2	3.4	—	—	9.3	32.0	270
1876	8.7	252	0.4	6.0	—	—	9.5	34.4	300
1900	12.6	367	4.0	50.0	1.0	14.7	10.6	79.0	400
1914	13.1	393	4.1	55.5	1.1	12.3	10.7	107.2	445

Summer 1914

by Brunello Vigezzi

War, *drawing by Giuseppe Scalarini (1873–1948), political cartoonist for the socialist newspaper* Avanti!.

"On July 31, 1914, at 3:30 P.M. a telegram from the Federal Council was posted up at Vevey station, announcing 'total mobilization in Russia and a state of war declared in Germany.' It had been one of the most beautiful days of the year and it was a wonderful evening. The mountains hovered above a light, luminous haze of palest turquoise; across the lake the moonlight spread a red-gold pathway starting from the coast of Savoy, from Bouveret and St. Gingolph, and ending at Vevey. The air was delicious, the scent of wisteria wafted through the night and the stars shone with such pure splendour! And in this divine peace, amidst this tender beauty, the sons of Europe were beginning the great carnage...."

Thus, with detachment, dismay and a feeling of utter helplessness and horror ("the great carnage"), Romain Rolland of neutral Switzerland recorded the event. Stefan Zweig, who was in Belgium on the same day of that "most beautiful summer ever," wrote that even thirty years later he could still vividly recall the feelings of shock and loss of faith.

In Le Coq too, the little seaside resort near Ostend, gaiety reigned. Holidaymakers sat on the beach under their multicoloured awnings, children were flying kites, boys and girls were playing about in front of the café and on the jetty. People from every nation mingled peacefully there, but German was the language most often heard because, as every year, the inhabitants of the Rhineland preferred to spend their summer holidays on Belgian beaches. The only vexation came from the newspaper sellers, who, to boost their sales, shouted out threatening headlines from the Parisian newspapers: "AUSTRIA PROVOKES RUSSIA," "GERMANY BEGINS TO MOBILIZE." The scene clouded over as the holidaymakers read the pages, but never for more than a few minutes.

There had been diplomatic scares like that for years, but everyone knew at bottom that the situation was always saved at the last moment, before things got really serious. Wouldn't it be the same this time? Except that now, Zweig tells us, the ever more menacing news sent the German visitors hurrying back to their own country, where, only just over the border, they saw with a shudder the not too carefully concealed preparations for violating Belgian neutrality: the military occupation of railway stations, the great German guns barely disguised under their covers, mounted on goods trains...

Europe in 1914 plunged into war with bewildering suddenness and dazed incredulity. "Europe has other things to think of at this moment..." until, at the end, the newspapers, speeches and interviews declared outright or let it be understood that this time all the belligerent statements meant what they said, and more. Yet, within very few days, the war met with spontaneous and overwhelming acceptance. The enthusiasm with which Europe went to war in the summer of 1914, once the fatal decision had been taken, has passed into legend. Romain Rolland, who sought at once to place himself "above the fray," to remember the words and obligations of peace and preserve the bonds of international collaboration, was an isolated figure, misunderstood if not despised. Zweig, too, had his difficulties. It was as if they were men out of their own time. A time, admittedly, that is not easy to understand. Had the *Belle Époque* been a preparation for war, then? Had it perhaps denounced war only to nourish it secretly in its bosom and, when it came, welcome it as its own favourite and fatal creation? "Even if it ends in ruin, it was beautiful," the Prussian Minister of War, von Falkenhayn, was supposed to have said on witnessing the mobilization and departure of the troops. Did the *Belle Époque* want peace or war? The change from one to the other had been too sudden, presenting two opposing pictures, almost as if it concerned two worlds quite out of touch with one another. For that very reason, perhaps, historians have never ceased to delve into the period in search of some important secret of Europe's history still to be found within those days at the end of July in the summer of 1914.

The Great Illusion

Pre-1914 Europe also wanted peace. Or, at least, it believed it had exorcised war and made it a thing of the past: that is to say, of course, European war, the only real and disastrous kind. Many people held that a civilized, progressive, industrial, capitalist society was in itself an insurance against any armed conflict, although they also, with an odd lack of consistency, warned that a general conflagration of that kind might break out at any moment.

From that point of view the case of Norman Angell is probably the most revealing. In 1914 he was a little over forty years old, having spent an eventful life between the old world and the new. He was born in Lincolnshire of an old county family, was partly educated in Switzerland and France and worked in America on the Atlantic Coast and in the West as a cowboy, gold prospector and journalist. Then he returned to Europe, where he became editor of the continental edition of the *Daily Mail*, then a new daily newspaper with a vast circulation. As a journalist he had experienced the disruptive force of many press campaigns, observed the amount of misinformation and the huge power of the popular press that had grown up so quickly. In particular, he had been in frequent contact with economic, political and military circles of influence and had been appalled to obsession by the gulf between the recent advances in economic and social life and the habitual politico-military standards, opinions and ideas. European politics struck him as antediluvian, in thrall to "arbitrary political phraseology" and "antiquated ideas." But what was at stake was Europe's very survival, and most of all because of the stubborn, lingering, common illusion about the effects of power politics.

Statesmen, governments, parties, "public opinion," applied to the modern economic world methods that dated back to the age of barbarism, the Middle Ages or the era of absolute states, pursuing, without realizing it, the ancient fantasy of "wars of conquest," which in capitalist Europe had become a practical impossibility...: Angell was finding his central theme. In 1909 he published a pamphlet entitled *The Optical Illusion of Europe*. He rewrote it in 1910, giving it a new title, *The Great Illusion: A Study of the Relation of Military Power in Nations to Their Economic and Social Advantage*. But what was significant and proved the degree of interest felt in such questions at the time was its indescribable success. The book went into one edition after another, and in the heat of debate for and against was continually reworked, and translated into twenty languages. Clubs were formed with reference to it, it was discussed in the papers and in parliaments; Angell was put up for the Nobel Prize. In its way the work became a brief summary of the epoch, useful for understanding the conditions and spirit of Europe on the eve of war.

The core of the book remained clearly defined. Angell extolled his new heroes with great precision: "a German manufacturer who sells film equipment to a suburb of Glasgow. Which, incidentally, lives by selling utensils to Argentinian planters who, in their turn, live by selling wheat to boilermakers in Newcastle...." During the last forty years, he adds, and still more during the last twenty, an extraordinary change had taken place, almost creating a new society, with its own hard and often brutal struggles, its gratifying progress but, above all, with its standards, customs and its unmistakable characteristics: the division of labour, the ease and frequency of communication, and financial interdependence. Credit is the new king, which achieves the "immense service" of providing "the sensory nerves of the whole economic and social organism," thus uniting and coordinating its different parts, putting them into harmony and, indeed, enabling them to survive. In such a situation any attempt at conquest designed (as so often it is) to change a country's prosperity by violence is unrealizable. Angell goes on to amuse himself by imagining the catastrophic general effects that would ensue if a German army plundered the vaults of the Bank of England or a British fleet annexed the free port of Hamburg. Those ideas belonged to the past... Then he compares the results of imperialist and colonial policy with those of economic expansion by mea is of world trade; the sterile, perilous fight for power over the island of Samoa, the widespread, fruitful and peaceful German penetration of Egypt as against the forced British withdrawal. 'The German colonies are *pour rire....*" The countries that feed the twenty million new Germans are "those Germany never possessed or hoped to possess: Brazil, Argentina, the United States, India, Australia, Canada, Russia, France and England."

Angell continues to list the series of accepted platitudes. He has various good ideas of his own too. And in the course of time, history has more than once confirmed his views. Basically his work is a legitimate expression of Europe in the *Belle Époque* described by Malcolm Falkus in the previous article of the present book. Nevertheless, reread today, *The Great Illusion* reveals its weak points, which are equally important for the understanding of what happened in the summer of 1914.

In the first place, Angell was convinced that war in Europe was a possibility and did his best to condemn it, demonstrating, among other things, how out of date it was. Yet, in the end, the reader has the curious impression that he felt obliged to report every possible opposition to his ideas to a point where even his most ardent supporters might lose heart. In his book the pages on "armed peace" based on the illogical "arms race" pack a much greater punch than those on peace entrusted to credit and trade.

Angell is too self-confident to admit of colonial or peripheral wars. His often impeccable observations on economic relations between the "more civilized nations" that ought to lead the world therefore remain, even if against his will, unilateral.

Finally, Angell is right when he protests against the too-easy confusion between economics and politics, as he is when he calls on Europe as a whole to use her expansive power and relations with the rest of the world to secure peace. He does so in a very characteristic way. And yet the defense of peace which he undertakes seems to fade away among hopes too fragile substantially to influence the course of events.

The Sarajevo Incident

"I am the son of a *khmet.* . . ." When Gavrilo Princip, the young Bosnian assassin of Franz Ferdinand, spoke those words at his trial he suddenly evoked another Europe, very remote from the one described in *The Great Illusion.* It brought to mind that in the Europe of 1914 serfdom still existed. The Christian *khmet*, that is to say the tiller of the soil, suffering under a twofold inferiority, both religious and social, was in a worse situation than many serfs in our own Dark Ages, and was as completely at the mercy of his Mohammedan landlord as if he had indeed been a slave. The tribute, forced services, subsistence farming, religious struggles, the very afflictions that Angell in his book had explicitly relegated to a buried past, reemerged almost unchanged. Capitalism, it is true, had knocked on the door of Bosnia Herzegovina, especially after the Austro-Hungarian occupation in 1878, which had taken it from the Turkish Empire, but not enough to change conditions of life and growth, or for it to feel that it shared in the prospects typical of democratic Europe.

Socialist organizations had begun to spread there too, but (like the growth of a middle class) were more or less a foreign phenomenon imported by means of German, Magyar and Polish workers drawn there by capitalist enterprises. In essentials the region remained agricultural, with the *khmet* at the base of the structure, and a class of intelligentsia beginning to develop, however tentatively.

In 1908 the Hapsburg Empire finally decided to annex Bosnia Herzegovina with its million or more Slavs; but the decision was not made in order to change the direction of things. The new constitution was absurdly limited. It was only with difficulty that it managed to overcome the internal division into Catholic Croats, Mussulman groups and Orthodox Serbs, thereby giving rise to a burning nationalism. The movement dreamed of independence, separation from the old Austria-Hungary and union with Serbia as a nucleus of all the southern Slavs. Among the young, secret societies pullulated, taking the political place of a party. Although they were all linked with the traditional peasant society, they took an interest, despite many difficulties, in the changes that were taking place in the world around them. Historical scholars who have studied the subject of Princip and his comrades have been able to identify a number of influences: the Russian populist movement, Mazzini, Masaryk's rationalism and, in the literary field (a much trodden field . . .), Ibsen, Wilde, Strindberg, and Kierkegaard, to say nothing of Walt Whitman and the American myth. The members of "Young Bosnia"—a rather vague term that can be taken to mean the whole collection of groups, circles and secret sects—aspired to a profoundly changed society and radical agricultural reform. They mistrusted discipline, approved of an aggressive individualism and wanted nothing to do with the Germanization or Magyarization that threatened their country. At the same time they were somewhat exclusive, reserved and bound up with their traditions. "Syphilis and clericalism are an unhappy inheritance from the Middle Ages. . . ." Thus Princip epitomized the prevailing winds of modern morality! These young men were abstemious, puritanical, virtuous if not ascetic, but were not without a taste for military glory. Anxiously they followed the trials of Serbia and strained to join in the Balkan Wars of 1912 and 1913, which allowed them, among other things, to tighten their bonds with the secret societies of Serbia, and, without very much difficulty, to hide supplies of arms in their houses. Their lives were enmeshed in hopeless contradictions. Between 1910 and 1914 they were involved in a dozen plots, while in Bosnia and Croatia one assassination followed another. "Sons of Yugoslavia, do you not feel that our lives must stand in blood, that assassination is the supreme god of all the nation's gods?" These were the young men who gathered in the road through which Franz Ferdinand, heir to the Emperor of Austria-Hungary, drove to attend the summer maneuvers at Sarajevo on June 28, St. Vitus' Day, the humiliating anniversary of the day six hundred years before, when Serbia had lost its independence to the Turks. They had decided to kill him.

A Miscalculated Risk

For his part, Franz Ferdinand was not a character who had much in common with the heroes of *The Great Illusion* either. He did have some connection with banks and industry, it is true, including armament makers such as Skoda (which gave rise to some fairly serious disagreements with the Serbian government); he also allowed himself to smile occasionally at the antiquated way in which the estates of the Hapsburg family were administered. But his habits, interests and ambitions were directed elsewhere. Convinced of the all-important role of the very Catholic (even superstitious), anti-Semitic aristocracy, a great landowner and a skilled sportsman, he did not care greatly for the new age. He proclaimed his dislike of "freemasonry, materialism, liberalism and Marxism." He had a very high idea of the empire, and he knew—unlike the young men of Bosnia—that many powers were still interested in his survival and, to that end, he was more than willing to adopt the necessary precautions. In spite of everything, he did not get on very well with the old Court. He knew the world, had travelled widely, and in his own way he loved the extraordinary mixture of peoples that made up the empire. Although he was an upholder of the aristocracy, he condemned the exclusiveness of the German and Magyar factions, who wanted to predominate to the detriment of all the other groups. He desired a stronger, centralized government and better treatment for all the minorities.

All in all, Franz Ferdinand personified well enough the state of the dual monarchy: the difficulties in which it was involved and the desire for survival. And yet on the morning of June 28 the attempt on his life succeeded, through the indescribable inefficiency of security measures and the incredible luck of the conspirators. The carefully planned route was blocked.

On his side, the old Emperor Franz Josef was not enthusiastic about the nephew who had become his heir. He could not forgive him his morganatic marriage with a noble lady below him in rank, and sometimes thought his politics at once old-fashioned and reckless. The funeral ceremonies in Vienna were dispatched without too much fuss. Europe had become used to assassinations and political murders. This time, however, things had gone too far, nor could Austria-Hungary ignore the main problems. If anything, the event simplified them. The assassination at least served to confirm that Yugoslav nationalism (identified with Serbia) was absolutely irreconcilable with the existence of the empire. Or, at least, that was how it seemed to Vienna. The chief of the general staff, Major Conrad, for example, boasted that he had suggested war with Serbia twenty-one times since January 1913, and certainly saw no reason to change his mind now. Paradoxically, as often happened in Austria, it was the head of the exclusive Magyar aristocracy who expressed his doubts. István Tisza, the Emperor's right-hand man, feared the excessive complications that would ensue (if Austria made a move, so would Russia). He was not eager for more Slavs to be annexed, for he knew it would upset the country's internal balance. And now Austria's choice of action began to concern the whole of Europe.

The affair had shifted, so to say, from the periphery towards the center, from Bosnia and Sarajevo to Vienna and Berlin. For, to come to a decision, Franz Josef and his counsellors had at last resolved to consult Germany, for some decades Austria's firmest if not her only remaining ally. He wrote directly to the Emperor of Germany, Wilhelm II: "After this last terrible happening in Bosnia, you too will be convinced that it is unthinkable to compound the differences between ourselves and Serbia, and that the maintenance of a policy of peace on the part of all the monarchs of Europe will be in danger as long as the focus of criminal agitation that is Belgrade remains unpunished...." A further message followed by special envoy: "In these circumstances it is incumbent on the monarchy to tear loose with energetic hands the net its enemy is endeavouring to throw like a noose over its head...." The proposal was Austrian, but in passing from Vienna to Berlin the question assumed new dimensions.

The Serbs were "bandits," "assassins," "criminals," "regicides." In his reply to the Austrian telegrams the Kaiser was not sparing of invective, nor did he distinguish very clearly between the murderers, the Serbian secret societies (there was doubtless some connivance) and the Serbian government. He assured the Austrian envoy of his complete solidarity with the Emperor, and said that he felt Austria should have *carte blanche* to put Serbia in its place as quickly as possible. Whether that should be achieved by war, a punitive expedition or some other form of punishment was for the Hapsburg Emperor alone to decide. So the idea of a "localized war" was already forming; but in the minds of Wilhelm II and his collaborators it was bound up with wider issues that would soon radically affect the whole European situation.

Moreover, Germany's alliance with Austria-Hungary went only so far; or rather, there was a point beyond which they might choose to go their different ways. The Foreign Secretary, Gottlieb von Jagow, and his ambassador in London were well aware of that. For the moment, however, the alliance still stood, and it was essential that its importance should not be diminished. "Austria hardly counted as a great power any more," and could not possibly accept any further humiliation in front of the southern Slavs, Russia and all Europe. Her behaviour was to some extent foreseeable. Apart from choosing the type of punitive action to be taken, she would react by adhering to her minor and slightly difficult allies, Italy and Rumania, but without informing them of her plans. Such was the advice of the German Chancellor, Bethmann-Hollweg, who also guaranteed German support during the trial of strength to come. So was Germany, under the pretext of the Sarajevo murder, really aiming at a European war? A perusal of the dispatches, minutes of the meetings and comments does not support that view. Wilhelm II expected to arrive at a peaceful settlement. Russia, the great protector of the southern Slavs, "was not ready for war and would certainly hesitate before resorting to arms...." Germany, in short, did not want general war, but... was accepting the risk of a general war. The fact was that the German government wanted Serbia punished, and desired above all to achieve a diplomatic triumph which, should occasion arise, would enable Germany to rearrange all European agreements to her own advantage. With such an end in view the risk seemed worth running. Meanwhile, time was on the side of her present adversaries: that was the other consideration preying on the government's mind. Russia, supported by France, was building up her army, and with the enormous population at her disposal, would in two or three years' time have an overwhelming influence. It would be better to thwart them now, not by a military victory, but with an affirmation of political power.

That was the German policy, but Austria, as usual, was equivocating. Once support was assured, might the Danubian monarchy hesitate to play its part? Might it discard the idea of a military expedition and delay the sending of an ultimatum to Serbia in the hope of not offering too open a "political affront" to the statesmen of France and Russia who were then conferring at Petersburg, preferring rather to wait till the meeting was over? In her own way, Austria too was hoping for political success without a European war. In the end, however, the ultimatum was presented at Belgrade on July 23, nearly a month after the assassination of Franz Ferdinand. The conditions were severe: patriotic societies and anti-Austrian propaganda must be suppressed, political and judicial inquiries must be held with Austrian officials participating, a positive answer must be delivered within forty-eight hours. And the German government, fulfilling its guarantee, sent a note on the following day declaring itself to be on the side of its ally. "Under the eyes, if not with the tacit consent, of the Serbian officials, propaganda for Greater Serbia has continually increased; and to that must be attributed the recent crime, which can be traced back to sources in Belgrade.... The Austro-Hungarian government, if it does not wish finally to abandon Austria's position as a Great Power, can only ensure that its demands are carried out by exerting the strongest pressure or adopting military measures.... It is a question that concerns only Austria-Hungary and Serbia...." And, on the part of Germany, the warning to the "Great Powers" was explicit: "The Imperial Government ardently hopes that the conflict will be localized, since in view of the diverse obligations inherent in the treaties, any intervention by another power would be fraught with incalculable consequences...."

The risk-taking tactic had been carried to its limit.

Great Powers, Alliances and General Staffs

If one examines the opinions and events of that period—as has often been done since—it seems as if, in fact, the Europe of 1914 was divided, if only momentarily, into a number of different levels or sectors. There was the Europe of credit and commerce so dear to Norman Angell; the Europe of backward peasants; imperial Austro-Hungarian Europe; Western as opposed to Eastern Europe; and the Europe of "armed peace," the Europe of the "Great Powers" that the German government was putting to the test. Each of these Europes was connected with the other, and interdependent if not superimposed; but each also enjoyed a relative independence and acted according to its own rules.

There were five or six Great Powers in Europe in 1914, according to whether Italy was counted as the first among minor powers or, as was more general, the last among the great. They differed widely among themselves but their position endowed them with certain qualities in common. As a definition of the time put it, a Great Power was one which was "inevitably involved in all major questions" and "could exert its influence in all the common deliberations," especially in those concerned with peace or European war. Perhaps the definition is not very precise, but it reveals the immense distance between a Great Power and an ordinary state.

The sharpness with which the German Foreign Secretary discusses with one of his ambassadors whether Austria is capable of maintaining her position, the freedom with which the German government comments on the same point to other nations, among many other examples, illuminate the situation all too clearly. A Great Power can, of course, favour conservation or expansion, be in the ascendant or declining, losing its importance or rising in the world. In the eighteenth century it was debated whether Spain ranked as a Great Power. It was during the nineteenth century that a distinction was first made between powers "with European interests," such as Austria and Italy, and those "with global interests," such as Britain, Germany, France or Russia (to which were now added two non-European nations, Japan and the United States of America). Even between the most powerful nations there were differences of opinion, but those would surely remain within acceptable limits.

"A question of prestige," as Friedrich von Holstein, the German Minister for Foreign Affairs, calmly remarked, referring to the first Moroccan crisis, when Germany, feeling herself diminished, nearly plunged Europe into war. And in summer 1914, the situation was comparable. Germany wanted to save Austria from a humiliation that was intolerable for a Great Power. The difficulty was that Russia, Serbia's protector, had never forgotten the "humiliation" she had suffered in 1908–09 when, after the annexation of Bosnia by Austria, her request for an international conference had been denied. Moreover, in European eyes, Russia had not yet redeemed the military defeat suffered in the Russo-Japanese War of 1904–05. Affairs were not in good shape.

The complications were further increased by Europe being divided into opposing alliances and spheres of interest. That is to say, the Great Powers were only nominally members of a hypothetical "Congress of Europe." In fact, they nearly always acted independently, although counting on their friends or allies. Thus Europe was usually thought of as being divided into two camps made up of the Austro-German alliance on one side and the Franco-Russian on the other, with Italy and Rumania to be added to the first and Great Britain to the second. Indeed, the situation had gone so far that after a meeting between Wilhelm II and Tsar Nicholas II of

Russia a communiqué was put out, acknowledging "the existence of two groups of nations in Europe," as well as the usefulness of such an arrangement for "maintaining equilibrium and peace." These alliances that were supposed to take the place of a Congress of Europe more often, alas, merely augmented the demands of the contracting parties. The alliances were, after all, inherited, based on the land boundaries of European history. Taken at their face value the alliances between the Great Powers might be merely defensive, but here too there was a margin of interpretation. Austria-Hungary alone facing the lesser Slav countries and Russia in the Balkans was one thing; doing so in the knowledge that she was supported by Germany was another. After her defeat by Germany in 1870–71 and her loss of prestige (and of Alsace-Lorraine), France, by herself, was not to be feared, but with Russia as her ally it was very different. Russia, in her turn, would be able to confront Austria in the Balkans, knowing that, in case of danger, France would be ready to invade the Rhineland.

Such was the simple logic to which European politicians had become accustomed. To which was now added Germany's clamorous naval policy, the decision to build a great fighting navy. The decision was partly inspired by economic considerations connected with heavy industry, and furthered by a publicity campaign of grandiose proportions in favour of German nationalism, but its chief purpose was to obtain a means of pressure against Great Britain—a typically "Great Power" move. After the adoption of this new naval policy in 1906 the rivalry between the two nations became fiercer and more serious than in the past, and England veered towards the dual alliance of France and Russia. Liberal Italy, allied to Austria and Germany, but faithful to her rule of never finding herself in the field against England, had already begun to loosen her ties to the Central Powers. Germany felt the danger of "encirclement" was increasing and did everything possible to break the circle. For a Great Power it could not be otherwise. Here, too, the crisis of 1914 was putting down roots. .It was one more troubling symptom.

Economic rivalry added to the tension. The spectacular rise of Germany, especially, was a case in point. In the 1800s England had exported twice as much as Germany to Russia, now its share had dropped to a third. Goods "made in Germany" flooded the markets of Europe and the world. England reacted; so did France. Russian loans were arranged in Paris, and the economic assistance had a distinctly anti-German flavour, as had the railway reorganization plans (corresponding only too well with the reinforcement of the new Russian army). French finance in the Balkans vied with that of Austria and Germany. Meanwhile, expanding Germany was creating new zones of dissension. Everyone was talking about the Baghdad railway, the Ottoman Empire and Russia's resentment.

Was the Europe of "armed peace" and "imperialism" eager for war, and was it thus a foregone conclusion in 1914? Some believed in the theory then, and many more have done so since. But it distorts reality. The theory overlooks, among other things, that alliances in the Europe of 1914 were always a reply to mutable situations. Europe seemed to be divided into two camps, but Great Britain kept a considerable margin of independence. Under the surface, the traditional Anglo-Russian antagonism still existed, even openly and suddenly as in Persia. The equally traditional cordiality between Britain and Germany continued, in spite of differences. Germany's encirclement was largely imaginary, in regard to both enemies and allies. Austria-Hungary still counted in Europe; Italy maintained many bonds with Germany; the partition of the Balkans had not yet ended. As to economic rivalry and its connection (still largely uninvestigated) with the direction of policies, the opposing sides affected were not always the same. It was indeed at the beginning of 1914 that the much desired Franco-German agreement was concluded, to say nothing of the Anglo-German agreement for the building of railways in Baghdad and the Middle East. France had invested five billion gold francs in the Ottoman Empire, which called for French collaboration in its application. Even armament manufacturers

followed political divisions only to a limited degree. In spite of everything, Russian rearmament was carried out with the help of French, British, Austrian and German firms, while in Petersburg the authorities had no hesitation in using the growth of their military power to negotiate a more favourable trade agreement with the Germans. Economy was sometimes the slave and at other times the beneficiary of "war policy." Or else it followed paths that led to bitter rivalry, fortunes or failures, but not, for those reasons, to war. Norman Angell's "world of commerce" undoubtedly has a strong constitution and tends to be on the side of peace. Although it is true that in 1914 Britain absorbed a good 14.2 percent of Germany's exports, while Germany absorbed only 6.4 percent of British goods, it is also true—and more important—that the two economies were logically complementary in regard to spheres of production.

There were, however, other dangers to peace. Diplomats and soldiers often enjoyed a prominent position in Europe during the *Belle Époque*, as Philippe Jullian has already recorded earlier in this work. But beneath all the spectacle, the uniforms, parades and reviews, or even the "summer maneuvers," the situation was genuinely threatening and not too controllable. To a great extent that was due to changes that had been introduced nearly everywhere among the armies of the Great Powers. The Prussian victory of 1870–71 had marked the end of long-term professional armies and the advent of compulsory conscription (except in Great Britain, where voluntary recruitment remained). Armies for a possible war were now composed of millions of men, to say nothing of arms, services and supplies, which had to be assembled, moved to the front and billeted. Plans for mobilization, therefore, required long preparation. For good or for ill, the general staffs had to provide for these huge armies and plan the gigantic troop movements that would be necessary. Towards what frontier? Alone or in collaboration? How would the alliances work in practice? . . . It seemed as if the entire delicate political situation in Europe would have to be reconsidered.

The Schlieffen plan was the most famous. Germany had to consider the problems that would arise if it became necessary to confront the Franco-Russian alliance. In the general's case that consideration had developed little by little into a precise strategy for a war on two fronts, absolutely demanding the violation of Belgian neutrality. Since it was practically impossible to invade by way of Alsace-Lorraine and swift action was vital, the only feasible way seemed to be a vast—and hazardous—outflanking maneuver to beyond Paris, in order to eliminate the French armies in four to six weeks, before turning east. On the eastern front, he calculated that the slow pace of Russian mobilization would allow the German forces to remain temporarily on the defensive. That involved—or should do so—coordination with the Austro-Hungarian army, divided in its turn between planning for action in the Balkans (or even against the ally-enemy Italy) or against the Russians.

The plan of the Italian general staff, should it be fighting at the side of the Central Powers in a war, was to send an army up the Rhine . . . But on that territory it was logical to suppose that the French and Russians would at least react, accelerating troop movements, coordinating plans, even if there were sometimes uncertainty and difficulties to overcome. The Russian general staff had to consider two alternatives, either war against Austria-Hungary alone, with partial mobilization, or an extended campaign against Germany, which would require general mobilization. It was a dilemma, for the two plans were mutually exclusive, while the political decision should be, had to be, delayed as long as possible to ensure that the better alternative was chosen. In 1912 Marshal Joffre, head of the French general staff, was also considering the possibility of violating the Belgian border. Later he veered to the idea of a central offensive, leaving the main defense of the northern frontier to a British expeditionary force. Meanwhile, for other reasons, the French fleet was diverted to the Mediterranean to take the place of the British navy, which was recalled to reinforce the Home Fleet for the defense of the Channel and the coast

of France. And so on . . .

The plans and drafts and conversations between the heads of the armed forces followed one another in close succession. They acted as if war were a foregone conclusion—whether it was actually to happen or not. Sometimes the politicians did not even know what was contained in the mobilization plans or the agreements between the general staffs. More or less explicitly, all the nations concerned adhered to the principle of "no commitment"—quite openly so in communications from Great Britain to the French. Plans and promises, even when they amounted to an obligation, were in reality mere technical studies of a problem. That was one more barrier that the Europe of 1914 had erected between itself and war, after having created a hundred occasions for hostilities.

Belligerent feelings remained as strong as ever. The rigidity of mobilization plans in case of crisis was particularly dangerous. Despite all distinctions of jurisdiction (often strictly observed) between politicians and the military, every Great Power ended by allotting huge sums for building up new armies millions strong. Here more (as in Germany), there less, there was a general air of militarization. During the same years in which *The Great Illusion* was so popular, Friedrich von Bernhardi published a book that was very widely read in Germany, namely *Germany and the Next War*, which went so far as to speak of "the duty to make war." Meanwhile, in France, at the École de Sciences Politiques, Lyautey declared, "What is most impressive about the youth of today is that it has no fear of war." The policy of the Great Powers had got people used to the idea of war; newspapers with wide circulations devoted a great deal of space to the subject. Even among contemporary novels, those on the "war of the future" had a surprising success; 180 books of that type were published between 1900 and 1914, and were sometimes best sellers. And in the meantime, rearmament went ahead. In addition to various naval measures, the army and artillery of Russia were being reinforced on a grand scale; at the beginning of 1913 Germany increased her peacetime military forces by one third; France, with her smaller population, lengthened the period of obligatory military service to three years. What was still missing?

Nevertheless, the whole picture, even then, was not entirely one-sided, and an observer of Europe "on the eve" would have seen not only the symptoms of war but also events unconnected with it. The United Kingdom was occupied with the social legislation proposed by Lloyd George, while the Irish question was bringing the country to the verge of civil war. In Italy universal male suffrage was being tried for the first time, and there was Red Week. The socialists had, relatively speaking, become the most powerful party in Germany, and voted that the burden of rearmament should fall only on the more prosperous classes. In France the election that followed the vote on conscription produced a majority for the radical socialists, who were against the three-year term of service and in favour of a progressively increased income tax. In various countries attention was abruptly directed to internal unrest, and turned ever more often to the important subject of European democratization. At the beginning of the summer, it must be remembered, it still seemed possible that there would be no war. But given the reigning circumstances, it was practically impossible, after the Sarajevo incident, that the German government's decision to test the whole policy of the Great Powers and the entire system of alliances could lead in a peaceful direction.

War is Declared

Austria-Hungary, to save her multinational empire, wanted to strike at Serbia and Yugoslavian nationalism; but on that pretext the Germany of Wilhelm II—planning for the application of pressure and diplomatic success, but not necessarily war—wanted to put the whole equilibrium of Europe at risk. Little by little, as the days passed, her line of action became clear and the initiative passed to the German government. After Austria-Hungary had declared the

Serbian reply to be unsatisfactory and had broken off relations, it was Germany that made the important decisions. Even the eventual declarations of war (which soon became inevitable) spoke for themselves. Germany declared war on Russia on the first of August, and on France on August 3, while Britain declared war on Germany on the fourth. The obligatory declarations of war between *Austria* and the *Entente*, however, did not take place till later, when, almost wearily, as it were, one was sent to Russia on August 6, but the others, to France and Great Britain, only on the tenth and twelfth respectively.

At the center of events was Berlin. And in recent years even the historians, in their attempts to pin down once more the exact point of no return, have abandoned their deeper researches, to concentrate instead on the German Chancellor then in office. Among the bitter polemics, recurrent arguments and remaining uncertainties, Theobald von Bethmann-Hollweg has almost come to be taken as the interpreter of the final crisis. As long as the idea is not pushed too far, there is a good deal of truth in it. His attitude, opinions, attempts at agreement, even the last settlement, were representative.

"Any future war which is entered into without real necessity will set at risk not only the Hohenzollern crown but also the future of Germany. To unsheathe the sword unless honour, safety and the country's future are at stake would be worse than an act of folly; it would be a crime. . . ." These words addressed by Bethmann-Hollweg to the Crown Prince at the end of 1913 were hardly those of a warmonger. A high Prussian official and great landed proprietor, he was always suspicious of parliamentary rule, yet felt acutely the need for certain reforms in Germany and Europe. However—and it was typical of him—he felt equally sure that the necessary support would not be forthcoming and that the right moment would pass. He was part and yet not part of the Prussian *Junker* world. His family originally belonged to the aristocracy of Frankfurt and had only gradually acquired a "nobleman's estate" in the Mark of Brandenburg. Perhaps for that reason Bethmann-Hollweg took it for granted that this patriarchal and authoritarian society would be forced to grant ever greater concessions. Sometimes he thought that the advance of social democracy was inevitable, although he still—and he had been chancellor since 1909—held it at bay and had conceded little or nothing. He felt the pressure of new forces that were difficult to hold back. From Brandenburg he warned of the Slavs' advance. "The future belongs to Russia and the forces she represents," he said. Therefore he sought agreement with Britain, but without granting any immediate concessions, without renouncing Germany's ambition to be a world power, and without relaxing his bonds with Emperor, bureaucracy, army or navy. He did not deny the differences between the two countries, but tried to smooth them over, always seeking to strengthen national unity. Although he liked to work "slowly, continuously, stubbornly," the manner in which he dealt with obstacles suggests that he was also the victim of a sort of fatalism, of resignation when faced with measures that were desirable but difficult to carry out.

That, in essence, was how Bethmann-Hollweg treated the crisis of July 1914; as a duty and an opportunity, a last great opportunity, to change a difficult situation both on the home front and abroad. Briefly stated, the difficulties were that Germany saw herself as being encircled, which stimulated the militaristic elements within the country, threatening to divide the nation, favour extremism and make new international alignments more problematical. After Sarajevo, on the other hand, it was possible to impose a favourable political scheme. Austria was on the side of reason. The Great Powers acknowledged it, even if somewhat unwillingly. It gave her the right to a reply or, failing that, to the waging of a "local war." That would place Russia in a difficult position since, owing to her lack of military preparation and perhaps to French counsels of moderation, she was not yet ready to support Serbia and might yield, leaving the path clear for Germany, rich in armed force and prestige, to approach Britain with a view to a global agreement. It was quite possible that, if Russia

submitted and not too many complications arose, Britain might not concern herself overmuch with insurgent troubles in the Balkans.

And so, after the ultimatum, after Serbia's reply, and after Austria had broken off relations with that country, Bethmann-Hollweg persisted, perhaps with an extra touch of impatience and intransigence, in order not to lose the advantage he had gained. Those were the standards of the period, standards typical of Great Powers, which Bethmann-Hollweg further stiffened and sharpened. The foundations of peace were crumbling.

The German Chancellor had his plan and kept to it with energy ... and with his usual dash of fatalism. His Emperor, Wilhelm II, saw things rather differently. Impressionable, vacillating, fond of theatrical gestures as he was, the Kaiser, once he had read Serbia's clever, compliant, if slightly elusive, reply, was appeased, or rather lost sight of what Bethmann-Hollweg saw as essential. The reservations that Serbia had made could, the Kaiser hoped, be arranged by negotiation with the Powers, but a temporary military occupation of part of Serbia would be necessary as a guarantee. The original object of the exercise, which had been to avoid the intervention of a third power and force Serbia to accept the full contents of the Austrian note in order to influence the grouping of European nations, seemed to have been forgotten. However, German policy at this time was in the hands of the Chancellor and had already changed direction. The German government had put pressure on Vienna for Austria to declare war on Serbia, and on July 28 that was done, Belgrade was bombarded and attempts at mediation weakened. The first thing needed was to create a situation clearly advantageous for itself, or, as Bethmann-Hollweg said, "It is a question of finding a way to cut the central nerve of propaganda in favour of a greater Serbia without at the same time unleashing a European war. Finally, if that war cannot be avoided, to see that the conditions in which it is waged shall be as advantageous to ourselves as possible...."

The significance of German policy to Europe was clear enough; but Bethmann-Hollweg had wound and set in motion an infernal machine.

The risk was too great and ill calculated: either there would ensue an endless stream of negotiations, or the smouldering embers of war would suddenly burst into flames. In spite of everything, Austria's declaration of war on Serbia had stiffened Prussia's attitude. What is more, if matters came to a head, the politicians might well be overruled by the military. "An ignoble war has been declared on a weak country. Russia's indignation is enormous, and I share in it," wrote Tsar Nicholas II to Kaiser Wilhelm. "I expect very soon to be overruled by pressure from the army, and forced to take measures that will lead to war...." The politicians, at least, were still considering counterpressure, a partial mobilization against Austria, or a campaign against Austria only. Russian military circles, however, were raising the objection that partial mobilization would exclude total mobilization. And what if Germany intervened? The German army, in its turn, was afraid of losing precious time for its Schlieffen plan (and, on the whole, it would be better to fight Russia then than later . . .) and wanted the situation brought into the open. Bethmann-Hollweg tried to keep to his own line of action. Just as he had disagreed with the Kaiser in regard to one policy, so he now opposed the chief of the general staff, Helmuth von Moltke, on another. He firmly maintained that it could not be "profitable to pursue political and military action at the same time." Meanwhile he endeavoured not to lose touch with Great Britain and to convince her that the wrong was on Russia's side and that Germany had no hankering after European hegemony. But his policies were at odds with one another and had lost their drive. They were reduced to pretexts or the basis of a much reduced plan. The German Chancellor insisted stubbornly on putting Russia "in the wrong." He was thinking of "a peace that will force us to go to war," and of the socialists, who, if they accepted war at all, would accept only one of defense. His arguments were weighty, but now he turned his attention to internal preparations. His peace strategy was lost; warlike moves followed one another in quick succession. On the late afternoon of the thirtieth the Russians decided on general mobilization. Austria-Hungary, foreseeing that she would be faced with Serbia and Russia at the same time, followed suit. On the thirty-first Germany declared a "state of threatened war" (a sort of premobilization, since for Germany, once more according to the Schlieffen plan, mobilization and war were practically the same thing), and sent ultimatums to France and Russia. Perhaps what Bethmann-Hollweg wrote in a dispatch of that time was the last word on the subject: "All the governments, Russian included, and most of the people, want peace at heart, but the direction has been lost and the machine set in motion...."

The last example of the workings of that machine, so long in preparation, concerned England. On August 1 news—vague and dangerous—reached Berlin that Britain might remain neutral as long as Germany did not attack France and the conflict was limited to Eastern Europe. Wilhelm II was delighted and ordered von Moltke to concentrate his troops on the Russian front, only to be told that it was impossible. The Schlieffen plan did not allow for such an eventuality. Belgium and France were to be attacked first, then Russia.

The discussion was pointless anyway, because, however reluctantly, Great Britain was swinging towards intervention. At the end of July the government was still undecided, several ministers threatened to resign if war were declared, public opinion fluctuated, the City, heart of the business world, preferred peace. But in the end general political considerations took the upper hand. Britain could not run the risk of France losing her position as a Great Power, or that there should be a sole dominant power in control of Europe. From that point of view the invasion of Belgium (whose frontiers were guaranteed by international treaties) was only the igniting spark. The conviction that British participation in the war was now inevitable spread quickly. Most of the ministers believed it, public opinion was swayed, the atmosphere changed. "Between Saturday and Monday," during the weekend between August 1 and 3, as Lloyd George, who had at first been very hesitant, said in London, "war suddenly became popular." On the third the British ultimatum regarding the violation of Belgium's neutrality was sent to Germany. On the fourth general war broke out.

The dam had burst and the floodwaters were pouring over the land.

Socialists, Church and Intellectuals

There were not a few obstacles, it had been hopefully predicted, that would bar the way to the outbreak of the Great War. Among them were expert diplomacy, the balanced system of alliances, the race for arms intended to discourage enemy attack, fear of a war that was already foreseen as "the most gigantic the world has ever known," economic interdependence, the love of comfort, the wisdom of governments, even, according to some, the authority of reigning monarchs, who—it was also said—were "warlords," but likewise "watchful shepherds of their flock." There were also other influences of long standing (even regarded with a certain fear) which would curb the Great Powers' will to wage war: the socialists, the Socialist International, the Christian churches and the intellectuals. Both old and new were an active part of Europe. They would oppose, denounce and hinder "the massacre of the people."

None of this, alas, came true. With a few exceptions, hardly noticed at the time, neither socialists, intellectuals nor the church stood out against war. It was one of the great surprises. The exceptions were the objects of scorn, and both at the time and during the ensuing decades were often referred to as traitors. Few episodes in European history have been so exhaustively discussed. Perhaps it is now time to drop the words "failure" and "treason" when trying to understand what really happened and what role was played in Europe at that time by the socialists, the intellectuals and the church.

It is often forgotten that the Socialist International had begun its opposition to war during the years before the outbreak of hostilities. In November 1911, and again in 1912, it organized international demonstrations against Italian aggression in Libya and Turkey, and against the Balkan wars with their possible European repercussions. The leaders of the party in various countries spoke in the capital cities of the opposing systems of alliances: Jaurès in Berlin, Scheidemann in Paris. Then, if ever, the European war might have been prevented. A sigh of relief went around, confidence returned; the conviction that there existed powerful economic, social and cultural forces working for peace was confirmed. "Financial imperialism," "shameless colonialism" and the "archaic antagonisms of religions and races" could constitute an explosive mixture, capable of leading to a general conflict. Jaurès, the socialist leader who was the most concerned with external politics, was explicit in his plans for action. He too, however, shared a new kind of "great illusion" that might be considered socialist. It led to much theorizing on the possibility of international collaboration, which at that moment found growing approval among the various socialist parties of Europe, although they saw reality from somewhat different viewpoints. The Socialist International was naturally also striving to find ways of preventing war and tried every means to unite the national sections which at that time formed part of its distinctive structure. Unfortunately they were not all in agreement and it was difficult to make them so. The proposal of a simultaneous general strike against war favoured the nations less advanced in socialism; the theory of the unequal development of socialism in Europe, with its related problems, increased the opposition of German and Austrian socialists to the idea. If the powerful German socialist movement sabotaged mobilization, it would open the way to the troops of Tsarist Russia, where socialists would get very short shrift. It was the classic reply and induced them to look for other methods, such as coordinated parliamentary pressure, or strikes to be settled by arbitration. In the summer of 1914, in view of its imminent international congress, European socialism was desperately searching for a peace formula.

After the breaking off of relations between Austria and Serbia there was a sharp feeling of impending danger. "Citizens, what I want to say to you this evening is that never have we, never for forty years has Europe, been in such a threatening situation," was Jaurès' diagnosis. The manifesto issued by the German socialist party had this to say: "A grave hour has tolled, the gravest for fifteen years. The danger grows nearer. The menace of a universal war is upon us." Here and there demonstrations were started, sometimes attended by huge crowds. On July 29 the International called a formal meeting at Brussels, where it was decided to advance the date of the Paris congress to August 9 in order to express "the proletariat's will for peace."

At this point further action was impeded by the prevailing uncertainty. "The nation is the indispensable nucleus of today's workers' movement and tomorrow's internationalism." The nation was still the basic unit in the Europe of 1914, and the succession of events did nothing but add to the perplexity. The question of the unequal development of socialism, seen in the light of a European war, seemed only to confirm that. The polemics hurtling between the various European countries were echoed inside the socialist world in a way now hard to believe. The German socialists would save their country from "'Muscovite barbarities": a sentiment that dated back to the days of Marx. Pleckanov, on the other hand, felt that Europe was threatened with Germanization and that it would be a good thing if Russia, allied to the Entente, defeated the German Empire. The Belgian socialists defended their invaded land; the same went for the French, who had always had a great deal to say about German socialist bureaucracy. Nor did the assassination of Jaurès by a fervid young woman nationalist do anything to change the ever more embittered polemics. The Russian Social Democrats, the Serbian socialists, some English Labour groups, the Italian socialists in their own way (Italy had remained neutral), others here and there, opposed the prevailing climate of opinion. Internal arguments, however, were often fiercer than appeared on the surface. The hard facts that decided the issue were as follows: Vandervelde, the president of the Socialist International, joined the Belgian government on August 4; on the same day the German socialists voted military credits; the French accepted the "inviolable union"; the secretary of the International moved to neutral Holland. Meanwhile a circular announced that "as a result of recent events, the Congress of Paris is postponed to a later date."

It seems to have attracted very little subsequent notice that during those same anxious days another congress was held by the most important Protestant churches of Europe and America to discuss "what contribution the church could offer to establish friendly relations between nations." On July 12 at Liège another meeting had been arranged, having a certain amount of liaison with the first, by the Congress of the International Catholic League for Peace, founded in 1911. But the war left no breathing space. At Constance, on August 2, such delegates as had been able to come started and finished their work on a single day. Each in his own tongue, "a German, an Englishman, a Frenchman, a Swiss and an American" prayed for peace and all sent an appeal to the heads of state to "avoid a war between millions of men . . . and to save Christian civilization from disaster." Then the German government informed them that after the third it would not be able to guarantee the delegates safe passage across its territory. Some arrived back in London shortly afterwards. "It is not the Christian idea of peace that has failed," said a delegate, "but a system that imagined security could be built on a basis of piled-up armaments." Controversy started again, there were plans to keep in contact, to ensure useful work in the future, especially in England and Germany. Then the meeting was dissolved . . . and the name of the association so recently founded changed from "the World Council of Churches to Promote International Peace" to the more modest and apt "Council for Promoting International Amity through the Churches."

In reality, far the most prevalent attitude, even among the churches, was quite different. The Catholic Congress at Liège had fallen through. Pope Pius X, for his part, called upon the clergy of all nations to lead "public prayer to the end that Our Lord, moved to compassion, will rid us as soon as possible of the grievous burden of war, and inspire the supreme rulers of nations to thoughts of peace and not of torment." But the Catholic journals were giving space to other considerations: "The sons of combatant nations, leaving their homes to take up arms in the name of national interests, will depart more encouraged, more confident, readier to fulfill their duty, when they know that they are accompanied by the prayers of pious souls...." The expectation of peace was postponed to an indefinite future; international action by the churches remained equally vague; religion was seen as a comfort during the ordeal, which, in the meanwhile, it accepted. A thousand compelling reasons drove Catholics, Protestants and Orthodox to that conclusion. Tradition was strong in the churches of Europe, as strong as the idea that war was some kind of salutary expiation for mankind. Or else they relied on the old distinction between thesis and hypothesis. Had everyone followed Christ's teaching, the war would not have occurred, but since it had not been followed, Christians must share in the common sacrifice, obey the authorities of this world, and each fight for his own country. Communication between the faithful of different nations was rare. "Except for the eucharistic conferences, there were no other international reunions," a contemporary witness said, speaking for the Catholics. In short, each one was imprisoned within his own viewpoint, each, all too often, argued in favour of his own country. Separation cut a deep trench between coreligionists of different nations and unfailingly set "brother" against "brother." On that theme Alfred Firmin Loisy notes in his memoirs: "During the war only national gods survived: the god of the Germans and the god of the French," and, he added sardonically, "it was very difficult to choose between the two...."

In the case of a war between European nations, the wisest course was still, perhaps, to explain it as a matter of power politics and fundamental interests that had set state against state, without necessarily seeing one's own country's part in the war as a crusade for justice, and to cling instead to the old values of civilization, objectivity and morality. Benedetto Croce, in an essay written in 1912, noted the capacity that great nations still enjoyed of retaining the loyalty of their citizens. He sought in this way to reconcile the duty of intellectuals with attachment to the mother country.

Romain Rolland was, indeed, an exception. For in some ways war itself exercised a fascination as a time of tragedy and grandeur, a recaller of forgotten virtues, a day of reckoning, or even just the experience of sharing a common fate which almost inevitably drew the intellectual to his own land. Freud confessed to "feeling himself Austrian for the first time for thirty years.... My whole *libido* went out to the Austro-Hungarians." Friedrich Meinecke at Fribourg experienced "one of the most beautiful hours of his life" and felt "the greatest happiness" at the news that the socialists had agreed to vote war credits, and at the spectacle of "national fusion." For varying reasons the most diverse men were converging towards the same point. Often, all too often, intellectuals, instead of patiently sorting out truth from falsehood, were believing and defending contradictory statements, peremptory, absurd or farfetched, that would justify the absolute necessity of victory for their own country, and of defeat for the enemy. As Croce wrote, between irony and anger, of still neutral Italy, "The ground of Europe is shuddering not only under the weight of arms, but under the weight of lies." That is to say the intelligentsia supported propaganda. Or, at least, they were struck by the novelty of a war that conscripted thought and imagination, and required one's whole soul. Or, again, they tried to combine the theories of yesterday with the facts of the present. As did Norman Angell himself, who, while not denying his past opinions, considered that now it was necessary to defeat Germany, which had been mainly responsible for the war. He was at first against "peace by conquest" and "beating the Prussian on his own ground," but at the end of the summer 1914 he published a book entitled *Prussia and Its Destruction*. In other words, as the reviews were quick to point out, he too wanted "a fight to the finish, a decisive military victory for the Entente Cordiale, full and irreversible defeat for the Central Powers."

The Armies and the People

The coming of war did not merely wipe out resistance. It won approval, even aroused enthusiasm. The approval of the various political parties, the churches and the intelligentsia was echoed on a wider scale by large, sometimes enormous, public demonstrations cheering the declaration of war and the departure of troops. In Paris as in Berlin, London, Moscow and Vienna ... Recently some historians collected and studied newsreels of the time and compared them with other contemporary film material. The verdict was unanimous: "The soldiers who were called up in 1914 made no objections. They all went willingly and, as they paraded through the streets, their faces were cheerful, even radiant."

Other significant news seeps through. In France the government quickly shelved the famous *Carnet D* with its list of subversives to be arrested in case of war. When, in Britain, where there was no obligatory conscription, it was decided to appeal to the country, the number of volunteers exceeded all expectations: by September there were already 750,000. In none of the combatant countries were there many men unwilling to be called to the colours, not even as many as foreseen by the military authorities. In Russia, too, for various reasons, conservatives and liberals found themselves in agreement in favour of war. During the decisive crisis a great majority in the Duma went over to the prowar camp. "The Russian people," it was said, "will never forgive a delay that could throw the country into chaos and misfortune." Patriotic accord extended to the moderate elements of the socialist party and the working classes.

The same happened in Germany on a much larger scale: "We are witnessing the magnificent spectacle of the awakening of a nation of seventy million.... Socialist ideals are fusing with those of the old military feudalism.... There are no more parties or factions, nothing that is false or arrogant. It is not a political movement, but the most elementary eruption of popular force that has ever been seen."

Internal national and social tensions, in some cases agonizing, were straightened out, slackened, or at least went underground. At the peak of the crisis the British Prime Minister, Asquith, declared the situation to be the gravest for fifty years, but that it might "drive the dark picture of the Ulster civil war into the background," which, indeed, was what happened within a few days.

The war, at least at first, instead of widening the cracks, seemed to blow a breath of life into the crumbling structure of the old Austro-Hungarian Empire. Not only were there huge prowar demonstrations in Vienna but, generally speaking, the various component nationalities confirmed their loyalty, as they did at Zagrabia (Zagreb), where large crowds gathered to show their approval of intervention, while among even the minority groups the traditional hatred of Serbia overcame Yugoslav solidarity.

There were exceptions, of course. The declarations of war were often accompanied by straitened living conditions and strict, even repressive, measures. The predominant attitude, however, was not resentful, or so one gathers from very diverse observers. Here and there some noticed a certain silence or resignation on the part of many peasant farmers who answered the call to arms in spite of distressing difficulties. It seems true to say that in every country the Great War was seen above all as a defensive war, a fight for survival. Alternatively—and not very differently in many contemporary eyes—it was to defend a vital principle, attain a centuries-old aspiration, or give vent to some more recent grudge that had been allowed to drop but was still dormant in the people's hearts and easily aroused, like the growing antagonism between English and Germans.

Perhaps, as some comments and incidents suggest, the war was even more closely integrated with the life of European society. After all, many of the great developments—industrialization, the growth of large cities, the spread of bureaucracy, increased social discipline, infinitely greater social mobility, the wearisome rat race for power—developments which had changed living conditions, customs and habits from top to bottom, were relatively recent and still provoked resistance which it would be idle to conceal. The war revealed, assimilated, sharpened deep anxieties of that nature, as we can see when we compare the words of such different and opposed observers as Trotsky and Stefan Zweig, who, on August 1, each on his own initiative, attended demonstrations in Vienna in favour of war.

"Hundreds of thousands of people," wrote Zweig, "then felt as never before what they should have felt in peacetime; that they belonged to one great unity. A city of two million inhabitants, a nation of nearly fifty million, understood in that hour that they were participating in world history and were living at a unique moment. All differences of class, language, religion were submerged in the powerful current.... Strangers exchanged friendly words along the way, people who had avoided each other for years wrung one another by the hand.... Each separate individual underwent an expansion of the 'I.' That is to say, the person was no longer isolated, but felt part of a great whole and of the people; his obscure self had found a reason for living. The humble post-office clerk who sorted letters from morning to night, the shop assistant, the cobbler, were suddenly aware of a new romantic possibility in their lives. Everyone was potentially a hero, and anyone in uniform was made much of by the women and given that title in advance.... All recognized that an unknown force was relieving the monotony of everyday life; even pain and anguish ... were concealed for very shame. But it may be that some deeper and more mysterious force played a part in the exaltation ... a desire, perhaps, to break away from the middle-class world of laws and paragraphs to give vent to more primitive instincts."

Trotsky saw things from a very different angle:

"There are so many people whose lives go on from day to day in a monotony without hope. It is they who bear the burden of contemporary society. Mobilization came into their lives like a promise. Everything they were used to and weary of was cast aside as the reign of the new and strange took over.... War had taken possession of everything, and consequently the oppressed, those whom life had disappointed, felt on a level with the rich and powerful...."

The Illusion of a Short War

So the Europeans did not oppose—even supported—war and awaited it with confidence. Perhaps, too, they had not lost their belief in the possibility of an easy victory. They may have thought of it as a leap in the dark into adventure and the unknown. At all events they were sure it would not last long.

It was the final, extraordinary error of July 1914.

The lessons that might have been learned from the American War of Independence or the more recent Russo-Japanese war were forgotten. The point of reference was the Franco-Prussian War, in which mass armies and universal conscription had made their first triumphal appearance, but within the limits of a war of maneuver. Now all the Great Powers disposed of armies numbering millions, and yet the fighting was expected to proceed according to the old rules.

"It could become another Seven-Year, or Thirty Years' war," with all the terrible additions imposed by the rise of the contemporary Great Powers. It was the victor of 1870, old von Moltke himself, who uttered the warning, but no one listened. Especially not von Schlieffen, who had no hesitation, if only because, in his opinion, no great industrial state could afford the "luxury" of a long-term war which would constitute a prolonged change in its economy. The episode was typical, and the illusion of a "short war" illuminates, perhaps better than any other, the general state of mind in that European summer.

"You will be back home before the leaves have fallen from the trees," the Kaiser promised. "It will be over by Christmas," was the English slogan. The words reveal how far they were from

reality. The destructive power of the Great War was largely derived from just such irremediable separation between intention and result.

When the illusion was inevitably abandoned the consequent change of mood was accompanied by a sort of somber resignation. Perhaps, with hindsight, historians are too apt to discern warning signs, but here the evidence is plain and the various witnesses confirm each other's testimony.

"A war with Russia would be the end of us. . . . The Emperor of Austria and the Tsar would hardly be the ones to cause each other's fall and open the way to revolution!" Those words uttered by the Emperor Franz Josef in 1913 make an ironical counterpoint with the sentiment expressed by Lenin in the same year: "A war between Austria and Russia would be of great assistance to the revolution, but it is unlikely that Franz Josef and Nicholas will give us that pleasure. . . ."

The Russian Minister of the Interior was fully aware of the situation. "In our land," he said, "war cannot be popular with the lower mass of the people. The idea of revolution means much more to them than a victory over Germany. . . ." There was nothing to do but resign oneself.

In 1914 the Europeans went to meet that fate in an irreparably divided spirit. The words spoken by the British Foreign Secretary, Sir Edward Grey, late on August 3, the day on which the House of Commons approved the harsh demands of power politics, might almost serve as an epilogue to the *Belle Époque*, and suggest that the illusion of a short war had already faded a little. "The lamps are going out all over Europe. We shall not see them lit again in our lifetime."

Chronology

1900

PORTRAIT OF HEROES—From the Atlantic to the Red Sea (*Revue Illustrée*, Paris, January 1, 1900)
A French expedition under the command of Captain Marchand crosses Africa from the Congo to Abyssinia.

PUCCINI'S *TOSCA* IN ROME (*Il Secolo*, Milan, January 13–14, 1900)
The first performance of Puccini's opera based on a celebrated drama by the French playwright Sardou.

BARONESS NATHANIEL DE ROTHSCHILD'S BEQUESTS TO THE LOUVRE (*Gazette des Beaux-Arts*, Paris, January 1900)
They include, among other things, a Botticelli Madonna and a Ghirlandaio.

HE IS DEAD (*Il Pasquino*, Turin, January 28, 1900)
John Ruskin, English painter, philosopher, social reformer and art critic, dies.

A NEW NOVEL BY COUNT TOLSTOY (*Revue des Deux Mondes*, Paris, February 15, 1900)
Resurrection by Leo Tolstoy published in two parts (by Perrin).

THE FIRST LECTURE ON GIORDANO BRUNO BY PROFESSOR LABRIOLA
In spite of opposition by the authorities, the Marxist historian gives a series of lectures in Rome on Giordano Bruno in honour of his third centenary.

RELIEF OF LADYSMITH— DUNDONALD ENTERS THE CITY, OFFICIAL (London news vendors' posters, March 1, 1900)
Announcement of an important military action in the Transvaal during the Boer War.

FIRE AT THE THÉÂTRE FRANÇAIS (*Illustrazione Italiana*, Milan, March 11, 1900)
The theater of the Comédie Française, founded in 1680 by Louis XIV and first directed by Molière, destroyed by fire, March 8. A young actress, Jane Herbert, perished in the flames.

ROSTAND'S *L'AIGLON* (*La Tribuna*, Milan, March 17, 1900)
First performance in Paris with Sarah Bernhardt. A great success with the public.

THE MODERN BICYCLE (*Illustrazione Italiana*, Milan, March 18, 1900)
An article on the spread of the bicycle, a new springtime means of locomotion for all classes.

For the European reader on the threshold of the twentieth century the most gripping newspaper articles were those dealing with the Far East: the Boxer Rebellion. As reports came through of violence against foreigners, the ambiguity of the Widow Empress Tz'u-hsi, the siege of the legations, the multinational military intervention, relief columns marching from the coast to Peking, the sacking that followed the Western victory, all set against a background of the "white" powers' political plans to divide up China, the events in the Celestial Empire were perhaps the first, embryonic opportunity for the new society of mass communication to realize how much the world and its destiny were interdependent. Below, in a contemporary photograph, a group of "Boxers" (the word was a rough translation of the secret society's name "Fists of Justice and Concord." The society was especially active in the provinces of Shantung and Chihli); on the right, a German cartoon: urged on by War, a pack of dogs—the Powers— prepare to attack the dying China.

THE BRIGAND MUSOLINO, AUTOBIOGRAPHER (*La Tribuna*, Rome, March 28, 1900)
A letter to the newspaper from the legendary Calabrian brigand, in which he declares himself to be a criminal not by nature, but through having been unjustly condemned.

GABRIELLANDO (*L'Uomo di Pietra*, Milan, March 31, 1900)
A humorous and satirical article on D'Annunzio, with sentences composed from the titles of his best-known works.

THE FIRE by Gabriele D'Annunzio (*Fanfulla della Domenica*, Rome, April 8, 1900)
A review of D'Annunzio's new novel.

THE 1900 UNIVERSAL EXHIBITION—The city of Paris's exhibition— The United States at the Exhibition— The Palace of Electricity—Old Paris— The Palace of Optics: the moon four

kilometers away—The moving staircase —The Avenue of Nations—The Decennial Exhibition of Fine Arts— The Centennial Exhibition of Electricity —Italy at the Exhibition—The British Pavilion—Music from all countries. (Extracts from *Exposition Universelle de 1900*, Paris, a guidebook to the Exhibition)

TERRIBLE CATASTROPHE IN A NORTH AMERICAN MINE. 250 VICTIMS (*La Sera*, Milan, May 2–3, 1900)
Huge gas explosion in a coal mine at Coalville (Utah, U.S.A.) near the Great Salt Lake.

GRAVE SITUATION IN SPAIN: FEARS OF A GENERAL REVOLUTION (*La Sera*, Milan, May 13–14, 1900)
Riots and demonstrations in the larger Spanish towns: an anarchist revolution is feared.

THE SENTIMENTAL SECRET (*Figaro*, Paris, May 20, 1900)
An article by Marcel Prévost on D'Annunzio's *The Fire*. Its aggressive tone leads to a fiery exchange of letters between the two writers.

THE VICTORY OF DEMOCRACY IN BELGIUM (*Il Secolo*, Milan, June 1, 1900)
Proportional representation adopted for the first time in the elections: politicians and journalists come from all over the world to act as observers.

THE BOXER REBELLION AND THE IMPOTENCE OF GREAT BRITAIN (*Il Secolo*, June 7–8, 1900)
Boxer rebellion breaks out in China. Britain fears intervention from Russia and is concerned for her economic interests, but the Boer War is using all her military resources.

EVENTS IN CHINA—EUROPEAN TROOPS—GRAVE EVENTS FORESEEN (*Il Secolo*, Milan, June 14–15, 1900)
30,000 men and many guns wait outside Peking for the arrival of the international troops.

WAR WITH CHINA INEVITABLE —FOREIGN LEGATIONS IN PEKING DESTROYED—THE GERMAN MINISTER ASSASSINATED (*Il Secolo*, Milan, June 17–18, 1900)

THREE HUNDRED EUROPEAN SOLDIERS KILLED—A HUNDRED THOUSAND MEN NEEDED IN CHINA (*Il Secolo*, Milan, June 25–26, 1900)
300 men of the European army massacred. It is reckoned that the Powers ought to intervene with 100,000 men to quell the revolt.

AUGUSTE RODIN EXHIBITION (*Revue Illustrée*, Paris, July 1, 1900)
This great French sculptor exhibits a wider selection of his works in Paris.

CORRESPONDENCE BETWEEN NIETZSCHE AND HEINRICH VON STEIN (*Neue Deutsche Rundschau*, Berlin, July 1900)
Appearing after the death of the great German philosopher, a hitherto unpublished correspondence between him and another prominent figure in the German cultural world.

A GALLANT LAW (*Il Pasquino*, Turin, July 8, 1900)
A matter that will be discussed for a long time: the proposal for a law allowing the adulterer responsible for a divorce to marry his mistress. (The Turin journal rejects the proposal with contempt, taking it to be put forward only as a joke.)

KING UMBERTO ASSASSINATED AT MONZA. The first report—The attack—THE KING IS DEAD!—The assassin named (*Corriere della Sera*, Milan, July 31, 1900)
The anarchist Gaetano Bresci murders King Umberto I at Monza. The nation's anger and sorrow is intense. The culprit is arrested.

OBITUARY: Death of Liebknecht (*Corriere della Sera*, Milan, August 1900)
Died in Berlin: one of the fathers of German socialism. With Bebel he founded the Social-Democratic Workers' Party.

CLEO DE MERODE (*Revue Illustrée*, Paris, August 15, 1900)
The life of one of the most celebrated dancers of Paris: very beautiful, she specialized in exotic dances, travelled in America and earned up to 200 francs a month [sic].

CHINA. "By the time these lines are in print, the Allied forces will probably be at any rate under the walls of Peking" (*The Illustrated London News*, August 18, 1900)

A JOURNALIST INTERVIEWS the famous brigand Musolino a thousand meters above sea level (*Corriere della Sera*, Milan, August 19–20, 1900)
He is a fair, handsome young man, intelligent, with lively eyes. He speaks feelingly of the sisters who cared for him, but says he has not yet completed the extermination of his enemies. What if he is captured? He displays a phial of strychnine.

THE TENOR BORGATTI IN DANGER OF BEING SHOT IN *TOSCA*! (*Corriere della Sera*, Milan, August 21–22, 1900)
At the Grand Theater, Brescia: during a rehearsal of the firing-squad scene a bolt came from the barrel of one of the guns and hit the actor in the groin. The singer staggered, clutched his hand to his lower abdomen and pirouetted two or three times, crying "Murderers!" But he was not badly hurt.

LONG-DISTANCE PHOTO-GRAPHY (illustrated Sunday edition of *Il Secolo*, Milan, September 2, 1900)
On the invention of the telephoto lens by Steinheil, Dallmeyer and Miethe, and on the more manageable, practical and popular version by Francesco Negri.

A JOURNALISTIC REVOLUTION (*Il Tempo*, Rome, September 5, 1900)
The invention of the first teleprinter (telegraphic typewriter) appears to open a new era in journalistic communication.

FINE ART AND UGLY ART (*L'Uomo di Pietra*, Milan, September 8, 1900)
A humorously ironical article on varnishing day at the Fourth Triennial Exhibition of Fine Arts at Brera (Milan).

HE HAS COME BACK! (*Il Pasquino*, Turin, September 9, 1900)
The Duke of Abruzzi has returned from his arctic expedition in the ship Stella Polare. Italy is proud of her famous and noble explorer.

PRESIDENTIAL ELECTION IN THE UNITED STATES. An overwhelming victory for McKinley. (*Corriere della Sera*, November 8–9, 1900)

DEATH OF OSCAR WILDE (*Corriere della Sera*, Milan, December 1–2, 1900)
"The famous English author Oscar Wilde died yesterday evening in Paris in a small hotel in the Rue des Beaux Arts under the assumed name of Sebastian Melmoth."

THE INTERNATIONAL SOCIALIST CONGRESS. Middle-class socialism (*Revue des Deux Mondes*, Paris, December 1, 1900)
An appreciation and report on the Congress of the Socialist International recently ended in Paris.

THE SEA DEVIL (*North American Review*, New York, December 15, 1900)
This refers to the submarine, here fully described by one of its inventors and perfectors, John P. Holland.

ZOLA WRITES TO LOUBET. Another campaign for Dreyfus—Unjust amnesty—The fifth act—The truth rests in the hands of Wilhelm II. (*Corriere della Sera*, Milan, December 22–23, 1900)
The French newspaper *L'Aurore* publishes a new letter from Zola on the Dreyfus affair. The pardon and amnesty granted by the government were designed only to suppress the truth.

SORMA WEEPS WHEN COMPARED TO DUSE. Theatrical tour interrupted (*Corriere della Sera*, Milan, December 23 24, 1900)
Vienna: On reading the newspaper reviews of her interpretation of Nora in Ibsen's *A Doll's House*, in which she was compared unfavourably to Duse, the famous actress fainted, wept all day, interrupted the tour and declared that she would retire from the stage for a long time.

THE HOLY YEAR OF 1900 (*Le Correspondant*, Paris, December 25, 1900)
A short history of the Holy Year, instituted by Pope Boniface VIII in the fourteenth century, is issued on the occasion of the closing of the Holy Year in Rome.

TRISTAN AND ISOLDE, musical drama in three acts by RICHARD WAGNER (*Corriere della Sera*, Milan, December 30–31, 1900)
The well-attended first night at the Scala, Milan, is conducted by Toscanini: a brilliant success.

1901

ROME SALUTES THE NEW CENTURY. 500 doves released. (*Corriere della Sera*, Milan, January 1–2, 1901)

THE REPUBLIC OF AUSTRALIA (*Il Secolo*, Milan, January 7–8, 1901) Australia declares itself a republic. The first parliament will be solemnly inaugurated on May 10.

COMMUNICATION BETWEEN THE EARTH AND MARS. Who believes in it and who doesn't. (*Corriere della Sera*, Milan, January 10–11, 1901) Sir Robert Ball holds a conference on "possible communication between Mars and earth." The celebrated astonomer says he is skeptical, but in the *Corriere* the Italian Nicola Tesia replies, "In a short while we shall be in communication with Mars."

A MASKED BALL BY PIETRO MASCAGNI in Italy (*Il Secolo*, Milan, January 18–19, 1901) Simultaneous first performances at the Scala, Milan, and in other Italian cities: Rome, Turin, Genoa, Venice and Verona. Triumphant success.

ARNOLD BÖCKLIN (*Il Secolo*, Milan, January 19–20, 1900) The great Swiss painter dies in Florence aged 74.

DEATH OF QUEEN VICTORIA OF GREAT .BRITAIN. The last moments—the death. (*Corriere della Sera*, Milan, January 23–24, 1901) National mourning in Britain for the death of the Queen. (A few days later Edward VII was proclaimed king.)

DEATH OF GIUSEPPE VERDI. Verdi is dead. After a final crisis lasting nearly fifty hours the glorious old man passed away at 2:50 A.M. (*Corriere della Sera*, Milan, January 27–28, 1901) (The newspapers, especially those of Milan, appeared edged in black for more than a week.)

THE PAN-AMERICAN EXHIBITION AT BUFFALO (*Frank Leslie's Popular Monthly*, New York, February 1901) How the coming Pan-American Exhibition will celebrate the triumph of electricity.

THE SAN MALATO–DALMOTTE DUEL, January 20, 1901 (*Revue Illustrée*, Paris, February 15, 1901) A photographic record of the duel at the Parc des Princes Stadium which has filled the pages of the Parisian press.

CRISIS OF FRENCH SOCIALISM (*Die Neue Zeit*, Berlin, February 2, 1901) Rosa Luxembourg (who signs the article) criticizes the participation of French socialists, led by Jaurès, in the bourgeois government.

TOLSTOY'S THOUGHTS ON GOD (*Die Zeit*, Berlin, February 16, 1901) "God does wrong! But if God does wrong, he is not good: hence he does not exist at all." Unpublished ideas of the great Russian writer.

THE STEEL KING (*Il Secolo*, Milan, February 23–24, 1901) Andrew Carnegie, the legendary American millionaire, is retiring from the world of business, yielding his place to Pierpont Morgan, another famous industrial magnate.

VIE PARISIENNE. The revival of pornography (*Il Secolo*, Milan, February 27–28, 1901) After the good work done by the Moralist League led by jurist René Bérenger (known as *Père-la-Pudeur*), it is to be regretted that pornographic displays, novels and publications are being revived.

A SCIENTIFIC–INDUSTRIAL REVOLUTION? THE SOLAR ENGINE (*Domenica del Corriere*, Milan, March 3, 1901) Perfected by Dr. W. Calver of Washington, it can raise 6300 liters of water per minute from a great depth. It is at present working on an ostrich farm in California.

FROM OUCHY: Déroulade and Buffet expelled from the canton of Vaud. The duel will not take place. (*Corriere della Sera*, Milan, March 15–16, 1901) The interminable preparations for a duel between these two politicians of opposing views have filled the newspapers for a month. But with all the journalists informed of the date and highly secret meeting place in Switzerland, the opponents were expelled by the local authority. Honour is satisfied and the duel will not take place.

RIOTS IN RUSSIA. Massacre of students in St. Petersburg. (*Il Secolo*, Milan, March 29–30, 1901) General Kleygel's cossack cavalry slaughters students and workers assembled in the Winter Palace Square. The cavalry charge continued through the streets. Dozens were killed or wounded.

A CURIOUS FASHION IN LONDON HIGH SOCIETY (*Corriere della Sera*, Milan, April 5–6, 1901) There is a craze for tattooing, which even gentlemen are having done on the less exposed parts of their bodies.

THE FRANCO–ITALIAN CELEBRATION AT TOULON (*Il Secolo*, Milan, April 12–13, 1901) Great festivities and ceremony mark the Italo-French meeting between the Duke of Genoa and President Loubet: speeches, naval reviews and banquets.

MILLIONAIRE STEALS "THE DUCHESS OF DEVONSHIRE"— Story of the discovery—A theological case. (*Corriere della Sera*, Milan, April 16–17, 1901) A mysterious robber-millionaire steals the famous painting and takes it (presumably) to New York. Then opens negotiations for its return.

TERRIBLE DISASTER NEAR FRANKFURT. 100 dead—150 injured. (*Il Secolo*, Milan, April 26–27, 1901) A terrible explosion destroys a chemical works at Griesheim.

OPENING OF THE VENICE EXHIBITION. The Venice Exhibition and foreigners (*Il Secolo*, Milan, April 28–29, 1901) The Fourth International (*Biennale*) of Venice is opened. Works by Rodin, Fontanesi, Leibl and Nono are on view.

FIELD DAY AT THE NEW YORK STOCK EXCHANGE. War between two coalitions—Frenzied scenes. (*Corriere della Sera*, Milan, May 11–12, 1901) Titanic struggle between the great names of industry and finance. Morgan and Vanderbilt fight Gould and Rockefeller for control of the Northern Pacific Railway.

THE AUTOMOBILE TOUR OF ITALY backed by *Corriere della Sera*. 15th day—arrival in Milan. (*Corriere della Sera*, May 12–13, 1901) The first motorcar rally around Italy comes to an end.

SUICIDE OF THE REGICIDE BRESCI (*Corriere della Sera*, Milan, May 24–25, 1901) In the Santo Stefano prison (Ventotene Island) the anarchist Gaetano Bresci committed suicide by hanging himself from the prison bars. Only much later was it suggested that he may have been murdered.

THE TRIBULATIONS OF ITALIANS IN CANADA. Unemployed—Exploited—False promises—Vain efforts—What can be done? (*Corriere della Sera*, Milan, May 26–27, 1901) A whole front-page article: the paper's extensive inquiry into the problems of Italian emigration to Canada.

THE LIVING TOMB IN POITIERS. Everyone knew, but no one talked (*Corriere della Sera*, Milan, May 27–28, 1901): a lady, Blanche Monnier, whose parents kept her locked in a filthy cellar for 25 years. Friends and relations knew of it, but thought she was mad.

EDMOND ROSTAND, AN IMMORTAL (*Scena Illustrata*, Florence, June 1, 1901)
The author of the highly successful play, *Cyrano de Bergerac*, is elected to the Academy. He is the youngest member of that renowned French cultural institution.

THE QUEEN'S BABY. A princess born. (*Corriere della Sera*, Milan, June 1–2, 1901)
At nine o'clock on the first of June Queen Helena gave birth to a baby girl who will be christened Yolanda.

THE GERMAN EXPEDITION TO THE PACIFIC FINISHES AS A MEAL FOR CANNIBALS (*Corriere della Sera*, Milan, June 7–8, 1901)
A scientific expedition led by Herr Monke and the ornithologist Heinroth is massacred by cannibals on the island of San Maltia (New Guinea).

GOVERNMENT POLICY ON STRIKES CLARIFIED by Giolitti in the Chamber of Deputies (*Corriere della Sera*, Milan, June 22–23, 1901)
The need for complying with the law and seeing that it is respected. The government should remain neutral in disputes between management and employees, or at most encourage reconciliation.

WHAT THE "PARIS–BERLIN RUN" MEANS TO US (*Corriere della Sera*, Milan, July 3–4, 1901)
An interview with the Frenchman Henri Fournier at the banquet celebrating his victorious motorcar run from Paris to Berlin in 16 hours, 55 minutes, 42 seconds.

EDISON'S ACCUMULATOR. Is the news true?—Its history—A chapter of accidents—What the "lead horses" cost and weigh—How Edison's accumulator is made—Comparisons—The accumulator and the motorcar—When will experiments begin in Italy? (*Corriere della Sera*, Milan, July 13–14, 1901)

EXPERIMENTS IN AERIAL NAVIGATION—SANTOS DUMONT'S BALLOON AROUND THE EIFFEL TOWER (*Illustrazione Italiana*, Milan, July 21, 1901)
An unlucky first attempt: the famous Brazilian aeronaut Dumont tries to win the prize offered by Deutsch de la Meurthe to anyone circling the Eiffel Tower in a balloon. He succeeded only partially and ended up hanging from a tree in a villa garden, where he was subsequently offered tea. He will surely succeed in his next attempt.

ARRIGO BOITO'S PLAY *NERO* (*Scena Illustrata*, Florence, July 1–15, 1901)
A new tragedy by Arrigo Boito published in two fine editions by Treves and Ricordio.

FROM LONDON: ANTI-TUBERCULOSIS CONFERENCE. Koch's view opposed. (*Corriere della Sera*, Milan, July 24–25, 1901)
The importance of prevention (avoid infection), as well as healing and public information, stressed by the great German scientist Robert Koch. His assertion that there was no possibility of man–animal infection roused debate.

DIFFERENT WAYS OF MAKING A LIVING—THE SCAVENGERS OF PARIS (*Domenica del Corriere*, Milan, August 25, 1901)
These are the people who scour the boulevards in search of money dropped by passersby. It seems they manage to pick up a franc or a franc and a half a day, or sometimes even two or three. Their favourite hunting grounds are roads reserved for equestrians.

ELECTRIC RAILWAY WITH A THIRD RAIL (*Illustrazione Italiana*, Milan, September 1, 1901)
A third electric rail used for the first time on the Milan–Gallarate–Varese railway.

A NEW WAGNER THEATER IN GERMANY. The Prince Regent Theater—A historic event—The building—*Tristan and Isolde*—German singing—A democratic prince—A rival to Bayreuth? (*Corriere della Sera*, Milan, September 6–7, 1901)
A grand-opera house built at Munich in honour of the regent, Leopold of Bavaria. The theater, which holds 1200 seats, will open with the Wagnerian opera *Tristan and Isolde*.

ANARCHIST ATTACK ON THE PRESIDENT OF THE UNITED STATES. McKinley wounded by two revolver shots (*Corriere della Sera*, Milan, September 6–7, 1901)
The president wounded at Buffalo, N.Y., during a visit to the Panamerican Exhibition. The assassin, a certain Leon Czolgosz, who declared himself to be a disciple of the notorious Emma Goldman, was arrested on the spot. The President's condition is grave. (He was to die about ten days later.)

A LITTLE ANTIFEMINISM (*Scena Illustrata*, Florence, September 15, 1901)
"Emancipation, in general, is a Utopia, because economically and legally women will always be inferior to men." Nature has not only endowed "the stronger sex with the necessary aptitude for ruling a family, but also with moral superiority...."

THE ANGLO–BOER WAR. Recent Boer victories—Critical conditions for the British—The effect of Kitchener's proclamation—The English press—A final disaster (*Corriere della Sera*, Milan, September 21–22, 1901)

UNFORTUNATE LITERATURE! (*Corriere della Sera*, Milan, October 13–14, 1901)
Trial of the anarchist poet Laurent Tailhade, accused of incitement to regicide in the journal *Le Libertaire*. The poet defended by Anatole France, Gustave Kahn and Émile Zola.

EXPLOITS AND CAPTURE OF THE BANDIT MUSOLINO (*Illustrazione Italiana*, Milan, October 27, 1901)
On October 9 the famous brigand Musolino was arrested in the mountains near Urbino, where for three years the police have been searching for him in vain. A price of 50,000 lire had been put on his now legendary head. The elusive bandit is charged with seven murders and six attempted murders.

A *CAUSE CÉLÈBRE*: THE PALIZZOLO TRIAL AT BOLOGNA (*Domenica del Corriere*, Milan, October 27, 1901)
Raffaele Palizzolo, several times deputy, holder of important government appointments at Palermo, Grand Officer of the Crown, is accused of having killed the administrator Francesco Miceli in 1892 and the commissioner E. Notebartolo in 1893. Palizzolo is conducting his own defense and the trial is expected to be long drawn out.

CROSSING NIAGARA by boat and barrel (*Corriere della Sera*, Milan, October 27–28, 1901)
A certain Peter Niszen of Chicago conquers the falls in a boat, while Mrs. Anne E. Taylor, a 43-year-old widow, throws herself over closed in a barrel, risking her life to pay a mortgage. She succeeds.

MECHANICAL AIDS FOR THE MIND (*La Lettura*, Milan, November 1901)
An article by the distinguished anthropologist Cesare Lombroso, in which he describes the new "wonderful machines that reduce physical and mental strain": the typewriter, voting machine, countmeter (ancestor of the calculator), the tachyanthropometer (an aid to forensic anthropology).

FROM PARIS—SCUFFLE BETWEEN THE BROTHERS. The right to remove (*Corriere della Sera*, Milan, November 16–17, 1901)
Brawls and fisticuffs between Italian Franciscans and Greek Orthodox monks at Jerusalem for the right to remove the small staircase leading to the

chapel of the Franks, adjacent to Calvary, and hence for possession of the same.

THE CABARETS OF MONTMARTRE (*Revue Universelle*, Paris, 1901)
Article on the celebrated bars and nightclubs where the Parisians used to, and still do, love to spend their evenings: the Tréteau de Tabarin, the Boîte à Fursy, the Grand Guignol and, above all, the Chat Noir, the legendary cabaret where Aristide Bruant, *chansonnier* of the Golden Age, used to perform.

GABRIELE D'ANNUNZIO'S *FRANCESCA DA RIMINI* AT THE COSTANZI IN ROME (*Corriere della Sera*, Milan, December 10–11, 1901)
The whole of the Roman world of literature and art present at the long-awaited first night of D'Annunzio's new work. Opinions were favourable but with reservations; some whistling, but more applause. Fights in the foyer between detractors and admirers. Duse a little nervous.

SOLEMN CEREMONIAL AT NOBEL PRIZE–GIVING (*Corriere della Sera*, Milan, December 11–12, 1901)
The first distribution of Nobel Prizes takes place in Paris: Roentgen for physics, van't Hoff for chemistry, Behring for physiology, Sully Prudhomme for literature, Dunant (founder of the Red Cross) and Passy for peace.

THE MOTORCAR AND BICYCLE SHOW (*Corriere della Sera*, Milan, December 15–16, 1901)
Huge crowds flock to the exhibition of motorcars, motor bicycles, bicycles and even vans and buses.

1902

BARNUM AND CO. (*L'Illustration*, Paris, January 4, 1902)
The great Barnum and Bailey Circus from America is in Paris.

THE NIGHTS OF THE PARISIAN MILKMEN. A matter of hygiene. (*Corriere della Sera*, Milan, January 17–18, 1902)
A real racket carried on by dairy delivery boys has been discovered: they deliver watered milk. They work with outside collaborators known as "acrobats" for the dexterity with which they load their vans with cans of milk, evading the watchful eyes of the police.

OBITUARY: FILIPPO MARCHETTI. The master musician and Queen Margherita—An anecdote. (*Corriere della Sera*, Milan, January 19–20, 1902)
The great Italian musician is dead. He was a great friend of the Queen, who once rebuked him for presenting himself without a tie. She was so amused by his embarrassment that she gave him one of her own.

THE DIVORCE PROJECT (*Corriere della Sera*, Milan, January 28–29, 1902)
The parliamentary commission is considering a proposal for new legislation: divorce after five years of separation if there are children; after three years if there are none. Alternatively, two years in the first case and one in the second if the family council gives its consent.

MARCONI'S VICTORY (*McClure's Magazine*, February 1902)
Marconi transmits a message across the Atlantic from Cornwall to Newfoundland.

FROM BERLIN: The new metropolitan electric line (*Corriere della Sera*, Milan, February 16–17–18, 1902)
The first stretch of the electric metropolitan railway was opened in Berlin.

FROM OUR PARIS CORRESPONDENT: the "*belle Otéro*" loses her case (*Corriere della Sera*, Milan, February 20–21, 1902)
The famous Otéro has lost her case for debt against the Englishman Bulpett, who, during his three-year relationship with her, spent a million and a half francs paid by the dancer for presents which he gave her.

FROM MADRID: REVOLUTIONARY RIOTS IN CATALONIA. Unrest continues—Mass arrests—Strange incidents—The anarchist Neri wounded —Attack on a convent—Parliament grants suspension of constitutional guarantees. (*Corriere della Sera*, Milan, February 20–21, 1902)
Diffused unrest among the people causes a general strike throughout the land. Result: the city and suburbs of Barcelona occupied by the military, workmen's clubs suspended, leaders arrested, schools, universities closed.

COMPLETION OF THE TRANS–SIBERIAN RAILWAY. A telegram from the Far East. How this colossal undertaking came into being. A look at Siberia. The original project. Rapidity of its construction. Across Baikal. A Russo-Chinese agreement. In Manchuria. (*Illustrazione Italiana*, Milan, February 23, 1902)
Conclusion of an immense and eagerly awaited enterprise. Running from Tcheliabinsk (Urals) to Vladivostok, the railway is the longest in the world. Passengers will be ferried across the Great Lake Baikal in a steamboat.

SCIENCE IN 1901 (*Popular Science Monthly*, March 1902)
Survey of scientific progress and discoveries during the past year: wireless telegraphy, electric underground railways, TB bacillus, liquid air, the mosquito as transmitter of malaria and yellow fever, radioactive bodies, ionization, etc.

THE TRAGIC POET (*L'Illustration*, Paris, March 22, 1902)
Catulle Mendès comes into a boulevard café: an excuse for describing the poet and playwright's appearance, character, gifts and refusal to compromise. Also his relationship with Sarah Bernhardt, great star and interpreter of his plays.

LAW ON WOMEN'S AND GIRLS' LABOUR (*Corriere della Sera*, Milan, March 26–27, 1902)
Passed in Parliament, it stipulates: children under 12 must not be employed (in cellars and mines, not under 14); children under 15 and underage women must not do dangerous work. Working hours: 8 hours a day for 12 years, 11 hours up to 15 years, 12 hours for women of any age.

EVENTS IN SOUTH AFRICA— DEATH OF CECIL RHODES (*Corriere della Sera*, Milan, March 27–28, 1902)
While the Boer War still continues Cecil Rhodes dies. Born a poor boy, then an Oxford student, makes a fortune in diamonds, becomes a "great man." Gave his name to Rhodesia.

ASSASSINATION OF SIPIAGUIN, Russian Minister of the Interior—The assassin's disguise—"An eye for an eye." (*Corriere della Sera*, Milan, April 16–17, 1902)
The murderer, Balschanev, Kiev student, wanted to vindicate his comrades, victims of police violence: discharged five bullets at point-blank range.

"CASQUE D'OR'S" LOVER ARRESTED IN BRUSSELS (*Corriere della Sera*, Milan, April 22–23, 1902)
Leca, the Parisian ringleader of the Apaches and the lover of "Casque d'Or" arrested in Brussels.

THE FIRST CONTRACT FOR TRANSATLANTIC WIRELESS TELEGRAPHY. From Great Britain to Canada—The charges— Competition for cables—At 60 percent!—25 centesimi a word— Provision for transmission from the United States to Europe. (*Corriere della Sera*, Milan, April 27–28, 1902)
Contract between Marconi's Wireless Telegraph Co. with Marconi's International Marine Communication Co. on the one hand and Mr. Wilfred Laurie, Prime Minister of Canada, on the other.

The Belle Époque *was punctuated by anarchist assassinations, successful or otherwise. The top picture shows the anarchist Leon Czolgosz shooting the President of the United States, McKinley, on September 6, 1901. In 1902 the Boer War was drawing to a close: the central illustration is a British propagandist cartoon of an armed Boer repelling the angel Peace, with her dove and olive branch. Below, Stephanus Johannes Kruger, the dictatorial governor of the Transvaal, one of the two Boer states (the Orange State was the other). Their incorporation into the British Empire was the cause of the war.*

GLEANINGS AND ODD FACTS. Demands of the actress Réjane (*Giornale della Donna*, Turin, April 30, 1902)
The celebrated actress Réjane insists on an author changing a part of his play because she does not want to be jilted, even on the stage. If he wants his heroine to be abandoned by the hero, he will have to find another actress. Incident at the Théâtre de Vaudeville, managed by Réjane's husband.

AERONAUTICAL CATASTROPHE IN PARIS due to the burning of the balloon Pax (*Corriere della Sera*, Milan, May 13–14, 1902)
The Brazilian deputy Severo fell from a height of 400 meters in his balloon and died immediately, together with the operator. The accident was due to a fire.

HERBERT SPENCER'S PHILO-SOPHICAL TESTAMENT (*Revue des Deux Mondes*, Paris, May 15, 1902)
Just published: *Facts and Comments*, in which the 82-year-old philosopher has collected the ideas left out of his other works.

THE CORONATION OF ALFONSO XIII—AN INCIDENT—On the throne of Spain (*Corriere della Sera*, Milan, May 18–19, 1902)
The son of Christina of Austria crowned King of Spain. False alarm of a supposed assassination attempt on the new sovereign as he goes to the Cortès.

INTERNATIONAL EXHIBITION of Modern Decorative Art opened at Turin (*Giornale della Donna*, Turin, May 31, 1902)
The exhibition confirms the triumph of Liberty and Co. and is accompanied by other public shows now in Turin: another art exhibition. *Strike* by Pellizza da Volpedo and paintings by Girardi, Calderini, Tavernier, Fontanesi, Previati.

PEACE BETWEEN GREAT BRITAIN AND THE BOERS. Statement in the House of Commons— Huge demonstrations of joy (*Corriere della Sera*, Milan, June 3–4, 1902)
The Boers surrender after three years of bloody war. Peace treaty signed by Lords Kitchener and Milner for Great Britain and Mr. Steyn and General de Wet for the Boers.

RETIREMENT OF WALDECK– ROUSSEAU and the ministerial crisis in France (*Corriere della Sera*, Milan, June 5–6, 1902)
His resignation after three years as President of the French Council leads to a crisis.

FROM HERE AND THERE: The hundred-million swindle—An extraordinary woman gets her deserts— Fantastic marriage—False diamonds—

A new labyrinth of Daedelus (*Giornale della Donna*, Turin, June 15, 1902)
Thérèse d'Aurignac weds Frédéric Humbert, professor of law and later president of the State Audit Office. Abetted by her sister, husband and brothers, she organizes a tremendous swindle. She claims to be the heiress to the hundred millions of a nonexistent Mr. Crawford and, on the basis of these expectations, runs up enormous debts. The fraud (known as the Humbert case) is discovered, fills the pages of the newspapers for months and takes its place in social-legal-political history.

CAFÉS, CONCERTS AND MUSIC HALLS (*Revue des deux Mondes*, Paris, July 1, 1902)
Hundreds of them in Paris alone, with an army of performers and singers coming from all classes of society. A few stand out above the crowd: Yvette Guilbert, who earns 25,000 francs a month; the "Belle Otéro," 30,000 francs in London; Gallois, 22,500 in Berlin; Cléo de Mérode, 40,000 francs at the Folies Bergères. Frégol, the quick-change artist, gets 400 francs a night at Olympia, more than 100,000 a month.

EDWARD VII GIVES A GIGANTIC BANQUET for half a million poor people in London (*Corriere della Sera*, July 6–7, 1902)
In various parts of London and neighbouring towns the poor received a personal invitation from the King to attend a banquet: tables for 90,000; 300,000 pounds of meat, 200 tons of potatoes, 36,000 gallons of beer.

A NEW PLANET BEYOND NEPTUNE? The limits of our planetary system—Marvellous astronomical discovery—An ultra-Neptunian planet? —A comet that saved a century of astronomical research (*Corriere della Sera*, Milan, July 7–8, 1902)
The astronomer Forbes reads a paper at the Royal Society of Edinburgh, basing his deductions on the modifications of a comet's orbit.

FALL OF THE ST. MARK BELLTOWER IN VENICE (*Illustrazione Italiana*, Milan, July 20, 1902)
The celebrated *campanile* of San Marco in Venice has collapsed, destroying the Sansovino balcony, a painting by Molin, two by Tintoretto and two by Schiavoni. The *Libreria Vecchia* also partly in ruins.

RELIGIOUS UNREST IN FRANCE. Demonstrations in the Place de la Concorde yesterday (*Corriere della Sera*, Milan, July 28–29, 1902)
The government orders the closing of all unauthorized sectarian schools. The public expresses violent dissent in a series of demonstrations.

THE TRIAL OF PALIZZOLO AND ACCOMPLICES—VERDICT AND SENTENCE. The last day. (*Corriere della Sera*, Milan, July 31–August 1, 1902)
The protracted trial started in 1901 ends in Bologna: the accused were pronounced guilty and sentenced to 30 years' imprisonment.

CORONATION OF EDWARD VII IN LONDON'S WESTMINSTER ABBEY. Britain's victory—The great day. (*Corriere della Sera*, Milan, August 19–20, 1902)

AN AMERICAN BANDIT. Tragic career—Two months of havoc—Dogs and men hunt the bandit—Unexpected end. (*Corriere della Sera*, Milan, August 19–20, 1902)
After a long criminal career Harry Tracy, run to earth by thousands of men and dogs, held the law at bay with incredible skill. He walked for over 1000 kilometers through parched and savage country. Surrounded at last, he shot himself rather than face arrest.

CLASS HATRED (*La Revue Bleue*, Paris, August 23, 1902)
Article by Theodore Roosevelt, suggesting that class hatred is growing because of a lack of communication between different social groups, the consequent impossibility of understanding one another and the ignorance of common feelings.

GRIEG'S OPINION OF VERDI (*Giornale della Donna*, Turin, August 31, 1902)
"Greater than Bellini, Rossini and Donizetti," Verdi is considered the only artist who can truly represent his country's emotional life. His masterpiece *Otello* was fully appreciated only by Wagner.

TOWARDS THE CONQUEST OF THE POLE. The return—A hero of the polar world—Hopes for the future—An Italian expedition. (*Corriere della Sera*, Milan, September 23–24, 1902)
Peary returns from the Pole beaten but not discouraged: after his 12 years of travelling he will try again.

A KING OF DANDIES (*Giornale della Donna*, Turin, September 30, 1902)
The banker Gordon has died in London. He used to buy 574 pairs of trousers a year and thousands of ties and gloves. He spent 50,000 francs a month on his clothes.

DEATH OF ÉMILE ZOLA (*L'Illustration*, Paris, October 4, 1902)
The great novelist died on September 29 in the hotel of the Rue de Bruxelles in Paris. There are rumours of suicide. The autopsy is poisoning, but it was probably from a gas stove left on by mistake.

JEAN JAURÈS and French socialism (*Die Zeit*, October 11, 1902)
Bernstein considers Jaurès a great speaker, an able writer, a historian of merit and the most French of French socialists.

THEATRICAL EVENT—THE GERMAN SOVEREIGNS AT SARAH BERNHARDT'S RECITAL (*Corriere della Sera*, Milan, October 30–31, 1902)
The great actress performs scenes from *Tosca* by the French playwright Sardou.

NEWS FROM PARIS—*Resurrection*, a play in 5 acts and a prologue, adapted from Tolstoy's novel by Henri Bataille (*Corriere della Sera*, Milan, November 14–15, 1902)
Interested expectation in the capital regarding the work drawn from Tolstoy, the apostle of the unabridged gospel, excommunicated by the Holy Synod.

ATTACK ON THE KING OF THE BELGIANS AT BRUSSELS (*Corriere della Sera*, Milan, November 16–17, 1902)
The culprit, the Italian anarchist Rubino, barely saved from the fury of the mob.

A BANQUET TO CELEBRATE THE COMPLETION OF THE ENCYCLOPAEDIA BRITANNICA (*Corriere della Sera*, Milan, November 23–24, 1902)

1903

A ROTHSCHILD SPORTSMAN, CONSTRUCTOR AND PHILANTHROPIST (*La Stampa Sportiva*, Turin, January 4, 1903)
Henri, of the French branch of the Rothschilds, portrayed while designing carriages, working at a lathe and mounting guard at a clinic for the needy.

SCIENTISTS' BANQUET TO HONOUR AN APE (*Corriere della Sera*, Milan, January 9, 1903)
A Congolese ape proves the validity of Darwin's theory, dining in a dinner jacket with some scientists and behaving in a perfectly civilized manner.

THE CAKEWALK (*L'Illustration*, Paris, January 10, 1903)
The new American Negro dance is the craze of Paris. The music hall star Fay Templeton popularizes the "kangaroo hop."

THE BIOGRAPHY OF A SKYSCRAPER (*The World's Work*, January 1903)
Description of how a great skyscraper (19 stories) is started and built in New York, and of the people who live and work in it.

BOXING. The champions of America and Europe (*La Stampa Sportiva*, Turin, February 1, 1903)
Portraits and careers of the famous boxers Sharkey (world champion), Ruklin, McGovern, Corbett, Munro and Fitzsimmons.

PETROL TRACTION. Advantages of the system—Experiments in Europe, America and Asia—Its use in Italy. (*La Tribuna*, Rome, February 22, 1903)

LAST DAY OF THE PARIS CARNIVAL (*La Tribuna*, Rome, February 26, 1903)
At least a million people crowd into the streets. By the evening there is a layer of confetti on the ground, at least 10 centimeters thick. The Apaches cause disturbances: 387 arrests.

A MANIFESTO FROM THE TSAR. Reforms in Russia. (*Il Secolo*, Milan, March 13–14, 1903)
As a result of strikes and riots, the Tsar promises certain reforms.

LOOPING THE LOOP (*L'Illustration*, Paris, March 14, 1903)
At Olympia and the Casino de Paris, Vandervoort, known as "Diavolo," and a certain Mephisto amaze the audience by performing acrobatic somersaults on a bicycle running along a vertically circular track.

EPIDEMIC OF SUICIDES (*Il Secolo*, Milan, March 26–27, 1903)
The widespread suicide mania (the newspapers are full of them) becomes worse with the coming of spring. In a single day in Milan there were two attempted suicides and one that succeeded.

NEW GHASTLY TRAGEDY IN RUSSIA. Details of a horrendous massacre (*Il Secolo*, Milan, March 31–April 1, 1903)
Replying to the Tsar's promises, the revolutionaries declare: "The people want deeds, not words." Arrests are followed by tumult in the streets, and the cossacks, infuriated, shoot at the crowd encircling them. More than 50 people are dead.

THE SARDINIAN NOVEL: GRAZIA DELEDDA (*Revue des Deux Mondes*, Paris, March 1903)
A long essay on the rising star of Italian literature appears in the authoritative French literary review.

The official visit of the new King of Great Britain, Edward VII, to Paris in May 1903, which greatly improved relations between the two powers who in 1898 had been close to war. Above, the King, on a later visit, is helping to plant a tree in honour of the Entente Cordiale alliance (1904).

The new century revolutionized clothes, including bathing costumes. The 1903 Punch *overleaf is eloquent.*

GENERAL STRIKE IN ROME a complete failure. Return to work. (*La Sera*, Milan, April 10, 1903)
The strike, started by 20,000 in a city garrisoned by 15,000 soldiers, ends miserably after only two days of nothing to do.

SANTOS DUMONT AT HOME (*La Stampa Sportiva*, Turin, April 19, 1903)
This keen aeronaut never forgets his life's aim, "to fly in space"—if only between domestic walls. For that reason (as the photograph shows) he eats sitting on a sort of raised armchair at a table 3 meters high.

LATEST EXECUTION IN VIENNA.
The criminal's extraordinary cynicism (*La Sera*, Milan, April 30–May 1, 1903)
Condemned man executed in Vienna for the murder of an old woman tobacconist. He went to the gallows smiling, head held high, and blasphemed before dying. Crime reporter greatly surprised when autopsy revealed that the hardened criminal's brain was "of perfectly normal conformation."

END OF A GREAT CARTHUSIAN MONASTERY. Vigil on the mountain. (*Corriere della Sera*, Milan, May 1–2, 1903)
The French government's campaign against religious orders continues. After nine hundred years the army turns the monks out of the famous monastery above St. Laurent. While soldiers break down the doors the brothers chant the *Parce Domine*.

A JOURNALIST'S PSYCHOLOGY (*La Revue*, Paris, May 15, 1903)
Andrew Carnegie has presented a library to Washington. In the opening speech his philanthropy was described as "helping people to help themselves."

VICE SQUAD IN PARIS (*Corriere della Sera*, Milan, May 21, 1903)
Prefect Lepine tells Paris municipal council that there are only 130 police officers to every 70,000 prostitutes. Councillors greatly perturbed to hear that 30,000 women are arrested every year.

TRAGIC MOTOR RALLY (*Revue Illustrée*, Paris, June 1, 1903)
A series of accidents casts a pall over the great, popular Paris–Berlin motorcar race. Marcel Renault loses his life.

BLOODY REVOLUTION IN SERBIA—KING ALEXANDER AND QUEEN DRAGA ASSASSINATED in their palace in Belgrade on the night between June 10 and 11 (*L'Illustration*, Paris, June 15, 1903)
Leader of the conspiracy, Karageorgevic, claimant to the throne, now proclaimed king. Declares intention to restore democratic constitution, and summon parliament June 18.

SPREAD OF CANCER (*The Nineteenth Century and After*, June 1903)
The disease of the century is found almost everywhere. Worrying radiographic evidence of its diffusion.

BIG AUTOMOBILE RACE IN IRELAND for the Gordon Bennett Cup (*Corriere della Sera*, Milan, July 2–3, 1903)
If the rally is a success, Gordon Bennett, owner of the *New York Herald*, will repeat it under the name of the Motor Derby. (The winner was the Belgian Jenatzky, driving at a speed of 60 mph.)

MOTORCAR ACCIDENT TO ITALIAN ROYAL FAMILY. King and Queen thrown from car—Queen sprains foot—Rest for a month—Grave rumours denied (*Corriere della Sera*, Milan, July 16–17, 1903)

AUSTRALIAN WOMEN TO THE POLLS—Their program (*Corriere della Sera*, Milan, July 18–19, 1903)
Equality of sexes and labour; hygienic control of imported foodstuffs; opium to be banned; voluntary army only; tribunals to arbitrate on management-worker disputes. Women are voting for the first time.

LEO XIII, PATRON AND SCHOLAR (*Illustrazione Italiana*, Milan, July 26, 1903)
Leo XIII dies after a long illness. He is succeeded by Pius X.

TOUR DE FRANCE (*La Stampa Sportiva*, Turin, July 26, 1903) End of long race: 2400 kilometers in 19 days. Won by Vince Garin in little over 94 hours.

UNDERGROUND DISASTER IN PARIS (*Illustrazione Italiana*, Milan, August 23, 1903)
Two trains (16 carriages) of Paris *métro* on fire. Scenes of panic. 84 victims.

CONVICTION OF HUMBERTS AT COURT OF ASSIZES. The last sitting—Teresa's latest revelation—Name of the false Crawford—The traitor: not Bazaine but Regnier—Who he was—Impressions (*La Tribuna*, Rome, August 24, 1903)
Hundred-million fraud trial ends. Humbert couple sentenced. Strong expression of public opinion.

BALKAN REBELLION. *Carte blanche* for the sultan?—Unrest in Sofia (*Il Secolo*, Milan, September 1–2, 1903)
Russia and Austria give the sultan *carte blanche*, knowing he will suppress the rebellion by whatever means. The Tsar wants everything to be over before his visit to Vienna.

INVENTOR OF THE TELEPHONE PROPHESIES A FLYING MACHINE (*Corriere della Sera*, Milan, October 1, 1903)
Professor Graham Bell is immersed in study. No one who studies birds, he says, can doubt that human beings are capable of flight. Experiments begin in a few months' time.

A MODERN ROYAL PAIR (*La Revue*, Paris, October 1903)

Portrait of Victor Emmanuel III and Queen Helena: culture, charm, dislike of pomp and splendour, love of right and justice. At Racconigi, the Queen receives groups of peasant children and hands out sweets.

FROM PARIS: PUCCINI'S VISIT. The maestro's leg—The first steps—Susceptibility of Italian doctors—*Tosca*. (*Corriere della Sera*, Milan, October 4, 1903)
The maestro takes his first steps after breaking his leg. He is in Paris partly to attend rehearsals of *Tosca*, but above all to buy a new car.

DUSE IN LONDON—Irving in America (*Corriere della Sera*, Milan, October 15, 1903)
Rain of flowers for Duse at first night of *Francesca da Rimini* in London; enthusiastic reviews. English actor Henry Irving has taken *Dante* to America, a play specially written for him by Sardou.

PARIS TO LONDON BY BALLOON (*Revue Scientifique*, Paris, October 24, 1903)
Daring flight across Channel to England by Henri de la Veaulx.

WHAT AMERICA SPENDS ON ADVERTISING (*The Chatauquan*, October 1903)
Total cost runs to hundreds of thousands: for these days an astronomical figure.

MORE THAN A HUNDRED "MIDINETTES" IN A RACE (*La Sera*, Milan, November 1–2, 1903)
The dressmakers' track event.

MISS LOIE FULLER (*Revue Illustrée*, Paris, November 1, 1903)
"An incomparable dancer admired and applauded all over the world": a portrait of Isadora Duncan's teacher.

NEW MINISTRY FINALLY SETTLED. There at last.
GIOLITTI CABINET COMPLETE (*La Sera*, Milan, November 1–4, 1903)

AFTER A THREE-AND-A-HALF-YEAR STRIKE (*La Sera*, Milan, November 8–9, 1903)
After three years the strike at Penryn mines has ended without result (Wales, Great Britain).

MATHILDE SERAO RESIGNS FROM EDITING *IL MATTINO*. Official announcement (*La Sera*, Milan, November 13–14, 1903)
Serao is the wife, separated by mutual consent, of Scarfoglio, the newspaper's director.

INSULT TO THE ITALIAN FLAG BY DENATIONALIZED COWARDS (*La Sera*, Milan, November 13–14, 1903)
At Trenton, New Jersey (U.S.A.) Italian socialist extremists and anarchists stoned the windows of their own consulate.

LUCA BELTRAMI AND A CRITIC'S FANTASIES (*Giornale d'Italia*, November 12–13, 1903)
Bitter argument between architects Calderini and Beltrami about the rebuilding of St. Mark's belltower in Venice.

A RUSTIC DUEL. The son of Senator Roux stands up to the notorious Ferri—Ferri the provoker. (*La Sera*, Milan, November 14–15, 1903)
To avenge an insult to his father, the senator's son had a fight with sticks and fists against the "notorious charlatan, Ferri," parliamentary socialist.

A NEW MEANS OF TRANSPORT. From gypsy van to motor-driven house (*La Stampa Sportiva*, Turin, November 22, 1903)
A luxurious, four-wheeled motor caravan divided into separate rooms, with kitchen and bunk for servant. Travels at 15–18 kilometers per hour.

FIRST NIGHT OF *TALES OF HOFFMAN* AT BOLOGNA (*La Sera*, Milan, November 29–30, 1903)
Brilliant success of Offenbach's opera, new to Italy.

"RADIUM" AND ITS PROPERTIES. Becquerel's discoveries—Madame Curie and "radium"—Development of spontaneous heat—Transformations of the atom—Latest experiments at Ramsay (*La Tribuna*, Rome, December 5, 1903)
Recent experiments on the new element isolated in 1898 by the French man-and-wife team, Pierre and Marie Curie.

FREE UNIVERSITY AT INNSBRUCK—ITALIAN UNIVERSITY AT TRIESTE (*Illustrazione Italiana*, Milan, December 6, 1903)
The former closed. Students fight and demonstrate because it may also happen to the latter. Frequent clashes

between Italian and German students and the police.

HERBERT SPENCER (*Il Regno*, Florence, December 13, 1903)
Giovanni Papini's article on the death of the famous English philosopher: "H.S. is an outstanding example of how in the Western world today it is possible to gain a reputation as a great philosopher without having done any philosophy."

THE SECOND VOLUME OF D'ANNUNZIO'S EULOGIES (*La Tribuna*, Rome, December 20, 1903)
The reporter says, "G. D'Annunzio gives his critics no time to draw breath. His pace is a forced march."

1904

SPORT: WOLF HUNTING (*La Tribuna*, Rome, January 12, 1904)
Wolf hunting in the Capannelle (Rome), outside the city. Colonels, dukes, princes, marquises, knights, ambassadors, both Italian and foreign, and even five ladies, take part.

DEATH OF PROFESSOR LABRIOLA (*La Tribuna*, Rome, February 3, 1904)
Professor Antonio Labriola has died in Rome. A Hegelian philosopher and later a Marxist, he was the pupil of Spaventa and author of the book *Historical Materialism*.

CITY OF BALTIMORE IN FLAMES. A hundred million worth of damage. No loss of human life (*La Tribuna*, Rome, February 10, 1904)
The famous burning of Baltimore City (U.S.A.): a terrible disaster that will pass into American folklore.

WAR BREAKS OUT. Naval battle at Chemulpo and Port Arthur—Bombardment of Vladivostok (*The Russo-Japanese War Fully Illustrated*, Tokyo, January–March 1904)
According to the Japanese, the Russo-Japanese War was caused by the insolent attitude of Russia and her refusal to give any explanation of the massing of ships and troops in Manchuria. For these reasons, after patient but fruitless negotiations, Japan sees herself as forced to declare war in order to preserve peace in the East.

FIRST PERFORMANCE OF *MADAMA BUTTERFLY* AT THE SCALA. Expectations—Account of the performance—The work of art (*La Tribuna*, Rome, February 19, 1904)
Puccini's long-awaited opera is shown before a large public and turns out to be a failure.

JORIO'S DAUGHTER AT THE LYRIC, MILAN (*La Tribuna*, Milan, March 4, 1904)
Great success, of course, for the new and much-looked-forward-to tragedy by Gabriele D'Annunzio. The poet himself was present.

THE PINI vs. SAN MALATO DUEL AT NEUILLY. Eighteen rounds—Pini scratched—Reconciliation (*La Tribuna*, Rome, March 7, 1904)
The duel took place in the Cherry establishment, to which a special train had brought a party of English spectators. General enthusiasm: "*Ce sont des lions!*" A blister on the hands prevents San Malato from continuing; the duel is suspended, the adversaries are reconciled and honour is satisfied.

THE CELEBRATED ARRIGO BOITO, artist, poet, musician, among many other things, says "*Lodo Odol*" (Italian for "I praise Odol"). People who clean their teeth with Odol keep them always white and healthy. (Advertisement for Odol toothpaste in *La Tribuna*, Rome, March 9, 1904)

SOMETHING NEW AT THE NATIONAL—*PETITS BOURGEOIS* BY MAXIM GORKY (*La Tribuna*, Rome, March 24, 1904)
Play, performed for the first time in Italy, only a moderate success, received without enthusiasm.

The Naval War. ATTACK ON PORT ARTHUR ON APRIL 13 (*The Russo-Japanese War Fully Illustrated*, Tokyo, April–June 1904)
Japanese attack Port Arthur. Russian Admiral of the Fleet Makarov dies. Replaced by Rodjestenwski.

REPUBLICAN AND SOCIALIST VICTORY. Paris reconquered. Tremendous success in the provinces (*L'Humanité*, Paris, May 3, 1904)

UNIVERSAL EXHIBITION AT ST. LOUIS. Viewed by car—The opening ceremony—THE IVORY CITY (*La Tribuna*, May 3, 1904)
Big International Exhibition opens in St. Louis (U.S.A.). Italy takes part in grand style.

APACHES IN HIGH SOCIETY. The exploits of the Countess de Chatillon—A true woman of the world—The will swindle—Numerous charges—The inquiry. (*L'Humanité*, Paris, May 5, 1904)
Shocking scandal in Paris: the misdeeds and criminal career of a high society lady come to light. Countess and the Count, her husband, grow rich through fraud!

THE PARISH PRIEST OF THE MOULIN ROUGE. Reverend gentleman's escapades—In Montmartre—*La Margot*—The cakewalk—Mockery of passersby—Arrival of the police—Belated repentance (*L'Humanité*, Paris, May 16, 1904)
Parish priest A. Robin (38 years old) goes around streets of Montmartre arm in arm with La Margot, well-known prostitute, both obviously tipsy. All of a sudden he lifts up the skirts of his cassock and does a wild cakewalk to great amusement of public. Annoyed, the priest removes his habit completely with an obscene gesture and continues to dance. Later he grovels in apologies and excuses to the commissioner of police.

THE POPE'S PROTEST—AUTHENTIC DOCUMENT. Text of papal note (*L'Humanité*, Paris, May 17, 1904)
The Pope, who still considers himself a prisoner of the Italian state, protests angrily at visit of French President Loubet to Rome.

THE BIG SCANDAL AT DEVERS (*La Tribuna*, Rome, June 9, 1904)
In the small French town a doctor, about to be married, gave a stag party to celebrate his last day as a bachelor. The guests, who included all the local dignitaries, "behaved more shamefully and indecently than can possibly be imagined." The madam of a brothel was obliged to call in the police to get rid of them. Even the guiltless mayor was involved and dismissed from office.

THE LOVERS OF VENICE. The last letters of Georges Sand and de Musset (*La Tribuna*, Rome, June 14, 1904)
Complete version of the amorous correspondence between the two writers, published in Brussels.

ADMIRAL SKRYDLOV'S DARING ATTACK. Japanese transports sunk—Kuropatkin's vanguard to the south—Contradictory reports of victory (*La Tribuna*, Rome, June 17, 1904)

NEW LAND VICTORY FOR THE JAPANESE. Four thousand Russians among dead and wounded—Danger of complete disaster—Admiral Komimura gives chase to Skrydlov—Expectation of decisive result (*La Tribuna*, Rome, June 18, 1904)

REPERCUSSIONS (*The Times*, London, June 27, 1904)
Long article by Leo Tolstoy, in which the Russian author expresses his pacifist ideals and bitterly condemns the Russo-Japanese War. The editor is obliged to accompany it with a paragraph of comment to soften the tone. The article has been long commissioned and cannot be omitted.

SLAUGHTER OF THE INNOCENTS ON BOARD THE STEAMER *GENERAL SLOCUM* IN NEW YORK (*Illustrazione Italiana*, Milan, July 3, 1904)
The old steamship, crowded with children on a school outing, catches fire in New York harbour: 938 dead, 179 injured, 93 missing.

SIEGE OF PORT ARTHUR SIMULATED AT GAETA (*Corriere della Sera*, Milan, July 3, 1904)
Planned for August; big land and sea maneuvers in the presence of the King. At Gaeta the siege of Port Arthur will be simulated.

ARRESTED AT MESSINA FOR HIGH TREASON, Captain Ercolassi and his wife (*Corriere della Sera*, Milan, July 7, 1904)
Convicted of spying for France, abetted by his wife, the captain is arrested. Desperate, he attempts suicide.

JUDGE PARKER WHILE BATHING learns of his selection as United States presidential candidate (*Corriere della Sera*, Milan, July 11, 1904)
Judge Parker, 52 years old, is the new Democratic candidate for the presidential election as rival to Roosevelt. Journalists tell him the news while he is swimming in the river at the back of his house.

FLYING MACHINE INVENTED BY AN AMERICAN (*Corriere della Sera*, Milan, 1904)
Engineer Holland, already inventor of a submarine, has now invented a flying machine. Four pairs of wings attached to shoulders and thighs are moved by pedals. He will try it himself next week and is sure that within a few years it will be more popular than the bicycle.

DIPLOMATIC BREACH BETWEEN FRANCE AND THE VATICAN, with its probable consequences—45 millions suppressed—Church abandoned to the municipalities—The unknown (*Corriere della Sera*, Milan, July 31, 1904)

SPINAL VERTEBRA REMOVED AND RECONSTITUTED (*Corriere della Sera*, Milan, August 9, 1904)
Scientific miracle at Philadelphia (U.S.A.). For a woman wounded by her lover's pistol shot in the back: a smashed vertebra was detached from the spine and sewn together with gold thread before being replaced.

THE FIVE DAYS OF THE FIRST EXPERIMENT IN PROLETARIAN DICTATORSHIP (*L'Avanguardia Socialista*, Milan, September 24, 1904)
On Thursday, September 15, a general strike lasting five days was proclaimed for the first time in Italy. The outcome was disappointing.

BIRTH OF A CROWN PRINCE (*Illustrazione Italiana*, Milan, September 25, 1904)
Born at Racconigi on September 15, a crown prince of the House of Savoy. He has been given the name Umberto, Prince of Piedmont.

1905

RUSSO–JAPANESE WAR. FALL OF PORT ARTHUR. Surrender conditions—Letter from Stoessel—Meeting of delegates—Last forts wiped out—Sufferings of the besieged. (*L'Humanité*, Paris, January 3, 1905)
Port Arthur surrenders to Japanese army. Russia now without a supply base.

There was another war, the war in the Far East, in which the "yellow" Japanese defeated the Russians. And after that war was lost, revolution in Russia. Below, Russian troops brought back from the front to quell the revolutionary unrest. Right, the Prussians in the train of Wilhelm II as he progresses through the streets of Tangiers during his state visit to Morocco in 1905. During the Moroccan crises that weighed on the European legations all through the year, the voluble Kaiser's initiative had the paradoxical result of strengthening the Anglo-French alliance.

RUSSIAN RETREAT AS DISASTROUS AS THE BATTLE. Half the Russian army lost—Kuropatkin will be recalled—The folly of national pride (*La Tribuna*, Rome, March 14, 1905)
Russia defeated yet again in the war against Japan.

THE 24th EXHIBITION OF THE ASSOCIATION OF WOMAN PAINTERS AND SCULPTORS (*Revue Illustrée*, Paris, March 15, 1905)
A great exhibition by French woman artists in Paris: remarkable success; numerous works on show.

ELEONORA DUSE IN PARIS (*La Tribuna*, Rome, March 17, 1905)
Duse plays in *The Wife of Claudius*. Crowds so great theater has to be closed.

THE NAVAL WAR. Defeat of the Russians—Encounter in the Strait of Sushima—Four Russian ships sunk—Others damaged. (*La Tribuna*, Rome, May 29, 1905)
Admiral Togo's ships sight the Russian fleet at Vladivostok. After one hour the battle ends in the complete defeat of the Russians, and practically ends the war at sea.

DEATH OF LOUISE MICHEL. The life of a revolutionary—During the Commune—In New Caledonia—Return to France—the Red Virgin—Last illness—Death (*L'Humanité*, Paris, January 10, 1905)
Died in Paris: the famous French revolutionary called the Red Virgin. She took part in the days of the Commune.

THE RUHR MINERS (*L'Humanité*, Paris, January 19, 1905)
The biggest strike ever known in the region is now on. The miners are demanding better wages and an eight-hour day.

BUSINESS IS BUSINESS (*Corriere della Sera*, Milan, January 21, 1905)
After a conference in Wichita, Kansas (U.S.A.), Booker T. Washington, Negro leader, received by Roosevelt in the White House, cannot find a hotel that will put him up. They are afraid of losing their patrons.

UPRISING AND REPRESSION IN ST. PETERSBURG. From Grand Duke Vladimir to Minister Witte—The truth about Sunday—Yesterday's revolt—Slaughter continues. (*Corriere della Sera*, Milan, January 24, 1905)
"Bloody Sunday" in St. Petersburg sparks off a series of repressive actions:

it is the first step towards a Russian revolution.

BOMBS IN PARIS (*Illustrazione Italiana*, Milan, February 12, 1905)
One at the Tivoli, where Jaurès and others were holding a meeting; one in front of a Russian colonel's house and two on the boulevards. They may be the work of anarchists in sympathy with the unrest in Russia.

HOW THE MURDER OF GRAND DUKE SERGE OCCURRED. Revolutionary tribunal: sentence of death!—The executioners arrested—Consternation at the palace: the people indifferent. What will the Tsar do? (*La Tribuna*, Rome, February 19, 1905)
Grand Duke Serge assassinated in Russia by revolutionary murderers.

THE SIMPLON TUNNEL. In the gallery—Water and heat (*La Tribuna*, Rome, February 26, 1905)
The two tunnels meet after a final explosion. The immense undertaking is nearly completed.

THE WOLF SHOWS ITS TEETH (*The Voice of Labor*, February 1905)
An American socialist severely condemns the great A.F.L. (American Federation of Labor) syndicate.

A BOMB MEANT FOR KING ALFONSO IN PARIS—Bomb under the carriage—King Alfonso and Loubet unhurt—Many injured—Arrests and searches—On the scent? (*La Tribuna*, Rome, June 2, 1905)
King Alfonso in carriage with French President Loubet during Paris visit: the attack left them unharmed but injured many in crowd. Naturally, anarchists are suspected.

RUSSIA AND JAPAN AGREE TO NEGOTIATE PEACE. The Japanese conditions—Russian counter-proposals—Warlike moves in Manchuria. (*La Tribuna*, Rome, June 12, 1905)
Roosevelt's mediation brings delegates from the two powers to the peacemaking table. The negotiations will proceed at Peterhoff and Portsmouth: Russians consent to withdraw from Port Arthur, Manchuria and Sakhalin, but refuse to pay war indemnity to Japanese.

HORRORS OF ODESSA. The bombardment—Ships set on fire—Battleship *Potemkin* fires on the city (*Il Secolo*, Milan, July 1, 1905)
On June 28, 1905, the sailors of the battleship *Potemkin* mutiny, refusing their rations of rotten meat. On the same day they fire on the city of Odessa in support of the rioting workers.

DR. MacLAUGHLIN WANTS MR. ROCKEFELLER'S FIVE MILLIONS. The physician who claims to have discovered five years earlier than Professor Loeb that electricity is life,

now declares that he can cure Mr. John D. Rockefeller and agrees to give twenty-five thousand francs to charity if he does not succeed. (*Il Secolo*, Milan, July 1, 1905)
A full-page announcement with huge headlines, ornate lettering and an article. The doctor, inventor of the electric girdle advertised every day in all the newspapers, hopes to win the prize which, it appears, has actually been offered by the celebrated American multimillionaire and patron.

JAURÈS AND BEBEL IN LONDON (*Il Secolo*, Milan, July 10, 1905)
The two socialist leaders are now attending a large meeting in the English capital.

A COLOSSAL THEFT AT EDISON'S. 1,000,200,000 lire. (*Il Secolo*, Milan, July 13, 1905)
This sum, stolen from the great electrical corporation by its treasurer, Alberico Catti, in the form of securities, may well be called colossal, even by today's standards. The thief was arrested.

A PARLIAMENT IN RUSSIA. A manifesto from the Tsar for the institution of a Parliament—The state *duma*—The articles (*Il Secolo*, Milan, August 19, 1905)
Popular agitation has forced the Tsar to institute a constituent assembly. It was to be elected by direct, secret, universal suffrage, the same for everybody. But as soon as the procedure was made public it was apparent that that was not how it would be.

PEACE (*Il Secolo*, Milan, August 30, 1905)
Peace negotiations between Russia and Japan have been concluded. Japan accepts Russian conditions.

INDUSTRIAL WORKERS OF THE WORLD (*International Socialist Review*, Chicago, August 1905)

Report of the historical reunion at Brand's Hall, Chicago (U.S.A.), held from June 27 to July 8. The most important exponents of American socialism and anarchism took part: Daniel de Leon, Eugene Debs, Bill Heywood, E. Trautman, Elizabeth G. Flynn. (Result: the drawing up of the statutes of the I.W.W., the anarcho-syndicalist organization which, between the years 1905 and 1914, was to rank as the greatest advance in all the history of the American workers' movements.)

THE PREMISES OF *THE NEW YORK TIMES* (*Illustrazione Italiana*, Milan, September 3, 1905)
The great newspaper's new building: a tall, flat skyscraper that goes 18 meters down below the ground. It is the second highest in New York or, if we include the subterranean part, the tallest building in the world.

REVOLUTION IN JAPAN— Against the peace—Sensational dispatches—Attack on British legation—State of siege confirmed (*Il Secolo*, Milan, September 9, 1905)
Crowd, infuriated by conditions of peace with Russia, turns to violence. Japanese journalists, all belonging to ancient samurai families, meet the crowd in front of the editorial offices, sword in hand.

DISASTROUS EARTHQUAKE IN CALABRIA (*Illustrazione Italiana*, Milan, September 24, 1905)
Bloodcurdling photographs of the terrible earthquake that has destroyed entire towns and villages in Calabria. Hundreds of victims.

MONTMARTRE: THE SONG MAKERS (*Revue Illustrée*, Paris, October 1, 1905)
It is in the musical cabarets of this quarter of Paris that the long or short careers of the best French *chanteuses* are born, flourish and finish.

TUBERCULOSIS CONQUERED. Behring's serum to the rescue (*Il Secolo*,

Milan, October 8, 1905)
Professor Behring describes his experiments for overcoming phthisis to the medical conference in Paris. He has discovered a serum more powerful than Koch's tuberculin.

THE GREAT VANDERBILT CUP (*Il Secolo*, Milan, October 15, 1905)
The motorcar race in New York circles the $29\frac{1}{2}$-mile track 10 times. Lancia, Nazari, Cedrino, Sartori and Chevrolet are entered for Italy; Hemery is the winner.

THE AUTUMN SALON. Paintings (*Revue Illustrée*, Paris, October 15, 1905)
Shown as a group at the Salon d'Automne in Paris are the fauves, the "wild beasts of colour," followers of Gauguin, Van Gogh and Cézanne. Their names are Matisse, Braque, Vlaminck, Derain, Friesz, Rouault, Marquet, Van Dongen. The critics ignore them, but give much prominence to the retrospective show of Manet, Cézanne and Ingres.

THE LAST GREAT TRAGEDIAN. Death of Sir Henry Irving—Personal recollections—Irving idolatry—His costumes—His artistic career—His *Marengo*—Was it true glory?—Irving, the theatrical producer—His artistic taste and sense of theater. (*Il Secolo*, Milan, October 17, 1905)
The great English actor is dead; an almost legendary figure in the theater of his day. Sardou wrote *Dante* especially for him.

THE VICTORIOUS REVOLUTION. The Tsar has yielded—A constitutional monarchy declared in Russia—Tsarism finished. (*Il Secolo*, Milan, October 30, 1905)
Finding it impossible to halt the revolution by force, the Tsar is obliged to sign the "October manifesto," which promises direct civil liberty and a legislative assembly elected by a very wide suffrage. Russia becomes a constitutional monarchy.

HENRI BATAILLE (*Revue Illustrée*, Paris, November 15, 1905)
Portrait of the celebrated French playwright of the avant-garde. An *enfant terrible* of the European theater.

RÉJANE AND HER THEATER (*Revue Illustrée*, Paris, December 1, 1905)
The great actress is to have her own theater in Paris, beside that of Sarah Bernhardt.

THE YELLOW BOOK AND BLACK TIMES (*Petite République*, Paris, December 15, 1905)
There are apprehensions regarding the publication of the government Yellow Book on the Moroccan question: it could prejudice the coming conference at Algeciras.

MEDICINE IN 1905 (*Revue Hebdomadaire*, Paris, December 15, 1905)
New medical discoveries during the past year: Behring's vaccine; serum therapy for diphtheria, plague and cholera; the introduction of anesthesia based on scopolamine injected subcutaneously together with morphine (but this is not expected to meet with success).

THE RUSSIAN REVOLUTION (*The Nineteenth Century and After*, London, December 1905)
In a long article Peter Kropotkin sums up the 1905 revolution and assesses its results: victory of the people over absolutism, power for the whole working class, liberty of the press. The people has shown itself united in its determination to create a new nation. Autocracy lies mortally wounded and will never rise again. Other victories are to come.

THE CITY OF DEATH—REVOLUTIONARIES GIVE UP THE BARRICADES. Fortified houses preferred—Ferocious order of the day—Situation in Moscow described—Will the revolutionaries surrender?—Bloodstained chapter. (*Il Secolo*, Milan, December 30, 1905)
The first Russian Revolution ends tragically, cut short by the bayonets of Prime Minister Witte. But Trotsky calls it "the dress rehearsal for the revolution."

1906

REVOLUTIONS PAST AND PRESENT (*International Socialist Review*, Chicago, January 1906)
Taking the failed revolution as his starting point, Karl Kautsky pieces it together with earlier revolutionary experiences to indicate a possible

strategy for the future.

THE ALGECIRAS CONFERENCE (*Illustrazione Italiana*, Milan, January 14, 1906)
On the eve of the Algeciras conference: France and Germany meet to resolve the colonial question in Africa and, together with the other European nations, to safeguard their respective interests in that continent.

LAFCADIO HEARN AND JAPAN (*The Nineteenth Century and After*, London, January 1906)
Born in Greece of Irish parents, Hearn, after working as a journalist in the United States and a correspondent in Japan, has settled in the latter country, where he is now a professor at Tokyo University. To him we owe our tenderest and most truthful descriptions of Japan.

SARAH BERNHARDT'S PET DOG (*Corriere della Sera*, Milan, February 2, 1906)
Articles and obituaries in the American papers on Spot, the actress's little dog, run over by a tram in New York. His mistress, prostrate with grief, has him buried in Deering Forest, described in poems by Longfellow.

M. ARMAND FALLIERES the new President of the French Republic (*Revue Illustrée*, Paris, February 5, 1906)

A VELÁSQUEZ PAINTING is sold for about a million and a half lire (*Illustrazione Italiana*, Milan, February 11, 1906)
A female nude (the only one by Velásquez) was bought by the National Gallery of London. One of the directors deplored wasting such a sum "on the acquisition of a naked figure."

THE ENCYCLICAL—POPE PIUS X PROTESTS TO THE FRENCH PEOPLE against the separation of church and state (*Corriere della Sera*, Milan, February 18, 1906)
After the breaking off of diplomatic relations between France and the Vatican (1904) comes the separation of church and state: religious liberty, end of the Concordat, ecclesiastical property inventoried and transferred to Christian cultural institutions, no governmental recognition or subsidy for any particular sect. These are the main points of the laws against which Pius X has reacted by issuing his encyclical *Vehementer nos*.

BLOODTHIRSTY ASSAULT BY "APACHES" ON A LODGING HOUSE at the gates of Paris (*Corriere della Sera*, Milan, February 19, 1906)
Night attack with revolver shots on lodging house known as the Swallows' Nest: tenants return fire and, after a fierce fight (one dead and a dozen wounded) drive back the assailants.

"SON OF JORIO" IN COURT (*Corriere della Sera*, Milan, February 21, 1906)
Actor Scarpetta, sued for forgery by D'Annunzio because of his parody, *Son of Jorio*, acquitted.

British soldiers photographed on the Sphinx in 1906. With the annexation of Egypt, Great Britain consolidated the "Imperial route" to India. On the left, the captain of Köpenick represented in a Danish caricature. Köpenick is a small town near Berlin: the captain, far from being a captain, was a shoemaker, Wilhelm Voigt, who on October 16, 1906, without any authority, put on a gold-braided uniform, lined up a number of soldiers, ordered three policemen to follow him and had the mayor arrested after handing over 4000 marks to the "captain." His crazy adventure ended six hours later; he had made a mockery of the proverbial respect of Wilhelm's subjects for anyone in uniform.

SARAH BERNHARDT'S THEATRICAL TOUR. A tent for 4000 people (*Corriere della Sera*, Milan, February 24, 1906)
The marquee has been ordered by her impresario for her tour in Mexico and California.

DREADNOUGHT, the world's biggest battleship (*Illustrazione Italiana*, Milan, February 25, 1906)
To maintain her naval supremacy, Britain has launched at Portsmouth the first battleship powered by turbine engines and equipped with large-caliber guns only. The most powerful ship in the world, she will immediately become the model that other countries will attempt to equal.

MULTIMILLIONAIRE VANDERBILT ARRESTED AT PONTEDERA (*Corriere della Sera*, Milan, February 25, 1906)
After having knocked a child over with his motorcar, he takes refuge in a tobacconist's and produces a pistol. The child is only bruised, but the police have difficulty in saving him from lynching by the crowd.

IBSEN CELEBRATES (*La Sera*, Milan, March 22–23, 1906)
The great Norwegian playwright celebrated his 78th birthday in London. (He died on May 27.)

TERRIBLE ERUPTION OF VESUVIUS. Burning river of lava advances —Boscotrecase invaded—Torre Annunziata and Torre del Greco in danger —Houses destroyed—Earth tremors— Volcano's cone collapses—Desperate flight—Rain of ashes and widespread darkness—Human victims (*La Tribuna*, Rome, April 9, 1906)

OLYMPIC GAMES—ITALIAN CHAMPIONS IN ATHENS (*La Tribuna*, Rome, April 11, 1906)
List of Italian athletes taking part in the Olympic Games in Athens.

THE SAN FRANCISCO EARTHQUAKE (*Illustrazione Italiana*, Milan, April 15, 1906)

Another huge catastrophe: city of San Francisco (U.S.A.) destroyed by terrible earthquake followed by raging fire. 1500 victims, hundreds of thousands homeless, suffering hunger, and thirst from lack of water. Opera singer E. Caruso on tour escapes death by a miracle.

CURIE (*Illustrazione Italiana*, Milan, April 15, 1906)
The famous scientist, discoverer of radium, has died in Paris after being run over by a cart.

RODIN'S *THINKER* UNVEILED at the Panthéon on April 21 (*Revue Illustrée*, Paris, April 20, 1906)
Rodin's famous statue will be unveiled at the Panthéon in Paris.

PIUS X AND THE FEMINIST MOVEMENT (*La Tribuna*, Rome, April 30, 1906)
The Pope has an audience with the Austrian feminist writer Theimir and declares himself in favour of feminism because it does not contravene Christian morals. He is also in favour of votes for women, but concedes that universal suffrage in countries with little education might have its dangers.

BUFFALO BILL AND HIS WILD WEST SHOW IN THE RING (*La Sera*, Milan, April 30–May 1, 1906)
The legendary Colonel William Cody, better known as Buffalo Bill, presents his great Far West Circus in the Milan Arena after successful tours in America and Europe.

HOW MANY NEWSPAPERS ARE PUBLISHED IN DIFFERENT PARTS OF THE WORLD? (*La Sera*, Milan, May 15–16, 1906)
The list of titles is impressive: 20,000 in Europe (of which 5500 in Germany, 3000 in England, 1400 in Italy), 3000 in Asia, 200 in Africa and 12,500 in the United States.

MARIONETTES IN PARIS (*Pall Mall Magazine*, London, May 1906)
The Parisians are mad about them. The most renowned puppeteer is an 11-year-old boy, Jean Louis Forain, manager of a company of real actors who supply the puppets' voices. The performances, staged in private houses, rival those in full-size theaters and draw enthusiastic crowds.

OFFICIAL OPENING OF THE SIMPLON TUNNEL (*Illustrazione Italiana*, Milan, May 27, 1906)
Simplon tunnel ceremonially opened in presence of King of Italy and President of the Swiss Federation.

SAVAGE ATTACK ON SPANISH ROYAL FAMILY—Bomb from third-floor window—Royal family unhurt— 12 dead and 50 injured— Anarchist plot—Impressions (*La Tribuna*, Rome, June 2, 1906)
Murder attempt in Madrid gives rise to rumours of anarchist plot, which later prove groundless. Culprit commits suicide to avoid arrest. As a precaution, royal carriage will be armoured in future.

THE HIGHEST POINT OF RUWENZORI reached by Duke of Abruzzi (*Corriere della Sera*, Milan, July 6, 1906)
Another great venture by the famous Italian explorer. The summit has never yet been reached.

NO RETRIAL (*Le Temps*, Paris, July 8, 1906)
Review of Dreyfus trial just ended: all evidence agrees in proving him innocent. The previous verdict of guilty is annulled and no appeal is allowed.

WARRANT FOR ARREST of multimillionaire Rockefeller (*Corriere della Sera*, Milan, July 11, 1906)
The American multimillionaire is accused of violating the antitrust law with his Standard Oil Company.

DREYFUS AND PICQUART REINSTATED AND PROMOTED—Formal demonstrations in the French Chamber—Zola at the Panthéon (*Corriere della Sera*, Milan, July 14, 1906).

SWIMMING THROUGH PARIS. Victory and 140 sugar lumps (*Corriere della Sera*, Milan, July 18, 1906)
Frenchman Bougoin wins, swimming 11 kilometers, 400 meters in 3 hours, 6 minutes, 6 seconds. Two women, Australian Kellermann and Austrian Frauendorfer, both make it in 3 hours, 59 minutes, 30⅖ seconds. During his swim Bougoin swallows 200 grammes of Madeira, 7 eggs and 140 pieces of sugar.

SHAW'S IRONICAL REPLY TO GERMAN SOCIALISTS. The most bourgeois party in Europe (*Corriere della Sera*, Milan, July 26, 1906)
Accused of having called them anarchists, Shaw replied, "The Socialist Party of Germany is not only free of anarchism, it is also untainted with socialism."

FALLIERES AMONG THE ACTORS. Coquelin's surprise decoration (*Corriere della Sera*, Milan)
The President of the French Republic visits rest home for retired actors founded by the famous player. Overcome with surprise and emotion, Coquelin is decorated with the gold medal for public service.

RED FLAG FLYING AT KRONSTADT—GENERAL STRIKE ARRANGED—DETAILS OF THE STRUGGLE AT KRONSTADT (*Il Secolo*, Milan, August 3, 1906)
Russian revolt against Tsarist repression still raging. The rebels barricade themselves inside the Kronstadt fortifications.

TERRIBLE WRECK OF GREAT ITALIAN LINER *SIRIO*—Disaster off Spanish coast—The first news—Many victims—Collision with reef (*Il Secolo*, Milan, August 6, 1906)

EPIC OF BEEF AND PORK. *The Jungle*, by Upton Sinclair (*Hebdo-Débats*, August 10, 1906)
Published in the United States (and serialized in *Il Tempo* in Italy) this new novel by the socialist American author, Upton Sinclair, deals with the horrors of the Chicago slaughterhouses and the appalling labour conditions in the tinned-meat industry. (The novel was to spark off the literary trend of "muckraking," as Roosevelt called it, and caused a huge scandal.)

PIERRE LOTI'S LATEST NOVEL: *THE DISENCHANTED* (*La Revue*, Paris, September 15, 1906)
Pierre Loti, romantic literary figure and adventurer in the East, writes a novel with a Turkish heroine. Fond of ancient customs, Loti is no champion of emancipation. His is a heroine in the sentimental tradition nearer his taste.

JOURNALISTS COME TO BLOWS (*La Sera*, Milan, September 25–26, 1906)
At the Caffè Aragno in Rome four journalists from *Avanti!* brawl with the editor of *Mattino* because the socialist newspaper insults the Queen Mother.

THE END OF CUBAN INDEPENDENCE. Governor Taft—Military occupation prepared (*La Tribuna*, Rome, October 1, 1906)
Independence conceded to Cuba after Spanish-American War comes to an end: on grounds of Platt amendment, United States intervenes in country's government.

ANTI–NEGRO MOVEMENT IN UNITED STATES. New torments and tormentors—Negroes pray to God. (*La Tribuna*, Rome, October 10, 1906)
Grave racist incidents including deaths and injuries in several American cities.

TOWARDS CONQUEST OF THE AIR. Successes of Santos Dumont and Zeppelin—Forlanini's flying boat. (*Illustrazione Italiana*, Milan, October 28, 1906)
Dumont flies his airplane for 50 meters at a height of 5 meters, while Zeppelin, after several failures, keeps his lighter-than-air craft aloft over Lake Constance for two hours. Forlanini is experimenting with a flying boat on Lake Maggiore.

POLAR RECORD—Peary reaches 87 degrees, 6 minutes N (*Corriere della Sera*, Milan, November 5, 1906)
The American explorer is 324 kilometers from the Pole.

FROM NEW YORK—ELECTION OF GOVERNOR—HEARST, the "man of mystery" (*Corriere della Sera*, Milan, November 7, 1906)
The great press magnate stands as candidate with the slogan "Down with trusts." (He was not elected.)

CYCLING TOUR OF LOMBARDY (*Corriere della Sera*, Milan, November 11, 1906)
First bicycle tour of Lombardy, organized by *Gazzetta dello Sport*, starts off with 60 competitors: course is 167 kilometers long.

THE "BELLE OTÉRO" WEDS ENGLISH SPINNER (*Corriere della Sera*, Milan, November 16, 1906)
The truth is that Renato Wep is owner of a spinning mill in America. La Otéro has applied to Lépine, the Paris prefect of police, to control the crowds on her wedding day. The event is certain to be a sensation.

STRANGE ADVENTURE OF CARUSO IN NEW YORK—CARUSO ARRESTED FOR FLIRTING (*Corriere della Sera*, Milan, November 18, 1906)
The singer, in New York to sing *Bohème*, was arrested in Central Park for making eyes at a lady. He was allowed out on bail for $500. It ended in a $10 fine.

NOBEL PRIZE FOR CARDUCCI—A simple and affectionate ceremony—The poet greatly moved—The speeches—"One thing only common to all mankind: the love of beauty." (*Il Secolo*, Milan, December 11, 1906) (The poet died early in 1907.)

1907

EPIDEMIC OF DUELS IN FRANCE (*La Sera*, Milan, January 5–6, 1907)
Another duel between journalists in Paris.

"APACHES" ACTIVE IN MARSEILLES (*Corriere della Sera*, Milan, March 7, 1907)
Shots exchanged between Apaches in the streets of Marseilles. Two arrests and some injured.

VOTES FOR WOMEN TURNED DOWN IN THE HOUSE OF COMMONS (*Corriere della Sera*, Milan, March 9, 1907)
Defeat for the British suffragettes. Document signed by 21,000 women against the vote on grounds that it would destroy their influence in society.

SINS OF THE "SMART SET" and a fashionable preacher (*Le Correspondant*, Paris, March 10, 1907)

The preacher is Father Vaughan, who compares the London "smart set" to canned meat from Chicago (having read *The Jungle* by Sinclair). Their sole god is money, they care only about "things." The smart set is "as casuistic as a pharisee, dissolute as the prodigal son, covetous as Midas, voluptuous as Herod, frivolous as Salome, sensuous as the Magdalene, vicious as Herodias." And the smart set comes in droves to hear him preach; it's the fashion.

"THE HUMAN SOUL WEIGHS ABOUT AN OUNCE" (*Corriere della Sera*, Milan, March 12, 1907)

After six years of research six doctors in Massachusetts (U.S.A.) have arrived at this conclusion. Experiments have shown that when dying patients are laid on a balance, their weight, after they have drawn their last breath, is one ounce less than before. Obviously that is the weight of the soul that has left their mortal remains. "At last the soul is being studied by scientific principles and experimental methods."

THE DANGERS OF PEACE CONFERENCES (*Daily Mail*, London, March 12, 1907)

A puzzle for the coming conference at The Hague: all attempts at securing peace and disarmament have been followed by a war. "Better to let sleeping dogs lie."

SUDDEN DEATH OF CHEMIST BERTHELOT (*Corriere della Sera*, Milan, March 19, 1907)

Permanent secretary of the *Académie des Sciences*, he discovered the synthesis of organic compounds, and was considered father of thermochemistry. His heart already weak, he never recovered from his wife's death.

THE TRANSVAAL RETURNED TO THE BOERS (*American Monthly Review of Reviews*, New York, April 1907)

The Boers have accepted British dominance. Revision of the treaty within four years. Meanwhile, General Botha presides over the government.

OH, THOSE AMERICANS! ONE MAN DOES IT WHILE

HUNDREDS ARE THINKING ABOUT IT (*La Tribuna*, Rome, May 29, 1907)

A big American financier collects funds to buy a strip of land 30 meters wide leading from the Vatican to the sea. In this way the Pope will have an extraterritorial corridor by which to leave his state and pay visits abroad.

AT THE MOTOR AND BICYCLE SHOW—The little American Ford (*Corriere della Sera*, Milan, June 5, 1907)

The little Ford motorcar ("a product of Detroit") arouses interest: solidly constructed at a low price, and can be driven without a chauffeur. The first utility car.

IN THE WORLD OF AERONAUTICS—NEW EXPERIMENTS BY SANTOS DUMONT—The airplane of the brothers Wright (*Corriere della Sera*, Milan, June 5, 1907)

Santos Dumont hopes to fly at 100 kilometers per hour in his new dirigible balloon. Meanwhile one of the Wright brothers has arrived in Paris. He maintains that on October 15, 1906, he flew 38 kilometers in 38 minutes in a machine built by him and his brother. The brothers have always refused to have their apparatus examined (perhaps they have sold it to Germany?) and are very reserved on the subject. It is not known why Wright is in Paris.

FROM NEW YORK—KISSING FORBIDDEN! Discussion at a medical conference. (*Corriere della Sera*, Milan, June 8, 1907)

In Atlantic City, U.S.A., more than an hour's discussion on the dangers of kissing on the lips. Proposal for a gradual campaign to overcome this unhygienic and perilous custom!

RECORD OF DARING IN THE LAND OF DREAMS. Preparations, difficulties and fear of novelty in the Peking–Paris race. (*Corriere della Sera*, Milan, June 8, 1907)

Departure on the 10th at 5 A.M. Five motorcars in the race: 3 French, 1 Dutch and 1 Italian. In the last, Prince Borghese and Luigi Barzini, the famous special correspondent of the *Corriere*.

COLOSSAL TRIAL IN AMERICA—Terrible deed of assassin hired by a federation (*Corriere della Sera*, Milan, June 9, 1907)

Law case in the United States against the Western Federation of Miners for the murder of Steunenberg, governor of Idaho. One of the accused, a certain Orchard, denounces leaders as instigators in confession obtained in prison by detective MacParlane. Principal defendant, leader "Big Bill" Haywood, is victim, like others, of colossal political "framing."

CLEMENCEAU'S BLOW AGAINST AGITATORS FROM SOUTH—DAY OF ARRESTS AT MONTPELLIER, NARBONNE AND ARGELLIERS—Flight of Marcelin Albert—DEAD AND INJURED AT NARBONNE—From the crisis spots (*Corriere della Sera*, Milan, June 20, 1907)

Fiscal strike in four whole provinces with 1200 municipal officials dismissed. Demonstration by crowd of 800,000 in Montpellier town square ends in bloodshed. Agitator Albert, called "the Liberator," avoids arrest by fleeing over the rooftops.

ORGANIZATION OF PEACE (*Revue Hebdomadaire*, Paris, July 13, 1907)

At the Hague Peace Conference the proposal to limit arms was dropped. There were long discussions on the competency rights and usefulness of the arbitration court in resolving disputes between nations.

THE GIRLS WHO MAKE OUR PARIS DRESSES (*Pall Mall Magazine*, July 1907)

They are the midinettes, the gay and celebrated assistant dressmakers of Paris, who throng the streets at midday (their lunch hour: hence the name). They earn a meager fifty francs a month.

A SERUM AGAINST TYPHUS (*Il Secolo*, Milan, July 27, 1907)

In Berlin Drs. Meyer and Bergell have discovered a serum that seems to achieve excellent results against that fearful illness.

THE REPRESENTATION OF LIFE AND MOVEMENT (*Revue des Deux Mondes*, Paris, August 1907)

Chronophotography, or motion analysis, invented in the late 19th century, preceded by very little that other sensational development, cinematography. In 1907 the French cinema industry is flourishing: the Compagnie Générale des Cinématographes at Joinville has an establishment extending over 10,000 square meters, including theaters, machines, technicians and artists, and produces 30 kilometers of film a day. Thousands of people are involved in a business turnover of 40 million francs a year.

FROM PARIS: THE AMAZING EXPLOITS OF THE THOMAS BROTHERS. Sacrilegious thefts, poisons—A bloodstained dagger—Scandalous revelations threatened. (*Corriere della Sera*, Milan, October 8, 1907)

Apparently honest coopers, sons of a good and pious mother (actually an accomplice), they robbed churches. Instruments for abortion, drugs, poisons and a bloodstained knife were discovered. Arrested, they threaten to disclose shocking scandals.

Woman at work under the capitalist system; woman in politics in the socialist opposition. Previous page, employed as office workers at the beginning of the century; above, Rosa Luxembourg speaks (with Klara Zetkin on her right), between the portraits of Marx and Lassalle, at the socialist meeting in Stuttgart in 1907.

EDWARDS–DE CROISSET DUEL —Poet wounded (Corriere della Sera, Milan, October 9, 1907)
Proprietor of the Matin and poet fight with sabers in Paris. Seconds: editor of Figaro and librettist Cain.

LUSITANIA RECORD—13 meters per second (Corriere della Sera, Milan, October 14, 1907)
The liner Lusitania has beaten the Kaiser Wilhelm II and the Deutschland by completing the Ireland–New York crossing in 4 days, 19 hours, 52 minutes, thus winning the Blue Ribbon at a speed of 24 knots.

SCANDALOUS VON MOLTKE– HARDEN TRIAL. Ministers, ambassadors and generals compromised— The Kaiser, Crown Prince, Bülow and the "Round Table"—TRIAL'S SENSATIONAL BEGINNING. Harden may examine the prosecution (Corriere della Sera, Milan, October 24, 1907)
One of the most brilliant and caustic of German journalists, Harden stirs up a cauldron of scandals, disclosing intrigues of men surrounding the emperor, a veritable mafia of power nicknamed "the Round Table." General von Moltke is suing him (but Harden won).

THE DUMA TAMED (Il Secolo, Milan, November 2, 1907)
The first Duma was revolutionary, and the Tsar dissolved it; the second Duma was constitutional, and the Tsar dissolved it. Now, at last, the third is genuinely reactionary. Tsarism has triumphed.

PERSISTENT AND WORRYING FINANCIAL CRISIS IN UNITED STATES (Il Secolo, Milan, November 5, 1907)
Europe and America concerned about the crisis. It is hoped that the President will intervene with special laws.

VIOLENT UPROAR IN GRAZ— THE GOVERNOR'S DUTY TO DEFEND ITALIANS (Il Secolo, Milan, November 15, 1907)
Skirmishes between Germans and Italians are becoming frequent: Austria refuses to provide an Italian university in Trieste but will not receive Italian students in her own colleges.

AMONG THE "APACHES" (Revue Bleue, Paris, November 16, 1907)
Portrait of the real Apache: a feeble, lazy youth attacking only in groups and running away at the least resistance. He rules over the outer boulevards at night and loiters about the lowest dance halls with his girls. The "slashers" (armed with razors) used to frequent Les Halles in 1903. On the Left Bank their usual haunt was the Père Lunette tavern.

FROM NEW YORK: CHEAP HOUSES—EDISON'S INVENTION (Corriere della Sera, Milan, December 2, 1907)
The cement is poured into an iron mould. When set, the mould is removed and the house is ready. Edison asks no recompense for his invention.

THE ADVENTURES OF A REPORTER ON L'INTRANSI- GEANT as the result of a strange competition (Corriere della Sera, Milan, December 10, 1907)
This is what happened: the reporter was to wander about Paris in disguise. The readers, who had seen his photograph and knew his route, were to stop him and announce their recognition. One reader decided to follow and stop him, crying "Stop thief!" The fortunate winner wants to join the secret police.

MAURICE DONNAY AMONG THE "IMMORTALS." The Académie makes friends with Montmartre. (Corriere della Sera, Milan, December 20, 1907)
The French Academy and the Montmartre bohemian have become reconciled: Paul Bourget, academician, gave a eulogy of the "long-haired brethren" on the occasion of Donnay's election. The two of them shared memories of the Chat Noir, Montmartre's most celebrated cabaret.

1908

PAINLESS EXECUTION—Experiments in electro-execution (*La Tribuna*, Rome, January 12, 1908)
In Paris Professor Laduc is investigating the possibilities of carrying out a death sentence by electricity.

SCATHING OPINION FROM THE TIMES (*La Tribuna*, Rome, January 16, 1908)
Appearance of a new play by D'Annunzio compared to a country circus announced in the press with fife and drum. Only difference: in the circus one sees animals behaving like humans; in D'Annunzio's works it's the other way around.

"IMPOSSIBLE TO SEND NEWS" (*Daily Mail*, London, February 4, 1908)
Wording of a telegram from Lisbon. Reason: the King has been assassinated.

ASSASSINATION OF THE KING AND CROWN PRINCE OF PORTUGAL (*L'Illustration*, Paris, February 6, 1908)
Band of ruffians in Lisbon shoot at King and crown prince. In ensuing tumult police kill six of the regicides. (News was fragmentary and inaccurate. In fact, the crown prince was only wounded and came to the throne as Manuel II.)

THE TROJAN HORSE OF THE ENGLISH SUFFRAGETTES—More pandemonium (*Corriere della Sera*, Milan, February 12, 1908)
After a first vain effort, the suffragettes tried to enter the yard of the House of Commons hidden in a horsedrawn cart. Driven back once more, they shouted slogans in favour of the vote.

HUGE TERRORIST PLOT IN RUSSIA against Archduke and Stolypin—70 agitators arrested—Fanatical courage of Italian journalist—A police error—Stolypin also threatened (*Corriere della Sera*, Milan, February 22, 1908)
Attempt on life of Nicholas Nicholayevich and Prime Minister Stolypin fails. Fifty revolutionaries found in possession of bombs and weapons. One attempts suicide, another kills a policeman.

PROSPECTS OF THE BLOND TYPE (*The Contemporary Review*, London, February 1908)
Men with fair hair and blue eyes have more resistance to pain and fatigue, wherefore they constitute the stronger and more enterprising races. They are, however, ill adapted to the unhealthy life of cities.

BEHIND THE CINEMA SCREEN (*L'Illustration*, Paris, March 28, 1908)
Full photographic report, in which the most practiced tricks of the cinema are revealed and illustrated

ARE THERE MEN ON OTHER PLANETS? (*The Nineteenth Century and After*, London, April 1908)
It is unlikely that human evolution has taken the same course in other worlds as on earth. Therefore, if there are other living creatures in the universe, they must be very different from us.

FEMALE VOTERS IN DENMARK (*La Sera*, Milan, April 14–15, 1908)
Both men and women may vote in Denmark after the age of 25.

THE FIRST CONGRESS OF ITALIAN WOMEN (*La Sera*, Milan, April 23–24, 1908)
Even the Queen and Princess Letizia, together with over 1000 other ladies, take part in the first Italian Women's Congress in the Campidoglio. The men present did not have the right to vote on the order of the day: political votes for women.

LITTLE GIRL PERISHES IN FIRE THROUGH EXCESSIVE MODESTY (*La Sera*, Milan, April 23–24, 1908)
It happened in Trieste: a little girl of ten refused to leave her burning room for fear of being seen in her nightdress.

RUSSIAN MUSIC IN PARIS (*Il Secolo*, Milan, May 20, 1908)
First night of *Boris Godunov* in Paris a great success.

DELAGRANGE TRIUMPHS AGAIN IN MILAN (*La Tribuna*, Rome, June 19, 1908)
In front of 6000 people the French aviator lifts himself between two and five meters above the ground and flies three kilometers in three minutes, twenty seconds.

STUPENDOUS SUFFRAGIST RALLY IN LONDON—20,000 demonstrate—700 flags (*Illustrazione Italiana*, July 5, 1908)

A WELCOME MOVE (*La Sera*, Milan, July 5, 1908)
General approval has greeted the newly formed Society against Suicide of Milan. A deserving social effort to counter the mania of the century.

OLYMPIC GAMES IN LONDON (*L'Illustration*, Paris, July 18, 1908)
On July 13 the Olympic Games were started in the new London stadium in the presence of several thousand sportsmen from all countries.

THE TURKISH CONSTITUTION (*L'Illustration*, Paris, August 1, 1908)
As a result of pressure from the "Young Turks" nationalist party "Union and Progress," the Sultan Abdul Hamid has been forced to renew the constitution granted in 1876 and then withdrawn.

ITALIAN HERO OF THE MARATHON IN LONDON (*Illustrazione Italiana*, August 2, 1908)
Italian Petri wins marathon but is disqualified for having been helped over last few meters by a games official.

PRESIDENTIAL CAMPAIGN IN UNITED STATES—Fight carried on by gramophone and cinematograph (*Corriere della Sera*, Milan, August 5, 1908)
Candidates Taft and Bryan both use these modern technical devices to win popular favour. The cinematograph has already been used by Teddy Roosevelt.

ZEPPELIN DIRIGIBLE BALLOON DESTROYED by engine explosion (*Corriere della Sera*, Milan, August 6, 1908)
During a halt between flights over Germany the balloon catches fire owing to a draft from the moorings fanning a spark from the engine. Count Zeppelin, imperturbable, announces construction of a fifth dirigible. "The future of my balloons now depends only on the engines." The state pays 500,000 marks' compensation.

FIRST FLIGHT OF THE WRIGHT BROTHERS IN EUROPE—3500 meters in three minutes (*Corriere della Sera*, Milan, August 9, 1908)
Wilbur Wright flies at Le Mans in presence of Blériot and other notables. The taciturn American does everything himself: the crowd is enthusiastic.

FROM NEW YORK: WAITERLESS RESTAURANTS—An American idea (*Corriere della Sera*, Milan, August 14, 1908)
One orders the meal, sits down and presses a button. The table sinks into the basement and comes back bearing the food. It is an American device, still in the planning stage.

SWORD THRUSTS AND PISTOL SHOTS (*Corriere della Sera*, Milan, August 29, 1908)
More about duels and the conditioning of public opinion that makes them necessary. Anecdotes and dramatic episodes.

VARNISHING DAY AT THE AUTUMN SALON—Eccentricity triumphs—The Italians (*La Tribuna*, Rome, October 2, 1908)
To be deplored are the obscene and incomprehensible works resembling those of primitive people and composed without design or colour sense.

THE MERRY WIDOW by Lehár (*La Tribuna*, Rome, October 8, 1908)
First performance in Rome of Lehár's operetta. A limited but undeniable success.

CUNNING NEW FASHION—The "toque" (*La Tribuna*, Rome, October 19, 1908)
The decline of large brims is welcome: they were too inconvenient.

WILLIAM THE TALKATIVE (*Evening Standard*, London, October 30, 1908)
Comments on the interview granted by Kaiser William II to the *Daily Telegraph*, in the course of which he let slip a number of indiscretions on friendly relations with Britain, and other more confidential matters. Needless to say, the interview caused a rumpus.

WILLIAM TAFT ELECTED PRESIDENT OF UNITED STATES OF AMERICA (*Illustrazione Italiana*, Milan, November 8, 1908)
Republican William Taft wins presidential election.

CAN LIFE BE PROLONGED? (*Journal*, Paris, November 13, 1908)
Article by famous French surgeon Doyen tells readers of fundamental importance of preventive medicine.

DEATH OF VICTORIEN SARDOU (*L'Illustration*, Paris, November 14, 1908)
Great and remarkable French playwright dies in Paris, aged seventy. For half a century he reigned over his country's theater.

CORRIERE FOR THE YOUNG (*Corriere della Sera*, Milan, November 15, 1908)
First announcement of imminent publication of new children's weekly.

ITALIAN TRIUMPH AT THE METROPOLITAN. Americans call Toscanini "best in the world." (*Corriere della Sera*, Milan, November 18, 1908)
Toscanini conducts *Aida* with Caruso, Scotti, Homer and other great singers. Tremendous success.

ITALIANS GO FROM VICTORY TO VICTORY IN AMERICA—**HOW DORANDO PETRI WON**—**EXCITING STAGES OF THE GREAT CHALLENGE**—**FIAT'S VICTORY** in Savannah tour (*Corriere della Sera*, Milan, November 27, 1908)
Dorando Petri, moral victor of London marathon, challenges official winner in New York's Madison Square Garden. Adversary Hayes beaten over 42 kilometers 182 meters of exhausting run. On same day Fiat won the Savannah race (Georgia, U.S.A.).

AT LAST TURKEY JOINS EUROPE—**TURKS ELECT MEMBERS OF PARLIAMENT BY VOTE** (*The Illustrated London News*, London, November 28, 1908)
Young Turks' revolution achieves its ends: Turkey changes from a closed and tyrannical form of government to a libertarian one. (The Union and Progress Party won the election and formed a government in February 1909.)

TRIUMPH OF THE GUILLOTINE IN FRENCH CHAMBER (*Il Secolo*, Milan, December 9, 1908)
Death penalty revived in France.

THE TRUTH ABOUT BOSNIA–HERZEGOVINA (*Fortnightly Review*, London, December 1908)
An attempt to clarify the annexation of Bosnia-Herzegovina by Austria-Hungary on October 6, one day after Bulgaria declared herself independent of Turkey. Thus two regions have been taken from the Turkish Empire. (The complex question, replete with international repercussions, was to keep Europe on the brink of war for half a year.)

IN THE LAND OF DEATH AND SORROW—More than 150,000 bodies—Searing details of destruction in Reggio Calabria and Messina—70,000 injured arrive in Naples—Magnificent example of Italian and international solidarity (*Il Lavoro*, Genoa, December 31, 1908)
Another great earthquake convulses Sicily and Calabria. Messina and Reggio Calabria are razed.

1909

STORMY FIRST NIGHT AT TURIN—**MARINETTI REBUKES AUDIENCE FROM STAGE** (*Corriere della Sera*, Milan, January 16, 1909)
La Donna È Mobile by Marinetti staged at the Alfieri. Large audience whistles and boos. Author appears on the boards to say, "I thank you for the whistling, which honours me greatly."

TOLSTOY ON GRAMOPHONE AND CINEMATOGRAPH (*Corriere della Sera*, Milan, January 23, 1909)
Two Americans, friends of Edison, film and record Tolstoy, who speaks in Russian, English, French and German.

ROOSEVELT OFFERED PART IN EQUESTRIAN CIRCUS SHOW (*Il Secolo*, Milan, February 3, 1909)
An impresario from Connecticut wanted to put Roosevelt at the head of a group of Rough Riders (soldiers who fought in Cuba) to reproduce episodes of life in the Far West. Salary: one and a half million francs for 30 weeks. The President declined.

JOURNAL RESURRECTED (*Gazetta di Messina et delle Calabrie*, February 4, 1909)
Daily newspaper resumes publication after terrible earthquake in Messina has destroyed the city.

TOWARDS THE MARRIAGE OF TWO OCEANS—Gigantic enterprise of the Panama Canal (*Il Secolo*, Milan, February 5, 1909)
According to estimates, it may be ready in 1915.

LONDON–CALCUTTA CABLE (*Il Secolo*, Milan, February 8, 1909)
Inauguration of direct line from London to Calcutta (11,000 kilometers), longest in the world.

CRIMES OF SLASHER CONTINUE—Another eight women stabbed (*La Sera*, Milan, February 17–18, 1909)
Berlin: police actively seeking criminal who terrorizes population. Twenty-three attacks in one week.

FOUNDATION AND MANIFESTO OF FUTURISM (*Figaro*, Paris, February 20, 1909)
F. T. Marinetti publishes first manifesto of futurist theory and program. He says, "We want to sing of the love of danger and the practice of energy and daring."

THE FOREIGN LEGION (*Bibliothèque Universelle*, Lausanne, February 1909)
A band of men recruited from every land and class to protect France's colonies. Description of the life and laws of the Legion.

THE GENTILE CASE and the dishonesty of Italian university life (*La Voce*, Florence, March 4, 1909)
Article by Benedetto Croce on the exclusion of Gentile from a course at Naples university.

ON THE EVE OF THE ELECTION—**THE FIRST WOMAN CANDIDATE!**—**GRAZIA DELEDDA AT NUORO** (*La Tribuna*, Rome, March 7, 1909)
After the dissolution of the Chamber and four years of government, the legislature is to be renewed. Some groups of intellectual electors have decided to vote for Grazia Deledda, largely to affirm the political vote for women.

MRS. WARREN'S PROFESSION BY G. BERNARD SHAW (*La Tribuna*, Rome, March 11, 1909)
Poorly received in London and censored in America, Shaw's play was

received in Italy with both enthusiasm and disapproval.

VIENNESE LITERATURE (WARLIKE CHARACTERISTICS) (*Illustrazione Italiana*, Milan, March 21, 1909)
On the Austrians' innate love of war and militarism.

ASSASSINATION OF DETECTIVE PETROSINO (*Minerva*, Rome, March 21, 1909)
Italo-American policeman murdered in full daylight in Palermo street while seeking clue to the Black Hand, Mafia organization against which he has long battled in New York.

ASSUNTA SPINA BY SALVATORE DI GIACOMO (*La Tribuna*, Rome, March 21, 1909)
First performance at Naples: "incomparable and unforgettable triumph."

RESULT OF GREAT MILAN–SAN REMO BICYCLE RACE—The arrival—GANNA'S VICTORY (*La Sera*, Milan, April 14–15, 1909)

CALM RETURNS TO THE GOLDEN HORN: FAILURE OF THE "YOUNG TURKS" (*La Sera*, Milan, April 14–15, 1909)
Strict Mohammedans revolt against Westernization introduced by Young Turks. Army marches on Salonika rebels and suppresses insurrection. But "Union and Progress" party has disappointed Liberal hopes of progressive government.

DUEL BETWEEN WRITERS (*La Sera*, Milan, April 17–18, 1909)
Marinetti and Hirshe fight with sabers because of latter's remarks about a lady in Parisian society. Marinetti wounds adversary: the two are not reconciled.

IN TURKEY: TWILIGHT OF AN EMPIRE—Sultan deposed—The new Caliph (*La Sera*, Milan, April 27–28, 1909)
The old Sultan, Abdul Hamid, who was behind the counterrevolution, deposed in favour of brother, Mahmud V. Power more firmly than ever in hands of Young Turks.

NEW YORK: WORLD'S GREATEST THEATRICAL CENTER (*World's Work*, New York, April 1909)
Grand productions with artists of world fame (Caruso, Tamagno, Toscanini, Jean de Reszke) in two famous rival opera houses: the Manhattan and the Metropolitan.

FROM NEW YORK: COMMUNICATION WITH MARS—Bizarre plan of Professor Todd (*Corriere della Sera*, Milan, May 3, 1909)
Already known through his Andes expedition and for having photo-graphed the canals of Mars, Professor Todd proposes to enclose a telegram in an aluminum box and put it in an airplane as high as possible above the disturbances of earth: it will capture the ether waves which undoubtedly radiate from the mysterious planet Mars.

BACCHUS by Massenet, libretto by C. Mendès, at the Paris Opéra (*Corriere della Sera*, Milan, May 3, 1909)

DREADFUL DAWN IN STAMBOUL—First hangings of the rebel soldiers (*Corriere della Sera*, Milan, May 4, 1909)

WHY THE DRUNK SEE DOUBLE (*Scientific American*, New York, May 8, 1909)
Before you see double, you have to have two eyes: the one-eyed can drink till they burst, but will never enjoy double vision. Fortunate possessors of both eyes owe the abovesaid phenomenon to the muscular contraction (an effect of alcohol) that pulls the eyes into asymmetrical positions.

ROOSEVELT'S OPINION OF TOLSTOY (*Outlook*, May 15, 1909)
"As a philosopher and moralist he has never exercised an effective and lasting influence on men of action." In short, while admiring the novelist, he casts a suspicious eye on his pacifist ideals.

FROM LONDON: DEATH OF NOVELIST GEORGE MEREDITH (*Corriere della Sera*, Milan, May 18, 1909)
Considered the greatest living English novelist, he dies at 81 in his villa at Box Hill.

THE RESOURCES OF AMERICAN SURGERY (*Corriere della Sera*, Milan, May 21, 1909)
Returned from the United States, Dr. Maiocchi declares himself dumbfounded by American hospital organization: 30 specialists available for consultation, and an anatomo-pathological laboratory for urgent diagnoses during operations; 8–10 operations every morning.

THEATER NEWS: *A FEAST OF HOAXES*, dramatic poem in 4 acts by Sem Benelli at the Lyric (*La Sera*, Milan, June 2–3, 1909)

THE END OF THE TOUR OF ITALY—Champions of the *Giro d'Italia*, in the Milan Arena—May 30 (*Illustrazione Italiana*, Milan, June 6, 1909)
Ganna of Varese, the winner, receives the *Corriere*'s prize of 3000 lire, plus prizes offered by the bicycle firms. In all, four times as much.

CONQUEST OF THE AIR—BLÉRIOT FLIES THE CHANNEL (*La Tribuna*, Rome, July 26, 1909)
Louis Blériot wins 1000-pound prize offered by *Daily Mail* with monoplane 7 meters long, weighing 22 kilograms. Triumphant welcome: afterwards promises wife to give up flying.

EIGHTH VENICE INTERNATIONAL EXHIBITION (*L'Art et les Artistes*, Paris, July 1909)
Shown at the Biennial Exhibition, works by Casorati, Alberto Martini, Emile Klaus, Pellizza, Nomellini, Lavery and Chiesa.

CANNON FIRE SUBDUES CATALONIAN REBELS—Grave situation in Morocco—Discontent in Spain continues (*La Tribuna*, Rome, July 31, 1909)
Rebellion smouldering in Catalonian capital for days ends in bloodshed. Socialists and anarchists lead ill-paid and discontented workers into the streets. (This episode was to be known as the Tragic Week of Barcelona.)

THE WAYS AND CUSTOMS OF THE EMINENT GUIDO GOZZANO (*La Voce*, Florence, August 12, 1909)
Article on the Piedmontese poet by Emilio Cecchi.

COLLEAGUES: THE DUEL (*La Voce*, Florence, September 2, 1909)
Why fight? Is the duel just for publicity, or to disguise a journalist's bad conscience under the manners of a gentleman?

SUFFRAGETTES FORCIBLY FED AGAIN—Laughter in the Commons (*Corriere della Sera*, Milan, October 1, 1909)
Letters from Mrs. Pankhurst, requesting that the prisoners subjected to forcible feeding should be visited by a doctor, caused much merriment in the House of Commons: "The suffragettes are bursting with health." *The British Medical Journal* considers that feeding through a rubber tube is neither dangerous nor an act of barbarism.

MARRIAGE OF ANATOLE FRANCE (*Corriere della Sera*, Milan, October 10, 1909)
There are rumours that the writer is to marry a girl of Slavonic origin.

DO YOU WANT TO HELP YOUR NEWSPAPER, whichever it is? Then don't leave it in carriages, cafés, restaurants or theaters without having first torn it up. (Notice published in the *Corriere della Sera*, Milan, October 12, 1909, and subsequently.)

PEARY AND COOK (*Deutsche Revue*, Stuttgart, October 1909)
Article by famous explorer Nordenskjoeld on controversy between Americans Peary and Cook. According

"STARS AND STRIPES NAILED TO THE NORTH POLE"

DR. FREDERICK A. COOK — APRIL 21 1908.

COMMANDER ROBERT E. PEARY — APRIL 6 1909.

TWO DAUNTLESS AMERICANS WHO REACHED THE GOAL OF A THOUSAND YEARS AND PLANTED THE STARS AND STRIPES UPON THE AXIS OF THE WORLD.

to author, both reached the Pole: Cook first, but unfortunately unable to say by what route; Peary second, but by a well-defined route.

GENERAL STRIKES AND DEMON-STRATIONS TO PROTEST ABOUT FERRER'S EXECUTION—Disorders in Rome and Florence—Soldiers wounded—Acts of vandalism—Mighty uproar—Confederation of Labour washes its hands like Pilate—Three hundred arrested in Rome—Serious violence in Florence (*Corriere della Sera*, Milan, October 16, 1909)
Francisco Ferrer, teacher and founder of the rationalist Modern School, champion of free education, arrested as instigator of "Tragic Week" disorders, tried and shot, in spite of manifest innocence. It happens that he was in London at that time and guilty only of attacking church's monopoly of education in Spain. Ferrer became first martyr of free thought.

THE COUNT, THE LADIES, ART AND FASHION ... Launching the Italian mode (*Corriere della Sera*, Milan, October 17, 1909)
A group of artists and lovely ladies seeks to start a movement for women's clothes of typically Italian style. President: Count Giuseppe Visconti di Modrone, supported by a host of noble ladies.

IN AMERICA WITH EMMA GRAMMATICA (*Corriere della Sera*, Milan, October 21, 1909)
Interview with actress in Latin America. Henri Bataille has offered to adapt one of his plays for her, provided she performs it in Paris. After seeing *Buridano's Donkey Cried*: we don't do plays like that in our country. "If I get

Characters from the Belle Époque. *The Stars and Stripes flutter over the North Pole—but who got there first? Cook, who may have been a fraud, on April 21, 1908, or Peary on April 6, 1909? The picture above pairs them as "dauntless Americans." On the right, Gabriele D'Annunzio with his dogs at Capponcina.*

bored," she said, "I'll start acting in German."

THEODORE ROOSEVELT'S AFRICAN SAFARI (*Daily Telegraph*, London, October 22, 1909)
The English newspaper is publishing Roosevelt's account of his African adventures as a serial.

TSAR'S ARRIVAL IN RAC-CONIGI—Journey on Italian soil—Meeting with our King and Queen (*Corriere della Sera*, Milan, October 24, 1909)

CESARE LOMBROSO AND CRIMINAL ANTHROPOLOGY (*Nuova Antologia*, Rome, November 16, 1909)
On October 19 Cesare Lombroso died suddenly in Turin, aged 73 years. One recalls his work as scientist and precursor of criminal anthropology.

BENEDETTO CROCE: PHILO-SOPHER OF ESTHETICISM (*Fortnightly Review*, London, November 1909)
International renown of Croce's *Esthetics*, published in 1902: Croce is considered the greatest Italian philosopher now living.

GABRIELE D'ANNUNZIO IN COURT—For breaking traffic police rules—Trusting to luck (*La Tribuna*, Rome, November 24, 1909)
People flock to court to see the poet. He

merely sends a telegram, declaring himself innocent and trusting to luck and Roman justice.

CONVERSATION WITH GEORGES SOREL (*La Voce*, Florence, December 9, 1909)
Sorel expresses his admiration for Croce, who has given Italy a feeling of nationality. Considerations on violence, the anti-Christianity of proletarian opinion, etc.

1910

E. H. SHACKLETON—Across the horrors of the Antarctic continent to latitude 88°23′ south (*La Tribuna*, Rome, January 2, 1910)
English explorer tells the Roman College, the city's geographical society, of his experiences in the Antarctic.

PAULHAN'S FLIGHT IN CALI-FORNIA—1524 meters: higher than the Sierra Madre! (*La Tribuna*, Rome, January 15, 1910)
Aviator achieves new altitude record, flying at height of 1524 meters. Previous record was Latham's of 1000 meters.

THE RESOURCES OF AMERICAN SCIENCE: human aura discovered by a professor of pedagogy (*Corriere della Sera*, Milan, February 8, 1910)
Dr. Doren, a clergyman, has discovered the aura. We each have one radiating a coloured nimbus all around us: purple if we are sad, green if jealous, red if angry. It will help to diagnose illness, especially of a mental or nervous type. If two people have clashing auras they cannot sit next to one another in a tram without feeling discomfort.

A **"RED SUNDAY" IN GER-MANY**—A dozen seriously wounded in the cause of electoral reform (*Corriere della Sera*, Milan, February 14, 1910)
45 socialist meetings in Berlin dispersed by police. Uproar in other cities, with dozens injured.

MADAME CURIE ISOLATES "POLONIUM"—New element's curious properties (*Corriere della Sera*, Milan, February 15, 1910)
Paris: widow Curie isolates new radioactive substance, which is rapidly transformed first into helium, then into a substance resembling lead and indestructible.

ANNA PAVLOVA, A WONDER-FUL DANCER. Of Little Russian origin, agile, exquisitely formed, she conquers the Metropolitan audience with her first waltz. Her debut in *Coppelia* (*New York Times*, March 1, 1910)

The triumphant American debut of the great Russian dancer, one of the stellar lights of ballet in the early years of the century.

CARUSO BLACKMAILED BY THE "BLACK HAND" (*Il Secolo*, Milan, March 6, 1910)
The Mafia organization has demanded 40,000 lire from the singer on pain of reprisals. Caruso has sought the protection of the New York Police.

EXPLOITS OF THE SUFFRA-GETTES—In the ventilation shaft of the House of Commons (*La Sera*, Milan, April 8–9, 1910)
A suffragette was found in the ventilation shaft. She had hidden there to jump out at the right moment and demand votes for women.

DEATH OF EDWARD VII (*Illustrazione Italiana*, Milan, May 15, 1910)
The king died on May 6 and will be succeeded by George Frederick, Prince of Wales, Duke of York, and cousin of Tsar Nicholas II, as George V.

HOW THE WORLD DIDN'T END
... The "last night" in Milan (*Corriere della Sera*, Milan, May 19, 1910)
The transit of Halley's much-feared comet passed off without incident. The end of the world, which was supposed to coincide with it, did not occur.

VERDICT AND SENTENCE IN TRIAL OF THE RUSSIANS. Three years' imprisonment for Naumow—Eight years for Tarnowska—Ten years for Prilukov—Perrier acquitted. (*Corriere della Sera*, Milan, May 21, 1910)
Venice: trial of Russian countess, Maria Tarnowska, accused of inciting Count Nikola Naumov to murder Count Kamarowsky in order to collect life insurance of which she was the beneficiary. All Venetian high society, cosmopolitans and idlers flocked to the hearing. One sensation after the other. Verdict: guilty.

PAULHAN'S SPLENDID VICTORY IN VERONA RACE—French flyer's aerial duel with Russian Efimov—Daring under test—Flying with Cheuret (*Corriere della Sera*, Milan, May 27, 1910)
Grand Prix for Altitude: minimum 500 meters. Paulhan tries to beat his own record of 1524 meters, and anyway wins the competition.

TRADE IN OBSCENITY (*Revue des Deux Mondes*, Paris, July 1, 1910)
Pornography causes juvenile delinquency and offends women. Its diffusion should be prohibited. The borderline between art and pornography is clear, however, so artists and writers need not fear for their liberty.

SOCIALISTS FROM ALL OVER THE WORLD MEET AT COPENHAGEN (*Il Secolo*, Milan, August 29, 1910)

RADIUM IN THE TREATMENT OF CANCER AND OTHER DISEASES (*Contemporary Review*, London, August 29, 1910)
The substance, discovered by the Curies at the beginning of the century, has shown itself useful in the treatment of cancer and moles. It is also an effective depilatory.

CHAVEZ FLIES OVER THE ALPS AT THE COST OF HIS OWN LIMBS—The sun rises—Chavez flies upwards. The Simplon crossed!—The feverish anxiety of waiting—Through the pass in 50 minutes—The victor crashes at Domodossola—Joy and anguish (*La Tribuna*, Rome, September 24, 1910)
Leg fractures and contusions of varying gravity the cost of the venture, although successful. (The pilot died a few days later.)

THE CINEMA AND PUBLIC MORALITY (*American Review of Reviews*, New York, September 1910)
The wide diffusion of the cinematograph is increasing its influence on social life. It is therefore desirable that censors should be appointed (as in the United States), recruited from intellectuals, police officials and representatives of the cinema industry, to prevent danger to public morals.

PROVISIONAL GOVERNMENT INFORMS POWERS THAT PORTUGAL HAS BECOME A REPUBLIC (*La Sera*, Milan, October 6–7, 1910)
A republic has been proclaimed in Portugal. Crowds rejoice in the streets and indulge in violent anticlericalism: police forced to defend churches from destructive fury of the mob.

HOW THE UNITED STATES ENCOURAGES THE "BLACK HAND" (*Outlook*, October 30, 1910)
Regrettably, laws regarding immigration are too lax. Immigrants should be admitted to the United States only if provided with a certificate of good conduct issued by their country of origin.

"SINS OF THE DOCTORS" (*New York World*, November 1, 1910)
Dr. Norman Barnesby's book of this title is causing an uproar in America: doctors, it says, care only for gain; the big teaching hospitals are guilty of serious organizational deficiencies.

FIRST WOMAN MEMBER OF THE ACADEMY (*Corriere della Sera*, Milan, November 1, 1910)
Judith Gautier is the first woman to be elected to the Académie Française, filling the place left vacant by the death of J. Renard.

DEATH OF LEO TOLSTOY—News of his death—False report of improvement—Invalid's last hours eased by music—The man (*Corriere della Sera*, Milan, November 17, 1910)
In the little station at Astapovo, Tolstoy is stricken by pneumonia, hemorrhage and cardiac weakness. Shortly afterwards comes news of his death. (In fact, the news was premature. Tolstoy survived for several days.)

NEW BIOLOGICAL DISCOVERY by Carrel and Bowers (*Corriere della Sera*, Milan, November 21, 1910)
The two scientists have discovered the possibility of preserving life artificially by means of cultures of living cells. Will

it become possible to transplant tissues and organs?

MEXICAN REBELLION against Porfirio Díaz—Bloody combat (*Corriere della Sera*, Milan, November 23, 1910)
Francisco Madero, leader of the only party in opposition to the Díaz government, heads a peasant revolt. Emiliano Zapata leads the peasants from the south: the password, used in the campaign of San Luis Potosi, inherited by Madero, is "restitution and distribution of the land."

THE GIRL OF THE GOLDEN WEST BY PUCCINI TRIUMPHS AT THE METROPOLITAN, NEW YORK (*Il Secolo*, Milan, December 11, 1910)

1911

NINE HOURS' BATTLE IN LONDON between two anarchists and a thousand policemen—Burned alive after appalling fight (*Corriere della Sera*, Milan, January 4, 1911)
Besieged in Sidney Street, Whitechapel, by a thousand policemen headed by Winston Churchill, two anarchists (Fritz and "Peter the Painter") engage in a gun battle and, after hours of fighting, let themselves be burned alive in the flaming house rather than be arrested. The *Corriere* praises the courage of Churchill, who "remained always in the front line, fearlessly facing the anarchists' fire."

THE GREAT ITALY–HUNGARY FOOTBALL MATCH IN MILAN—Splendid achievement by Italy's team, which loses by only one goal to nil—Public enthusiasm (*Corriere della Sera*, Milan, January 7, 1911)

CRISIS OF AMERICAN FEMINISM (*Revue Bleue*, Paris, January 7, 1911)
Something is stirring in America: the first protests against the matriarchy which actually rules in the United States.

JAPANESE ANARCHISTS CONDEMNED TO DEATH (*Corriere della Sera*, January 20, 1911)
After a trial behind closed doors, 25 anarchists are condemned to death for a supposed plot against the Mikado. Twelve of the condemned men have their sentences commuted to life imprisonment.

RUSSIAN BALLET *SCHEHERAZADE* **AT THE SCALA** (*Illustrazione Italiana*, Milan, January 22, 1911)

More characters from the Belle Époque: *the suffragette and the unemployed. A suffragette, above, under arrest (London, 1910); right, the unemployed march through the streets (election poster, 1910).*

Rimsky-Korsakov's ballet greeted with both praise and disapproval, but gets talked about. During the interval the audience discusses Tolstoy and Gorky—and the Tarnowska affair.

FIRST NIGHT OF *ROSENKAVALIER* by Richard Strauss in Dresden (*Illustrazione Italiana*, Milan, February 5, 1911)
Strauss's new opera wins the audience over; prolonged applause. The critics, on the other hand, seem puzzled.

LADY IN A "DIVIDED SKIRT" IN THE VITTORI EMANUELE GALLERY (*La Sera*, Milan, February 27–28, 1911)
Curiosity, excitement, scandal and annoyance (even a little violence) at the first, timid appearance of the new feminine fashion launched in Paris: women in trousers!

THE DUTY OF REMEMBRANCE (*L'Idea Nazionale*, Rome, March 1, 1911)
With this article in favour of Italian colonialism in Africa, plentifully illustrated by heroic episodes, the nationalist daily newspaper founded in 1910 by Enrico Corradini begins its series of publications.

GARIBALDI'S GRANDSON FIGHTS WITH THE REBELS—Contradictory reports on his fate (*La Tribuna*, Rome, March 14, 1911)
Faithful to his grandfather's example, Garibaldi's grandson enrolls on the side of the Mexican insurgents.

LOETSCHBERG TUNNEL COMPLETED—Enthusiastic scenes and rejoicing as miners meet (*Corriere della Sera*, Milan, April 1, 1911)
At last the two branches of the great tunnel have met. Starting from Briga and Thun, they join the Simplon with the Bernese Oberland. The ground levels at meeting fitted perfectly.

CHILDREN UNDER CANVAS (*Outlook*, May 27, 1911)
The idea of camping as an inexpensive holiday, even for children, is spreading in the United States.

FLIGHT FROM PARIS TO ROME ACHIEVED—Beaumont flies from Nice to Rome in 11 hours—Garros and Frey held up in Pisa—The winner—To Rome!—Beaumont tells our reporter of

impressions and enthusiasm (*Corriere della Sera*, Milan, June 1, 1911)
First half of Paris–Rome–Turin aerial rally completed. Tomorrow Garros too will reach Rome.

DEVASTATING EARTHQUAKE IN MEXICO—Madero's triumphant entry—More than 100 dead—"Vengeance from Heaven"—Madero arrives (*Corriere della Sera*, Milan, June 8, 1911)
Madero enters Mexico City as victor after defeat of Porfirio Díaz. Crowd acclaims him: he could be their candidate at next election in a few months.

TIME TO AWAKEN (*Fremdenblatt*, Vienna, June 9, 1911)
Coercive methods used by Turkey towards Albania are looked on with disfavour. Article arouses Turkish indignation and lively comment from entire foreign press. Albanian revolt causes great anxiety in Vienna.

TEXT OF ELECTORAL REFORM LEGISLATION. Printed ballot papers—Parliamentary indemnity of 6000 lire (*Corriere della Sera*, Milan, June 11, 1911)
Franchise for citizens over 30 years of age (or, in certain cases, over 21). Change in the ballot paper, organization of polls, manner of voting.

DEATH OF CARRIE NATION, the enemy of drinking saloons. Millions of dollars' damage done by her hatchet. (*Corriere della Sera*, Milan, June 12, 1911)
The fearsome president of the American Temperance Society has died aged 66. She was the terror of saloon bars, which she and her followers attacked with their hatchets.

GEORGE V CROWNED KING OF GREAT BRITAIN AND IRELAND. Magnificent traditional ceremony in

Westminster Abbey—Splendours of regal procession and spectacle for the crowd (*Corriere della Sera*, Milan, June 23, 1911)

FUTURISM IN ACTION IN FLORENCE—Punches and slaps exchanged between futurists and reporters from *Voce* (*La Tribuna*, Rome, July 1, 1911)
Marinetti, Boccioni and Carrà come to blows with some reporters from the Florentine literary review because of an article it published attacking futurism.

TELEGRAPHIC TRANSMISSION OF PHOTOGRAPHS (*Nuova Antologia*, Rome, July 16, 1911)
A new invention, at present used by only a few, major papers, may become useful to police, meteorologists and armies.

THE MODERN AESOP—Trilussa at home—How he works—The Austrian delegate and Trilussa's works—The "famous poet"—New fables—An unpublished fable, "Gratitude"—Trilussa abroad—D'Annunzio and Trilussa in a lady's album (*La Tribuna*, Rome, July 19, 1911)
An affectionate portrait of the Roman poet: anecdotes of his life and literary production.

PEARL OF THE LOUVRE STOLEN (*Illustrazione Italiana*, August 27, 1911)
The *Gioconda* stolen! Parisians dismayed: the picture is beyond price. May be revenge of dismissed employees or act of madness. Meanwhile the painting, missing since August 22, has not been found.

THOMAS EDISON SAYS AVIATION WILL PUT AN END TO WAR (*Il Secolo*, Milan, July 31, 1911)
According to the scientist, flying, with its possibilities, will be an effective material and psychological deterrent to any nation contemplating war.

FEMINIST'S DUEL WILL NOT TAKE PLACE—FIERCE LITTLE WOMAN (*Corriere della Sera*, Milan, September 1, 1911)
Arria Ly, ardent feminist and founder of the Feminist Struggle group in Provence, challenges journalist to a duel. After some hesitation he refuses. Accused of cowardly wish to save his skin—Ly is unbeatable with a pistol.

CROSS–CHANNEL SWIM achieved by Burgess after 13 attempts—Victory after 23 hours' swim—How Burgess repeated Captain Webb's feat (*Corriere della Sera*, Milan, September 7, 1911)
Leaving from Dover, he swims across to Cap Griz-Nez. The straits of Dover have only been swum once before, by the English Captain Webb in 1878.

THE *MONA LISA* STOLEN BY WORTH, the celebrated international thief, declares novelist Strauss (*Corriere della Sera*, Milan, September 8, 1911)
Only supposition: Worth is a "gentleman crook" who has already stolen a painting by Gainsborough, restoring it later for a ransom. He opens locks noiselessly, owns a yacht and stables. No sooner had he escaped than he made off with two million in the Place de la Bastille in plain daylight.

ATTACK ON STOLYPIN IN TSAR'S PRESENCE—Stolypin and his policies—Life in Russia now—How the attack occurred in a Kiev theater—wounded minister's condition desperate (*Corriere della Sera*, Milan, September 16, 1911)
Prime Minister condemned to death by revolutionary party for his reactionary policy. Assassin a certain Bagrov, who appears to be involved with important police officials. (Stolypin died shortly afterwards. Bagrov was hanged.)

CHURCH AND MUNICIPAL AUTHORITIES against boxing match between Johnson and Wells (*Corriere della Sera*, Milan, September 17, 1911)
Meeting between the American world champion Johnson and the English heavyweight Wells may not take place, because of a previous, too-violent match ending in bloodshed.

VIOLENT ERUPTION OF ETNA (*Illustrazione Italiana*, Milan, September 17, 1911)
Lava flow 400 meters wide crushes observation post and destroys fields and vineyards. Railways and roads sundered.

THE SALON D'AUTOMNE (*La Tribuna*, Rome, September 3, 1911)
Annual Paris show once more open to the avant-garde and the young, "with all the risks that implies." Cubists in the Chamber of Horrors.

THE "PEOPLE'S" BUDGET
GENIAL FOREIGNER:—
HOW THEY MUST WISH THAT MR LLOYD GEORGE HAD TAXED US INSTEAD OF THEM

1912

ITALY DECLARES WAR ON TURKEY. Reasons for conflict explained by Italian government—Turkish navy bombarded—Troops landed in Tripoli?—Consuls dismissed from Benghazi—Fall of Turkish government (*Corriere della Sera*, Milan, September 30, 1911)
Strengthened by Powers' support and tacit consent, Giolitti declares war on Turkey, which is opposing Italy's occupation of Libya.

IN FERTILE CYRENAICA (*Illustrazione Italiana*, Milan, October 8, 1911)
Marvellous description of African territory recently annexed by Italy: a rich and fertile land.

PACIFIST'S VILE VIEWS (*Il Secolo*, Milan, November 10, 1911)
Stands up and shouts "Down with war!" during running of film on Italo-Turkish conflict. Crowd attacks and beats him up.

IN CHINA — REVOLUTION TRIUMPHS—DYNASTY IN DIRE PERIL (*Il Secolo*, Milan, November 11, 1911)
Revolutionary officials and Chinese army lead revolution against Manchu dynasty, forming independent governments in almost all southern cities. General Yuan, nominated Prime Minister, stops rebels' advance, but nurses ambitions of power.

SUICIDE OF LAFARGUE AND MARX'S DAUGHTER (*Il Secolo*, Milan, November 27, 1911)
Husband and wife commit joint suicide to avoid approaching old age. Lafargue nearly seventy; wife chose to share his fate.

DISASTROUS AFFAIR OF TRIPOLI—Conclusions of a conservative economist—Present sacrifices ... future benefits ... and meanwhile debts and taxes—Colony will never be productive for the State—Tripolitania is not and never will be suitable for poor immigrants (*Avanti!*, Milan, December 3, 1911)
Economist in question is Luigi Einaudi, who writes in the *Corriere della Sera*.

END OF INCIDENT BETWEEN BOARD OF SCALA OPERA HOUSE AND BOARD OF *AVANTI!*—*Avanti!* returns Scala's press card—Intervention of Socialist councillors (*Avanti!*, Milan, December 27, 1911)
Turati puts a question to the mayor: a reporter from the paper was beaten black and blue because he did not stand up during playing of the royal march.

ANARCHY AMONG ARABS IN TURKISH CAMP? Closing of inquiry into identity of Turks on *Manouba*—Double sentence of death for soldier's murderer—German Red Cross Mission on way to Turkish camp (*Corriere della Sera*, February 1, 1912)

CHURCHILL SPEAKS FOR "HOME RULE" in citadel of Irish unionists, protected by 3000 soldiers (*Corriere della Sera*, Milan, February 9, 1912)
Belfast in state of siege for Churchill's meeting in Ulster Hall in heart of Protestant quarter. The prospect of submitting to an independent Irish parliament (as envisaged in the Home Rule Bill) with a Catholic majority enrages the four Protestant counties of Ulster. The inhabitants of Belfast meet Churchill at the station with cries of "We'll hang him from an apple tree!"

MOROCCAN TREATY APPROVED BY FRENCH SENATE—Strong speech by Clemenceau (*Corriere della Sera*, Milan, February 11, 1912)
Morocco to be French protectorate: so ends the Algeciras conference. In exchange, some territorial concessions to Germany: too many, according to some, including Clemenceau, who maintains Morocco can be won by peaceful penetration and a few gunshots.

FROM PARIS: 100,000 REVOLUTIONARIES accompany the body of a soldier—Violent skirmishes with police—Letter from Dreyfus (*Corriere della Sera*, Milan, February 12, 1912)
Soldier died from ill treatment in Algeria in 1911. In a letter Dreyfus deplores great antimilitarist demonstration.

HISTORICAL EVENT IN CHINA—End of the monarchy and proclamation of a republic (*Corriere della Sera*, Milan, February 13, 1912)
Emperor abdicates; republic established under conditions dictated by Yuan Shi-kai and the revolutionaries.

DEATH OF COUNT AERENTHAL—Final illness and death—Count Berchtold nominated as successor—The statesman and his work (*Corriere della Sera*, Milan, February 18, 1912)
"One of the oustanding figures in European politics" has died in Vienna. Supporter of annexation of Bosnia-Herzegovina, adviser to St. Petersburg

embassy, then ambassador, finally Foreign Minister, Aerenthal decided the entire foreign policy of Austria-Hungary.

VAST ENGLISH STRIKE—800,000 miners put down tools (*Il Secolo*, Milan, March 1, 1912)

NORWEGIAN AMUNDSEN REACHES SOUTH POLE ON DECEMBER 14, 1911—Mystery still surrounds fate of English expedition under Scott (*Il Secolo*, Milan, March 9, 1912)
Amundsen attains coveted goal before Scott (who was to find traces of Norwegian occupation when he reached the Pole).

PARIS POLICE OFFICERS AS CRITICS OF ART—Works withdrawn from Salon (*La Tribuna*, Rome, April 10, 1912)
The Société Nationale de Beaux Arts removes some exhibits from the celebrated show "for reasons of public decency."

WORLD'S GREATEST TRANS-ATLANTIC LINER SINKS—1500 people go to the bottom—Mourning in New York (*La Tribuna*, Rome, April 17, 1912)
Titanic, built in Belfast, 1911, largest transatlantic liner in the world, the one that "not even God could sink," struck an iceberg at midnight on April 16, and sank. Of the 2340 passengers and crew only 745 were saved.

TRAGIC GANG DESTROYED—Garnier killed. Valet wounded after night battle with bombs and gunfire (*Corriere della Sera*, Milan, May 15, 1912)
Anarchist Jules Bonnot, head of group to which Victor Serge, intellectual, once belonged, killed in conflict with police on April 28. What remains of gang is surrounded by police in a hovel near Paris. Police, headed by prefect Lépine, plan to blow them up with grenades. (Valet was, in fact, already dead.)

THE FEMINIZING OF ART (*Atlantic Monthly*, Boston, June 1912)
In America and the Anglo-Saxon countries women are beginning to monopolize the liberal arts. The cause is thought to lie in greater economic prosperity, which frees many women from domestic work and impels them towards culture.

"BLOWS OF A HOSTILE FATE"—A RUSSIAN NOVEL—The difference between Russian and Anglo-Saxon types of realism, the latter succeeding only in being stupidly indelicate (*New York Times*, June 30, 1912)
The Macmillan Company of New York publishes F. Dostoyevsky's *The Brothers Karamazov*. The Russian writer's novel is compared with those

produced by Wells, Galsworthy, Bennett and Herrick, who do not escape without bruises.

THE RADICALS' MEXICO—Why we are going into Morocco—*La Compagnie Générale Française* (*L'Humanité*, Paris, July 10, 1912)

Commercial interests, land speculation: the socialist newspaper tells its readers the true motives behind the Moroccan campaign. The C.G.F. is one of the companies speculating in Moroccan land.

FIFTH OLYMPIC GAMES AT STOCKHOLM (*Illustrazione Italiana*, Milan, July 21, 1912)

On July 6 the King of Sweden officially opens fifth Olympiad at Stockholm.

CAPITALIST CRIME IN UNITED STATES—Ettor and Giovanitti tried—Our comrades must be saved—C.G.T.'s protest (*L'Humanité*, Paris, August 11, 1912)

Lawrence, Massachusetts: Four textile mills with mainly female workers go on strike against wage reductions. The strike, led by IWW, will be famous in the history of the labour movement both in and outside America for its slogan "We want bread, but roses too," as well as for the case of Ettor and Giovanitti, the two leaders unjustly arrested for the murder of the Italian millhand, Anna Lo Pizzo. (In November their acquittal coincided with the successful outcome of the strike.)

TENSION BETWEEN NATIONS IN ARMS (*Corriere della Sera*, Milan, October 6, 1912)

Luigi Barzini, *Corriere*'s celebrated correspondent, on the scene of the imminent conflict between Bulgaria, Greece and Serbia on one side and Turkey on the other. (Montenegro declared war on October 8; Bulgaria, Greece and Serbia followed her example a week later.)

ATTEMPT ON ROOSEVELT'S LIFE—Dramatic account of the incident—Life-saving manuscript—Serious wound (*Corriere della Sera*, Milan, October 16, 1912)

Unbalanced Bavarian opponent fires at Roosevelt in Milwaukee. Manuscript of speech halts bullet and prevents fatality: Roosevelt is to rest in bed for ten days.

PEACE OF OUCHY—October 15 (*Illustrazione Italiana*, Milan, October 20, 1912)

Italy and Turkey sign preliminary peace treaty at Ouchy. Turkey grants independence to Libya, which will become Italian colony.

Contrasting pictures of the Belle Époque. *Above, the races at Auteuil: lovely ladies wearing veils, gentlemen in bowler hats, smartly uniformed officers. Elsewhere the* Belle Époque *wore a different face. In China, for example, men were dying for the republic: below, revolutionaries killed at Hanyang.*

VICTORIOUS BULGARIANS ON THE ROAD TO CONSTANTINOPLE—Turks flee, abandoning cannon, flags and prisoners—Turkey desires peace—Intervention of Great Powers (*Corriere della Sera*, Milan, November 1, 1912)

PRESIDENTIAL ELECTION IN UNITED STATES—Wilson's victory (*La Tribuna*, Rome, November 7, 1912)

Wilson elected President. Roosevelt and Taft defeated.

BERLIN THE SINFUL—Lively night life—Service with women—War of the red lights—Low but enterprising taverns—Courtesans and dancing girls—Campaign for sending Berliners to bed early (*La Tribuna*, Rome, November 13, 1912)

How the Berlin authorities are waging fairly unsuccessful war on organized prostitution in the "red-light district" of the German capital, and how they try in vain to introduce more sober habits to its inhabitants.

TURKEY ASKS BULGARIA FOR ARMISTICE. Bulgarians reply: "We shall enter Constantinople, if only for 24 hours" (*La Tribuna*, Rome, November 15, 1912)

ALBANIAN INDEPENDENCE PROCLAIMED AT DURAZZO (*La Tribuna*, Rome, November 24, 1912)

In spite of threats from Austria-Hungary that "If the Serbs reach Durazzo, they will find cannon there." Austria fears Serbs may gain ports on the Adriatic.

SOCIALISTS AGAINST WAR—INTERNATIONAL CONGRESS AT BASEL—Opening of Congress (*La Tribuna*, Rome, November 25, 1912)

Second International convenes Extraordinary Congress in Basel to show solidarity of international socialism against possibility of Balkan war leading to European conflict.

ARE THE FEDERATED STATES OF EUROPE A POSSIBILITY? (*Deutsche Revue*, Stuttgart, November 1912)
Federation would be a remedy for war: a common army and abolition of customs duty.

PEACE CONCLUDED? Peace treaty signed between Turkey and Balkan states—Adrianople surrendered to Bulgaria with honours of war. (*Avanti!*, Milan, December 1, 1912)
(In reality, peace was not concluded, the Bulgarians were not satisfied, the Greeks continued to fight, Turkey was not agreeable to allied proposals. If agreement proved impossible, the Powers were to intervene.)

TRIPLE ALLIANCE RENEWED (*Il Secolo*, Milan, December 8, 1912)

1913

EDISON'S NEW INVENTION—THE CINEMATOPHONE (*La Tribuna*, Rome, January 1, 1913)
Famous American inventor continues experiments in field of the cinematograph. (The cinematophone was the first, rudimentary attempt at sound films.)

CENSORSHIP IN THE LONDON CINEMA (*La Tribuna*, Rome, January 7, 1913)
Scenes of cruelty, reproductions of disasters that have deeply moved the public and scenes that lack propriety will be prohibited. Also banned are mixed bathing scenes on beaches.

POINCARÉ ELECTED PRESIDENT OF FRANCE (*La Tribuna*, Rome, January 18, 1913)

HEREDITY AT THE SERVICE OF MAN (*Outlook*, January 25, 1913)
First hints of possible practical application of laws of heredity as studied and expounded by Mendel in second half of nineteenth century: knowledge of them may serve to improve agriculture and stock raising.

TRAGEDY AT THE SOUTH POLE—Explorer Scott and four of his companions perish (*Illustrazione Italiana*, Milan, February 16, 1913)
The tragic news arrived on February 10: Scott reached the South Pole after the Norwegian Amundsen, but died of hunger and cold during return journey, only eleven miles from safety.

NOTE ON ART (*New York Times*, February 17, 1913)
A paragraph announces the opening of an international exhibition of modern art at 69th Regiment Armory, Lexington Avenue. The show, organized by A. B. Davies for the Association of American Painters and Sculptors, has gathered together works by the foremost European and American artists, including Picasso, Redon, Duchamp, Braque, Vlaminck, Matisse, Derain, Picabia, Brancusi ... In all more than 1300 works, from the impressionists to the avant-garde. The review is disturbed and indignant: "The propaganda of the cubists, futurists, postimpressionists and their fellows is not only a direct threat to art, but also constitutes a grave danger to public morality."

PIERPONT MORGAN DIES IN ROME—Master of millions—Illness and death (*Corriere della Sera*, Milan, April 1, 1913)
American Steel King dies at Grand Hotel, Rome. His nervous system never recovered from fatigue and strain of action brought by American government against trusts. Rockefeller was also implicated.

WELL–KNOWN SUFFRAGETTE PANKHURST SENTENCED TO THREE YEARS' HARD LABOUR (*Il Secolo*, Milan, April 4, 1913)
Leader of English feminism sentenced for incitement to crime. Suffragettes demonstrate their protest by acts of vandalism and condemn not only the sentence but also marital subservience: men too should vow obedience. Mrs. Pankhurst was freed after nine days of hunger strike.

NEO–MALTHUSIAN PROPAGANDA (*Il Secolo*, Milan, April 11, 1913)
Author of pamphlet entitled *The Art of Not Having Children* has been acquitted of charge of obscenity.

ATTEMPT ON KING ALFONSO'S LIFE—THREE REVOLVER SHOTS AT POINT–BLANK RANGE—KING ESCAPES DEATH BY MAKING HIS HORSE REAR (*Corriere della Sera*, Milan, April 11, 1913)
King saved by miracle; would-be assassin arrested: turns out to be an anarchist.

REHABILITATION OF CHARACTER UNSUCCESSFUL—Friend of Oscar Wilde loses his case (*Il Secolo*, Milan, April 23, 1913)
The now forty-year-old Admiral [sic] Lord Douglas loses his case for defamation of character against the author of a book. His relationship with Wilde was above suspicion. At the same time, a hitherto unpublished part of *De Profundis*, one of the late poet's most significant works, is published.

INFURIATED MOB TRAMPLES ON TWO SUFFRAGETTES IN HYDE PARK (*Il Secolo*, Milan, April 28, 1913)
London: a suffragist meeting ends tragically. An angry crowd attacks the women.

ANXIETY ABOUT STABILITY OF AMERICAN SKYSCRAPER (*Corriere della Sera*, Milan, April 28, 1913)
It is feared that the mania for skyscrapers may be dangerous. Experts will inspect New York buildings to see whether, as seems likely, electricity could seriously corrode the steel framework.

TERRIBLE LOSS FOR ISADORA DUNCAN—A premonition of tragedy and the "dance of sorrow" to Chopin's funeral march (*Corriere della Sera*, Milan, April 21, 1913)
The children of the famous English [sic] dancer drowned in the Seine. The whole of artistic Paris feels for her and comforts her in her grief.

TO IMPROVE THE HUMAN RACE (*La Tribuna*, Rome, May 26, 1913)
Doctor proposes annual organization in England and America of shows of children in perfect health. As with analogous horse and dog shows, it could be of great use to scientists and, of course, to entire human race, which could improve its products on a scientific basis.

PEACE TREATY BETWEEN TURKEY AND BALKANS SIGNED IN LONDON TODAY—Between the old and the new Albania (*La Tribuna*, Rome, May 31, 1913)
Official end of first Balkan War: Turkey and the Allies sign preliminary peace treaty. Turkey cedes all European territories beyond Enos–Midia line; Crete goes to Greece. Meanwhile, the ambassadors of the Powers have the task of solving complex territorial questions regarding Aegean islands and borders of new states.

THE INTERPRETATION OF DREAMS BY PROFESSOR SIGMUND FREUD (*New York Times*, June 1, 1913)
Published for the first time in English, Freud's basic work on the interpretation of dreams, till now accessible only in the original German.

FUTURIST EVENING IN MODENA—Presentation of the "detonator" (*Il Secolo*, Milan, June 3, 1913)
As usual, whistles and applause for Marinetti (who read poetry) and company. Musician Russolo presents his new invention: the "detonator," an instrument to harmonize noises. As

The economic world has discovered that wealth can be multiplied. At that time there was not much idea of sharing it out, quite the contrary.... The caption under this cartoon of J. P. Morgan, who died in Rome in 1913, says: "This amazing American wants to carry off all the wealth in the world." On the right, the beautiful, well-dressed (and rich) young woman of the late Belle Époque, *in a fashion drawing by Erté (1913).*

futurist procession leaves theater, skirmishes and fisticuffs.

NEW DANCE, THE TANGO, REACHES PARIS (*Illustrazione Italiana*, Milan, July 6, 1913)
Paris conquered by new South American dance: if you don't dance the tango, you're not in fashion.

WOMEN POLICE (*Corriere della Sera*, Milan, July 11, 1913)
First women police enter service in Hereport (U.S.A.). In uniform they are more suited than others to maintain good behaviour and give assistance in cases of juvenile delinquency.

BUFFALO BILL RETIRES (*Corriere della Sera*, Milan, July 30, 1913)
Legendary Colonel Cody, better known as Buffalo Bill, leaves his circus and retires to stud farm to breed horses.

GENERAL STRIKE A MAGGOT GNAWING ITS WAY THROUGH ITALY (*La Sera*, Milan, August 11, 1913)
On August 3, general strike in Milan starts with meetings and demonstrations. It will last ten days, also involving Rome and other cities. (The result, however, was negative.)

DEATH OF BEBEL (*La Sera*, Milan, August 13, 1913)
German socialist leader dead. Converted to Marxism by Liebknecht, he directed German Social-Democratic Party in open opposition to revisionists of Second International.

THE "BLACK HAND" BOSS OF NEW YORK'S ITALIAN QUARTER (*Outlook*, August 16, 1913)
The criminal organization called "the Black Hand" controls practically all Italo-American workers in New York. The police are powerless.

D'ANNUNZIO'S ADMIRER (*La Sera*, Milan, August 19, 1913)
Young kleptomaniac steals all of D'Annunzio's books she can lay hands on. Curious case of veneration, to which police put an inglorious end.

PANAMA CANAL—LAST BARRIER BREACHED (*La Tribuna*, Rome, September 3, 1913)

JOURNALIST'S BRAINWAVE—25,000 copies of cookery book sold through newspaper advertisement (*Corriere della Sera*, Milan, October 9, 1913)
The advertisement went as follows: "What a young girl ought to know before getting married—Cash on delivery." The sly journalist ended up in the dock but was acquitted: none of the recipients, it turned out, had dared to protest.

SIGNIFICANCE OF SUNDAY'S BALLOT—Increase of socialist and Catholic votes (*Corriere della Sera*, Milan, October 28, 1913)
Going to the polls for the first time in Italy, enlarged electorate consequent on Giolitti's electoral reform bill. Women are still excluded. "The time is not yet ripe," says Giolitti.

"WANT TO BE HEALTHY? EAT HUMAN FLESH," say two distinguished French doctors (*La Sera*, Milan, November 11, 1913)
The two specialists maintain that the human organism keeps in better health if fed on cells similar to its own. A cannibalistic diet is thus the best way to prevent premature aging and death.

LEONARDO'S *GIOCONDA* FOUND IN FLORENCE (*Illustrazione Italiana*, Milan, December 21, 1913)

Thief turns out to be Lombard labourer Vincenzo Perugio, who worked as a porter at the Louvre. Perugio claims to have taken the painting for patriotic reasons: he wanted to restore it to Italy, where it rightfully belongs.

1914

GREECE TO LEAVE ALBANIA ON DAY FIXED BY POWERS (*La Sera*, Milan, January 6, 1914)
Aftereffects of Balkan war trail on: London conference decrees independence of Albania. Date fixed is January 18.

COLLABORATING FOR THE CINEMA (*Il Marzocco*, Florence, January 18, 1914)
Unusual combination will shortly make a film. Socialist deputy Enrico Ferri and composer Mascagni will bring epic of Garibaldi to the screen.

PRIESTS OF MILAN AGAINST TANGO (*La Sera*, Milan, January 27, 1914)
Milanese parish priests thunder from pulpits, warning congregations not to indulge in the immoral dance; better still not even to watch it for fear of temptation.

D'ANNUNZIO'S NEW QUIP (*La Tribuna*, Rome, February 18, 1914) Awaited at a tea party, the poet failed to appear. Instead came one of his charming letters of excuse containing the following words written in huge letters: *"Je m'en frotte."*

CLAUDE DEBUSSY AT THE AUGUSTUS MAUSOLEUM (*La Tribuna*, Rome, February 24, 1914) Concert of music by the avant-garde French composer in Rome. Its great success makes up for critical incomprehension in earlier years.

THRONE OF ALBANIA FORMALLY OFFERED TO PRINCE VON WIED (*Illustrazione Italiana*, Milan, March 1, 1914)

MINISTERIAL CRISIS STILL UNSETTLED—Radical group discusses dismissal of government—Hon. Giolitti will inform King of cabinet's resignation today (*Il Secolo*, Milan, March 8, 1914)

THE *VENUS WITH LOOKING GLASS*. Wonderful Velásquez painting ruined by suffragette (*Il Secolo*, Milan, March 11, 1914) Suffragette enters London's National Gallery and disfigures picture with blows of ax. Says: "I tried to destroy the most beautiful woman of mythology as a protest against a government that seeks to destroy Mrs. Pankhurst, the most beautiful character in modern history."

POLITICAL TRAGEDY IN PARIS. Editor of *Figaro* murdered by wife of minister Caillaux (*Illustrazione Italiana*, Milan, March 22, 1914) Editor of *Figaro* was Calmette. It appears he refused to give Mme. Caillaux back intimate personal letters and photographs, planning instead to publish them in order to disclose scandals that could implicate her husband. The minister's wife waited for Calmette in front of his newspaper office and killed him with six pistol shots.

AMERICANS LAND IN VERA CRUZ AND OPEN FIRE (*La Tribuna*, Rome, April 23, 1914) While revolution rages in Mexico, Wilson occupies Vera Cruz by military force as protest against arrest of American marines and to block supply of arms to President Huerta. (Wilson detested Huerta and wanted to teach the revolutionaries to "elect decent people." At any rate, the clumsy intervention had no significant result other than to be considered by all as an unwarranted interference in a nation's internal affairs.)

FIRST PERFORMANCE OF *CABIRIA* AT COSTANZI (*La Tribuna*, Rome, April 24, 1914) D'Annunzio's cinematic drama shown for the first time in Rome. (In reality, the film, a mythological-historical jumble lasting four hours, was written by producer Pastrone, who paid D'Annunzio 50,000 lire for a few pompous captions, the characters' names and the famous signature. The completed work, which brought the figure of Macista, played by Bartolomeo Pagano, to the screen for the first time, was a great success in the United States and influenced directors such as De Mille and Griffiths.)

ARE JOURNEYS TO OTHER PLANETS FEASIBLE? (*La Revue*, Paris, April 5, 1914) Ideas are in the air about the construction of a mechanical catapult for launching a projectile carriage into space. Many problems, however, remain to be solved.

MEXICAN REBELS ADVANCE ON CAPITAL (*Il Secolo*, Milan, May 8, 1914) After their victory at Torreon, Pancho Villa's revolutionary troops march towards Mexico City. President Huerta orders destruction of some railways. Representative of United States government rejoices with Villa at his victory.

SYLVIA PANKHURST'S HEROIC DECISION (*La Tribuna*, Rome, June 18, 1914) Suffragist leader, daughter of Emmeline Pankhurst and founder of a second movement, independent of her mother's, decides to starve till Prime Minister Asquith consents to receive deputation of women. (Her action met with success.)

WHERE IS ANARCHIST MALATESTA?—Maneuver to hide his tracks?—Flight to London (*La Tribuna*, Rome, July 24, 1914) Police fire on workers, who abandon Villa Rossa at Ancona (June 7), where anarchist Errico Malatesta held meeting. Three dead, 15 wounded. (This was the beginning of the so-called Red Week of Ancona. Hunted by the police, Malatesta left the country and took refuge in London.)

HEREDITARY ARCHDUKE OF AUSTRIA AND WIFE ASSASSINATED BY SERBIAN STUDENT AT SARAJEVO (*La Tribuna*, Rome, June 29, 1914)

1914, the fateful year. Dancing in the streets on New Year's Day (on the right). Left, Emiliano Zapata (center, with wide-brimmed hat) and Pancho Villa (beside him in uniform) enter Mexico City.

THE MURDERS—Condolences—An unexploded bomb—Attack planned from afar—Impressions of the catastrophe (*Bosnische Post*, Sarajevo, June 28, 1914)
First attempt (a hand grenade) fails. Procession continues nevertheless. Imperial couple slain by expert gunman Gavrilo Princip's unerring shots.

ANTI–SERBIAN DEMONSTRATIONS (*Vorwaerts*, Berlin, July 1, 1914)
Anti-Serbian demonstrations begin, while Austria-Hungary mourns her imperial dead.

DEATH OF GREGORY RASPUTIN—His influence at the Imperial Court (*L'Humanité*, Paris, July 15, 1914)
The terrible monk, grey eminence of the Tsar's Imperial Court, dies at his Pokrovsky home, stabbed to death by a woman [sic].

MME. CAILLAUX AT THE ASSIZES. Very simply but with feeling she replies to judge's questions, saying, "The *Figaro* articles were like knife wounds in my heart ... I seemed impelled by some will other than my own ... I wanted to stop the horrible publication, not to kill." (*L'Humanité*, Paris, July 21, 1914)
The trial of Mme. Caillaux begins in Paris. She is accused of assassinating the editor of *Figaro* to save her husband, the deputy, from a scandal. (To everyone's great surprise, she was acquitted.)

WAR OR PEACE? THE PEOPLE MUST CHOOSE (*Vorwaerts*, Berlin, July 28, 1914)
Austria-Hungary has sent Serbia an ultimatum. Official journal of German social democracy sternly rebukes Austria's attitude: "unreasonable demands such as have never been put to a free nation in the whole of history, and which were formulated with the express purpose of provoking war."

DECLARATION OF WAR AGAINST REASON AND THE PEOPLE'S WILL (*Vorwaerts*, Berlin, July 29, 1914)
"By the supreme decision of His Apostolic Royal and Imperial Majesty" a declaration of war, written in French, was sent to Serbia on July 28. Hostilities had, in fact, already begun with frontier skirmishes between Austrians and Serbs.

GENERAL MOBILIZATION IN RUSSIA AND STATE OF WAR IN GERMANY (*La Sera*, Milan, July 31, 1914)
The European powers prepare to intervene in the conflict.

CROWD PSYCHOLOGY AND WAR PANIC (*Deutsche Revue*, Stuttgart, July 1914)
The problem of soldiers' panic on the battlefield is already under consideration: if they run away they must be stopped by a danger as great as the one they are fleeing from. In other words, their officers should shoot them in the back.

JAURÈS ASSASSINATED—His life —The assassin—Death (*L'Humanité*, Paris, August 1, 1914)
(The whole page is edged in black in mourning for Jaurès, director and founder [1904] of the newspaper, murdered in the café restaurant below the editorial offices.) The assassin, probably a prowar interventionist, killed him with two revolver shots. Messages of sympathy and condemnation from the Socialist Party (of which Jaurès was the head), and from President Poincaré, the state and the editorial staff.

GERMANY DECLARES WAR ON FRANCE—Belgian neutrality violated yesterday—Britain mobilizes army and navy—Italy announces neutrality (*L'Humanité*, Paris, August 4, 1914)

BRITAIN DECLARES WAR ON GERMANY (*Corriere della Sera*, Milan, August 5, 1914)

AUSTRIA'S OFFICIAL DECLARATION OF WAR ON RUSSIA (*Corriere della Sera*, Milan, August 7, 1914)
While conflict spreads all over Europe, German troops enter Liège.

DEATH OF THE POPE (*Illustrazione Italiana*, Milan, August 23, 1914)
Pope Pius X died on August 19. (He was succeeded by Benedict XV on September 3.)

BRUSSELS, CAPITAL OF BELGIUM, OCCUPIED BY GERMANS (*Illustrazione Italiana*, Milan, August 30, 1914)
Capital invaded and occupied by German troops on August 20.

GERMAN SOCIALISTS AND THE WAR—Doubtful justification of their attitude—Frank reply from Italian socialists (*Il Secolo*, Milan, September 12, 1914)
Italian socialists, against the war, indignant and disillusioned with policy change of German socialists, now in favour of war. Citing as justification their fear of Russian invasion, which could end all hopes of revolution, they vote war credits desired by generals.

D'ANNUNZIO ARRESTED IN PARIS (*Il Secolo*, Milan, September 12, 1914)
Poet, arrested in Paris while "taking literary notes," is quickly released and comments with amusement on his experience.

MARINETTI AND BOCCIONI IN JAIL (*Il Secolo*, Milan, September 18, 1914)
The two futurists arrested in Milan while, with their followers, they demonstrate against Austria-Hungary.

BOMBARDMENT OF RHEIMS CATHEDRAL—German command makes vain excuses—Pope telegraphs Kaiser (*L'Humanité*, Paris, September 23, 1914)

Indignation at irresponsibility of German artillery, which has bombarded and seriously damaged Rheims Cathedral, in spite of orders to spare works of art as far as possible.

ANATOLE FRANCE WANTS TO JOIN UP (*La Tribuna*, Rome, October 3, 1914)
Writer, now in his seventies, tries to enlist to help his country.

LEONCAVALLO ON THE INDEX ... IN GERMANY (*La Tribuna*, Rome, October 16, 1914)
Performance of *Pagliacci* banned at Cologne because of statements by Leoncavallo.

TURKEY BREAKS OFF DIPLO-MATIC RELATIONS WITH TRIPLE ALLIANCE POWERS (*Corriere della Sera*, Milan, November 1, 1914)

MUSSOLINI, HIS NEW PAPER AND THE PLEA FOR IMMEDIATE INTERVENTION (*La Sera*, Milan, November 11, 1914)
Mussolini announced publication on October 15 of new paper, edited by himself, *Il Popolo d'Italia*, which will support policy of direct intervention. Socialists discuss his possible expulsion from party. (The journal was published. It was later discovered to have been financed by the French.)

Europeans go to war: Germans, above, and French (left) leave for the front.

ANARCHISTS HAVE FOR-GOTTEN THEIR PRINCIPLES (*Freedom*, London, December 1914)
Errico Malatesta, exiled in London, publishes forceful article, condemning attitudes of many socialists and a few anarchists, who have become prowar: they must keep themselves "above all compromises with governments and ruling classes, be ready to profit by every favourable occasion, and continue with preparations and propaganda for the revolution."

Index

Abercrombie, Lady *16*
Abruzzi, Duke of 293, 306
Abstract art 242, 244, 248
Académie Française 85, 94
Adamov 179
Adorno, T. W. 182
Aerenthal, Count 316
Aiglon, L' (Rostand) 292
Aircraft—*see* flying machines
Alain-Fournier 182
À la Recherche du Temps Perdu
    (Proust) 46-7, 93, 196-7
Albert I of Belgium *61*
Albert, Marcelin 307
Album, L' 20
Alexander, King of Yugoslavia
    299
Alexandra, Queen 91
Alfonso XIII of Spain *61*, 92, 111,
    297, 302; murder attempt on
    318
All Done from Memory
    (Lancaster) 83, 89
*À l'Ombre de jeunes Filles en
    Fleurs* (Proust) 13
Alsace-Lorraine 11
American Review of Reviews 307,
    313
Amsterdam 39, *39*
Amundsen, Roald 316, 318
Anarchic Movement 84, 85, 295,
    298, 300, 302, 303, 314, 316,
    320, 322
Anderson, Sherwood 69
Angell, Norman 274-5, 278, 280,
    287-8
Anouilh, Jean 179
Apaches, the 296, 298, 301, 304,
    306, 308
Apollinaire, Guillaume 228, *228*
Archipenko, Alexander 226, *227*
Art Deco 109
Art et les Artistes, L' 311
Art Nouveau 45, 114, 115, 127,
    134, 139, 148, 152, 156, 166,
    168-9, 172-3, 186
Ashbee, Charles R. *170*, 171
Asino 64, *64*
Asquith, Herbert Henry 89, 288,
    320
Asquith, Margot 94
Astronomy 294, 297, 311, 313,
    320
Aurore, L' 12
*Au Temps des Marronniers en
    Fleurs* (Clermont-Tonnerre) 93
Automobiles, growth of 20, *49*,
    50, *51*, 65, *65*, 86, 107-8, 109,
    122-3, 222, 296, 303, 307, 310;
    racing/rallying 294, 299
Avanguardia Socialista, L' 301
Avant-garde Movement 84, 89,
    198, 210-58, 315, 318
Avanti! *272*, 306, 316, 318
Avanti della Domenica 45
Aymé 179

Bacchus (Massenet) 311
Bacon, Francis 190
Baillie-Scott, M. H. *148-9*, 149
Bagrov 315
Bakst, Léon 54, 59, *59*, 165, 236
Balkan War 64, 85, 317, 318;
    aftermath of 319

Ball, Sir Robert 294
Balla, G. *212*, 222, *223*
Ballet Russe 54, 91, 96, 97-8, 109,
    165, 236, 314
Balloons 297, 300, 306, 309
Balzac, Honoré de 186
Barbier 109
Barney, Nathalie 101, 102
Barnesby, Dr. Norman 313
Barnum and Bailey's Circus 296
Barrès, Auguste Maurice 182
Barroja, Pio 179
Basile, Ernesto 143, *143*, 151
Baryatinsky, Prince Alexander 46
Barzini, Luigi 49, *49*, 123, 307,
    317
Bataille, Henri 298, 304, 312
Bauhaus School of Architecture
    253
Beardsley, Aubrey Vincent 171,
    182, *183*, *188*, *195*, *202*, *207*
Beaudoin, Paul Albert 176, *176*
Beauvoir, Simone de 179
Beaux-Arts, Gazette des 292
Bebel, August 39, 303, 319
Beckett, Samuel 179
Becquerel, Henri 33, 300
Behrens, Peter 213, *213*, 252-3
Behring, Emil von 303, 304
Belboeuf, Marquise de 102
Bell, Graham 299
Belle Époque, animals/vegetables
    in art 168-9, *168-72*, 171-2;
    architecture in 125, *125-6*, 127,
    130, *131-2*, 132, 134, *136-9*, 137,
    139-40, *140-3*, 143, 145, *213*,
    214, *214-14*, 250-3, *250-1*;
    assassination in 18, 76, *77*, 78,
    80, 84-5, 91, 275, 276-8, 286, 293,
    295-7, 299, 302, 307, 309, 311,
    315, *320-1*; at-home days 98;
    Austria and 9, 28, 38, 41, 53,
    86, 88, 105, 124-5, 127-8, 139,
    152, 179, 196, 250; *Blaue Reiter*
    Group 89, 232-3, *233*, 247, 255;
    Brücke, Die, Movement 220,
    232, *232*; cinema, art of 73,
    181, 222, 256, 307, 309-10, 313,
    318-20; cinematophone 318;
    cities in 125, 127-8, 130, 132,
    132-3, 134, 289; contradictions
    of 179-80, 181; cosmetics 164,
    165; criteria of 182, 184; decay
    of 112; decorative arts 166,
    168-9, *168-74*, 171-4; *demi-
    monde* 100; economy,
    European, of 259-70; English
    contribution to 17, 88-9, 91-2,
    94, 96-7, 105, 140, 149, 163,
    171, 179; esthetics in 186,
    192-4, 197, 312; euphoria of
    85-6, 89, 108; exhibitions—*see
    also* under Paris, Salon
    d'Automne *and* Universal
    Exposition—116, *117*, 118, 174,
    228, *228*, 236-8, 244, 293-4, 297,
    301-3, 307, 309, 311, 314-16,
    318; exploration in 298, 306,
    311-12, 316; fashion—*see*
    fashion; flowers in decoration
    115, 173-4, *174-5*; furniture
    design 168-9, 168-70; Germany
    and 36, 89, 102, 104, 179, 187,
    189, 213, 218-19, 247, 252-3,

256, 317; grand hotels 107, *141*, 143, 145, *145*; high finance in 97; holidays, invention of 62, *62-3*, 84, 140; Hungary and 9, 159, 166, *167*, 179; interior design 143, 145, 148-51, 152, *152*; Italy and 13, 91, 116, 118, 122-3, 130, 132, 134, 137, 140, 143, 151, 159, 179, 192, 211, 214, 218-19, 222, 226, 235, 254, 301ff; jewelry design 168, *168*, 176, *176*; Latin-American influence 66, *66*, 109, 111, 165; literary figures 179, 181-2, 192-4, 203-4, 208, 298, 306, 315; literary problems 186-7, 189-90, 192-4; migration during 72, *72-3*, 259, 267-8; movements within 55, 70, 84, 114-15, 118, 152, 160, 186-7, 189-90, 192-4, 196-8, 200-1, 203-4, 206, 208, 210-56, 275-6, 285-6, 292-3, 303, 306, 311, 314; Paris avant-garde capital 238-40, 248; Persian influence 109; philosophies of 194, 196-8, 200-1; politics of 11, 13, 18, 34, 37, 39, 53, 83, 85, 94, 273-90; portraiture in 152, *152-3*, 160, *160-3*, 163, 240; prostitution in 101-2, 104, 204, 299, 317; psychology, growth of 186, 190, 192, 196-8; racist action 306; resorts 137, 140, 145; Russia and 37, *37*, 42-3, *43*, 85, 89, 91, 105, 151, *151*, 160, *160-1*, 166, *166*, 206, 217, 226, 236-7, 240, 248, 298; scientific approach 187, 189, 264, 296, 301, 312; social strata 83-6, 98, 107, 298; sociology in 200-1, 203-4, 206, 208; Spain and 179, 208; sport in 20, 107-8, 294-5, 298-300, 303, 306-7, 309, 311, 314, *317*; technology in 9, 20, 24, 30, 32-3, *48*, 49, 73, *73*, 85-6, 107, 116, *121*, 122-4, 130, 184, 259, 262, 293-6, 299, 303, 307, 310; theater in 54, 71, 91, 96, 97-8, 100-1, 154, 156, 204, 298, 300-2, 304, 310-11; thought changes in 187, 189-90, 192-4, 196-8, 200-1, 203-4, 206, 208, 232, 234-56; *Tout Paris* 100, 107; United States and 105, 107, 311; Exposition Universelle, Paris—*see* under Paris; Viennese Secession Movement 55, *55*, 70, *71*, 152, *152*, *157*, 160, *161*, 250; woman's image in 111, 154, 156-7, 159, 160, 163-5, *319*

Beltrame, Achille 115, 174, *175*, 211
Beltrame, Luca 300
Benelli, Sam 311
Benjamin, Walter 181
Benn, Gottfried 190
Bennett, Arnold 203
Bennett, Gordon 299
Béraud, Jean 8, 60, *60*
Berchtold, Count Leopold von 316
Bérenger, René 294

Bergler, E. de Maria *142-3*, 143
Bergson, Henri 182, 194, 196-7, 200, 208
Bernhardi, Friedrich von 281
Bernard, Nissim 107
Bernhardt, Sarah 13, 46-7, *46*, 104, 154, 156, 292, 296, 298, 304, 305
Berthelot, Pierre 307
Bethmann-Hollweg, Chancellor Theobold von 277, 282-4
Bibesco, Princess Marthe Lucie 108
Bicycles 107, 292, 296, 307; racing 107, 299, 306, 311
Bilibin, I. J. 172, *172*
Bismarck, Count Otto von 265
Björnson, Björnsterne 182
Blaue Reiter Group 89, 232, *233*, 247, 255
Bleichroder, Baron 97, 101
Blériot, Louis 111, 124, 309, 311
Boccioni, Umberto 50, *50-1*, 122, *122-3*, *210*, 211, 214, 218, *218*, 219, 222, 225, *225*, *234*, 235, *235*, 254-5, *254-5*, 315; jailed 321
Böcklin, Arnold 294
Boelsche, E. Wilhelm 189
Boer War 18, 85, 292, 295-7, 307
Boito, Arrigo 295, 301
Boldini, Giovanni 6, 8-9, 13, 58, *58*, 97, 132, *133*, 163
Bonnard, Pierre 10, *56*, 57, 105, 152
Bonnemain, Marguerite de 11
Bonnot, Jules 316
Bonzagni, Aroldo *144*, 145
Borgatti 293
Borghese, Prince Scipione 49, *49*, 123
Borghese, Valerio 307
Boris Godunov (Mussorgsky) 309
Bosnia-Herzegovina 310, 316
Botha, General Louis 307
Boulanger, General Georges 11
Bourget, Paul 94, 308
Boxer Rebellion 18, *292*
Boxing 298
Bragaglia, Anton Giulio 222, *223*
Braque, Georges 69, 238, 244, *246*, 306, 318
Bresci, Gaetano 293-4
Breuer, Josef 196
British Medical Journal 311
Brothers Karamazov, The (Dostoyevsky) 316-17
Brown, Father 179
Brooks, Romaine 13
Bruant, Aristide 104, 296
Brussels, occupation of 321
Bucharest 9, 91
Buffa, Giovanni 172, *172*, 174, *175*
Buffet, Gabrielle 228, *228*
Bürck, Paul 76, *76-7*
Burgess (Channel swimmer) 315
Bute, Lord 94
Byros, Marquis de 105

Cahen of Antwerp 97
Cabiria (D'Annunzio) 320
Caillaux, Joseph 13, 79
Caillaux, Mme. 13-14, 79, 112,

320, 321
Caillavet, Mme. Armand de 94
Calderini 297, 300
Calmette, Gaston 13, 79, 112, 320
Calvé, Emma 102
Calver, Dr. W. 294
Camoin, Charles 35
Campanini, Alfredo 38
Camus, Albert 179
Candida (Shaw) 204
Canudo, R. 73
Cappiello, Leonetto 13, 28, *28*, 159
Carabin, R. 166, *167*
Carco, Francis 41, 104
Carducci, Giosué 179; Nobel Prize for 306
Caricaturists 10
Carnarvon, Lord 101
Carnegie, Andrew 294, 299
Carnot, Sadi 11
Carrà, Carlo 218, 235, *235*, 254, 315
Carrière, Eugène 10
Caruso, Enrico 105, 305, 306, 310, 311, 313
Casati, Marchesa Luisa 13, 58, *58*, 91, 97
Caserio, Sante 11
Cassel, Sir Ernest 97
Castellane, Count Boni de 9-10, 11, 92, 94
Cavalieri, Lina 46, *46*
Cavazzoni, A. *136-7*, 137
Cézanne, Paul 242, 244, *244*, 245, 247, 303
Chabrilland, Mme. de 109
Chamberlain, Austen 89
Chandos, Lord 190
Charcot, Jean Martin 9, 196
Charlus, Baron de 58
Chatillon, Count and Countess de 301
Chavez 313
Chekhov, Anton 179
Chéret, Jules 104-5, 156-7
Chimay, Prince de 88
China 292-3; death of revolutionaries *317*; end of monarchy 316; revolt against dynasty 316
Chini, Galileo 145, *145*
Chirico, de, brothers 13
Churches, and the First World War 286-7
Churchill, Lady Randolph 96
Churchill, Winston 314, 316
Claudel, Paul 179, 181
Clemenceau, Georges 11, 307, 316
Clermont-Tonnerre, Duchesse de 93, 109
Cocteau, Jean 104
Cody, Colonel (Buffalo Bill) 305, 319
Colette, Sidonie-Gabrielle 101-2, 104, 179
Congress of Berlin 85
Conrad, Joseph 203-4
Conrad, Major 277
Contemporary Review 309, 313
Cook, James 311-12, *312*
Cooper, Gladys 105
Coquelin, Benoit Constant 306
Corbett, James J. 298

Correspondant, Le 293, 306
Corriere della Sera 49, *75*, 293 *et seq*
Courths-Mahler, Hedwig 182
Craig, Gordon 47
Crécy, Odette de 58
Croce, Bernedetto 179, 287, 310, 312
Cubism 237-8, 240, 244-5, 247-8, 315, 318
Curie, Marie 33, 300, 312-13
Curie, Pierre 300, 305, 313
Curtiss, Glenn 30
Cust, Henry 96

Dadaists 235, 249
Daily Mail 274, 307, 309
Daily Telegraph 310, 312
Dali, Salvador 69
D'Annunzio, Gabriele 13, 30, 47, 91, 93-4, 97-8, 107-8, 112, 179, 182, 192-4, 292, 296, 300-1, 304, 309, 312, *313*, 319-20; and Trilussa 315; arrest of 321
Dario, Rubén 182
D'Aronco, Raimondo *117-18*, 118
Darwin, Charles 187, 189, 196, 208, 298
Daudet, Léon 112
D'Aurignac, Thérèse 297, 299
Davidson, John *202*
Death in Venice (Mann) 31, 62, 194
Debs, Eugene 303
Debussy, Claude-Achille 54, 86, 108, 320
Decadent Movement 84
Degas, Edgar 10, 101
Degeneracy (Nordau) 84
De la Fayette, Mme. 197
De la Meurthe, Deutsch 97, 295
Delaunay, Robert 10, 217, *217*, 219, 247
De la Veaulx, Henri 300
Deledda, Grazia 298, 310
De Morgan, William 171
Depero, Fortunato 226
Derain, André 54, 229, *228-9*, 303, 318
Derby, Lord 94
Deslys, Gaby 105
Deutsche Revue 311, 318, 321
Deutsche Werkbund 253-4
Devonshire, Duchess of 94, 294
Devonshire, Duke of 96
De Wet, General Christiaan Rudolph 297
Diaghilev, Serge 54, 91, 97-8, 108, 109, 236
Diaz, Porfirio 314-15
Dilthey, Wilhelm 190, 192
Disasters 32, 107, 292, 294, 300, 303, 306, 310
Disenchanted, The (Loti) 306
Dix, Otto 221, *221*, 256, *256*
Domenica del Corriere 114, 115, 211, 295
Don Carlos of Portugal 92
Donnay, Maurice 13-14, 308
Dorgelès, Roland 41
Dostoyevsky Fëdor 316-17
Doucet, Jacques 26, 108
Draga, Queen of Yugoslavia 299
Dreiser, Theodore 206

Dreyfus, Albert 11-12, 17, 85, 293, 306, 316
Dreyfus, Mathieu 12
Dubliners (Joyce) 204
Duchamp, Marcel 69, *224*, 225, 238, 249, *249*, 318
Du Côté de chez Swann (Proust) 12, 112
Du Cubisme 238
Dudovich, Marcello *122*, 123, 159
Duelling 294, 300-1, 306, 308-9, 311, 315
Du Gard, Roger Martin 111
Dumont, Santos 295, 299, 306-7
Duncan, Isadora 97, 300, 318
Duran, Carolus 10
Duras 179
Durkheim, Émile 200-1
Duse, Eleonora 47, *47*, 293, 300, 302

Earthquakes 310, 315
Eberlein, Gustav 66, *66*
Echegaray, José 182
Eckermann, Johann Peter 184
Economy, the agriculture 260-1, 265, 267; Britain's lead 260-2, 263-6; Britain's lessening influence 268; capital, movement of 259-60, 262-3, 265-8, 280; colonies 269-70; communications, developments in 184, 262-3, 266, 289; foodstuffs, markets 263, 265; free trade 260, 262; gold standard 259-60, 262, 267-9; industrialism spread 184, 259-62, 264-5, 268, 288; population changes 259, 261, 264; raw materials movements 263-5; steam shipping 261, 263-4; United States part 259-69
Edison, Thomas 295, 308, 310, 315, 318
Edward VII of Great Britain 8, *61*, 89, 91-2, 96-7, 101, 104, 294, 297-9, 313
Edwardians, The (Sackville-West) 96
Ernaudi, Luigi 316
Einstein, Albert 41, *41*, 182, 187, 189
Electricity 18-19, 86, 116, *116*, 295; and executions 309
Encyclopaedia Britannica, completion of 298
Engels, Friedrich 186
Ercolassi, Captain and Mrs. 301
Esterhazy, Major Marie Charles 12
Esthetics (Croce) 192
Etna, eruption of 315
Eucken 182
Eugénie, Empress 108
Eulenberg, Prince 102, 104
Evening Standard 310
Everybody's Autobiography (Stein) 69
Expressionism 198

Fabergé, Carl *2*, 43, *43*, 91
Falkenhayn, Erich von 273

Falla, Manuel de 97
Fallières, Armand 304, 306
Fanfulla della Domenica 292
Faragó, Géza 159, *159*
Farago, Odön 151
Fashion, importance of 8, 26, 55, 60, 100, 108-9, 111, 132, *299*, *317*; men's 8, 58, 66; women's 8, 59, 66, 159, 163-5, *163*, 310, 312, 314, *319*
Faure, Félix 12, 86, 101
Fauré, Gabriel 97
Fauves, les 229-32, 238, 245, 303
Ferdinand I of Bulgaria *61*
Ferrer, Francisco 312
Fersen, Comte d'Adelsward de 102
Feuillatre, Eugène 168, *168*
Feydeau, Georges 86, 101
Figaro, Le 56, 57, 98, 110, 112, 222, 235, 310, 320-1
First World War 75-6, 78, 83, 108, 111, 165, 179-80, 192, 210, 254-6, 261, 269; prelude to 273-9, 321; support for 288-9
Fischer, Jens Malte 186
FitzGerald, Francis Scott Key 69
Fitzsimmons, Robert Prometheus 298
Flame of Life, The (D'Annunzio) 192
Florio, Vincenzo 123
Flying machines 30, *30*, 124, 299, 301, 306-7, 309, 311-15
Flynn, Elizabeth G. 303
Fontanesi 297
Forbes, astronomer 297
Ford, Henry 20
Foreign Legion, The 310
Forlanini 306
Formigé, Jean Camille 32
Forse che si, forse che no (D'Annunzio) 97, 108
Forster, E. M. 203
Forsyte Saga (Galsworthy) 111, 179
Fortnightly Review 310, 312
Foulds of Paris 97
Fourquet, Georges 22, *155*
Fournier, Henri 295
Fourth Estate, The (Pellizza da Volpedo) 22
France, Anatole 94, 295, 311, 322
Francesca da Rimini (D'Annunzio) 296, 300
Franco-Prussian War 11, 289
Franz Ferdinand, Archduke of Hapsburg 76, *76*, 275-6, 278, 320-1
Franz Joseph, Emperor 28, 88, 276-7, 290
Frederick VIII of Denmark *61*
Freedom 322
Frege, Gottlob 189
Fremdenblatt 315
Fresnaye, Roger de la 50, *51*
Freud, Sigmund 41, 88, 182, 196, 287, 318
Friesz, Émile Othon 303
Fruits of the Earth, The (Gide) 197
Fuller, Loie 156, 300
Functionalism 53
Futurist movement 232, 234-56

Gallé, Émile 169, *168-9*, 174, *174*
Gallois 297
Galsworthy, John 111, 203-4
Gambini, Silvio 124, *124*
Garden, Mary 98
Garibaldi, Giuseppe 314, 319
Garin, Vince 299
Garnier, Tony 216, *216*
Gasset, Ortega y 179
Gaudi, Antonio *148*, 149
Gauguin, Paul 303
Gaulois 98, 110
Gause, Wilhelm 28, *29*
Gautier, Judith 313
Gazzetta dello Sport 306
Genêt, Jean 179
Genoa, Duke of 294
Geoffroy, Gustave 85
George V of Great Britain *61*,
    313, 315
George, Stefan 182, 194
Gérôme, Jean Léon 46
Giachi, Giuseppe 134, *137*
Giacomo, Salvatore di 311
Gibson, Charles Dana 105
Gibson Girls 105
Gide, André 84, 94, 179, 181-2,
    196-8
Gigi (Colette) 101
Gioconda, La theft of 62, 315, 319
Giolitti, Giovanni 300, 316,
    319-20
Giornale della Donna 297-8, 300
Girardi 297
Girl of the Golden West, The
    (Puccini) 314
Guisti, Ugo 145, *145*
Gobedska, Missia 97
Goethe, Johann Wolfgang von
    184, 192
Goloubeff, Comtesse N. de 13
Goncharova, Natalya 236, *237*
Gorky, Maxim 179, 206, 301
Gould, Jay 9, 294
Goulue, La 104
Goursat, Georges (Sem) *6*, 10, 49,
    49, *82*, *90*, 93, *95*, 97, *103*,
    109-10, *110*
Gracq 179
Gramophones 105, 309-10
Gramsci, Antonio 192
Granville-Barker, Harley 204
Great Illusion, The (Angell) 274-6,
    281
Green 179
Greffulhe, Countess 92-3
Grey, Lady 96
Grey, Sir Edward 290
Grieg, Edvard 298
Gris, Juan 239
Gropius, Walter 252-3, *253*
Guesde, Jules 39
Guggenheim, Mrs. Simon 211
Guilbert, Yvette 104, 297
Guimard, Hector 127
Gyp 28, *28*

Haakon VII of Norway *61*
Haas, Charles 71, *71*, 97
Haeckel, Ernst 187
Hague Peace Conference 307
Halley's Comet 313
Hamid, Sultan Abdul 309, 311
Hari, Mata 69, *69*

Haselberg, P. V. 182
Harkness, Margaret 186
Hasenclever, Walter 71
Haute couture see under fashion
Hearn, Lafcadio 304
Hearst, William Randolph 306
Heart of Darkness, The (Conrad)
    203
Hebdo-Débats 306
Heckel, Erich 232
Helena, Queen 295, 300
Helleu, Paul *87*, 93, *99*, *106*, 110
Hemingway, Ernest 69
Henry, Major Hubert Joseph 12
Hermant, Abel 11, 107
Hesse, Grand Duke Ernst Ludwig
    of 89, 152
Hesse, Hermann 179
Heyse 182
Heywood, W. 303
Hirsch, Baron and Baroness de
    83, 97
History of Creation, The
    (Haeckel) 187
Hogfmannsthal, Hugo von 88,
    179, 182, 190, 193-4
Hölderlin, Friedrich 182
Holland, John Philip 293, 301
Holmes, Sherlock 179
Horta, Victor 130, *130*
Holstein, Friedrich von 279
Huerta, President 320
Humanité, L' 79, 301-2, 317, 321
Humbert, Frédéric 297, 299
Huysmans, Joris-Karl 179

Ibsen, Henrik 47, 179, 182, 198,
    204, 276, 293, 305
Illustrated London News 108, 293,
    310
Illustration, L' *48*, 49, 84, 108-9,
    111-12, 296, 298-9, 309-10
Illustrazione Italiana 292, 295-7,
    299-304, 305, 306, 309-11,
    313-21
Impressionism 198, 242, 244, 318
Immoralist, The (Gide) 197-8
Ingres, Jean 303
Innocenti, Camillo 152, *152*
International Amity through the
    Churches, Council for 286
International Catholic League for
    Peace 286
International Socialist Review
    303-4
Interpretation of Dreams, The
    (Freud) 41, 196
Intransigeant, L' 308
Iribe, Paul 164, *164*
Irving, Henry 300, 303
Istanbul 9
Italo-Turkish War 316-17

Jacob, Max 69, 239
J'ai vécu 1900 (de Pange) 93
Jagow, Gottlieb von 277
James, Henry 108
James, William 203
Jarry, Alfred 181
Jaurès, Jean 14, 34, *34*, 39, 80, 86,
    285-6, 294, 298, 302-3, 321
Joffre, Marshal 281
Journal 110, 310
Joyce, James 204, 206

Jugendstil 105, 114-15, 152, 166

Kafka, Franz 30, 190
Kahn, Gustave 295
Kaiser, Georg 71
Kammerer, Marcellus 128, *128-9*
Kandinsky, Vassily 232, *233*, 240, *240*, 242, 247-8
Karsavina, Tamara 54, 98
Kautsky, Karl 304
Keppel, Mrs. 92, 96
Kierkegaard, Sören 276
Kipling, Rudyard 182
Kirchner, Ernst Ludwig 220, *220*, 232, *232*
Kitchener, Lord 295, 297
Klee, Paul 232, 247, *247*
Klein, César 256
Kleygel, General 294
Klimt, Gustav *4*, 88, 97, 105, 160, *161*
Koch, Robert 295
Kokoschka, Oskar 71
Koppen, Erwin 182
Kropotkin, Peter 304
Kruger, Stephanus Johannes *297*

Labriola, Professor Antonio 292, 300
Laduc, Professor 309
Ladysmith, Relief of 292
Lalique, René *44*, 45, *45*, 154, 173-4, *173-4*
Lancaster, Osbert 83, 89
Langtry, Lillie 96
Lanthelme 111
Larche, Raoul *156*, 157
Larionov, Mikhail 54, 236, *236-7*
Laszlo de Lombos, Philip Alexius 92
Late Mattia Pascal, The (Pirandello) 198, 200
Latouche, Gaston 111
Lavedan, Henri 100
Laurie, Wilfred 296
Laverrière, A. 127, *127*
Lavoro, Il 310
Leautaud 104
Léger, Fernand 226, 238, 244
Léhar, Franz 88, 310
Leiris, Michel 179
Lenin, Nikolai 26, *27*, 42, 181-2, 290
Lenz, Maximilian 41, *41*
Leo XIII, Pope 299
Leon, Daniel de 303
Leoncavallo, Ruggiero 322
Lepape, Georges 109, 164, *165*
Lesseps, Vicomte Ferdinand de 11
Letizia, Princess 309
Lettura, La 295
Léveillé, A. 78, *78-9*
Liberty, Arthur Lasenby 45, *45*
Liberty style 114, 118, 140, 163, *163*
Liebermann, Max 39, *39*
Liebknecht, Karl 293, 319
Life of Don Quixote (Unamuno) 208
Lloyd, Marie 105
Lloyd George, David 89, 94, 282, 284-5
Locati, Sebastiano 118, *120*
Loeb, Professor 302

Loisy, Alfred Firmin 287
Lombroso, Cesare 295, 312
London, Buckingham Palace 38, 92; eminence of 89, 91, 261; National Gallery 320; Olympic Games in 309; Ritz Hotel 38, *38*, 88-9, 105, 107; Savoy Hotel 105, 107; Westminster Abbey 315
London, Jack 179, 206
Londonderry, Lady 94, 96
Loos, Alfred 250-2, *250-2*
Lorrain, Jean 86, 100, 101-2, 107
Loti, Pierre 94, 306
Loubet, Emile 12, 293-4, 301-2
Louÿs, Pierre 102
Ludwig-Victor, Archduke 104
Lumière brothers *48*, 49, 181
Lunarcharsky, Anatoli Vasilievich 206
Lusitania 308
Luxembourg, Rosa 294, *308*
Ly, Arria 315
Lyautey, Louis 281

McClure's Magazine 296
McGovern 298
McKinley, President William 293, 295, 297
Mackart 88
Macke, August 255
Mackintosh, Charles Rennie *148*, 149
MacLaughlin, Dr. 302
Madama Butterfly (Puccini) 300
Madero, Francisco 314-15
Maeterlinck, Maurice 181
Mafia, the 311, 313
Mahmud V of Turkey 311
Malatesta, Errico 320, 322
Malevich, Kasimir 226, *226*, 237, 245, 248, *248*, 249, 252
Maljutin, S.V. 151, *151*
Mallarmé, Stéphane 97, 190
Malraux, André 179
Manet, Edouard 10, 303
Manguin, Henri *229*
Mann, Heinrich 179
Mann, Thomas 31, 62, 111, 179, 182, 186, 194
Manuel II of Portugal *61*, 309
Man without Qualities, The (Musil) 180
Marc, Franz 232, 247, 255
Marchetti, Filippo 296
Marconi, William 24, 296
Margherita, Queen 296, 299, 309
Maria, Sophia of Naples 8
Marie, Princess of Thurn and Taxis-Hohenlohe 180
Marie, Queen of Rumania 91-2
Marinetti, Filippo T. 57, 184, 194, 208, 213, 234-5, *235*, 236, 254, 310-11, 315, 318; jailed 321
Marlborough, Duchess of 93
Marquet, Albert 303
Martini, Alberto 168, *168*
Marty 109
Marx, Karl 181, 286, *308*; suicide of daughter 316
Masaryk, Tomáš 276
Mascagni, Pietro 294, 319
Masefield, John 179
Massenet, Jules Émile Fréderic

311
Matin, Le 62
Matisse, Henri 54, 69, 229,
  229-30, 231, 303, 318
Matter and Memory (Bergson)
  194
Mattino, Il 300, 306
Maugham, William Somerset 88,
  96
Mauthner, Fritz 189
Max, Edouard de 104
Mayakovsky, Vladimir 76, 236
May, Karl 179
Mayerling affair, the 85
Mazzini, Giuseppe 276
Mazzucotelli, A. 134, *137*
Medicine, progress of 9, 295, 300,
  302-4, 307, 311, 313-14, 319
Meinecke, Friedrich 287
Meissonier, Jean Louis Ernest 10
Melba, Dame Nellie 83, 98, 105
Méliès, Georges 73, 181
Melograni, Piero 182
Menard-Dorian, Mme. 94
Mendel, Gregor 318
Mendès, Catulle 296
Meredith, George 311
Merode, Cleo de 293, 297
Merry Widow, The (Léhar) 88,
  310
Metchnikoff, Elie 9
Metlicovitz 159
Metternich, Princess 88
Meyer, Baron de 97
Michel, Louise 302
Middle classes 9, 98, 114, 139,
  145, 159, 163, 180-1, 204, 206
Millerand, Alexandre 19, 34
Milner, Lord 297
Minerva 311
Mirabeau, Sybille-Marie-
  Antoinette *28*, 29
Mir Iskusstva 151, 236
Moderne Bauformen 127-8, *127-8*,
  139, 150, *151*
Modes, Les 108
Modigliani, Amedeo 41, 105, 240,
  240-1
Molnár, Ferenc 179
Moltke, Count Helmut von 284,
  289; trial of 308
Mona Lisa, theft of 62, 315
Mondrian, Piet 245, *245*, 248
Monet, Claude 242, *242-3*
Monte Carlo 38, 100-1
Monneret de Villard, Ugo 140
Montesquiou-Fezensac, Count
  Robert de *6*, 9, 58, 102
Moore, Mrs. 92
Morelli, Domenico 58, *59*
Moretti, Gaetano 116, *116*, 214,
  215
Morgan, Pierpont 294, 318, *319*
Morris, William 171
Moser, Koloman 157, *157*
Mother, The (Gorky) 206
Mountbatten, Lord 97
Mrs. Warren's Profession (Shaw)
  203-4, 310-11
Mucha, Alphonse 22, *23*, 115,
  115, 154, *154-5*
Mugnier, Abbé 102
Munch, Edvard *178*, *185*, *191*,
  198-9, *205*

Munro 298
Murders in the Rue Morgue (Poe)
  188
Musil, Robert 53, 86, 180
Musolino 292, 295
Musset, Alfred de 301
Mussolini, Benito 322
Mussorgsky, Modeste P. 54

Napoleon III 86
Nation, Carrie 315
Negri, Francesco 293
Neue Deutsche Rundschau 293
Neue Zeit, Die 294
New York Times 303, 312, 316,
  318
Nicholas II, Tsar 42-3, 78, 92,
  279, 284, 290, 298-9, 303, 308,
  312-13
Nicholayevich, Archduke
  Nicholas 309
Niepce, Joseph 24
Niermans, Édouard 134, *134-5*
Nietzsche, Friedrich 89, 179,
  196-7, 208, 293
Nijinsky, Vaslav 54, 109
Nineteenth Century, The 299
Nineteenth Century and After, The
  304, 309
Nittis, Giuseppe de 13
Nobel Prize 181, 296, 306
Nolde, Emil 62, *63*
Nordau, Max 84
North American Review 293
Novissima 114, 115
Nurkse, Ragnar 263

October Revolution 181, 206,
  303-4
Offenbach, Jacques 300
Olbrich, Joseph Maria 89, 152,
  152
*On the Electrodynamics of Moving
  Bodies* (Einstein) 41
Opera 292-5, 300, 309-11, 314,
  322
Orazi, Manuel 154, *155*
Orient Express 88, 91
Origin of Species (Darwin) 187
Otello (Verdi) 298
Otero, the Belle 35, 101, 296-7,
  306
Outlook 311, 313-14, 318-19

Pailleron, Mme. 8
Paléologue, Maurice 112
Palizzolo, Raffaele 295, 298
Pall Mall Magazine 195, 307
Panama Canal 310, 319; scandal
  of 11, 85-6
Pankhurst, Mrs. Emmeline 311,
  318; Sylvia 320
Pange, Comtesse de 93
Papini, Giovanni 179, 300
Paquin 26
Paris, Bois de Boulogne 8, 100;
  Eiffel Tower 116, *217*, 295;
  Folies Bergère 88, 156, 297;
  Lapin Agile Tavern 41, *41*;
  Longchamp 38, 78, 132; Louvre
  62, *62*, 292, 315, 319; Maxim's
  Restaurant 26, *26*, 38, 100, 105,
  110; Metropolitain *126*, 127;
  Montmartre 35 41, 83, 101,

104-5, 239-40, 296, 303, 308;
Moulin Rouge 11, 35, *35*, 104,
301; Passy viaduct 32, *33*;
Sacré-Coeur 104; Salon
d'Automne 228-9, 236-7, 303,
315; Universal Exposition, 1900
10-11, 18-19, 85-6, 115, *115*,
118, *118-19*, 151, 156, 292
Parker, Judge Alton Brooks 301
Pascoli, Giovanni 179, 182, 192
Pasquino, Il 292-3
Pasteur, Louis 9, 101
Paulhan, Louis 312-13
Pavlova, Anna 54, *54*, 312-13
Peacock, depiction of *170*, 171,
171
Peary, Robert Edwin 298, 306,
311-12, *312*
Pechstein, Max 256
Pécs 166, *167*
Pelayo, Marcelino Menéndez of
208
Pellizza da Volpedo 22, 297
Petite République 304
Petits Bourgeois (Gorky) 301
Petri, Donando 309-10
Photography, rise of 24, *24-5*, *48*,
49, 73, *73*, 97, 293
Piacere, Il (D'Annunzio) 93
Picabia, Francis 69, 228, 238, *239*,
318
Picasso, Pablo 54, *68*, 69, 105,
231, *231*, 239, 244, 318
Picquart, Georges 12, 306
Pinero, Arthur Wing 96
Pirandello, Luigi 179, 182, 192,
198, 200
Pirchan, Emil *70*, 71
Pisanelle 13
Pius X, Pope 37, 286-7, 299, 301,
304, 305, 321
Planck, Max 187, 189
Plekhanov, Georgi Valentinovich
206, 286
Pless, Princess Daisy of 96
Poe, Edgar Allan *188*, 189
Poincaré, Raymond 13, 14, 111,
318, 321
Poiret, Paul 26, 59, 108-9, 164-5,
164-5
Polignac, Princesse Edmond de 97
Popular Science Monthly 296
Porter, Edwin S. 73
*Portrait of the Artist as a Young
Man* (Joyce) 206
Pougy, Liane de 101
Pound, Ezra 69
Pourget, Paul 85
Pourtales, Comtesse Edmond de
92
Pratella, Balilla 235
Prévert, Jacques 80, 179
Previati, Gaetano *121*, 122-3, 297
Prince Igor—ballet 54
Princip, Gavrilo 275, 320
Printing, development of 184
Prévost, Marcel 13, 292
Proust, Marcel 9, 12-13, 46-7, 60,
71, 83, 86, 93-4, 96, 98, 102,
112, 196-7
Psychotherapy of Everyday Life
(Freud) 41, 196
Puccini, Giacomo 292, 300, 314
Puvis de Chavannes, Pierre 10

Queneau 179

Radio, growth of 24
Radium 300
Raffaelli, Jean François 10
Railways, as symbol of progress
91, 118, *121*, 122, 184, *258*,
259-60, 262-3, 266, 280, 296,
302, 314; underground 125,
125-6, 127, 296, 299
Rasputin, Gregory 321
Ravel, Maurice 54, 97
Redfern 108
Regno, Il 300
Réjane 297, 304
Renan, Joseph Ernest 194
Renault, Marcel 299
Renoir, Jean 57, *57*, 83
Reszke, Jean de 311
Resurrection (Tolstoy) 298
Revue, La 299, 306, 320
Revue Bleue, La 298, 308, 314
Revue de Paris 98
Revue des Deux Mondes 292-3,
297-8, 307, 313
Revue Hebdomadaire 304, 307
Revue Illustrée 292-4, 299, 300,
302-5
Revue Scientifique 300
Revue Universelle 296
Rheims Cathedral, bombing of
321-2
Rhodes, Cecil 296
Ribbesdale, Lord 96
Rictus, Jehan 104
Riddle of the Universe, The
(Haeckel) 187
Riemerschmid, Richard 254, *254-5*
Rilke, Rainer Maria 86, 180-1,
190
Rimbaud, Arthur 6, 182
Rimsky-Korsakov, Nikolai
Andreevich 54, 59, 314
Riots/revolts 18, 294, 302-4, 307,
309, 311-16, 318, 320
Rire, Le 102
Ritz, César 38, *38*, 88-9
Riviera, the 105, 107
Rizzi, Emilio *162*, 163
Robida, Albert 21, *21*
Rockefeller, John Davison 294,
302-3, 306, 318
Rodin, Auguste 88, 96, 225,
293-4, 305
Roisin, Maxime 128, *129*
Rolland, Romain 273, 287
Roosevelt, Theodore 298, 301-2,
310-12; attempt on life 317
Roquentin, Antoine 190
Rosebery, Lord 97
Rosenkavalier, Der (Strauss—
Hoffmannstahl) 86, 314
Rostand, Edmond 292, 295
Roth, Joseph 28, 38
Rothschilds, the 12, 92, 97, 101,
292, 298
Rouault, Georges *299*, 303
Rousseau, Henri (Le Douanier)
239
Rubino 75, *75*, 298
Rubinstein, Ida 98
Rudini, Carlo de 46
Rudolph, Archduke 28
Ruklin 298

Ruskin, John 292
Russo-Japanese War 300-2, *302*, 303
Russo-Japanese War . . . 300-1
Russolo, Luigi 222, *222*, 235, *235*, 318

Saarinen, Eliel *150*, 151
Sackville, Lady 96
Sackville-West, Vita 96
St.-Exupéry, Antoine de 179
Sala, A. 116, *117*
Salmon, André 239
Salome (Wilde) 182, *183*, *207*
Sand, Georges 301
Sant' Elia, Antonio 214, *214*, 216, *234*, 235, 250, 254-5
Sarajevo 76, 78, 88, 275-7, 282-3, 320-1
Sardou, Victorien 292, 298, 300, 303, 310
Sargent, John Singer 8, 94, 96-7
Sarraute, Nathalie 179
Sarrazin 139
Sartre, Jean-Paul 179, 190
Sauvage 139
Savinio 13
Savoy, The 182
Scalarini, Giuseppe *272*
Scarpetta 304
Scene Illustrata 295
Schéhérazade (Rimsky-Korsakov) 59, *59*, 314
Scheidemann, Philipp 285
Scherer, William 189-90
Schlieffen, von 289
Schlieffen Plan 281, 284
Schmidt-Rottluff, Karl 232
Schnitzler, Arthur 190
Schöntal, Otto 139
Schopenhauer, Arthur 89, 194
Schufinsky, Viktor 55, *55*
Scientific American 311
Scott, Robert Falcon 316, 318
Scott, Sir Murray 96
Second Empire, The 84, 88
Secolo, Il 292-4, 298-9, 302-4, 306-10, 313, 315-16, 318, 320-1
Second World War 192
Sedan, defeat at 11
Sem—*see* Goursat, Georges
Sera, La 292, 299, 300, 305, 306, 309-11, 313-14, 319, 322
Serao, Mathilde 300
Sescau, Paul 25
Seurat, Georges 8
Severini, Gino 219, *235*, 254
Sezession Stil (Secessionist) 114, 118, 128, 176
Shackleton, Ernest Henry 312
Sharkey 298
Shaw, George Bernard 179, 204, 306, 310-11
Shop design 130, *130*
Sickert, Walter 105
Sidney Street Siege 314
Siebelist, A. 31, *31*
Sienkiewicz, Henryk 182
Simenon, Georges 179
Simon, Claude 179
Sinclair, Upton 206, 306-7
Singer, Paul 34
Sipiaguin 296
Sironi, Mario *234*, 235, 254

Slevogt, Max 36
Socialism, development of 34, 285-6, 293-4, 298, 301-3, *308*, 313, 321
Socialist International 285-6, 293, 317-19
Soffici, Ardengo 218-19, *219*
Somerset, Lord Henry 102
Sommaruga, Giuseppe 140, *141*
Sorel, Georges 312
Spanish American War 306
Spencer, Herbert 194, 297, 300
Sphere, The 67
Stacchini, Ulisse 130, *131*
Stampa Sportiva, La 298-300
Stein, Gertrude 64, 69
Stein, Heinrich von 293
Stenheil, Mme. 101
Steinlen, Théophile-Alexandre, 32, 104
Sternberg, Joseph von 83
Steuenberg, Governor 307
Stevens, Alfred 8
Steyn, Martinus Theunis 297
Stockholm, Olympic Games at 317
Stolypin, Prime Minister Pëtr Arkadevich 309, 315
Strauss, Johann 88-9
Strauss, Richard 314
Stravinsky, Igor 54, 97, 236
Strikes 295, 299-302, 306, 312, 316-17, 319
Strindberg, August 179, 182, 198, 276
Stroheim, Eric von 83
Strozzi, Prince 101
Studio, The 45, 149, 182
Submarine, invention of 293
Suez Canal, scandal of 11
Suffragettes 306, 309-11, 313, 318, 320
Sully-Prudhomme, René François Armand 182, 296
Surrealism 249
Sutherland, Duchess of 94
Sykes, Charles 108
Symons, Arthur 182

Taft, Governor William 306, 310
Tamagno, Francesco 311
Tango dance 66, *66*, 109, 165, 319
Tatler 97
Tatlin, Vladimir 237
Tavernier 297
Tchaikovsky, Pëtr Iljitch 91
Technology, advances in—*see under Belle Époque*
Teleprinter, invention of 293
Templeton, Fay 298
Tempo, Il 293, 306
Terzi, Aleardo *114*, 115, *158*, 159
Tesia, Nicola 294
Thaïs (Massenet) 83
Thomas brothers 307
Thousand and Second Night, The (Roth) 28
Tiffany, Louis Comfort 174
Times, The 301, 309
Tissot, James 71, *71*
Tisza, István 277
Titanic 66, *67*, 107; sinking of 316
Tolstoy, Count Leo 83, 179, 292, 294, 298, 301, 310, 311, 313

Tommasi, Angiolo 72, *72-3*
Tosca (Puccini) 292-3, 300
Tosca (Sardou) 298
Toscanini, Arturo 293, 310-11
Toulouse-Lautrec, Henri de 9, 10, 20, *20*, 24, *24-5*, 84, 102, 104-5, 157, 198
Tracy, Harry 298
Trautman, E. 303
Tredegar, Lord 94
Tribuna, La 292, 298-302, 305, 306-7, 309-20, 322
Tristan and Isolde (Wagner) 293, 295
Trotsky, Lev D. 289, 304
Twain, Mark 179, 182
Tz'u-hsi, Empress 292

Umberto I, King 18, 293
Umberto, Prince of Piedmont 301
Unamuno, Miguel 182, 208
Uomo di Pietra, L' 292-3
Utrillo, Maurice 41, *41*, 240

Valadon, Suzanne 41
Valentino, Rudolph 105
Valéry, Paul 89, 182, 189-90
Valta, Louis *229*
Vanderbilt, Cornelius 294, 303, 305
Vandervelde, Emile 286
Vandervoort 298
Van der Velde, Henry 159, 169, *170*, 171
Van Dongen, Kees 105, 239, 303
Van Gogh, Vincent 303
Vanity Fair 97, 108
Vaughan, Father 307
Veber, Jean 34
Veblen, Thorstein 182, 200-1, 203
Venice 98, 294, 301; Biennale 57, 294, 311; Lido 62, *62*; San Marco *campanile 30*, 31
Verdi, Giuseppe 294, 298
Verlaine, Paul 6
Vernes, Jules 179
Victor Emmanuel III, King of Italy 299-300, 305
Victoria, Queen of Great Britain *16*, 85, 294
Vienna 9, 28, 53, 105, 128, 315; Ringstrasse 41, *41*; Sacher Hotel 38, 88, 105; underground railway 125, *125*, 127
Vie Parisienne, La 102, 294
Vie Parisienne, La (Offenbach) 88
Villa, Pancho 320, *320*
Villeparisis, Marquise de 107
Visconti, Luchino 83, 93
Vivien, Renée 102
Vladimir, Grand Duchess 91; Grand Duke 302
Vlaminick, Maurice de 303, 318
Voce, La 310-12, 315
Voice of Labor, The 302
Volpedo, Pellizza da 22, *22*
Vorwaerts 321
Voysey, C. F. A. 140, *140*
Vrubel, Michail A. 160, *160-1*, 166, *166*
Vuillard, Édouard 97, 152

Wagner, Otto 53, *53*, *125*, 127
Wagner, Richard 89, 293, 298

Waldeck-Rousseau, Pierre Marie René 297
Wallace, Sir Richard 96
Waller, Lewis 105
Ward, Clara 88
Washington, Booker T. 302
Webb, Captain (Webb, Matthew) 315
Weber, Max 200-1
Wedekind, Frank 71, 179
Weill, Kurt 179
Wharton, Edith 108
What is to be done? (Lenin) 26, *27*, 181
Whistler, James McNeill 10, 171
Whitman, Walt 276
Wied, Prince William of 320
Wilde, Oscar 85, 96, 182, 204, *207*, 276, 293, 318
Wilder, Thornton 69
Wilhelm II, Kaiser 36, *61*, 85, 89, 92, 96, 102, 104, 111, 182, 277-8, 282-4, 289, 293, 302, 310
Willy (Henri Gauthiers-Villars) 28, *28*
Wilson, Thomas Woodrow 317, 320
Wireless telegraphy 296; photos sent by 315
World of Yesterday, The (Zweig) 180
World's Work, The 298, 311
Worth, Charles Frederick 108
Wright, Orville and Wilbur 30, 307, 309
Wyndham sisters, the 94, 96

Yellow Book, The 182

Zapata, Emiliano 314, *320*
Zarathustra (Nietzsche) 208
Zeit, Die 298
Zeller, Rudolf 52, *52*
Zeppelin, Graf Ferdinand von 306, 309
Zetkin, Klara *308*
Zola, Émile 12, 179, 182, 293, 295, 298, 306
Zweig, Stefan 179-80, 273, 289

333

Photographic Sources

Academy Editions, London: 55l, 70, 154, 155a. A.D.A.G.P., Paris: 224. Albi, Musée Toulouse-Lautrec: 20b, 24-5. Architektursammlung der Technische Universität, Munich: 245b, 255b. Archivo Casasola: 330. Bairati: 129b, 252l. Belli: 64-5. Bibliothèque Nationale, Paris: 17, 33b, 66-7, 324, 325. Bonzagni: 144. Bulloz: 60. Bürck: 76-7. Coll. Estorick, London: 210, 223a. Coll. Jucker, Milan: 254-5. Coll. Felix Klee, Bern: 247. Coll. Riccordi, Milan: 122l, 158. Cisventi: 52a. Clari: 227b. Conservative Research Department: 321. Costa: 235. Courath: 46r. Culver Picture Inc.: 318, 320, 328. Cunard Hotels Ltd.: 38a. Dani: 22l, 32, 37b, 44, 45a, 48, 61b, 65a, 75b, 79r, 114-5, 121, 162, 168a, 172a, 175, 219. De Maré: 258. De Selva: 168b. Detaille: 49a. Documentation Photographique de la Réunion des Musées Nationaux: 57. Dubout: 78-9. EMME Edizioni: 172b. Ender: 236a. Farabola: 27b. Feltrinelli Editore-Mondadori Archives: 234c. Firmenarchiv AEG Telefunken: 213. The Forbes Magazine Coll., New York: 2, 43r. Fotochronika Tass: 237. Fototeca 3M: 62a. Fototeca Storica Nazionale: 75a. Fratelli Fabbri Editori: 63, 217, 233, 248, 250. Galerie Welz, Salzburg: 4. Giacomelli: 30a. The Solomon H. Guggenheim Museum, New York: 227a. Haags Gemeente Museum: 245. Hamburger Kunsthalle: 31, 52b. Harlingue-Viollet: 300. Held: 243a. Historisches Museum der Stadt Wien, Vienna: 28-9. Hunterian Art Gallery, University of Glasgow, Mackintosh Collection: 148a. Interfoto MTI: 159, 167a, 176r. Josse: 26, 54, 59a, 82, 87, 90, 95, 99, 103, 106, 110, 156l. Kodansha Ltd.: 249. Kunstbibliothek, Berlin: 152-3a. Kunsthaus, Zürich: 242-3. Lalance: 18-9, 21, 28, 33a, 151, 155b, 222, 228l, 229, 234a. Landesbildstelle Württemberg, Stuttgart: 256. Lartigue: 20a. Lauros Giraudon: 23b, 34, 51a. Lemaire: 238b. Liberty & Co. Ltd.: 163. Lichtbildwerkstätte Alpenland: 156-7. London Express News: 61a. Mangin: 146-7, 168-9. MAS: 148b. Mathildenhöhe, Darmstadt: 36. Arborio Mella: 22r, 252. Mercurio: 228 br, 239. Meyer: 53, 125, 176l, 251. Minnella: 142, 143. Mondadori Archives: 24l, 30b, 39b, 40b, 41a, 46l, 47, 49b, 66l, 67a, 72-3, 77b, 115a, 130, 174al, 174br, 215, 216a, 218, 228ar, 232, 234b, 238al, 238ar, 240, 253, 272, 290, 293, 297b, 297a, 301, 310, 311, 329, 331, 333. Mori: 38, 118a. Munch-Museet, Oslo: 178, 185, 191, 199, 205. Musée, Lyon: 216b. Musée des Arts Décoratifs, Paris: 56. Musée Toulouse-Lautrec, Albi: 20b, 24-5. Museen der Stadt, Vienna: 41b, 161r. Museo Civico, Como: 214. Museo Teatrale della Scala, Milan: 69b. Museum of Modern Art, New York: 211, 212. National Portrait Gallery, London: 16. Nicolini: 131, 132, 137r. Nimatallah: 133. Nordfjelske Kunstindustrimuseum, Trondheim: 170a. Novelli: 124. Novosti: 27a, 42-3, 160-1, 166, 306. Nunes Vais: 319. Orbis Publishing Ltd.: 164, 165. Paltrinieri: 36-7, 62b, 114a, 136-7, 148-9, 183, 188, 195, 202, 207. Parchitelli: 23a. Paris-Match, Segonzac: 71. Perrin: 230. Photo Reger: 221. Picturepoint: 55r. Punch: 297c. Radio Times Hulton: 312. Rampazzi: 73a.

Riva e Lanza: 116b. Roger Judlin: 35a. Roger Viollet: 35b, 236c, 236b. Rolls-Royce Motors: 64l. Sansoni Editore: 223b. Saporetti: 69a, 74, 116a, 117, 118-9, 120, 127, 128, 129a, 134-5, 138, 139, 140, 141, 150. Savio: 122-3, 152-3b. Scafidi: 45b. Scala: 7, 40a, 50-1, 59b, 68, 225, 231, 244, 246. Scarnati: 80. Schindler: 174ar. Simion-Ricciarini: 58-9. Snark: 292, 313, S.P.A.D.E.M. and A.D.A.G.P., Paris: 241. Südd-Verlag, Munich: 307. Tosi: 145. Ullstein: 332. Victoria and Albert Museum, London: 170b, 171. Villiers le Moy: 167b, 173. Wallraf-Richartz Museum, Cologne: 39a, 220. Yale University Art Gallery: 226. Ziolo: 126.

©A.D.A.G.P., Paris: 35a, 56, 217, 224, 233, 237, 243a, 246, 249l, 249r. Bild Kunst, Frankfurt: 213. S.P.A.D.E.M., Paris: 7, 21, 28l, 32, 40a, 49a, 51a, 58-9, 59a, 60, 68, 82, 87, 90, 95, 99, 103, 106, 110, 133, 165, 222, 227r, 228ar, 230, 231, 239, 242-3, 247.

The Works of Art illustrated in this volume are to be found in the following collections:

Grafische Sammlung Albertina, Vienna: 55, 70, 156-7. Architektursammlung der Technische Universitat, Munich: 254b, 255b. Centre Pompidou, Paris: 222. Chicago Art Institute, Joseph Winterbotham Coll.: 241. Galleria Nazionale d'Arte Moderna, Rome: 58, 59b, 152-3b. Galerie der Stadt, Stuttgart: 256. The Solomon R. Guggenheim Museum of Art, New York: 227a. Gulbenkian Collection, Lisbon: 174br. Haags Gemeente Museum, The Hague: 245. Hamburger Kunsthalle: 31, 52b. Historisches Museum der Stadt Wien, Vienna: 28-9. Jeu de Paume, Paris: 57. Kunstbibliothek, Berlin: 152-3a. Kunsthaus, Zurich: 242-3, 244. The Metropolitan Museum of Art, New York: 68. Munch-Museet, Oslo: 178, 185, 199, 205. Musée des Arts Décoratifs, Paris: 56, 156l. Musée Carnavalet, Paris: 23, 34, 51a, 60. Musée des Deux Guerres Mondiales, Paris: 78-9. Musée de l'Ecole de Nancy, Nancy: 146-7, 168-9. Musée Nationale d'Art Moderne, Paris: 7, 40a, 230, 246. Musée Luneville: 46r. Musée Lyon: 216b. Musée Municipal, Menton: 35a. Musée Toulouse-Lautrec, Albi: 20b, 24-5. Museum der Stadt, Vienna: 41b, 161r. Museo del Cinema, Turin: 73a. Museo Civico, Como: 214. Museo Teatrale del Burcardo, Rome: 46l. Museo Teatrale della Scala, Milan: 69b. Museum of Art, Philadelphia: 224. Museum für angewandte Kunst, Vienna: 174ar. Museum of Modern Art, New York: 211, 212, 231. Museum of the Revolution, Leningrad: 42-3. National Portrait Gallery, London: 16. Nordfjelske Kunstindustrimuseum, Trondheim: 170a. Pinacoteca di Brera, Milan: 218, 219. Rheinland-Pfalz Museum, Mainz: 36l. Schmuckmuseum, Pforzheim: 176l. Stedelijk Museum, Amsterdam: 248. Tretjakovskaja Gallery, Moscow: 160, 166, 237. Victoria and Albert Museum, London: 170b, 171. Wallraf-Richartz Museum, Cologne, 39a, 220.